Image © Bill Brooks / Alamy - Image Ontario

W9-DEC-696

Contents

1

Introduction

11

Fishing

207

Index

Eastern Ontario
Zone 17: Kawarthas
Zone 18 & 20: Eastern

Testimonials

"With their guides you will be an expert on the lake even before you get there."

~ *Fishing4Fools.com*

"...Mussio Ventures gets a big two thumbs up from this angler!"

~ *Richard A. Cuffe*

"The absolute best selling fishing guides in the store."

~ *George Chenge, Angling Specialties*

Ontario

Land Area...1 076 395 km2
Population...12 686 952
Capital...Toronto
Largest City...Toronto
Highest Point...Ishpatina Ridge
693 metres (2 274 feet)
Tourism info...1-800-ONTARIO
www.ontariotravel.net

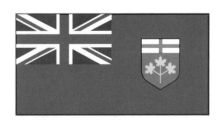

Acknowledgements

BRMB
BACKROADMAPBOOKS.COM

#106- 1500 Hartley Ave,
Coquitlam, BC, V3K 7A1
Toll Free: 1-877-520-5670
E-mail: info@backroadmapbooks.com

Backroad Mapbooks

DIRECTORS
Russell Mussio
Wesley Mussio

VICE PRESIDENT
Chris Taylor

COVER DESIGN & LAYOUT
Farnaz Faghihi

COVER PHOTO
© Bill Brooks / Alamy - Image Ontario

CREATIVE CONTENT
Russell Mussio
Wesley Mussio

PROJECT MANAGER
Andrew Allen

PRODUCTION
Farah Aghdam, Joana Maki,
Shaun Filipenko, Courtney Fry, Oliver Herz,
David Mancini, Matthew Steblyna,
AJ Strawson, Dale Tober

SALES / MARKETING
Chris Taylor / Nazli Faghihi / Basilio Bagnato

WRITER
Jason Marleau

Library and Archives Canada Cataloguing in Publication

Library and Archives Canada Cataloguing in Publication

Marleau, Jason, 1972-

Eastern Ontario fishing mapbook / Jason Marleau. -- 3rd ed.

Includes index.
ISBN 978-1-897225-78-3

1. Fishing--Ontario, Eastern--Maps. 2. Fishing--Ontario,
Eastern--Guidebooks. 3. Ontario, Eastern--Maps. 4. Ontario,
Eastern--Guidebooks. I. Title.

G1147.S62E63M374 2011   799.1'1097137   C2011-903447-6

Copyright © 2014 Mussio Ventures Ltd.

Acknowledgements

This book could not have been compiled without the help of the Backroad Mapbooks team working for Mussio Ventures Ltd. Thank you Jason Marleau, Trent Ernst and Mike Manyk for your efforts and knowledge to pull together the research and writing. You did a fabulous job of relaying countless fishing hot spots and tips and describing them in a creative, yet appealing way. When combined with the talented team of Farah Aghdam, Andrew Allen, Farnaz Faghihi, Nazli Faghihi, Shaun Filipenko, Courtney Fry, Oliver Herz, Joana Maki, David Mancini, Matthew Steblyna, AJ Strawson, Chris Taylor, and Dale Tober we were able to produce this comprehensive guidebook.

We would also like to thank Steve Coombes, Larry Bradt and the staff of the Ministry of Natural Resources for their assistance and patience in helping us track down the best lakes and streams in the area. We would also like to thank the countless other ministry personnel for their help. In addition, we would like to thank all those individuals, retailers and tourism personnel for their knowledge and expertise to help bolster the information on these lakes. We would also like to express our gratitude to Heather Marleau, Ron Marleau, Carmine Minutillo and Jeremy Pooler for their help over the years in exploring the waterbodies of Eastern Ontario.

Finally we would like to thank Allison, Devon, Jasper, Nancy, Madison and Penny Mussio for their continued support of the Mapbook Series. As our family grows, it is becoming more and more challenging to break away from it all to explore our beautiful country.

Sincerely,

Russell and Wesley Mussio

Disclaimer

The lake charts contained in this book are not intended for navigational purposes. Uncharted rocks and shoals may exist. Mussio Ventures Ltd. does not warrant that the information contained in this guide is correct. Therefore, please be careful when using this or any source to plan and carry out your outdoor recreation activity. Also note that travelling on logging roads, trails and waterways is inherently dangerous, and you may encounter poor road conditions, unexpected traffic, poor visibility, and low or no road/trail maintenance. Please use extreme caution when travelling logging roads, trails and waterways.

Please refer to the Ontario Recreational Fishing Regulations Summary for closures and restrictions. It is your responsibility to know when and where closures and restrictions apply.

Help Us Help You

A comprehensive resource such as Fishing Mapbooks for Eastern Ontario could not be put together without a great deal of help and support. Despite our best efforts to ensure that everything is accurate, errors do occur. If you see any errors or omissions, please continue to let us know.

All updates will be posted on our web site: www.backroadmapbooks.com

Please contact us at:
Mussio Ventures Ltd.
Unit 106- 1500 Hartley Ave
Coquitlam, BC, V3K 7A1

Email: updates@backroadmapbooks.com
P: 604-521-6277 toll free 1-877-520-5670
F: 604-521-6260 , www.backroadmapbooks.com

Introduction
Fishing Eastern Ontario

Welcome to the Third Edition of the Fishing Mapbook for Eastern Ontario!

Get ready to reel in the catch of a lifetime! With so many lakes and streams to choose from, this Fishing Mapbook is sure to become the go-to guide for all your fishing excursions.

Featuring many of your favourite lakes and streams found in the popular Kawartha Lakes region (Zone 17), the familiar lakes and rivers of Eastern Ontario (Zone 18), and the big water around Lake Ontario (Zone 20), no other source offers as many fishing hot spots or details on where to fish in the area. In addition to hundreds of lakes and streams, you will find countless fishing tips, coloured depth charts, information on surrounding facilities, directions and fish stocking data.

This information allows you to explore the lakes and rivers of Eastern Ontario with the confidence of a good guide. Whether you are a local fishing pro or visiting an Ontario fishing hot spot for the very first time, our detailed information is sure to prove valuable in your success rate as you take in the natural beauty and colonial history behind the oldest settled region of the province.

Boasting a great reputation as one of the premiere fishing destinations in Ontario, Eastern Ontario is home to hundreds of beautiful lakes and waterbodies. The unique collection of cool and warm bodies of water in the area provides an endless array of angling opportunities. Smallmouth or largemouth bass are prolific in the region, with the majority of fishing holes being inhabited by either species. Brook trout and lake trout are also quite popular. Anglers targeting these sport fish can expect to find a combination of natural and stocked fishing opportunities. Larger predatory fish such as the ever popular walleye (pickerel) and northern pike can also be found throughout the region in decent quantities.

The lakes and streams in this region vary from the popular Rideau and Trent-Severn Waterway chain of lakes to small backcountry lakes. As an added bonus, we also feature some of more popular river hot spots in the area. The popular lakes are home to cottages and can be busy destinations during the summer months, but they do offer great boat launch facilities and the convenient amenities to help make a perfect fishing holiday. If serene surroundings are what you seek, lakes found between the main highways (e.g. areas between Highway 28, 62 and 41 or north of Highway 7) would be the ideal spot to bait your hook, sit back and relax: until you get your first bite, that is.

Although Eastern Ontario's well-developed road systems provide easy access to most fishing hot spots in the region, there harder to reach lakes that require a 4wd vehicle, ATV or are only accessible by trail or portage. Let us also be your guide on the road to your fishing adventures and pick up your very own Backroad GPS Maps or the Cottage Country Ontario and Eastern Ontario Backroad Mapbooks. In addition to the detailed backcountry maps, our Mapbooks and Backroad GPS Maps provide detailed information on everything from camping areas to other fishing opportunities and are the perfect companion to the Fishing Mapbook Series. So cast your line, sit back and relax.

Happy fishing everyone!

BACKROAD HISTORY

The Fishing Mapbook Series evolved from research done when creating the Backroad Mapbooks. Russell and Wesley Mussio, as well as their team of researchers, really enjoy exploring and fishing new lakes but would get frustrated trying guess where to fish. After stumbling across the depth charts for a few lakes, they learned how to read a lake a lot quicker and start working the right areas much sooner.

Although there were a few other companies producing individual lake charts and selling them for a premium, in typical entrepreneurial fashion the brothers decided to take it one step further. Rather than selling individual charts, they put several lakes in a single reasonably priced book and added valuable information on everything from directions and facilities to fishing tips and stocking information.

Today, the series have evolved into even bigger books and now cover the popular streams in the area. We also work with key people in the industry to help gain valuable insight into each lake, river and region we cover.

Legend

Fishery Zones

Lake Chart Classifications

+ + + + + + + + Rocks	Sand Bars
Swamps, Marshes	Parks, Private Areas
→→→ Stream	Lake
Highway	Side Road
Main Road	---------- Old Road, Trails
Railway	Management Zones

MNR's Regional Offices

Natural Resources Information Centre.......................
.... English 1-800-667-1940
.................................French 1-800-667-1840
MNR's Website .... ontario.ca/mnr
Outdoors Card (Licenses, Customer Service)...............
.... (800) 387-7011
Greater Toronto .... (905) 713-7400
Bancroft MNR Office .... (613) 332-3940
Minden MNR Office .... (705) 286-1521
Parry Sound MNR Office .... (705) 746-4201
Bracebridge MNR Office .... (705) 645-8747
Pembroke MNR Office .... (613) 732-3661
Peterborough MNR Office............... (705) 755-2001
Tweed MNR Office .... (613) 478-2330

Recreational Activities and Miscellaneous

(A)	Access: put-in,take-out	5	Highway / Secondary
⚓	Anchorage		Hiking
⛺	Backcountry Campsite		Hut / Cabin
	Beacon		Paddling (canoe-kayak)
	Boat Launch	P	Parking
	Biking		Picnic Site
	Bridge	★	Point of Interest
	Campsite / Limited Facilities		Portage
	Campsite / Trailer	R	Resort
●	Community		Swimming
‖	Dams		Viewing
☐	Dock / Wharf		Viewpoint
	Float Plane Access		Waterfall
5	Highway / Primary		

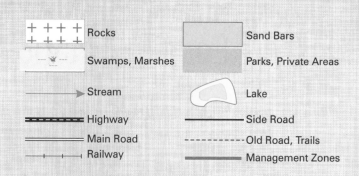

Map Key
Eastern Ontario

7B

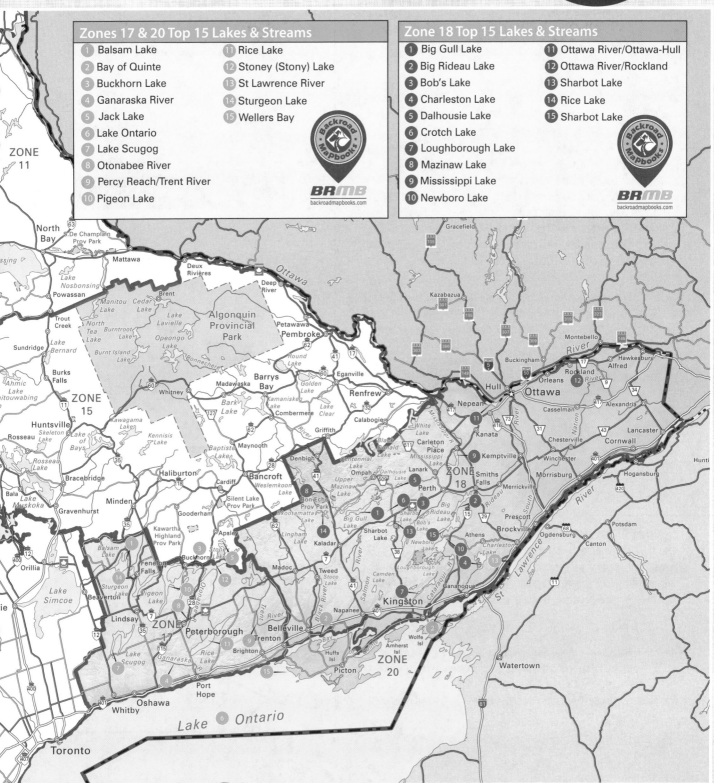

Zones 17 & 20 Top 15 Lakes & Streams

1. Balsam Lake
2. Bay of Quinte
3. Buckhorn Lake
4. Ganaraska River
5. Jack Lake
6. Lake Ontario
7. Lake Scugog
8. Otonabee River
9. Percy Reach/Trent River
10. Pigeon Lake
11. Rice Lake
12. Stoney (Stony) Lake
13. St Lawrence River
14. Sturgeon Lake
15. Wellers Bay

Zone 18 Top 15 Lakes & Streams

1. Big Gull Lake
2. Big Rideau Lake
3. Bob's Lake
4. Charleston Lake
5. Dalhousie Lake
6. Crotch Lake
7. Loughborough Lake
8. Mazinaw Lake
9. Mississippi Lake
10. Newboro Lake
11. Ottawa River/Ottawa-Hull
12. Ottawa River/Rockland
13. Sharbot Lake
14. Rice Lake
15. Sharbot Lake

Backroad Mapbooks
BRMB
backroadmapbooks.com

How to use this Mapbook

Fish Species

The book begins with a rather elaborate section on the main sportfish species in the region. In it we give pointers on how to identify and fish for these sometimes elusive fish. These tips should not be overlooked, as they are an accumulation of many years of personal experience and research. Of course there are many anglers out there that know a lot more than we do, but few sources put it all together in such a convenient, compact package. Whether you are new to the area or new to fishing or have fished these holes for years, we guarantee that following these tips will help you find more fish.

The Lakes (Bathymetric Charts)

The lake fishing section of this book features all of the favourites as well as some of those lesser know lakes that can produce that lifetime fishing memory. With so many lakes to choose from, the task was indeed a challenge to try to get that right mix in our book.

Similar to this book's predecessors, Fishing Ontario Kawarthas, Haliburton and Muskoka, we have highlighted many of the better lakes with depth charts. These charts, if read properly will help you pinpoint the likely areas on a lake to start fishing. These charts show the contours of the lake and help readers figure out where the shoals, drop-offs, hidden islands or basically any sort of water structure that will likely hold fish is located. Reviewing these charts before visiting the lake for the first time could reveal where to find the fish. At the very least, they will help you know where to start fishing.

We have also included the fish species and whether they are stocked or not for each listing. In some cases we even tell you how and what to fish with. If there are no fishing tips included under the individual listing, you can refer to the front or back of the book to refresh yourself on tactics and fly patterns of the prominent species in that lake. Of course, when you get to the lake and there are other anglers there do not be shy to ask where to fish and what to use. Most people are more than willing to help out.

Rivers & Streams

The river or streams section is new to the series, but follows the similar pattern of including fish tips, access, and facilities for each stream that is highlighted. Of course, the river maps are a popular feature that include popular access points where possible.

Fishing Tips & Techniques

Near the back of the book this is another excellent resource to refer to. In this section, we give pointers on how to fish using the various lake and stream fishing techniques, as well as some useful fishing tips. Constant referral to this section will help anglers new and old to the sport.

Map Key & Index

There are also handy planning tools such as the Overview Map and an Index. If you know the waterbody you are planning on visiting, you simply turn to the lakes or river section and find the listing you are interested in. Alternatively, you can look it up in the index to see what page it is listed on.

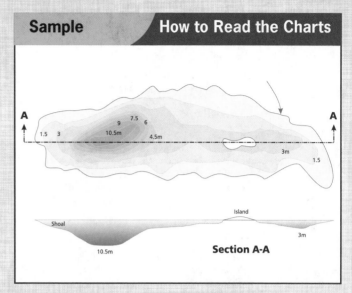

Sample — How to Read the Charts

Section A-A

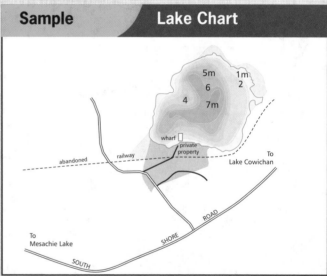

Sample — Lake Chart

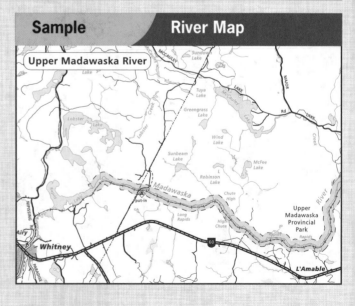

Sample — River Map

Eastern Ontario Fish Species

Brook Trout are native to Ontario and inhabit cool streams and smaller lakes across the province. Brook trout (which are not actually a trout, but a char) are also known as speckled trout due to the red spots with blue halos on their sides. Brookies are renowned for being a fickle and difficult fish to catch. One of the best times of year to increase your success for brook trout is in the spring just after the ice comes off the lakes and into early June. Once the ice retreats, the oxygen content of the lake enables trout to feed near the surface. After a long winter brookies readily feed off new insect larvae and small minnows. Brookies have been known to be quite aggressive at this time of year and can be caught readily from shore with small spinners or even bobber fishing with a hook and worm. Once the heat of summer sets in, brookies sit in the middle of the lake in an area called the thermocline layer in about 11.5°C (53°F) of water. At this time they can still be caught, but it is definitely much more challenging.

Flyfishing in spring can be very productive for brookies, as the bulk of their diet in the spring is insects such as chironomids and other insect larvae. For spincasters, try small spinners or trolling small spoons. Some proven spoons include the Little Cleo, smaller sized Williams Fishlander, Luhr Jensen Diamond King or Gibbs Gypsy. As for spinners, almost anything with a smaller profile can work well in silver or gold, such as a Blue Fox or Panther Martin. For smaller creeks and rivers, spoons are not the best choice, but small spinners can be deadly when they are tossed along banks and beside sunken logs. You can potentially increase success by adding a worm or small dead minnow to the end of your presentations. The Ontario record brook trout was caught on a fly in the Nipigon River and weighed a whopping 6.58 kg (14.5 lbs).

Lake Trout (which aren't actually a trout, they a misnamed char) are one of the most sought after fish species in the province, but must be protected to ensure a healthy future. In many parts of Ontario, especially in Central Ontario, lake trout populations have been in steady decline and have become extinct from hundreds of lakes. The dramatic decline is due mainly to over harvesting by anglers, as well as pollution from the numerous cottages and motorboats on Ontario lakes. Stricter regulations around fishing for lake trout, as well as pollution, has seen the population in many lakes stabilize, but lake trout have a long way to go to fully recover.

However, there remain hundreds of great lake trout lakes in the region. The key is to respect lakers and realize that they are indeed a fragile sportfish. This fall spawning fish is recognized by its forked tail, long head and large snout as well as an abundance of spots. They grow very slowly and mature at an older age (6-8 years) than most other species; therefore, catch and release fishing can go a long way in helping maintain populations.

Similar to brook trout, lake trout are readily found near the surface in spring and will aggressively take spoon and spinner presentations. Although trolling is the preferred method, when the lakers are hitting, it is possible to fish for them from shore. When spring fishing for lakers is slow, you may even want to try a simple bobber and a dead minnow. Lakers will cruise by and pick up any decent looking meal.

As the water warms, lakers will seek the solace of the cooler water in the deeper parts of the lake and they become increasingly difficult to catch. Trolling becomes a necessity and gear to reach the depths of the lake where the trout are is vital to success. Down rigging equipment can certainly help with this task, although if you are fishing out of a canoe or simply prefer fishing without the down rigging gear, try a steel line or a lead core line rod set up. And remember the bigger the spoon the bigger the laker!

Largemouth Bass are found throughout Central Ontario in mainly the warmer water lakes and streams in the region. Despite the name, largemouth are actually a sunfish, not a bass. The largemouth bass is an aggressive feeder and puts up a commendable fight when hooked. Largemouth often frequent the quiet back bays of lakes where plenty of weed growth or shore structure is found. The great thing about largemouth bass is that they will often strike top water presentations.

Classic bass lures like the jitterbug or new classics like the hula popper can be a ton

The breadth and variety of fish species in Central Ontario is a testament to how good the fishing can be here. At any given time, there is quality fishing for one sportfish or another. There are over twenty five fish species that are angled for sport in the Province of Ontario and most species are regulated to some degree. We have listed the most popular sportfish found in the area along with tips on how and when to fish each species.

EASTERN BROOK TROUT

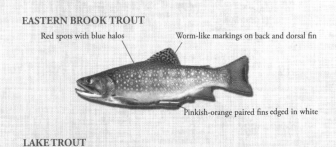

Red spots with blue halos

Worm-like markings on back and dorsal fin

Pinkish-orange paired fins edged in white

LAKE TROUT

Worm-like markings on back and dorsal fin

Tail deeply forked

LARGEMOUTH BASS

Large wide lower jaw slightly longer than the upper jaw

The anal and pelvic fins are green to olive with some white

MUSKELLUNGE - (Clear, Spotted, Barred)

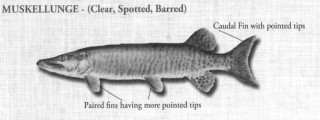

Caudal Fin with pointed tips

Paired fins having more pointed tips

of fun when fishing for largemouth. Top water action is usually best on calm overcast days or in the evening period. Often the calm before a storm can create a frenzy of action. Other lures to try when top water action is slow are jigs, spinner baits and crank baits. In the heat of summer largemouth bass will often sit in tight in heavy weed cover and weedless presentations are needed to pry them out of their slumber and convince them to take the lure. If you do entice a big bucket mouth to take your bait, it is likely you will be fighting a bunch of weeds on your line as well.

Muskellunge is the largest freshwater sportfish species in Ontario and can reach over 16 kg (35 lbs) in size. The Ontario record muskellunge was caught in 1989 in Blackstone Harbour of The Massasauga Provincial Park and weighed a whopping 29.5 kg (65 lbs). Muskie are an aggressive creature with sharp teeth used to decimate their prey. Every angler in Ontario knows a great muskie story or two, even if they have never fished for the predatory sportfish.

Fish Species

There are angling regulations in effect on all water bodies in Ontario in order to preserve the future of the resource. Some of the more specific regulations may include bait bans, special limits, slot size restrictions and closures. These regulations are having positive effects on fishing quality in the province and are in place strictly for the benefit of future angling.

NORTHERN PIKE

Dorsal fin set far back

Long flattened snout

PANFISH -BLACK CRAPPIE

Mouth extends to front edge of pupil

RAINBOW TROUT

Small black spots mostly restricted to above the lateral line

Radiating rows of spots on tail

No teeth in throat at back of tongue

SMALLMOUTH BASS

Jaw extends to about middle of eye

Three short spines on anal fin

Muskie fishing in Ontario has become a real specialty form of fishing over the past decade or so. Some anglers fish only for muskie and nothing else. While there is plenty to learn on how to become a better muskie angler, the basics are that muskie feed on mainly baitfish and often, large baitfish. In addition muskie are often on the move, cruising shoal areas where baitfish congregate or cruising weed lines waiting for an unsuspecting meal to venture out of the safety of the weed cover. Trolling is a popular method for finding muskie season long, but usually it is the unsuspected bass or walleye angler that hooks into these big fish and is surprised when they see their catch. One of the best times for muskie fishing is in the fall by trolling or casting larger crankbaits and presentations along weed lines and off underwater structure.

Northern Pike is the cousin of the muskellunge and inhabit weedy, murky waters throughout Ontario. They are found in hundreds of lakes and rivers in Central Ontario. Pike are very aggressive and readily strike fast moving spoons and spinners or anything imitating a good meal. In the spring, pike will be often found in the calm bays of lakes and you will often see a significant increase in success for pike on calm overcast days in quiet back bays. Generally, you will find small to medium size pike in

the quiet bays, whereas big pike are often found in the areas leading into bays. They will also hang around rocky points, shoals, islands and other places where there are larger fish that they can feed on.

When it comes to lures, there are the old classics like the Daredevil and the five of diamonds, but realistically, often pike will hit just about any lure. When specifically targeting pike in quiet bays, casting spoons along weedlines and other bottom structure can produce results or alternatively spinner baits or crankbaits or anything that looks like a good meal can entice strikes. For larger pike, trolling a larger spoon or plug is a good method of finding these aggressive fish.

Panfish of various types such as bluegill and sunfish are quickly becoming a popular target for Ontario anglers. In addition to being easily caught from shore or off a dock with a simple bobber and worm setup, panfish can also produce non stop action. While fishing for the larger sportfish species in some of the more popular lakes takes significant patience at times, it is quite possible to pull out dozens of these smaller fish in an hour. For younger anglers, this is the best way to get them interested in fishing. No kid wants to sit in a boat all day just to catch two or three fish, they want action.

While the bobber and worm is still the mainstay for panfish fishing, there are a wide variety of small spinners, jigs and jig bodies that have revolutionized this form of fishing. In addition to the steady action, the new lures that come in bright colours and in all different shapes and sizes are fun for kids too.

Rainbow Trout are native to the Pacific Northwest and get their name from the colourful stripe they get when spawning in the spring. They have also been introduced into many inland lakes and streams and are stocked by the Ministry of Natural Resources on a put and take basis. Like brook trout, rainbow take readily to small spinners, trolling small spoons or lake trolls as well as bobber fishing with a hook and worm.

While rainbow trout have similar characteristics as brook trout, rainbows are known to be more aggressive, and at times they will even launch right out of the lake while chasing down a meal. Flyfishing can certainly increase your success since rainbow trout prefer aquatic insects, either in larvae form or in adult stage. More specifically chironomid larvae are a favourite of rainbows as well as caddis, damselfly or dragonfly larvae. Additionally rainbows also will feed aggressively on leeches at times.

For stream fishing, surface flies can be fantastic for rainbows especially during the mayfly or caddis fly hatch periods. Even though there are periods where top water presentations are hot, the vast majority of the time rainbows are feeding on larvae. Because of this, it is recommended to have a number of different coloured bead head nymphs or simply nymph patterns in your fly box.

Smallmouth Bass are the close cousin of the largemouth bass (although technically, neither is a bass: both are members of the sunfish family) and are native to portions of Ontario. In this region, they are found throughout the majority of the lakes and streams. The smallmouth has a reputation of putting up a great fight when hooked and can be a very aggressive feeder at times. Smallmouth fans will tell you that pound for pound, smallmouth are the best fighters out there.

Smallmouth love structure and will gravitate to anything that they can use as cover. Look for boulders, underwater drop-offs and along rocky shoals or shoreline. Smaller smallmouth tend to hang out in the shallows through the summer, feeding on crayfish and insect nymphs. Working a crayfish fly or lure along a rocky bottom is often deadly for smaller smallmouth bass. As they get bigger, though, smallmouth will move into relatively deeper water, and begin feeding on baitfish. This can make them infuriatingly difficult to find, as they move around a lot.

While typical largemouth bass lures will work for smallmouth, including top water presentations, underwater presentations are usually more effective, as smallmouth are not as willing to come to the surface. On calm evenings, especially in the late spring, they will rise to the surface, though. Try working spinners, jigs and crankbaits along the structure areas and if fishing is slow, slow the retrieve down significantly.

Splake is a sterile cross between lake trout and brook trout and was developed specifically to stock lakes uninhabited by other trout or lakes where trout were either extinct or near extinction. In the 1960s, they were stocked in many of the Great Lakes to replace lampreydecimated lake trout stocks. The great thing about splake is that, unlike brook trout, they can grow quite big and unlike lake trout, they grow quite quickly. Success is best in spring and they regularly feed on insect larvae and smaller baitfish.

Splake mature in about three years, and can get to 4.5 kg (10 lbs). They are an aggressive predator, and love feeding on smaller fish, especially perch. They prefer to hold in water that is around 12–14°C. Like brook trout, they like to hold along shorelines and around cover, but they don't dig themselves into fallen timber the same way. They tend to be found around points that have deep water, shorelines with cover (fallen trees or a jumble or rocks), sand and mud flats and around the inflow and outflow of creeks.

Jigging for splake with a metal spoon like a Blue Fox Pixie or a William's Wabler works well, but jigging with a spoon and minnow works even better. Silver and gold work well, though sometimes pink or metallic blue and green will work, too. Work around the edge of dropoffs around 3–4 m (8–12 ft).

Walleye, or pickerel, is perhaps the most prized sportfish in Ontario due in part to its acclaim as a great tasting fish. The walleye's diet is made up of mainly baitfish, although they do take leeches and other grub like creatures. Walleye travel in loose schools and once you find them you should be able to catch more than one. The Central Ontario region is one of the most popular areas for walleye fishing.

Walleye will often cruise a lake or river for their prey and one of the most proven methods of regularly finding walleye is to troll a lake or if a spot is not producing, move on. One of the favourite lures or set ups for trolling for walleye is the worm harness. The worm harness is a spinner type lure specifically designed to hold bait and be trolled at various depths and speeds. Casting jigs is also quite popular as well as still jigging over a structure area such as a rock pile, weed hole or dropoff. Other lures that can produce results include crankbaits and spinners, but basically anything that will imitate the walleye's preferred food, the minnow.

Whitefish are a silvery fish with large scales that are found in many lakes in Ontario from the Great Lakes to the Hudson Bay. The species is not known as a sportfish due to its boney nature, although it is increasingly becoming more popular. The biggest attraction of having whitefish in a lake is that that often signals that the other sportfish in the lake (lake trout, pike, etc.) are going to be bigger than average. Whitefish provide a bountiful supply of food for some of the larger sportfish species, but they are also fun to catch. While they will strike small spinner presentations, whitefish feed quite heavily on insects and flyfishing can be quite exciting, especially in the spring during the mayfly hatches.

Yellow Perch are aggressive feeders and are best caught by still fishing worms with a float. Perch are active throughout the year, especially during ice fishing season. The fish is becoming so popular that the Ministry of Natural Resources has had to install a limit for the panfish. Perch are generally small, rarely getting to more than 0.5 kg (1 lb), but they are feisty and provide the bulk of the action on many walleye lakes when the walleye are nowhere to be found. Outside of a worm presentation, perch love small minnows, which is why they are so easy to catch while ice fishing. Small jigs and bodies will also work quite well for perch.

Please Note: There are angling regulations in effect on all water bodies in Ontario in order to preserve the future of the resource. Some of the more specific regulations may include bait bans, special limits, slot size restrictions and closures. These regulations are having positive effects on fishing quality in the province and are in place strictly for the benefit of future angling. For up to date information on the fishing regulations for this region and in Ontario, be sure to consult an up to date copy of the Ontario Recreational Fishing Regulations Summary or visit online http://www.mnr.gov.on.ca/MNR/pubs/fishing.

For up to date information on the fishing regulations for this region and in Ontario, be sure to consult an up to date copy of the Ontario Recreational Fishing Regulations Summary or visit online

http://www.mnr.gov.on.ca/en/Business/LetsFish/Publication/STEL02_163615.html

SPLAKE

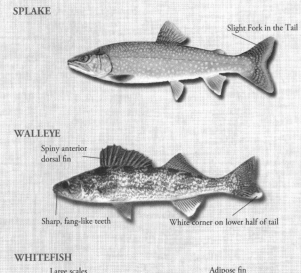

Slight Fork in the Tail

WALLEYE

Spiny anterior dorsal fin

Sharp, fang-like teeth

White corner on lower half of tail

WHITEFISH

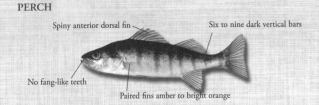

Large scales

Adipose fin

Teeth weakly developed or absent

PERCH

Spiny anterior dorsal fin

Six to nine dark vertical bars

No fang-like teeth

Paired fins amber to bright orange

Anstruther Lake

Location: 10 km (6 mi) west of Apsley
Maximum Depth: 39 m (128 ft)
Mean Depth: 22 m (72.2 ft)
Way Point: 44° 45′ 00″ Lat - N, 78° 12′ 00″ Lon - W

Fishing

This large cottage destination lake makes a scenic backdrop for several cottages and offers fishing opportunities for a range of sport fish. Fishing is best for bass as success can be good at times for decent sized smallmouth and largemouth bass. Bass can be found in any of the quiet bays found around the lake. Another good spot to look for bass is around cottage docks and other shore structure.

Unknown to many visitors to Anstruther Lake, the lake is home to a naturally reproducing strain of lake trout. These lakers have been fished heavily in the past but the increased use of catch and release has helped maintain the current lake trout populations. To further help protect the lake trout stocks, the lake is part of the winter/spring fishing sanctuary. Fishing success peaks just after the season opens in late spring. During the summer, down rigging equipment is required to find lake trout. At this time, a good region to try is in the deep area found in the southwest end of the lake. The shoals in this area often hold summer lake trout.

Facilities

Anstruther Lake is home to the well-established public boat access as well as a small marina. West of the main public access, there is another boat launch and marina. The lake also provides access to two fabulous canoe route systems that continue north and south to other lakes in the area. Paddlers looking for Crown Land areas to camp at will find Crab Lake to the south and Rathburn Lake to the north are better suited for camping.

Other Options

A good fishing alternative to Anstruther Lake is **Rathburn Lake**, which is found to the north. The lake is part of the Serpentine Lake Canoe Loop and is accessible via a 162 m (531 ft) portage from the north side of Anstruther Lake. Fishing in Rathburn Lake is rumoured to be decent lake largemouth and smallmouth bass. The lake is also home to a natural population of walleye and is regularly stocked with lake trout.

Directions

Anstruther Lake is part of the series of lakes in the Kawartha Highlands. The larger lake is found not far off Highway 28 north of Lakefield. Just south of Apsley off Highway 28, Anstruther Lake Road leads west. The road is well marked and should not be difficult to find. Follow Anstruther Lake Road west all the way to the public access area along the east side of Anstruther Lake. The access area is a rough boat launch complete with a parking area.

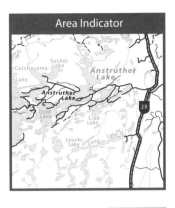
Area Indicator

Species
Lake Trout
Largemouth Bass
Smallmouth Bass

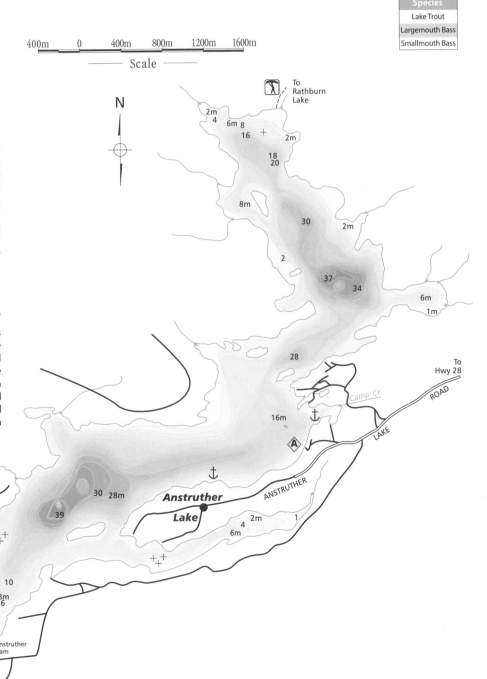

© Backroad Mapbooks

Zone **15**

Location: 1 km (0.6 mi) east of Apsley
Maximum Depth: 12 m (40.4 ft)
Mean Depth: 5 m (16.4 ft)
Way Point: 44° 46' 00" Lat - N, 78° 04' 00" Lon - W

Apsley Lake

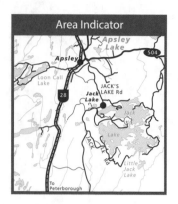

Area Indicator

Fishing

Apsley Lake is one of those small lakes that can surprise an angler at times. The lake provides fair fishing for smallmouth bass that can be picked up pretty much anywhere around the lake. There are also rumours of the odd largemouth bass being caught in the lake. One particular area to concentrate your efforts is the drop-off area along the western shore of the lake. Some nice sized bass are regularly caught in this area. During slower periods, try working a jig or similar bait close to the bottom.

A unique attraction about Apsley Lake is that the lake supports a small muskellunge population. The musky are not usually very big, but musky hunters may find this lake quite an interesting lake to fish. The deep 12 m (40 ft) holes along with the definite 6 m (20 ft) shoal area make interesting structure to find muskellunge.

Species
Largemouth Bass
Muskellunge
Smallmouth Bass

Directions

To find Apsley Lake, follow Highway 28 north from Peterborough to the County Road 504 cut-off and the small town of Apsley. Continue east on the 504 to a crossing of Apsley Creek, which can be paddled north to Apsley Lake.

Facilities

There are no facilities available at Apsley Lake, although **Silent Lake Provincial Park** is mere minutes away along Highway 28 north. The park offers full amenities including flush toilets and showers. There are also a few local private campgrounds and tent & trailer parks found in the area. Chandos Lake to the north and Jack Lake to the south are both home to private campgrounds.

Other Options

There are several fine angling alternatives available in the immediate area. The closest lake, **Lower Apsley Lake**, lies to the southwest of Apsley Lake and is accessible off County Road 504. The lake offers fishing opportunities for both smallmouth and largemouth bass.

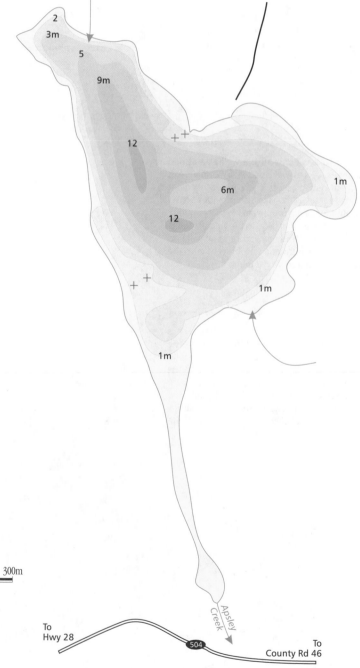

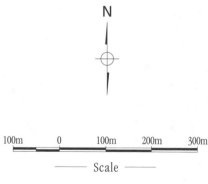

N

| 100m | 0 | 100m | 200m | 300m |

Scale

Balsam Lake

Location: Rosedale
Surface Area: 4,665 ha (11,528 ac)
Elevation: 256.3 m (841 ft)
Maximum Depth: 9.1 m (30 ft)
Mean Depth: 5.5 m (18 ft)
Waypoint: 44° 35′ 00″ Lat - N, 78° 50′ 00″ Lon - W

17 Zone

Area Indicator

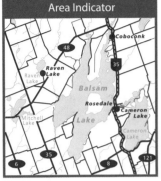

Species
Largemouth Bass
Muskellunge
Smallmouth Bass
Walleye

Fishing

As one of the more popular Trent-Severn Waterway lakes, Balsam Lake receives significant angling pressure throughout the season, especially during the summer months. Despite the heavy fishing pressure, the lake continues to produce decent results for several sport fish.

Walleye are the main species sought after in the lake and fishing for walleye can be good at times. One area in particular to concentrate efforts is the 4 m (13 ft) shoal hump found in the western portion of the lake. This hump is a natural attractant for weed growth and baitfish, which the predatory walleye mainly feed on. Anglers should also look for other shoal areas that walleye will congregate at in search of easy meals. Alternatively, the various stream mouths found around Balsam are decent holding areas for early season walleye as well as the elusive muskellunge. Musky hunters boast that the lake is quite productive for good-sized muskellunge. In order to maintain the fishery, there have been several regulation changes including reduced limits and slot sizes for walleye.

Largemouth bass and smallmouth bass are the other main sport fish found in Balsam Lake. Good numbers of bass can be found anywhere from the weedy shoreline areas to the rocky shoals bordering the islands around the lake. In fact, the South Bay is a well-known largemouth bass holding area. Top water flies and lures can be a lot of fun in the bay for largemouth during overcast periods or at dusk. As on any lake, bass can become lethargic at times, especially during the heat and bright of summer. To entice these reluctant bass, try working grub type bait such as a jig in a much slower fashion along the bottom structure of known holding areas. Often the less aggressive bass will suck in a well-presented jig as it is worked through their holding area.

Directions

The easiest way to find Balsam Lake is to take Highway 35 north from Highway 401. Highway 35 leads directly past the eastern shore of Balsam Lake providing access to all the local boat launches and marinas. Alternatively, you can take County Road 45 east from Highway 12 to access the west side of the lake.can take County Road 45 east from Highway 12 to access the west side of the lake.

Facilities

Balsam Lake is one of the larger Kawartha Lakes along the Trent-Severn Waterway. There are a few full service marinas and boat launches available. Overnight facilities include a number of tent and trailer parks along with the **Balsam Lake Provincial Park**. The provincial park is a full service park, offering all the basic amenities including flush toilets and showers. The park is very busy throughout the summer months and it is recommended to make reservations prior to arrival. For supplies and roofed accommodations such as motels, the towns of Coboconk and Fenelon Falls are both within minutes of the lake. For provincial park reservations call (888) ONT-PARK.

Map labels

To Norland · Gull River · Coboconk · weeds · Indian Point · North Bay · Balsam Lake Prov Park · NORTHBAY · 48 · Gull River · 5th CONC · 35 · PARKSIDE Rd · To Mitchell Lake · DRIVE · INDIAN POINT · Prov Park · Ball Isl · Hogg Isl · 5m · 4 · Delamere Isl · LAKE · BLANCHARD Rd · Mackenzie Pt · BALSAM · Trent Canal · Grand Island · Rosedale · Trent Canal · Long Pt · 9m · 7 · 6m · 4 · 2m · Long Point · 3rd CONC Rd · West Bay · 7 · Daniels Pt · Camp Kagawong · South Bay · 7 · To Lindsay · N · 2m · Birch Pt · KILLARNEY BAY · Staples River

Scale
500m 0 · 1km · 2km · 3km
Scale

Zone 17

Location: 11 km (7 mi) north of Bobcaygeon
Elevation: 244 m (800 ft)
Surface Area: 115 ha (285 ac)
Maximum Depth: 9 m (29.5 ft)
Way Point: 44° 41′00″ Lat - N, 78° 32′00″ Long - W

Bass Lake- Lindsay/Bobcaygeon

Area Indicator

Species	
Largemouth Bass	Smallmouth Bass
Muskellunge	Walleye
Rock Bass	Yellow Perch

Fishing

As the name suggests, the Bass Lake found north of Bobcaygeon is inhabited by bass. Smallmouth and largemouth bass are the targeted species, but there are also rock bass that can all be taken throughout the open season. Adding to the mix are muskellunge, walleye and perch.

The lake has productive weed growth, providing good cover for bass. For this reason, top water presentations such as poppers, prop-baits, or stickbaits can create a stir on the lake at times. Try just off the small island found southwest of the boat launch for ambush ready bass. While these typical largemouth bass lures will work for smallmouth, underwater presentations are regularly more effective. Try working spinners, jigs and crankbaits along the structure areas and if fishing is slow, slow the retrieve down significantly. When smallmouth bass are lethargic, they will often simply suck in the lure or fly as it passes by.

Those looking for musky or walleye will find the fishing generally slow, while perch can be a little easier to find. Those looking for the aggressive muskellunge are best to start with traditional spoons such as the Daredevil and the Five of Diamonds. Good muskie lures are 12–15 cm (4–5 inch) floating fire-tiger or orange Rapalas. The odd lunker is caught each year.

Facilities

The closest facilities to Bass Lake can be found in the town of Bobcaygeon. The town offers a number of private campgrounds as well as a few motels in the area. If you prefer, **Balsam Lake Provincial Park** is located west of Bass Lake, just outside of the town of Coboconk.

Directions

The easiest way to access Bass Lake is to travel northeast along County Road 36 from the town of Lindsay through the town of Bobcaygeon. Look for the Bass Lake Road and follow this road north past Nogies Marsh eventually reaching the fire access roads that access the east side of the lake. There is an informal launch area on this side of the lake off the 405 fire access road, but there are also several private cottages in this area that may limit public access

Other Options

Concession Lake to the east of Bass Lake is accessible by 4wd type trails and offers fishing opportunities for smallmouth and largemouth bass as well as for stocked lake trout. Due to the rough access to the lake, fishing remains fairly steady. To the south, Nogies Creek is a good alternative for walleye, smallmouth and largemouth bass as well as panfish.

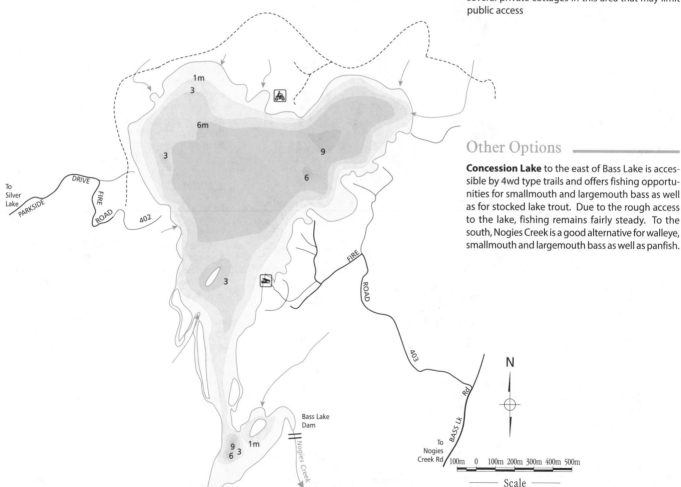

Bass Lake- Perth/Rideau

Location: 15 km (9 mi) southwest of Smiths Falls
Elevation: 134 m (439 ft)
Surface Area: 290 ha (716 ac)
Maximum Depth: 22.5 m (74 ft)
Mean Depth: 8.2 m (27.1 ft)
Waypoint: 44° 49′00″ N, 76° 08′00″ W

18 Zone

Fishing

Found near Big Rideau Lake, this Bass Lake is best known as a smallmouth bass lake. However, it is full of a good variety of fish species that range from bass, pike and walleye to rainbow trout, perch and other panfish. Anglers looking for largemouth and smallmouth bass will find better success along structure areas such as shoals, rocky drop-offs and even near cottage docks. When working these areas be prepared for the odd northern pike or even walleye that can surprise the unsuspecting angler with their size. Alternatively, younger anglers might have better luck casting for perch in these same areas.

In Bass Lake, there are a couple of significant points that jut out into the lake and continue underwater forming large shoal areas. These are the prime areas to focus your angling efforts. Your best bet for success is to troll along these shoals and points to find feeding bass and northern pike. The big shallow bays found along the southern end of the lake are other hotspots to try. These bays are home to significant weed growth that provides ample structure for both bass and northern pike. Bass can be found in these holding areas even during the hottest of days, while pike tend to roam into the areas during overcast periods or in the evening.

Facilities

Along with the tent and trailer park, there are numerous cottages and camps located along the shoreline of Bass Lake. Some of these cottages and camps can be rented for a fee throughout the summer months. The only boat launching facilities available are at the tent and trailer park.

Directions

To reach Bass Lake, begin by following Highway 15 south from Smiths Falls to County Road 1 or the Rideau Ferry Road. County Road 1 traverses west past Pegg Road (which leads to the east shore of Bass Lake) to Bass Lake Road. Follow this road to the private tent and trailer park along the northeastern shore of the lake that provides boat launching facilities for a small fee..

Other Options

Otter Lake is literally minutes away from Bass Lake and is readily accessible via Highway 15. The lake is quite developed and offers fishing opportunities for bass, northern pike and the odd stocked rainbow trout.

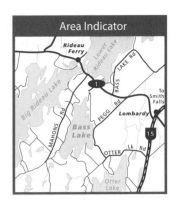

Species	
Largemouth Bass	Smallmouth Bass
Northern Pike	Walleye
Rainbow Trout	Yellow Perch

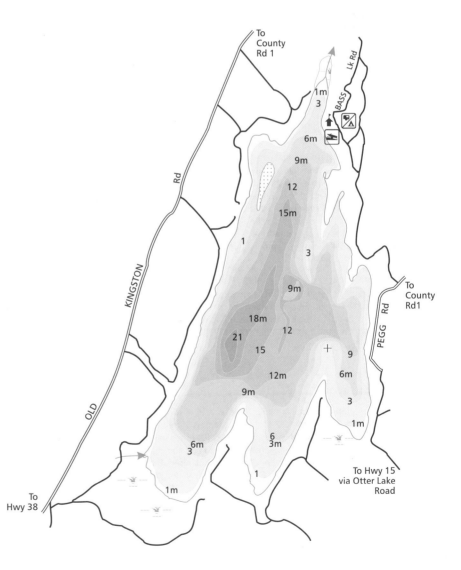

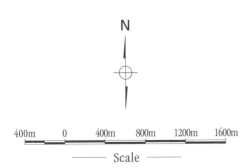

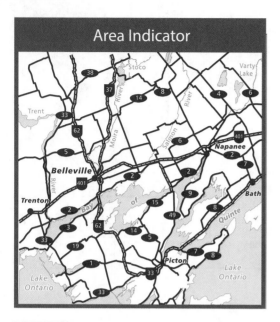

Area Indicator

Species
Largemouth Bass
Northern Pike
Smallmouth Bass
Walleye

Directions

Bay of Quinte is a large waterbody that can be easily accessed from many areas including the cities of Belleville and Trenton to the south of Highway 401. Trenton provides good access to the most northern stretch of the bay. Look for boat launch sites south of town off the east side of County Road 33. Continuing east, the city of Belleville offers a launching area near the northwest side of the Bay Bridge of Highway 62. Belleville also provides the main access to the Big Bay portion of the Bay of Quinte. There are other access areas around Big Bay on Big Island and near the settlements of Northport.

Further south, Highway 62 links to Highway 33 and eventually takes you to Picton and the southern tip of the Bay of Quinte. The scenic, original loyalist community is also found at the south end of County Road 49. Continuing east Highway 33 leads to the Glenora Ferry and along the north shore of Adolphus Reach and the North Channel of the bay where several access points are found en route to Bath and Kingston beyond. Alternatively, follow County Road 7 west to the community to Cressy and one final launch site.

Facilities

Similar to the tremendous number of access points, visitors to the Bay of Quinte area have plenty of options to choose from. Motels, hotels, grocery stores and other amenities are readily found in the cities of Belleville and Trenton in the northwest. If you prefer, there are the odd bed and breakfast that can be found in the smaller villages like Crofton. For campers, there are a few tent and trailer parks available on the Tyendinaga First Nations Reserve found east of Belleville.

As a popular boating and vacationing spot, there are numerous facilities available around this portion of the Bay of Quinte. The town of Picton is a beautiful bay side town complete with numerous amenities, including grocery stores, bed and breakfasts, motels and other retail establishments. Outside of the Picton area, you can find a number of different access areas around the bay as well as a few marinas and facilities like tent and trailer parks.

Finally, the North Channel is well serviced from Bath and Kingston. Of course there are cottage resorts and a variety of other amenities in this area too.

Fishing

The Bay of Quinte is synonymous with fishing. The bay has long been home to fine catches of everything from bass to pike, but is best known for its walleye. In fact, Bay of Quinte is called the "Walleye Capital of the World" and is host to one of North America's largest freshwater sports fishing derbies. Partly due to its fame and partly due to its close proximity to cities like Belleville, Kingston and Trent the bay remains a very popular destination.

This is definitely evident in the stretch of water between Trenton and Belleville and the North Channel west of Kingston. Every year anglers flock to these sections of the bay in search of the fabled walleye. Fishing for walleye can be productive throughout the year, as the shallow, weedy nature of this portion of the Bay of Quinte provides a good source of habitat. One of the favourite lures or set ups for trolling for walleye is the worm harness. The worm harness is a spinner type lure specifically designed to hold bait and be trolled at various depths and speeds. While worm harnesses and jigs are the mainstay for most anglers when fishing for walleye, be sure not to overlook minnow type crankbaits and lures like the classic Rapala or even Shad Rap or X-Rap.

Big Bay found east of Belleville is perhaps the most famous angling area as the bay is notorious for producing some good sized walleye. It is also a very busy section of the bay as it is easily accessed the city of Belleville. The inlet areas around the Moira River and Salmon River are often decent holding regions for walleye during various times of the year. Locating the shoal areas around the Salmon River can definitely increase your chances of success. The deeper areas near Northport are also popular angling locations.

Further south, the bay around the Picton area is not as popular as some of the other regions, although the fishing remains productive. Fishing for walleye can be good at times, with some of the more productive areas found in the Mohawk Bay area and the Hay Bay region. As with most other waterbodies, success is often linked to finding underwater structure. Look for shoal areas and weed growth to increase your success.

With so much attention focused on walleye, other species such as bass and pike are often overlooked and underutilized. However, anglers in the know will often go home with decent catches of these sportfish. Some big northerns can be hooked in the Bay of Quinte and the word is slowly getting out.

There is a lot of weed growth and other structure around the bay that can hide lurking predators like bass and pike. Look for rocky shoal areas for smallmouth, while largemouth bass and smallmouth bass can be found anywhere around weed structure. Northern pike are often caught in the morning or at dusk around weed beds when they cruise the shallows in search of prey.

For smallmouth bass, largemouth bass and northern pike, Muscote Bay, Mohawk Bay and Hay Bay are all good choices. The shallow nature of the bays coupled with the usually good weed structure makes for great bass and pike habitat. Of course, you can always find walleye in these type of areas as well. The bay around the Picton area is another good area to target bass. Success is usually always better for smallmouth bass or even largemouth bass than walleye or pike here. As with most other waterbodies, success is often linked to finding underwater structure. Look for shoal areas and weed growth to increase your success.

Ice fishing is also very popular here with the chance to land nice sized walleye and pike along with panfish.

Other Options

If you are a big water type angler, the best fishing alternative to the Bay of Quinte in this region would be Lake Ontario. The expanse of **Lake Ontario** is accessible to the west of Trenton by vehicle or by boat via the Murray Canal. A large watercraft is needed to fish the lake, as trolling is the main method of angling. Salmon and rainbow trout are the focus of fishing in the giant lake, although you can experience good success for bass and northern pike closer to shore. If your luck is slow, try the many bays along the shore for the abundance of pan fish like crappie and rock bass.

Bay of Quinte -
Trenton to Northport

Location: Trenton-Belleville
Maximum Depth: 10 m (32.8 ft)
Mean Depth: 5 m (16.4 ft)
Waypoint: 44° 09' 00" Lat - N, 77° 18' 00" Lon - W

20 Zone

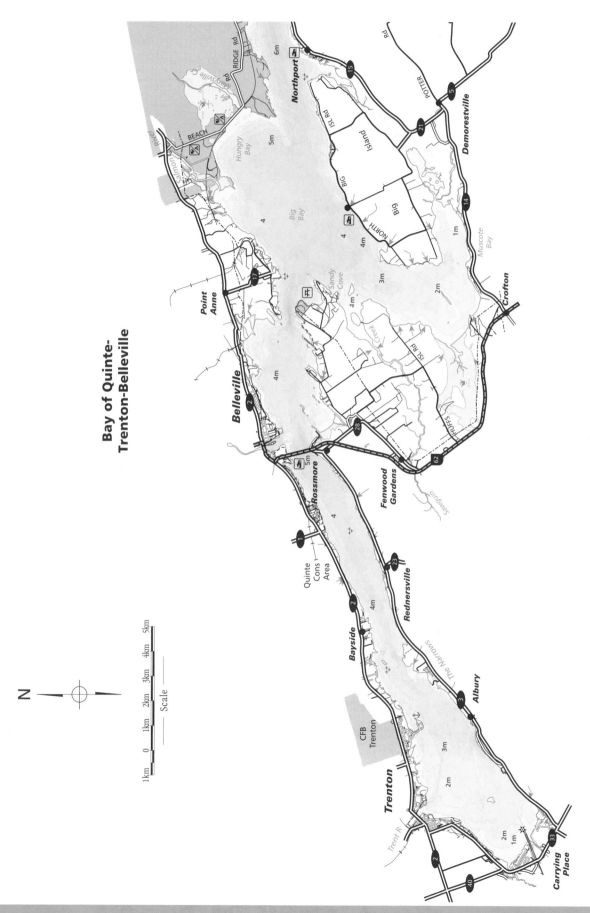

Bay of Quinte-
Trenton-Belleville

N

5km
4km
3km
2km
1km
0
1km
Scale

Zone 20

Location: Bath
Maximum Depth: 66 m (216 ft)
Mean Depth: 19.4 m (63 ft)
Waypoint: 44° 10′ 58″ N, 76° 46′ 36″ W

Bay of Quinte -
North Channel

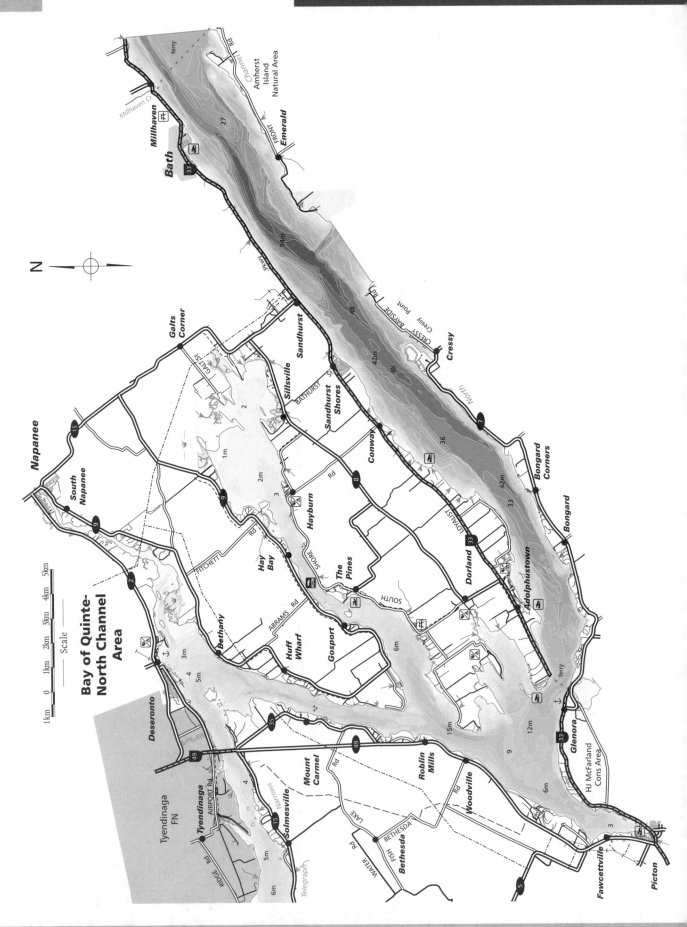

**Bay of Quinte-
North Channel
Area**

Scale

1km 0   1km 2km 3km 4km 5km

Beaver Lake - Kawarthas Highlands

Location: 9 km (5.5 mi) east of Catchacoma
Surface Area: 502.2 ha (1,241 ac)
Maximum Depth: 12.0 m (39.3 ft)
Mean Depth: 2.4 m (7.9 ft)
Geographic: 44° 30' 00" Lat - N, 77° 02' 00" Lon - W

Fishing

You can find fair numbers of largemouth and smallmouth bass in Beaver Lake. Bass provide the bulk of the fishing opportunities on the lake and are generally located along almost any of the rocky shoreline or weed structure areas. Off Maniece Island is a known holding area for bass, while the 1-4 m (3-10 ft) shoal area in the middle of the lake almost always produces bass.

A natural population of lake trout also exists in Beaver Lake and the lake is part of the winter/spring fishing sanctuary in order to protect the low lake trout stocks. Lake trout can be caught by trolling during the open season and are usually around the deeper 18 m (59 ft) hole found in the lake. Be sure to practice catch and release whenever possible.

Facilities

The boat launch onto Cavendish Lake is the main access point for Beaver Lake. A marina, boat launch and tent and trailer park can also be found on Catchacoma Lake to the west of Beaver Lake. Beaver Lake is accessible via boat from Catchacoma, Mississagua and Gold Lakes.

Directions

Beaver Lake is another fine fishing lake found in the Kawartha Highlands. This area can be busy with boat traffic and is part of a series of canoe routes. To reach the lake, follow County Road 36 north from the town of Buckhorn to Flynn's Turn and head north along County Road 507. County Road 507 passes by the west side of Mississagua and Catchacoma Lakes, which are home to access points to the lake chain. The interconnected chain of lakes include Mississagua, Catchacoma, Gold and Beaver Lakes.

Other Options

The closest angling alternative to Beaver Lake is **Catchacoma Lake** to the west. The bigger lake offers consistent fishing for smallmouth bass, largemouth bass and the odd resident lake trout.

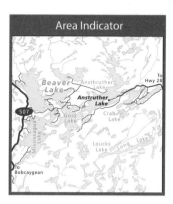

Area Indicator

Species
Lake Trout
Largemouth Bass
Smallmouth Bass

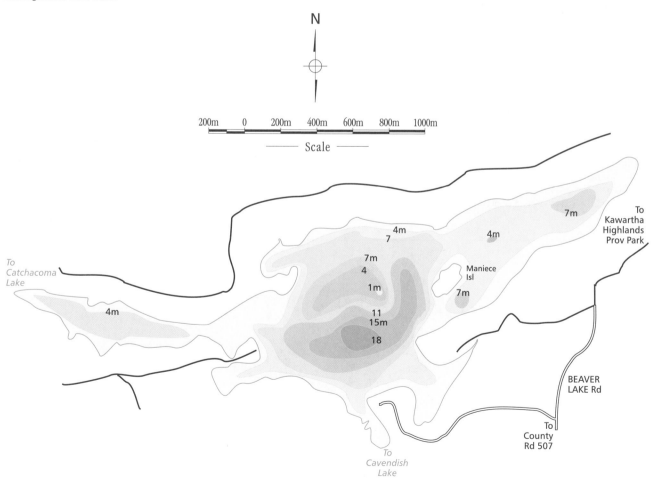

N

| 200m | 0 | 200m | 400m | 600m | 800m | 1000m |

Scale

To Catchacoma Lake

4m

7m
4
1m

11
15m

18

4m
7

4m

7m

Maniece Isl

7m

7m

To Kawartha Highlands Prov Park

BEAVER LAKE Rd

To County Rd 507

To Cavendish Lake

Location: 22 km (13.7 mi) south of Kaladar
Elevation: 167 m (548 ft)
Surface Area: 529 ha (1,307 ac)
Maximum Depth: 12 m (39.3 ft)
Mean Depth: 2.4 m (7.9 ft)
Waypoint: 44° 30' 00" N, 77° 02' 00" W

Beaver Lake- Tweed

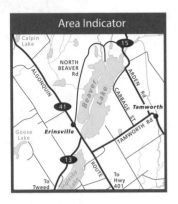

Area Indicator

Species	
Black Crappie	Walleye
Largemouth Bass	Yellow Perch
Northern Pike	Other
Smallmouth Bass	

Fishing

Near Erinsville, Beaver Lake is a clean, beautiful body of water that has many homes and summer cottages. As part of the Salmon River system, the lake is also a popular fishing lake that is home to populations of most warm water species found in the region. Northern pike, smallmouth bass, largemouth bass, walleye, perch and a host of other species are all found in the lake. The presence of abundant baitfish makes it possible to find a good sized pike or walleye on occasion.

Walleye are the most sought after and most difficult sportfish to catch in Beaver Lake. A good holding area for the prized walleye in the spring or the late fall is the inlet and outflow of the Salmon River. During the summer months, walleye will still cruise the river area, although they are mainly found in the deeper water of the lake. As the water warms up in summer, the walleye will hit faster moving bait, so it's possible to speed up to cover more area. Crankbaits like Shad Raps, Redfins and other hard minnow baits. Drifting works well if the wind is cooperative since there is no engine noise to spook the walleye.

Fishing success for northern pike is generally slow to fair for pike that are usually quite small, while success for both smallmouth and largemouth bass can be good on occasion. The good areas to find northern pike and largemouth bass are the weedy shallows found around the lake. In particular, the region around the outflow of the Salmon River seems to attract fish. Try working a top water lure or popper fly for both largemouth and northern pike here. Smallmouth bass can sometimes be found amid the weedy shallows, although are most predominant off the rocky shoreline areas found around various portions of Beaver Lake.

Directions

Centrally located, Beaver Lake is just 35 minutes from Kingston, 2 hours from Ottawa and about 3 hours from Toronto. It is found south of Kaladar and Highway 7, just off County Road 41. The access area for Beaver Lake is located along the southern shore. There is plenty of parking and a gravel boat launch for visitors to access the lake.

Facilities

The village of Erinsville has a large Catholic Church and school along with sports facilities including an arena, soccer field and baseball park. Around the lake, there are many cottages with a few that are available for rent. Inquire locally for information for rental information. Alternatively, the village of Kaladar is only minutes away by vehicle to the north of Beaver Lake and is home to a hotel, a few restaurants and a general store.

Other Options

Inglesby Lake is located to the southwest of Beaver Lake and can be easily reached via County Road 13. The lake is about half the size of Beaver Lake and is inhabited by smallmouth and largemouth bass. The success rate and size of bass in Inglesby Lake is quite similar to Beaver Lake.

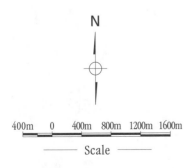

N

400m	0	400m	800m	1200m	1600m

Scale

Belmont Lake

Location: 6 km (3.5 mi) east of Peterborough
Elevation: 195 m (644 ft)
Surface Area: 758 ha (1,873 ac)
Maximum Depth: 16.1 m (51 ft)
Mean Depth: 6.2 m (20 ft)
Geographic: 44° 31'00" Lat - N, 77° 49'00" Lon - W

Fishing

Belmont Lake is part of the Crowe River system and offers fishing opportunities for smallmouth bass, largemouth bass, walleye and northern pike. Fishing is best for bass as the weedy and shallow nature of the lake has created some fantastic habitat. While bass can be found away from the weed structure, to find consistent fishing you will need to work your presentation deep into the cover. Working subsurface flies, such as weedless leech or streamer fly patterns, or a tube jig is best to coax these deep holding bass into striking. Look for bass holding in every bay and notably in King Bay, North River Bay and Deer Bay.

Walleye remain a popular sport fish on the lake, while a few northern pike can also be found on occasion. Try trolling worm harnesses or other walleye lures along the weed lines for cruising walleye. A good holding spot is the 6 m (20 ft) shoal found just off the northeast side of Big Island. Reports are that fishing is generally slow to fair for average sized walleye and small pike.

Directions

To reach Belmont Lake follow Highway 7 east from Peterborough past the village of Havelock. Just as you are coming out of the village, watch for County Road 48 off the north side of Highway 7. County Road 48 provides access to the southern and eastern portions of the lake. The road also passes over Crowe River. At the bridge a canoe can be launched into the river providing access to the lake.

Facilities

Other than the possibility of renting a cottage on Belmont Lake, there are no facilities available in the immediate area. For cottage rentals, there are a number of resources on the web or inquire with a local real estate agent. All amenities, including groceries, gas, bait can be found in the nearby town of Marmora.

Area Indicator

Species	
Black Crappie	Smallmouth Bass
Largemouth Bass	Walleye
Muskellunge	Yellow Perch
Northern Pike	

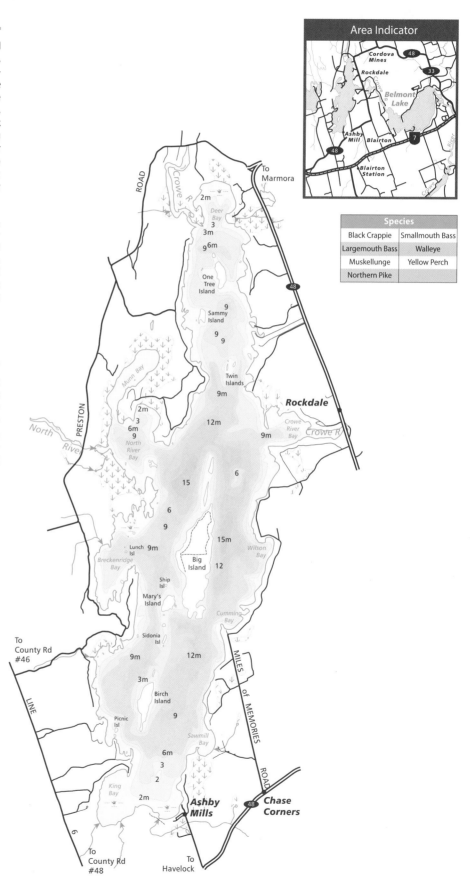

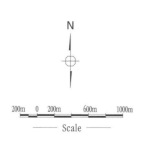

Zone **18**

Location: 15 km (9 mi) west of Perth
Elevation:158.2 m (519 ft)
Surface Area: 762 ha (1,882 ac)
Maximum Depth: 12.2 m (40 ft)
Mean Depth: 4.4 m (14.4 ft)
Waypoint: 44° 55'00"N, 76° 28'00"W

Bennett Lake

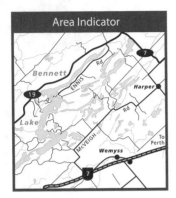

Area Indicator

Species
Largemouth Bass
Northern Pike
Smallmouth Bass
Walleye

Directions

Bennett Lake is a long lake that lies just west of the town of Perth. The lake can be accessed by following Highway 7 west to County Road 36. Follow County Road 36 north to County Road 19 (Bennett Lake Road). Bennett Lake Road travels east passing by numerous cottage access roads along the northern length of the lake. Permission is required from private land owners to access the lake.

Facilities

Bennett Lake is a well developed cottage lake that is home to a few camps and cottages that rent to the public privately. For supplies and other accommodations, the nearby town of Perth has plenty to offer visitors. It is best to inquire locally for information on camps and cottage rentals.

Fishing

This odd shaped lake is quite popular throughout the summer and winter months with anglers in search of smallmouth and largemouth bass, northern pike and walleye. Anglers will find numerous prime holding areas in the many bays, rock drop-offs and weed lines scattered around the lake. Bass anglers usually have good success on Bennett Lake.

Bennett Bay, located in the southeastern corner of the lake is a good holding area for bass and northern pike. Bass can often be picked up in the deep weeds of the bay, while northerns roam the area in the spring and during the evening periods in the summer. Another prime area for both northerns and bass is the weedy, shallow, northern end of the lake. This region offers plenty of structure for cover weary bass and pike, although anglers will find fishing here can create a lot of snags. A good way to avoid snags along heavy weed cover like this area to work either a weedless spinner bait, a jig or top water lure or fly.

Ice fishing is a popular winter activity on Bennett Lake with numerous huts found on the lake in search of walleye, perch and northern pike. Through the ice, try a small jig, tipped with a minnow or worm. Currently, if you plan to keep your walleye, there is a minimum length limit of 41 cm (16 in) in place to help aid reproduction rates.

Other Options

In the southwest corner of Bennett Lake, you can reach0 **Fagan Lake** by canoe during high water periods. There is a small stream that flows between the two lakes providing a possible water connection. Fagan Lake is much smaller that Bennett Lake and is also home to a few cottages. Fishing in Fagan Lake is fair for smallmouth and largemouth bass, while success for walleye and northern pike is often slow.

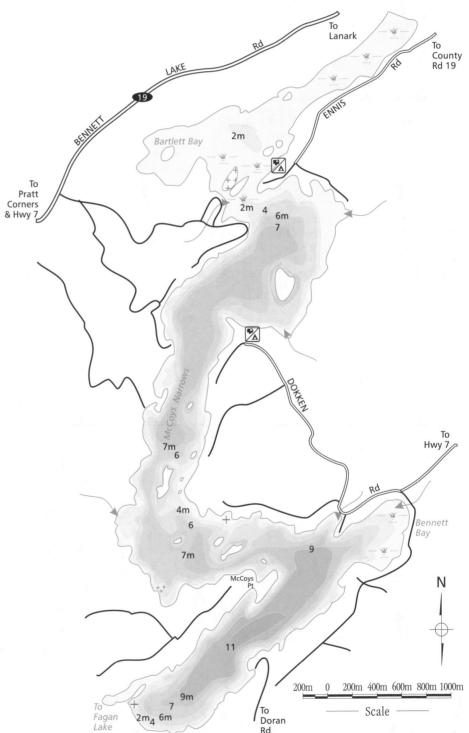

Big & Little Bald Lakes

Location: 12 km (7.5 mi) east of Bobcaygeon
Elevation: 249 m (808 ft)
Maximum Depth: 9.2 m (30 ft)
Mean Depth: 5.2 m (17.7 ft)
Waypoint: 44° 34' 00" Lat - N, 78° 23' 00" Lon - W

17 Zone

Fishing

The Bald Lakes are just a northern extension of Pigeon Lake; therefore, the fishing quality of the lakes is quite similar. The most predominant sport fish found in the lakes are both smallmouth and largemouth bass. The shallow nature of the lake, coupled with the endless shoal areas, weed lines and underwater rock piles, make for a myriad of bass holding areas in the Bald Lakes. Try off any one of the small islands or in one of the many bays for good bass action throughout much of the season. Topwater lures and flies can be a lot of fun, especially in the quiet bays as dusk approaches.

Walleye and muskellunge also attract a lot of attention throughout the year. Fishing for walleye can be fair to good at times, while angling is slow to fair for musky. The Big Bald Narrows is a known hot spot for walleye, although the sport fish can literally be found throughout the lake. During late spring and summer, weed lines can be a prime holding area for walleye as the predator cruises the structure in search of food. In and around the mouth of the Squaw River is a popular spot to try during the spring opening.

If your luck is slow for the bigger fish, there are always smaller fish to keep you occupied. Sport fish like crappie, perch and rock bass, can be a ton of fun to catch, especially on lighter angling gear.

Directions

Both Big Bald and Little Bald Lakes lie south of County Road 36 east of the town of Bobcaygeon. The lakes are accessible via cottage roads that branch south off the county road. The main access road to the lakes is Northern Avenue, which can be picked up via Kennedy or Nichols Cove Roads from County Road 36.

Facilities

There are no public facilities available on Big Bald Lake or Little Bald Lake; however, there are a number of resorts, motels and private campgrounds in the region that are within easy access to both lakes. Alternatively, **Balsam Lake Provincial Park** lies to the west and offers full facility camping with all the basic amenities of home. The nearby town of Bobcaygeon has numerous retail operations available to supply anything that may be required to make your adventure a success.

Other Options

There are several other fishing options available nearby including a number of large Kawartha Lakes. For a more out of the way alternative, **De Gaulle Lake** and **Concession Lake** to the north offer fishing for bass, while Concession Lake also offers fishing for stocked lake trout. Both lakes are accessed by rough 4wd trails branching off Nogies Creek Road.

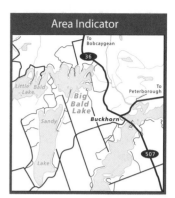

Area Indicator

Species
Largemouth Bass
Muskellunge
Smallmouth Bass
Walleye

N

| 200m | 0 | 200m | 400m | 600m | 800m | 1000m |

Scale

Zone 15

Location: 2 km (1 mi) west of Haultain
Maximum Depth: 18.5 m (61 ft)
Mean Depth: 9.3 m (30.5 ft)
Waypoint: 44° 36′00″ Lat - N, 78° 10′00″ Lon - W

Big Cedar Lake

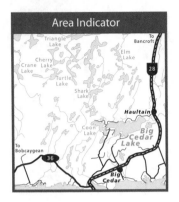

Area Indicator

Species
Largemouth Bass
Muskellunge
Rock Bass
Smallmouth Bass
Walleye

Fishing

Big Cedar Lake is a scenic spring fed lake with many islands to explore and a lovely granite shoreline surrounded by pine trees. Although there are reports of walleye, the main sportfish found in Big Cedar Lake is smallmouth bass, which provide fair to good fishing for nice sized fish. Similar to walleye, look for smallmouth off any one of the islands or along drop-off areas. Flipping jigs in deeper water or working spinners in the more shallow areas near structure seem to provide success. Working jigs and crankbaits along the structure areas can also be productive. But if the fishing is slow, slow the retrieve down significantly. When smallmouth bass are lethargic, they will often simply suck in the lure or fly as it passes by.

A small population of muskellunge also inhabits the lake but these creatures are very elusive. Although challenging, many musky hunters fin d success by trolling the lake. Try working a jointed Rapala in a Fire Tiger pattern, or an X-Rap Jointed Shad in Gold. Muskie are very sensitive to sound, and scatter when they hear a boat approaching. They will return to where they were once the boat has past, but it is good to have your lure at least 70 m (200 ft) behind the boat. The jointed lures have a very pronounced swimming motion which can draw strikes from these big predators.

Other sportfish reported in Big Cedar Lake are largemouth bass and rock bass. The latter are easily caught from shore and make a fine alternative for children.

Directions

Found about half an hour north of the city of Peterborough, you will find Big Cedar Lake by travelling north along Highway 28 past the town of Lakefield and the popular tourist area of Burleigh Falls. Just northeast of Burleigh Falls, look for Julian Lake Road off the west side of the highway. Julian Lake Road travels past Julian Lake to the boat launch area on Big Cedar Lake. Alternatively, Haultain Road branches west from the highway and leads to another launching site off the east side of the lake.

Facilities

Big Cedar Lake is part of the **Buzzard Lake Canoe Route** and offers a public beach and boat launch along with few other access sites and rustic camping. There are a number of cottages located along the shoreline including cottages for rent, while a few private campgrounds and resorts are found in the immediate area. Locally there is a convenience store with gas and food and nearby restaurants.

Other Options

This is a region of seemingly endless lakes and there are plenty to choose from. The chain of lakes found to the north, such as **Coon Lake** and **Buzzard Lake**, offer fishing opportunities for mainly bass. A few of these lakes are stocked with lake trout. Otherwise, **Buckhorn Lake** and **Stoney Lake** to the south are two very popular lakes that can provide a great day worth of fishing.

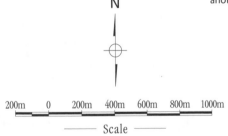

N

200m   0   200m   400m   600m   800m   1000m

Scale

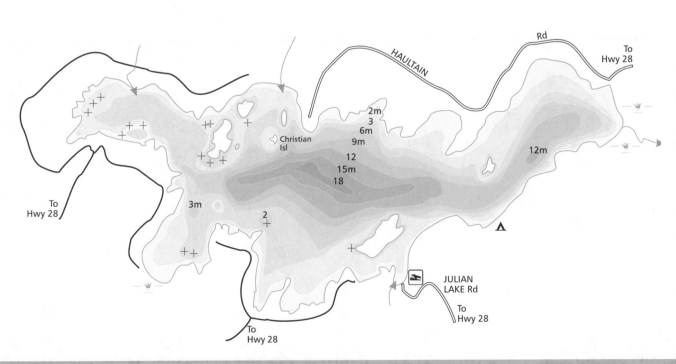

Big Gull Lake

Location: 48 km (30 mi) northeast of Kaladar
Elevation: 253 m (831 ft)
Surface Area: 2,364 ha (5,840 ac)
Maximum Depth: 26 m (85 ft)
Mean Depth: 4 m (12.9 ft)
Geographic: 44° 50′ 00″ N, 76° 58′ 00″ W

18 Zone

Fishing

Big Gull Lake is a popular summer cottage destination lake that is inhabited with smallmouth bass, largemouth bass, northern pike and walleye. Due to the popularity of the lake, the lake receives significant angling pressure throughout the year.

Fishing is fair for smallmouth and largemouth bass in the 0.5-1.5 kg (1-3.5 lb) range. Smallmouth are often found along rock walls and off any of the islands around the lake. Try working a jig or tube jig along the bottom. A crayfish imitation fly or lure can also work quite well. Largemouth bass are predominately found in the shallower more weedy areas of the lake. There are a number of quiet weedy bays around the lake that are good holding areas for largemouth. As evening approaches, top water flies and lures can be productive for largemouth, with the odd pike adding excitement to well presented offerings.

Fishing success for northern pike and especially walleye is much slower than for bass. This is due primarily to over fishing over the years. Walleye is the number one targeted species in Southern Ontario and Big Gull Lake is no exception. Anglers will still find pike in the shallower sections of the lake as well as cruising along island areas at times. Trolling a spoon or casting spinner baits along these structure areas can entice northern pike strikes.

Facilities

A number of cottages and tourist operators are located around Big Gull Lake. Private launching and accommodations can be found at the lake. The lake is also home to four public boat launches that provide good access to different bays on the big lake.

For the adventurist at heart, the **Mazinaw/ Mississippi Canoe Route** passes through Big Gull. As a result, there are several rustic Crown Land campsites scattered around the lake. All campsites are quite basic with only a few offering a fire pit and privy.

Directions

Sometimes referred to as Clarendon Lake, Big Gull Lake is found to the southeast of Bon Echo Provincial Park. To reach the lake, follow Highway 7 to the Henderson Road located at the yellow flashing light near Arden. Head north along this side road and look for the Veley Road off the northeast side. Veley Road leads to a couple of public launching areas. If you continue west along Henderson Road, you will pass by the access road to Earls Bay where another boat launching area and small marina are located.

Visitors wishing to access the east side of the lake can follow Ardoch Road to a launching area near the dam at Coxvale. Ardoch Road can be reached by following Highway 509 north from Highway 7 at Sharbot Lake.

Other Options

There are two small lakes that can be accessed by portage off the north side of Big Gull Lake. **Quebec Lake** can be reached from the northern middle part of Big Gull and offers fishing opportunities for smallmouth bass, largemouth bass and the odd small northern pike. **Mosquito Lake** can be found by a short portage along the northeast end of Big Gull. Mosquito Lake is inhabited by largemouth bass, which provide for fair fishing on occasion. Both Mosquito Lake and Quebec Lake are home to rustic Crown Land campsites.

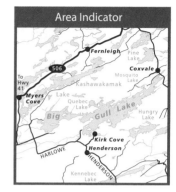
Area Indicator

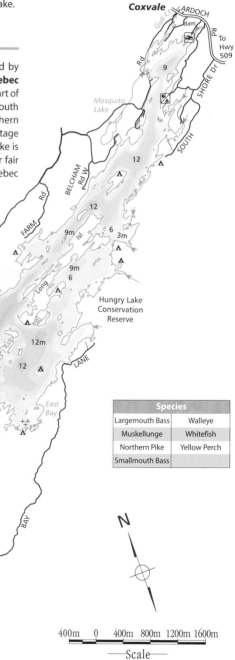

Species	
Largemouth Bass	Walleye
Muskellunge	Whitefish
Northern Pike	Yellow Perch
Smallmouth Bass	

Scale: 400m 0 400m 800m 1200m 1600m

Location: 32 km (19 mi) north of Sydenham
Elevation: 160 m (525 ft)
Surface Area: 112 ha (366 ac)
Maximum Depth: 42.4 m (139 ft)
Mean Depth: 13.2 m (43.4 ft)
Way Point: 44° 32′ 00″ N, 76° 30′ 00″ W

Big Salmon Lake

Area Indicator

Species
Lake Trout
Largemouth Bass
Smallmouth Bass

Fishing

Big Salmon Lake is another rocky, clear Frontenac Lake that is very deep. In the northern end of the lake there is a spot that reaches up to 40 m (130 ft) deep. Fishing in the lake is fair to good at times for smallmouth and largemouth bass that can reach up to 1.5 kg (3.5 lbs) in size on occasion. Bass frequent the various weedy bays as well as rocky drop-off areas and points found around the lake. Flipping jigs along the rocky structures is a good method in finding bass. Fly anglers should note that a crayfish imitation worked off the drop-off areas can also work quite well at times.

The other main sportfish found in Big Salmon Lake is lake trout. These big fish are a naturally reproducing strain that can be quite difficult to find most of the time. Trolling spoons along the drop-offs and over shoal areas can increase your success. One area that should attract lakers is the 18 m (30 ft) shoal found in the northern end. Lake trout will revert from the cooler deeper waters during overcast periods in search of food along these shoal areas.

Directions

Big Salmon Lake lies within the heart of Frontenac Provincial Park and can be accessed from the western end of the park. Follow Highway 38 to Harrowsmith and then travel east along County Road 5 to the small town of Sydenham. From Sydenham, follow County Road 19 north to the Salmon Lake Road just past Gould Lake. The Salmon Lake Road traverses northwest to the southwestern end of the lake.

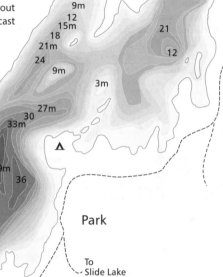

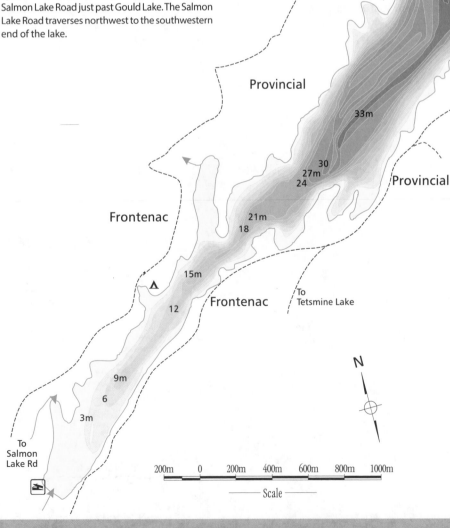

Facilities

Visitors to Big Salmon Lake will find a public canoe access with a parking area along the southwestern shore. The lake is also home to twelve interior **Frontenac Provincial Park** campsites for rustic overnight camping. For basic supplies and other necessities, the nearby towns of Sydenham and Harrowsmith are merely minutes away.

Other Options

Little Salmon and **Little Clear Lakes** lie to the north of Big Salmon Lake and can be reached by trail or portage from Big Salmon Lake. The two picturesque Frontenac interior lakes offer fishing opportunities for mainly smallmouth and largemouth bass, although natural populations of lake trout do exist in each of the lakes. There are nine interior campsites available on Little Clear Lake and six available on Little Salmon Lake.

Scale
200m 0 200m 400m 600m 800m 1000m

Birch Lake

Location: 18 km (29 mi) north of Sydenham
Elevation: 134 m (440 ft)
Surface Area: 148 ha (485 ac)
Maximum Depth: 40.2 m (132 ft)
Mean Depth: 13.1 m (43.3 ft)
Way Point: 44° 33′ 00″ N, 76° 32′ 00″ W

Fishing

Similar to many of the Frontenac Provincial Park area lakes, Birch Lake is very deep in sections. In the southern portion of the lake, the water level has been recorded at over 40 m (132 ft) deep, making for fantastic summer holding areas for the resident lake trout population. Other sportfish species that are found include northern pike, smallmouth bass and largemouth bass. The ample supply of lake herring and other minnow life helps maintain both the quality of the fishery and the decent size of trout and pike that are caught on occasion.

Your best bet to find lake trout is to fish right after the season opens in June. Although the water temperature has usually increased by this time, you will still find that lakers will be roaming in the upper layer of the lake, especially during cooler, overcast days. Try trolling a spoon along the rocky drop-off areas or over the 12 m (40 ft) shoal found in the middle of the lake.

During the spring, northern pike frequent the many bays around the lake and are best caught on a jig worked through cover. You will also find largemouth bass and on occasion smallmouth bass by using this method. Smallmouth tend to favour the rocky structures around the lake; therefore, try a jig or crayfish fly imitation off points and other structured areas.

Facilities

There is no established public boat launch directly on Birch Lake but you can launch a canoe into Mitchell Creek for access to the lake. The southeastern shore of the lake is part of the serene **Frontenac Provincial Park** and is home to interior campsites. The sites are rustic, equipped with a privy and fire pit at the most, and make a great way to escape the stresses of urban life. Supplies and other basic amenities can be picked up in the towns of Sydenham or Harrowsmith to the south. To reserve an interior campsite call (888) ONT-PARK. For more information on Frontenac Provincial Park, call (613) 376-3489.

Directions

Birch Lake is a scenic lake that is flanked by the popular Frontenac Provincial Park. To find the lake, follow Highway 38 north from Highway 401. At the small village of Verona, look for County Road 19 (Desert Lake Road) off the east side of the road. County Road 19 travels east. Just after passing by Desert Lake, look for a road heading north named Snugharbour Road. You will find it near the substantial curve in the road. Follow this road north to the crossing of Mitchell Creek. You can park off the side of the road and launch a canoe into the creek. It is a short paddle down the creek to Birch Lake. An alternate access to Birch Lake is by trail through Frontenac Provincial Park to the southeast.

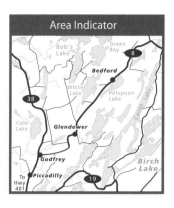

Area Indicator

Species
LakeTrout
Largemouth Bass
Northern Pike
Smallmouth Bass

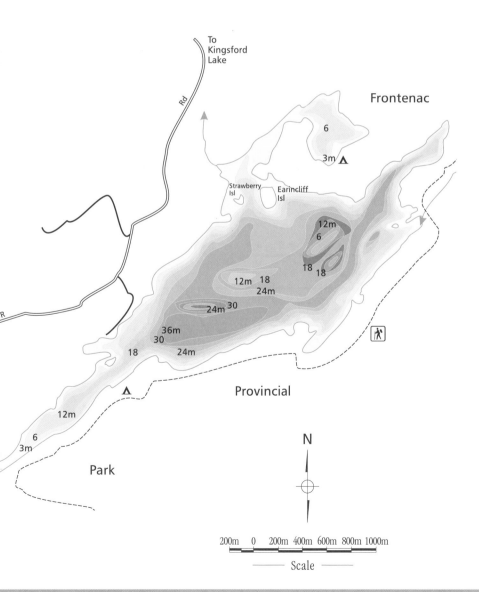

Location: 30 km (18 mi) southeast of Calabogie
Elevation: 250 m (820 ft)
Surface Area: 1,618.7 ha (4,000 ac)
Maximum Depth: 44 m (140 ft)
Mean Depth: 22.3 m (71.3 ft)
Way Point: 45° 13′ 00″ N, 76° 56′ 00″ W

Black Donald Lake

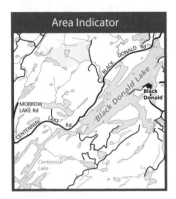

Area Indicator

Species	
Muskellunge	Walleye
Northern Pike	Whitefish
Smallmouth Bass	Yellow Perch

Fishing

Black Donald Lake is one of the larger lakes in the area and is home to several cottages as well as a significant portion of shoreline that remains Crown Land. A few of the islands on the lake are also a part of Centennial Lake Provincial Nature Reserve.

Some of the best fishing in the lake comes from its resident smallmouth bass. Smallmouth regularly hold near any of the many islands and can be found in bunches off a number of the drop-offs. A few larger catches (over 1.5 kg/3.5 lbs) have been reported.

Walleye are the most sought after sport fish in Black Donald Lake and average about 40 cm (16in) in size. Walleye success is fair at times and often peaks during overcast periods. Look for walleye in similar areas to smallmouth such as along drop-offs or off island areas. Trolling with a worm harness is popular, although still jigging along suspected holding areas can also produce results.

Northern pike also reside in the lake and while the odd big pike roams its waters, anglers should expect generally smaller pike throughout. Northerns can be found roaming the numerous shallower bays on this lake. Locating weed beds or any weed structure is a good area to try for evening pike. Try jigs, minnow imitation lures or even top water presentations for aggressive pike.

Directions

Set amid the beautiful rolling hills of the Madawaska Highlands, Black Donald Lake is a very scenic fishing destination in Eastern Ontario. To find the lake from the southeast, follow Highway 7 to Highway 511 at the town of Perth. Take Highway 511 north all the way to Calabogie and Calabogie Lake. Look for Centennial Lake Road in the village of Calabogie. The road heads west along the northern shore of Calabogie Lake, eventually passing by the northern shore of Black Donald Lake.

To reach the lake from the west, follow Highway 41 northeast to the village of Griffith. Once in town, look for the Matawachan Road near the Rapids End Store. The Matawachan Road travels south along the Madawaska River eventually reaching the Centennial Lake Road, which branches east. This road passes over the river and access to Centennial Lake before eventually reaching Black Donald Lake.

The main public access to Black Donald Lake is from the boat launch located along the northwest shore. There are also a few camps or lodges around the lake as well as a more remote launch on the south side of the lake that visitors can use.

Facilities

There are two boat launches found on Black Donald Lake. The main one is on the northwestern shore, while there is another one on the southern shore near the inlet to Norcan Lake. Along with the boat launches there are the odd camp and lodge found around the lake. For the campers at heart, there are a few established, user maintained Crown Land campsites available.

Other Options

With **Centennial Lake** to the west and **Calabogie Lake** to the east there are plenty of big water bodies in the area that see fairly constant pressure. For a quieter alternative, why not give **Norcan Lake** to the south a test? It is linked to Black Donald Lake via the waterway and also offers bass, walleye and northern pike in fair numbers.

Scale: 500m 0 1km 2km 3km

Black Lake

Location: 33 km (20 mi) north of Sydenham
Elevation: 140 m (460 ft)
Surface Area: 258 ha (846 ac)
Maximum Depth: 21.3 m (70 ft)
Mean Depth: 7.2 m (23.8 ft)
Geographic: 44° 46' 00" N, 76° 18' 00" W

18 Zone

Fishing

Although Black Lake receives consistent angling pressure throughout the year, it can still produce decent angling results. Fishing is best for both smallmouth and largemouth bass, as these species are the least targeted sportfish in the lake. Northern pike and walleye are also found in the lake.

There are plenty of structures for both bass species to roam with numerous small islands and other underwater structure throughout the lake. The weed growth in the lake is also a great hiding area for both bass species. Northern pike in Black Lake also tend to lurk near weed structure. Many unsuspecting anglers have been surprised by the pull of these large predatory fish when attempting to catch bass. Try working a weedless spinner or jig through the weeds to try to coax bass and pike into strikes. Other presentations that can work well include top water lures such as the rapala or top water popper flies.

Walleye are the most sought after sportfish in Black Lake and fishing pressure can be significant for these feisty fish throughout the year. As a result, fishing success for walleye does suffer. Try jigging a minnow or worm tipped jig along weed structure or near one of the many shoals found around the lake. Trolling a crankbait or rapala can also provide results.

Ice fishing for walleye and northern pike is a popular winter activity on Black Lake. Anglers will find using a small jig can provide success for both species. Jigging a small spoon can also be good for catching cruising northern pike.

To help maintain the fishery, please practice catch and release.

Other Options

Round and **Long Lakes** are found to the east of Black Lake and are only a short drive away. There are a few cottages on Long Lake, which is inhabited by smallmouth bass, largemouth bass and northern pike. Round Lake lies mainly within Murphy's Point Provincial Park. The quiet lake also sports populations of both bass species but the main attraction to Round Lake is its stocked splake.

Directions

The aptly named, Black Lake is found south of the Trans Canada Highway (Highway 7) near the town of Perth. To find the lake from the south end of Perth, begin by following County Road 10 (Scotch Line) west. Just past Allan's Side Road, turn south along the Lower Scotch Line and look for the Stanleyville Road. Take the Stanleyville Road south and it will eventually turn into the Black Lake Road.

Facilities

A good portion of Black Lake is made up of private land and there are a few private establishments that may allow access for a fee. To find out more information about rental cottages or other lodging on the lake, it is best to inquire locally. For full services, the town of Perth has plenty to offer, including motels and other amenities.

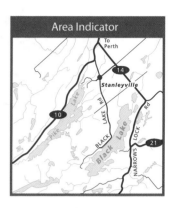
Area Indicator

Species
Largemouth Bass
Northern Pike
Smallmouth Bass
Walleye

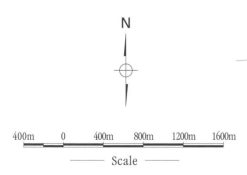

N

| 400m | 0 | 400m | 800m | 1200m | 1600m |

Scale

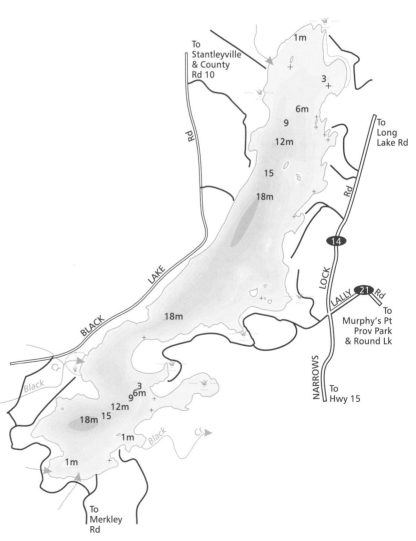

Location: 16.5 km (10.3 mi) south of Sharbot Lake
Maximum Depth: 24 m (78.7 ft)
Mean Depth: 11 m (35.8 ft)
Geographic: 44° 39' 00" N, 76° 37' 00" W

Bob's Lake

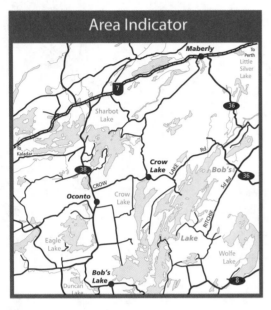

Species	
Lake Trout	Walleye
Largemouth Bass	Whitefish
Northern Pike	Yellow Perch
Smallmouth Bass	Other

Directions

Bob's Lake is one of the larger lakes in Eastern Ontario and is found south of Highway 7, not far from Sharbot Lake. To reach the East Basin, travel along Highway 7 to County Road 36 near the village of Maberly. Head south along County Road 36 to the village of Boilingbroke, where you can find Bob's Lake Dam and the eastern tip of the lake. Look for the Crow Lake Road, a branch road that provides access to the northern portion of the basin. Further south, the Long Bay Road is the main artery to the south end of the lake. There are numerous branch roads off the Long Bay Road that lead to the southern shore of the East Basin.

To access the West Basin of Bob's Lake, it is best to follow Highway 7 to Sharbot Lake. From here, follow the smaller Highway 38 south past Oconto and look for the Bradshaw Road 3 off the east side of the highway. Travel east along Bradshaw Road approximately 1 km (0.6 mi) and look for Bob's Lake Road off the south side. Bob's Lake Road traverses south to the western shore of Bob's Lake.

Facilities

As one of the larger lakes in Eastern Ontario, Bob's Lake is also one of the more popular lakes in the region. The lake is well developed with hundreds of cottages, numerous lodges and resorts available. There is no official public access to the lake but most lodges, tent and trailer parks and resorts do offer boat launch facilities for a fee.

Basic supplies can be picked up in any of the nearby villages such as in Bob's Lake or Boilingbroke, while the towns of Westport and Sharbot Lake are within a half hour drive. For information on cottage rentals or local resorts and lodges, it is recommended to surf the internet or inquire with the local tourism or real estate office.

Fishing

Bob's Lake is a big lake. Stretching over 24 km (15 miles) long and offering about 800 km (500 miles) of shoreline and numerous islands, there is plenty of area to explore. Its waters are clean and clear which makes Bob's Lake an excellent choice for fishing and other water sports. The lake is well known for the plentiful numbers of walleye, northern pike, smallmouth and largemouth bass as well as an abundance of panfish including perch, bluegill, rock bass and sunfish. Also, if you get lucky, lake trout can be found in some areas too.

Bass are the predominant sportfish found in the lake and can be found in the 1-2 kg (2-4.5 lb) range. Fishing for northern pike and walleye is much slower than for bass and is regarded as fair. Pike and walleye average around 1 kg (2 lbs) although can be found to 3.5 kg (8 lbs) on occasion.

The East Basin is the shallower portion of Bob's Lake and is known as the better area for bass and northern pike. While bass can be found near any type of shore structure, the northern more shallow areas of the basin seem to hold better numbers of bass and pike. There is plenty of weed structure in this area, making for prime holding areas for big largemouth bass and the odd northern pike.

Walleye are also found in the East Basin. One known hot spot is the 6 metre (20 foot) shoal found in the northeastern portion of the basin. This hump is an attractant for baitfish, the main food source for walleye. Try trolling the area with a worm harness or still jigging just off the hump.

Lake trout are not that common in the East Basin but there is potential. Try trolling along the middle portion of the lake. The use of downrigging equipment is a requirement to find lakers most of the season as they will hold quite deep. A depth sounder can also aid in finding the holding areas and the required depth to troll.

The West Basin is certainly the deeper of the two basins. As a result, lake trout prefer to roam this area. In particular, the deep eastern arm is a known holding, especially during the summer months. Other than during the first few weeks of the season, a downrigger or leadcore line is required to reach the fish. Try trolling a silver or gold spoon in the approximate depth the lake trout are holding to entice strikes.

There is also plenty of bass structure around the West Basin. The key to finding consistent success for bass in this part of the lake is to locate underwater rock structure. There are a number of underwater rock piles, which are magnets for big bass. Flipping jigs off these areas or casting a spinner into the fray can produce exciting results. The odd northern pike will also be caught using these methods.

For walleye, working the deeper narrows can create success. Loose schools of walleye continuously travel through the narrows and your odds of success are much higher here than compared to some of the more open areas of the lake. Still jigging or trolling a minnow imitation Rapala or plug can be effective.

Panfish like bluegill, perch and rock bass are a great way to introduce youngsters to fishing with. They like to hang around docks, and can be easily caught on a simple bobber and bait set up. While these fish are usually quite small, they seem to like getting caught and virtually anyone can snag a whole bunch in just a few hours. Perch in particular are also quite a tasty fish, too.

The lake was once inhabited by a natural population of lake trout but over fishing and shore development in the 1960's collapsed the stock. Today, thousands of lake trout are stocked in the lake annually and provide for fair fishing throughout the season. Success rates for lakers are certainly higher just after the season opens when the fish are closer to the lake surface.

Other Options

There are several fishing alternatives near Bob's Lake. Two small lakes in the area are **Duncan Lake** and **Little Silver Lake**. Duncan Lake is located just to the west of the village of Bob's Lake and offers fair fishing for smallmouth and largemouth bass in the 0.5-1 kg (1-2 lb) range. A small population of walleye and northern pike also exist in the lake. Little Silver Lake lies to the east of Bob's Lake and is accessible north of Boilingbroke off the east side of County Road 36. Little Silver provides fair fishing opportunities for average sized largemouth and smallmouth bass.

Bob's Lake

Location: Bob's Lake
Maximum Depth: 24 m (78.7 ft)
Mean Depth: 11 m (35.8 ft)
Geographic: 44° 39′ 00″ N, 76° 37′ 00″ W

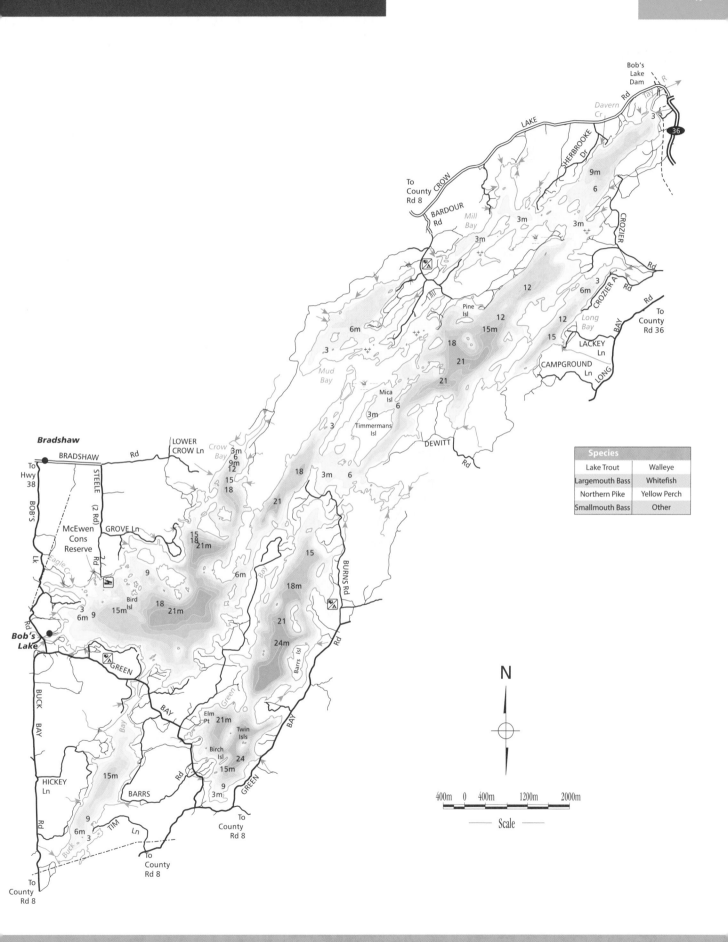

Species	
Lake Trout	Walleye
Largemouth Bass	Whitefish
Northern Pike	Yellow Perch
Smallmouth Bass	Other

N

400m 0 400m 1200m 2000m
— Scale —

Zone **15**

Location: 13 km (8 mi) east of Catchacoma
Elevation: 385 m (1,263 ft)
Maximum Depth: 22.6 m (74 ft)
Mean Depth: 8.1 m (26.5 ft)
Way Point: 44° 46'00" Lat - N, 78° 17'00" Lat - W

Bottle Lake

Fishing

Bottle Lake is actually a fairly deep lake at a maximum depth of approximately 22 m (72 ft) making for suitable habitat for the resident lake trout. The resident lake trout in Bottle Lake are a naturally reproducing strain that has sustained itself into the 21st century. Angling for lakers is generally slow.

Smallmouth bass can provide for good fishing much of the time. A good concentration area for bass is around the creek inlet during the beginning of the season. The rocky drop-off found along the middle portions of the lake also holds smallies. The few small bays along the east side of the lake are also good action areas at times during overcast periods and at dusk.

Even though Bottle Lake is a portage access lake, the lake still receives enough fishing pressure throughout the year to endanger the resident lake trout population. There have been more restrictive regulations and sanctuary periods imposed on the lake to help sustain the natural population. Regardless, the practice of catch and release will go a long way in aiding the trout.

Directions

This scenic lake is part of the original designation of the Kawartha Highlands Provincial Park. The park area has since been expanded substantially creating one of the largest provincial parks in Southern Ontario.

Bottle Lake can be reached by taking County Road 507 off County Road 36 north of the town of Buckhorn. Put in your canoe at one of the Catchacoma Lake boat launch areas and proceed east to Bottle Creek. There is a short portage around the Bottle Creek Dam and it is a short paddle up the creek to reach Bottle Lake.

Facilities

The **Kawartha Highlands Provincial Park** is a non-operating provincial park that was established to help protect some of the wilds of this fascinating portion of the Kawarthas. Facilities at the park are very basic with user maintained, primitive campsites offering rustic fire pits and not much else. Be sure to carry out all off your garbage and leave the campsites cleaner than when you arrive.

Other Options

Sucker Lake to the east of Bottle Lake is accessible via a short portage and is a fabulous Kawartha Highlands interior lake offering rustic, user maintained campsites and fishing for smallmouth bass and natural lake trout. Similar to above, be sure to watch for special restrictions and sanctuary periods for lake trout.

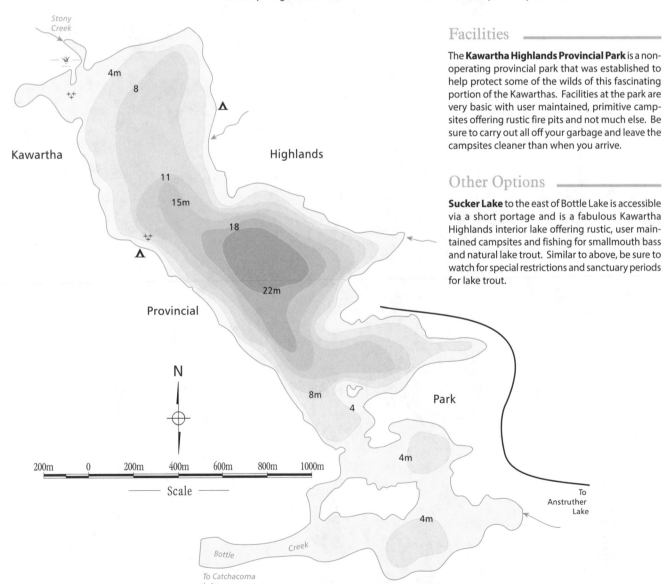

Buck Lake

Location: 20 km (12.4 mi) southwest of Westport
Elevation: 132 m (434 ft)
Surface Area: 744 ha (1,837 ac)
Maximum Depth: 40.8 m (134 ft)
Mean Depth: 13.2 m (43.3 ft)
Geographic: 44° 32′00″ N, 76° 32′00″ W

Fishing

Buck Lake is riddled with rocky islands that offer anglers plenty of interesting terrain to fish. In addition, the lake is not as clear as some of the other lakes in the region. This helps to reduce the spooky aspect of some of the sportfish. Smallmouth bass and largemouth bass are both found in fair numbers and decent sizes. The two larger sportfish found in the lake are northern pike and lake trout.

Lake trout are best caught at the beginning of the season on the troll. Try working a flashy spoon along the deeper drop-off areas for your best bet for success. Although rare, the odd laker has been caught from shore on a spoon or spinner.

Northern pike also cruise the drop-off areas, although these predators are usually found in the upper layer of the lake. A good way to find northerns during the summer is to work the sheltered bays around the lake during dusk or overcast periods. Pike will cruise into the bays in search of food and can often be taken on a streamer, popper type flies or a top water lure.

Smallmouth bass seem to be the more dominant bass species in Buck Lake but there are a good number of largemouth bass caught regularly. There is plenty of fine bass structure found around the lake, from rocky points and small islands to weedy bays and even cottage docks. The shallower areas found in the northern portion of the north bay are good holding areas for both bass and northern pike.

Directions

Visitors can find Buck Lake south of the town of Westport via Perth Road (County Road 10). From the north, follow Highway 15 to Crosby and head west along County Road 36 past the village of Newboro. Just before you reach the town of Westport, look for County Road 10 (Centreville Road) heading southwest. This road travels a short distance before it veers south along what is now referred to as Perth Road.

From the south, Perth Road (County Road 10) travels north from the Highway 401 near Kingston. Whether you take the Perth Road from the north or south, it eventually passes right through the middle of Buck Lake.

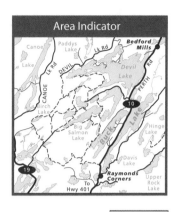

Area Indicator

Species
Lake Trout
Largemouth Bass
Northern Pike
Smallmouth Bass

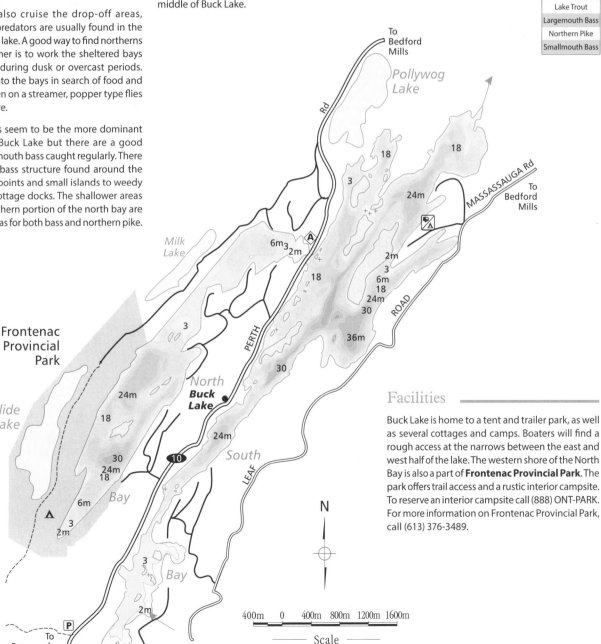

Facilities

Buck Lake is home to a tent and trailer park, as well as several cottages and camps. Boaters will find a rough access at the narrows between the east and west half of the lake. The western shore of the North Bay is also a part of **Frontenac Provincial Park**. The park offers trail access and a rustic interior campsite. To reserve an interior campsite call (888) ONT-PARK. For more information on Frontenac Provincial Park, call (613) 376-3489.

Location: Buckhorn
Elevation: 254 m (833 ft)
Surface Area: 3,188 ha (7,878 ac)
Maximum Depth: 14.3 m (47 ft)
Mean Depth: 2.1 m (6.8 ft)
Way Point: 44° 29' 20" N, 78° 23' 29" W

Buckhorn Lake- Upper

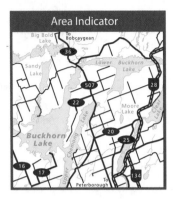

Area Indicator

Species	
Black Crappie	Walleye
Largemouth Bass	Yellow Perch
Muskellunge	Other
Smallmouth Bass	

Directions

Buckhorn Lake is another famous Kawartha Lake that is a part of the Trent Severn Waterway and can be reached via several different routes. From the south, follow Highway 7A north to Fowler's Corners and County Road 26. County Road 26 travels north to County Road 14, which leads east to County Road 16. County Road 16 can be followed north from County Road 14 providing access to the southwest shore of Buckhorn Lake.

From the east, Highway 134 leads north form Highway 7 just east of Peterborough. Highway 134 eventually changes to Highway 28, which continues north to the village of Burleigh Falls. From Burleigh Falls, take County Road 36 west to the village of Buckhorn on the northeast end of Buckhorn Lake.

Fishing

Since Buckhorn Lake is a part of the Trent Severn Waterway, the lake sees an abundance of anglers throughout the season. Similar to other Kawartha Lakes, Buckhorn Lake is found in nutrient rich terrain and supports a productive fishery. Angling success is often best for largemouth and smallmouth bass, as the shallow weedy nature of the lake makes for prime bass habitat. You can literally find bass anywhere in the lake, the key is to find weed beds and other structure where bass hold out in the greatest numbers. However, due to the heavy boat traffic on the lake, bass can be quite spooky at times. If the bass are not hitting, try subtler, slower presentations, such as a grub type lure worked off the bottom.

Anglers will tell you the most popular sportfish in the Kawartha Lakes is walleye. Buckhorn Lake is no exception. The prized sport fish offers generally fair fishing for average sized walleye. Muskellunge are the other main species in the lake and success can be fair throughout the season. Some big musky can be found throughout the lake. Adding to the mix are black crappie, perch and a host of other panfish species.

As a heavily fished lake, the practice of catch and release should be used whenever possible to help maintain the fishery.

Facilities

As a part of the Trent Severn Waterway, Buckhorn Lake is a popular lake throughout the summer months. The lake is home to many cottages, resorts and camps, making for plenty of boater activity on the lake. There are numerous marinas and boat launches available around the lake as well as a few tent and trailer parks for overnight camping. The village of Buckhorn offers basic supplies along with some roofed accommodations. For more lush amenities and retail operations, the town of Lakefield to the southeast has plenty to offer.

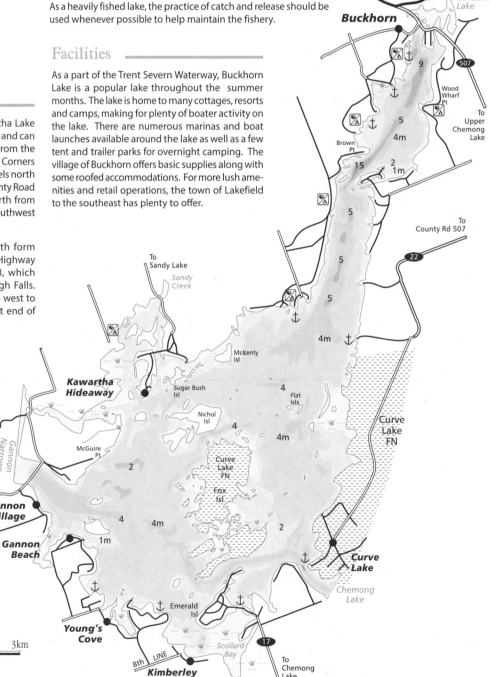

Buckshot Lake

Location: 32 km (19 mi) northwest of Ompah
Elevation: 299 m (980 ft)
Surface Area: 439 ha (1,085 ac)
Maximum Depth: 33.5 m (110 ft)
Mean Depth: 9.7 m (31.9 ft)
Way Point: 45° 00' 00" N, 77° 04' 00" W

18 Zone

Fishing

Anglers looking for naturally reproducing lake trout will be happy to note that Buckshot Lake still holds a small population. Unfortunately, with the shoreline development and the fishing pressure on the lake, the trout species is under siege. Other sportfish species, like the resident bass and walleye are much more adaptable to changes in their environment and continue to produce well in the lake. If you do happen to hook into a lake trout, be sure to release it unharmed to help preserve the fishery.

For the smallmouth and largemouth bass in Buckshot Lake, shoreline and island structure is your best bet for success. The creek inlets found at the southern end of the lake can also be a good holding area for bass.

Walleye are often found frequenting the creek mouth areas, especially early and late in the season. Another hot spot for walleye is the 6 m (20 ft) shoal found near the east middle portion of the lake. This abnormality in the lake bottom attracts baitfish, which in turn attract walleye, especially during summer evenings.

Be sure to check your regulations before heading out onto Buckshot Lake. There are special size and ice fishing restrictions in effect to help preserve lake trout and other fish stocks.

Facilities

Anglers with a boat or canoe can access Buckshot Lake from the public access area at the southern end of the lake. Although the boat launch is a little rough, there is ample parking available. A few tourist lodges have been long established on the lake and provide lodging and rentals for a fee. For supplies, you will find a general store in nearby Plevna offering all the basics.

Other Options

To the west of Buckshot Lake, you can reach **Brooks Lake** and **Long Mallory Lake** by dirt roads that can be quite rough at times. Both lakes are picturesque Eastern Ontario Lakes that offer undeveloped boat access areas. Brooks Lake is stocked with splake every few years that provide good fishing periodically for decent sized splake. Smallmouth and largemouth bass, a small population of northern pike as well as a stocked population of lake trout inhabit Long Mallory Lake. Fishing is best for the resident bass, although northern pike can be surprisingly aggressive in the spring. Winter and early spring is the best time to try for lake trout.

Directions

Found in the Madawaska Highlands, Buckshot Lake makes a fine fishing destination. The easiest route to the lake is to take Highway 7 to the junction with Highway 41 at the town of Kaladar. From Kaladar, head north along Highway 41 to Highway 506, just south of the village of Cloyne. Trek east along Highway 506 until the road swings north on what is now Highway 509. Eventually, you will come to the small village of Plevna where the Buckshot Lake Road can be found off the west side of the road. Buckshot Lake Road is a gravel road that eventually veers north passing by the southwestern shore of Buckshot Lake.

Species
Lake Trout
Largemouth Bass
Smallmouth Bass
Walleye
Yellow Perch

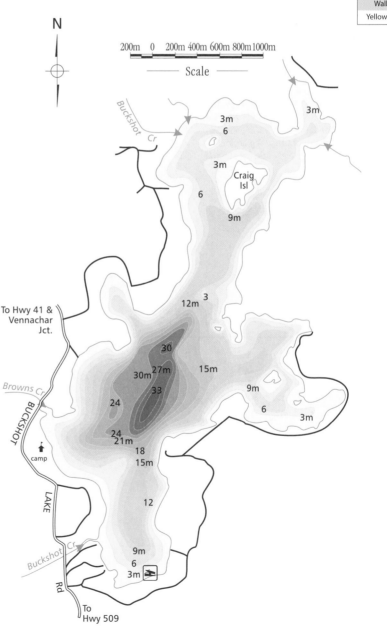

Location: 24 km (15 mi) southwest of Apsley
Elevation: 308 m (1,010 ft)
Maximum Depth: 41.7 m (137 ft)
Mean Depth: 17.3 m (57 ft)
Way Point: 44° 40' 00" Lat - N, 78° 13' 00" Lon - W

Buzzard Lake

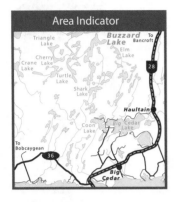

Area Indicator

Species
Lake Trout
Largemouth Bass
Smallmouth Bass

Fishing

Although Buzzard Lake is a canoe access only lake, the lake still receives significant angling pressure. It is an easy overnight trip from Long Lake, making it a favourite canoe camping destination.

Fishing in Buzzard Lake is usually fair for largemouth and smallmouth bass in the 0.5-1 kg (1-2 lb) range. There is plenty of rock structure around the lake that holds smallmouth bass, while largemouth are found predominantly in the quiet shallow bays. Topwater action for largemouth is usually best on calm overcast days or in the evening period. Often the calm before a storm can create a frenzy of action. When topwater action is slow for largemouth bass try jigs, spinnerbaits and crankbaits amid shoreline structure or weed growth. While typical largemouth bass lures will work for smallmouth, including topwater presentations, underwater presentations are regularly more effective.

Buzzard Lake is also home to a small population of naturally reproducing lake trout. Lake trout are quite active just after ice off when they are found closer to the surface. Anglers will find success by trolling silver or gold spoons or larger streamer type flies that imitate baitfish. For trolling, the Little Cleo or Diamond King are good bets, while fly fishers should try a grey and white streamer with some crystal flash.

Lakers were heavily fished in the past by winter ice anglers and winter/spring ice fishing sanctuary and specific slot size restrictions have been put in place to aid the low stocks. If you do catch a lake trout, the practice of catch and release is recommended to help the stocks recover.

Directions

Buzzard Lake is part of a popular series of canoe access lakes. To reach the chain, follow Highway 28 north from the town of Lakefield past Burleigh Falls to Long Lake Road. Long Lake Road lies off the west side of Highway 28 and leads to the access area on Long Lake. Buzzard Lake is accessible via a 540 metre portage from the southwest end of Long Lake and makes for a nice overnight trip. A marginal fee is charged to park your vehicle at Long Lake Lodge.

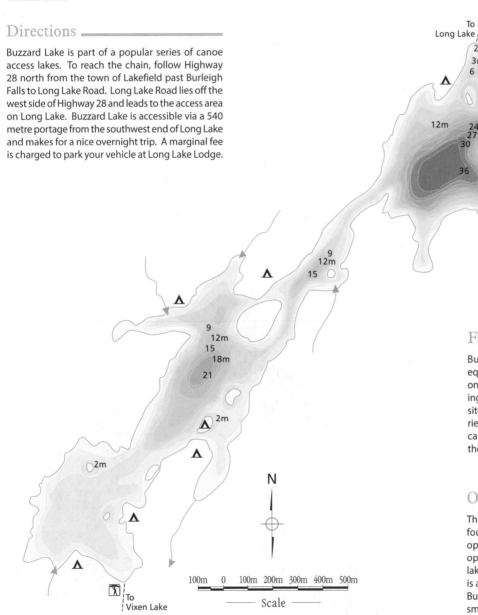

Facilities

Buzzard Lake is an interior access lake that is equipped with established rustic campsites. The only development at these sites are a cleared tenting area with a fire pit and possibly a pit toilet. The sites are basic but a great way to rough it and experience some nature. Please remember that these campsites are user-maintained; therefore, leave them as clean or cleaner than when you arrived.

Other Options

There are a number of different fishing options found around Buzzard Lake. The most obvious option is **Long Lake**. Long Lake offers fishing opportunities for smallmouth bass and natural lake trout. **Vixen Lake** is another nearby lake that is accessible via portage from the southern end of Buzzard Lake. Vixen Lake is known to have a decent smallmouth bass fishery available.

Calabogie Lake

Location: Calabogie
Surface Area: 1,315 ha (3,250 ac)
Maximum Depth: 25 m (82 ft)
Mean Depth: 11.6 m (37 ft)
Waypoint: 45° 16'00" N, 76° 44'00" W

18 Zone

Fishing

With a large resort, cottages and a ski hill located on the lake, Calabogie Lake is a popular year round fishing destination. In general, fishing opportunities are decent, with fair fishing for resident northern pike that can reach up to 6 kg (13 lbs) in size. During most of the season, try along any shallow area such as those in Grassy Bay as evening approaches. In winter, shallower areas where weeds typically develop in the open water months often see cruising pike.

Smallmouth bass can reach sizes of 2 kg (4.5 lbs) and there have been rumors of bigger fish caught on occasion. Crayfish fly or lure imitations and jigs can be good for smallmouth. Try off any of the drop-offs near islands or along the drop-offs in the deeper southern portion of the lake.

The close cousin of the smallmouth bass, largemouth bass also reside in Calabogie Lake and can reach similar sizes to that of smallmouth. While largemouth can be found in any shallower section of the lake, the main holding area for largemouth is Grassy Bay. Try flipping weed less presentations through the thick weeds found in the bay or even try top water presentations.

As with most areas in Eastern Ontario, walleye are the most sought after species here. Fishing for walleye is slow to fair, but success can increase during overcast periods. Walleye can be found to 3 kg (6.5 lbs) and a popular hot spot seems to be near Indian Island and the shoal just west of the island. Be sure to check provincial regulations for sanctuary areas.

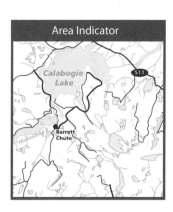

Area Indicator

Species
Black Crappie
Largemouth Bass
Northern Pike
Smallmouth Bass
Walleye
Yellow Perch
Other

Directions

This man-made lake is the reservoir formed by the damming of the Madawaska River to provide local hydroelectric power. To locate Calabogie Lake from the south, follow Highway 7 to Highway 511 at the town of Perth. Take Highway 511 north all the way to the village of Calabogie and Calabogie Lake. From the north, Highway 508 links Highway 17 to Calabogie. There is a public access areas found near town along the north shore of Grassy Bay.

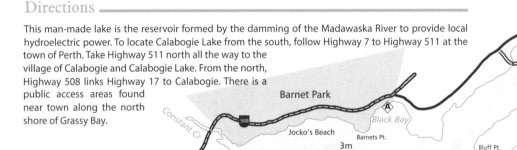

Facilities

Calabogie Lake is a popular recreational lake that hosts numerous facilities for visitors to enjoy. Do it yourselfers can take advantage of a public access point, while those looking for more pampering can visit the popular resort on the lake. The village also offers a few shops and dining options for area visitors.

Location: Fenelon Falls
Surface Area: 1,376 ha (3,400 ac)
Maximum Depth: 18.2 m (60 ft)
Mean Depth: 9.3 m (30.6 ft)
Waypoint: 44° 33′ 00″ Lat - N, 78° 46′ 00″ Lon - W

Cameron Lake

Area Indicator

Species
Largemouth Bass
Muskellunge
Smallmouth Bass
Walleye

Fishing

Cameron Lake is a popular spot for boaters and anglers alike. Fishing in the lake can be good for bass in the 0.5-1 kg (1-2 lb) range. Largemouth bass are the main bass species in Cameron Lake, although smallmouth bass can be found from time to time. Look for largemouth in weedy areas such as in Sackett Bay or around Deweys Island.

Walleye and muskellunge round out the main sport fish species in Cameron Lake. Fishing for walleye can be good at times, while success for muskellunge is usually much slower. Cameron Lake has a very unique lake bottom as it sports a number of different shoal areas of various shapes and depths. The key to increasing your success on this lake is to locate these shoal areas as they regularly hold baitfish that attract sport fish such as walleye and muskellunge.

Directions

The town of Fenelon Falls is blessed with the scenic backdrop of Cameron Lake. The main access to Cameron Lake is located in Fenelon Falls near the mouth of the Fenelon River and Cameron Lake. To reach Fenelon Falls, travel north from the town of Lindsay along Highway 35 to County Road 121. County Road 121 travels northeast through the downtown core of Fenelon Falls, crossing the Fenelon River along the way.

The lake is also part of the Trent Severn Waterway and many boaters access the lake from the popular water route.

Facilities

Cameron Lake is home to a number of facilities including a boat launch, marina and a few tent and trailer parks. For the explorers at heart, the **Victoria Rail Trail** traverses along the east side of the lake. The trail is a popular route throughout the year for everything from snowmobiling to hiking. Supplies can be readily found in the town of Fenelon Falls.

Other Options

As a part of the Trent Severn Waterway, there are several nearby angling alternatives to Cameron Lake. To the east you will find **Sturgeon Lake** and to the west **Balsam Lake**. Both of these larger lakes are accessible by boat from Cameron Lake and offer similar fishing opportunities. Populations of smallmouth bass, largemouth bass, walleye and muskellunge inhabit these large lakes. If your luck is slow for these more popular species, there is an abundance of other exciting fish to try for, such as crappie, perch or rock bass.

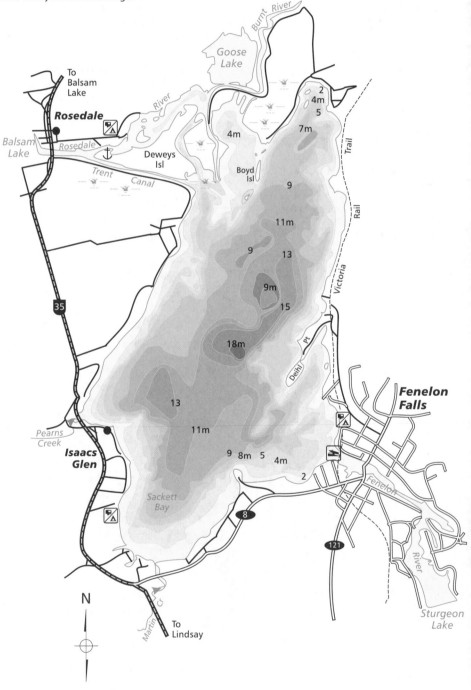

Canal Lake

Location: 35 km (21 mi) east of Orillia
Surface Area: 1085 ha (2681 ac)
Maximum Depth: 4.3 m (14 ft)
Mean Depth: 1.3 m (4.2 ft)
Geographic: 44° 34' 00" Lat - N, 79° 03' 00" Lon - W

Fishing

Canal Lake is a very shallow lake with a maximum depth of only 4.6 m (15 ft) and an average depth of approximately 2-3 m (4.5-10 ft). The lake is lush with vegetation throughout the summer months providing ample habitat and cover for all sport fish species. Smallmouth and largemouth bass create most of the fishing action on the lake and can be a lot of fun to catch, especially when they can be convinced to hit surface lures or flies. Surface action is best during overcast periods and in the evening, although the early morning can also be an active period on occasion.

The two most popular sport fish found in Canal Lake are muskellunge and walleye. Fishing for muskellunge is regarded as fair, while success for walleye can be good periodically. Both species reach respectable sizes when compared to the catches in other Trent Severn Waterway lakes. Look for both walleye and musky along weed lines, especially at dusk when they cruise these regions in search of dinner.

Directions

This Trent Severn Waterway Lake is found between Lake Simcoe and Balsam Lake. Many boaters access the lake as they travel along the waterway. By land, Canal Lake is found near Highway 12, southeast of Orillia. Follow Highway 12 to the junction with County Road 48 near the small town of Beaverton. Follow County Road 48 east to Centennial Park Road (County Road 33) and then head north again. Centennial Park Road actually traverses across Canal Lake about 1 km north of the junction with County Road 48.

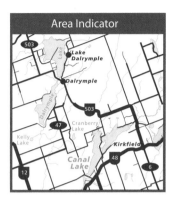

Area Indicator

Species	
Black Crappie	Smallmouth Bass
Largemouth Bass	Walleye
Muskellunge	Yellow Perch
Northern Pike	Other

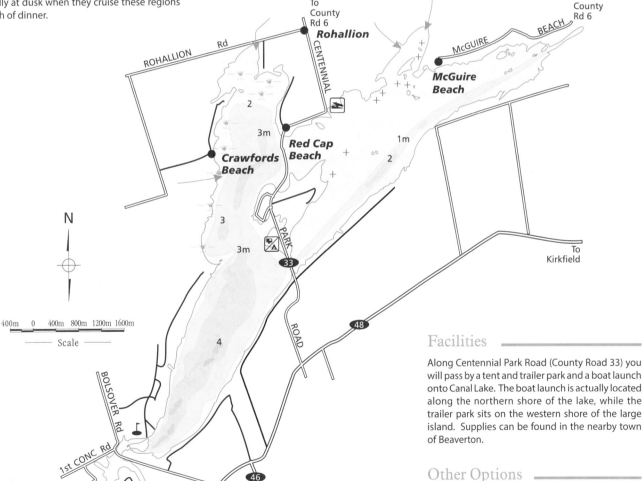

Facilities

Along Centennial Park Road (County Road 33) you will pass by a tent and trailer park and a boat launch onto Canal Lake. The boat launch is actually located along the northern shore of the lake, while the trailer park sits on the western shore of the large island. Supplies can be found in the nearby town of Beaverton.

Other Options

Nearby **Mitchell Lake** forms part of the Trent Severn Waterway and therefore is accessible by boat from Canal Lake. By vehicle, you can reach Mitchell Lake by continuing east along County Road 48. Fishing in the smaller lake is similar to Canal Lake, as largemouth bass, smallmouth bass, walleye and the ever-predacious muskellunge inhabit the lake.

Location: 30 km (18 mi) north of Sydenham
Elevation: 145 m (475 ft)
Surface Area: 291 ha (720 ac)
Maximum Depth: 47.2 m (155 ft)
Mean Depth: 22.6 m (74 ft)
Waypoint: 44° 35' 00" N, 76° 33' 00" W

Canoe Lake

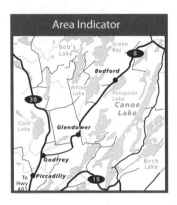

Area Indicator

Species
Lake Trout
Largemouth Bass
Northern Pike
Smallmouth Bass

Fishing

The rocky shoreline that borders Canoe Lake provides a geographical clue to the depth of the lake. At its deepest point, Canoe Lake reaches up to 46 m (150 ft) deep. As a result, the lake provides the cool waters needed for its resident lake trout. Alongside the lake trout, anglers can expect to catch smallmouth bass, largemouth bass and northern pike.

Fishing success is best for smallmouth and largemouth bass. Bass can be found almost anywhere along the shoreline of the lake and spinners and jigs produce results regularly. While fishing for bass, do not be surprised to hook into a good sized northern pike. If you plan to target pike specifically, try trolling a spoon or rapala along the shoreline drop-off areas.

Lake trout fishing is best in the spring. Although fishing success for lake trout is usually slower, you may get lucky and hook into one during the first few weeks of the season. Trolling a flashy silver or gold spoon is the best way to find these big fish. In the summer, like in most lakes, lake trout will revert to the depths of the lake in search of cooler waters. During this time, the only way to catch these naturally reproducing fish is by using down rigging equipment.

Directions

Canoe Lake is a long, slender lake found near Frontenac Provincial Park. To find the lake from Highway 401, travel north along Highway 38 to the village of Verona. At Verona, look for Desert Lake Road (County Road 19) heading east. Just past Desert Lake, take the Snugharbour Road north. Snugharbour Road passes by Eels Lake, eventually turning into Canoe Lake Road and reaching the eastern shore of the lake.

Canoe Lake Road can also be reached from the north by following Highway 38 south from Highway 7 near Sharbot Lake. Another popular northern access point is found west of the town of Westport along County Road 8. Canoe Lake Road is found off the south side of County Road 8.

Facilities

There is no official public boat launch available on Canoe Lake but it is possible to access the lake just off Canoe Lake Road near the southeastern end of the lake. A canoe can be easily launched into the lake from the road. Along with a number of scenic cottages, a few tourist lodges have been established on the lake.

Other Options

Canoe Lake flows south into **Eel Lake** through a small bay under a road bridge. It is possible to launch a canoe into the lake at the bridge. Fishing in Eel Lake is known to be good at times for decent sized smallmouth bass. The odd largemouth is also found around in the lake along with walleye. Although the walleye seem to get most of the sportfishing attention, fishing can be painfully slow at times.

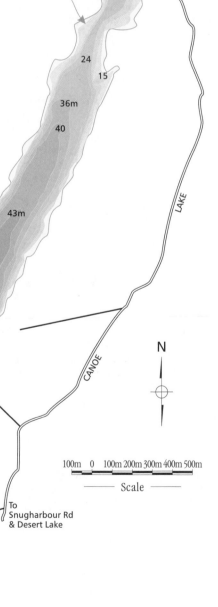

Canonto Lake

Location: 8.5 km (5.3 mi) north of Ompah
Elevation: 262 m (858 ft)
Surface Area: 221 ha (546 ac)
Mean Depth: 21.3 m (70 ft)
Max Depth: 3.8 m (12.6 ft)
Way Point: 45° 03′ 00″ N, 76° 47′ 00″ W

18 Zone

Fishing

Fishing in Canonto Lake is fair for smallmouth and largemouth bass that average 0.5-1 kg (1-2 lbs) in size. The best areas for bass are in the channel areas next to Arcol Island. Rock piles and weed beds can be found around the island and make prime bass habitat. Another hot spot for smallmouth bass is around the rock shoal located in the southern end of the lake. Smallmouth hang out around rocky areas and can be picked up with tube jig presentations and spinners on occasion. In the heavy weed areas, top water flies and lures can create some exciting action during dusk periods.

A small population of northern pike also exists in the lake. Pike usually can be picked up along shoreline areas with bass type presentations.

A few years ago, Canonto Lake was stocked with walleye to help supplement resident walleye populations. There were reports that fishing success had improved but it is unclear whether the lake will be stocked with walleye in the future. Trolling is the most effective angling method for walleye, although still jigging near the small islands can produce results on occasion. When trolling, try a worm harness or a deep diving Rapala.

A natural population of lake trout once existed in Canonto Lake, however it is thought that the population is now extinct. The demise of the lake trout can be attributed to over fishing, although shore development is sure to have played a role as well.

Directions

Visitors can find Canonto Lake northeast of the small village of Ompah. Follow Highway 7 to the junction with Highway 509, north of Sharbot Lake. Head north along the quiet highway past the hamlet of Donaldson, eventually reaching the Canonto Lake Road just east of Ompah. Canonto Lake traverses northeast to the southeastern shore of the lake.

Highway 509 can also be reached from the west via Highways 506 and 41 north of Kaladar and Highway 7. Once on Highway 509, continue north past Plevna to Canonto Lake Road.

Permits for road use, parking and camping must be picked up in Plevna before travelling to Canonto Lake. Plevna is found west of Ompah on Highway 509.

Facilities

The **Palmerston/Canonto Conservation Area** near the dam between Canonto and Palmerston Lakes adds to the scenic nature of the lake. The area preserves a portion of the western shoreline of Canonto Lake and is home to some rustic hiking trails. At the northeast end of the lake, near the dam on Cruse Bay, a boat launch is accessible via Canonto Lake Road. For supplies and permits, a small general store is located west of the lake via Highway 509 at the village of Plevna.

Other Options

North of Canonto Lake anglers can find **Summit Lake** and **Wolfe Lake** via a local access road. Summit Lake is stocked every few years with brown trout, while Wolfe Lake is stocked annually with rainbow trout. Both lakes provide fair to good fishing periodically for decent sized trout.

Area Indicator

Species
Largemouth Bass
Northern Pike
Smallmouth Bass
Walleye

Location: 24 km (14.9 mi) north of Buckhorn
Elevation: 293 m (962 ft)
Surface Area: 688 ha (1,699 ac)
Maximum Depth: 44 m (144 ft)
Mean Depth: 25 m (84 ft)
Way Point: 44° 45′ 03″ N, 78° 19′ 36″ W

Catachacoma Lake

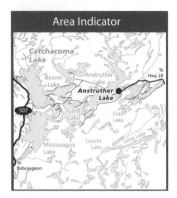

Area Indicator

Species
Lake Trout
Largemouth Bass
Panfish
Smallmouth Bass

Fishing

Catchacoma Lake was originally an exclusive lake trout lake over a century ago. However, with the introduction of panfish and bass, the lake is now home to several sportfish species. Fishing for the natural lake trout population can be challenging at times, although the smallmouth and largemouth bass fishery can be quite good at times.

Lake trout enthusiasts are best to troll in the early spring or fall otherwise you will need to use barrel weights, downriggers or steel line to get down to the trout throughout the summer months. Similar to most Ontario lakes, try larger Williams silver or silver gold combo spoons, with a salted minnow or preserved minnow on the end. Other good spoons for lakers include your classic Little Cleo silver blue or pure silver. Work plenty of water, specifically near the drop offs. When you get one, go back and work that area as there should be more holding in the same area.

In the late spring and throughout the summer bass fishing can be a ton of fun flipping topwater baits along shorelines. This rocky lake is prefect for jigs and deep water baits for smallmouth. Work jigs and tubes along shoreline drop off and rock walls or even among submersed logs for increased bass success. If the slower presentations don't get the bite, trying a Mepps Aglia or Blue Fox spinner with or without a worm to entice lethargic bass into striking.

Directions

Resting on the western boundary of the Kawartha Highlands Provincial Park, Catchacoma Lake is best accessed from the west off Highway 507. This highway links Highway 503 in the north with Buckhorn in the south. Buckhorn is found west of Highway 28 to the north of Peterborough and Lakefield. Simply follow County Road 36 west from Burleigh Falls to get to Buckhorn or follow Buckhorn Road (County Road 23) north from Lakefield Road (County Road 29) outside of Peterborough. Once in Buckhorn, continue north on Highway 507 to Beaver Lake Road, which leads to the south end of Catchacoma Lake. There is an alternate access at the north end of the lake off the highway.

From the north, Highway 507 leads south from Gooderham. To get to Gooderham, follow Highway 118 to Tory Hill, where Highway 503 branches west. Highway 503 can also be pickup at Kinmount in the west, not far from Minden and Highway 35.

Facilities

There are two public access points on Catchacoma Lake, as well as a small camping/cottage establishment that can provide access to the lake for a fee. The access points are found at each end of the lake. Private cottages for rent can also be found through the internet. The nearby village of Buckhorn is home to a grocery store, bank and other necessities.

Other Options

Catchacoma Lake is at the edge of a vast array of fishing lakes that lie just north of the Kawartha Lake lowlands. Some great alternatives that can be accessed directly from Catchacoma Lake by canoe are **Beaver Lake**, **Bottle Lake** and **Sucker Lake**. The latter two lakes are within the Kawartha Highlands Provincial Park boundary and make for a great overnight interior camping destination. All three lakes are home to a fair natural lake trout population, as well as a healthy population of smallmouth and largemouth bass.

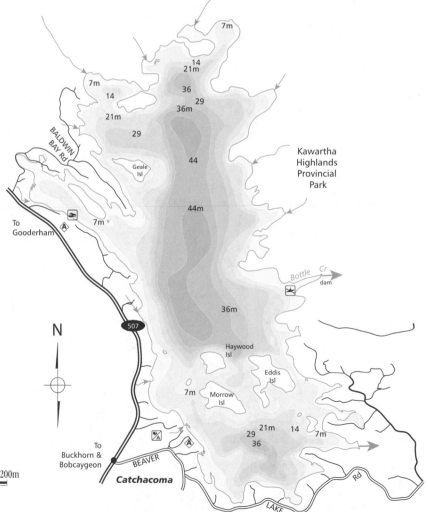

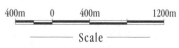

400m   0   400m   1200m

Scale

Centennial Lake

Location: 30 km (18 mi) southeast of Griffith
Surface Area: 3,439 ha (8,498 ac)
Maximum Depth: 44.2 m (145 ft)
Mean Depth: 13.9 m (45.6 ft)
Waypoint: 45° 09' 00" N, 77° 03' 00" W

Fishing

There are many bays and inlets located around Centennial Lake that are ideal holding areas for numerous sport fish species. In particular, both largemouth and smallmouth bass are found in decent numbers. Largemouth tend to hold in the shallower areas of the lake such as the shallow middle bays and small shallow inlets. Smallmouth on the other hand are often located in the deeper sections near drop-offs and love to hold near any one of the islands. Working a crayfish imitation fly or lure can be deadly for smallies here, while top water flies and lures can be a ton of fun for finding lunker largemouth.

Northern pike frequent the shallow bays in spring and tend to move to deeper water as the water warms up through the summer months. However, pike can still be found in the summer evenings roaming along the shallows in search of prey. Try minnow imitation lures and flies or top water presentations for decent sized northerns.

Walleye are probably the most heavily fished for species and fishing tends to be fairly slow for these sharp-toothed predators. Look for walleye in the north portion near the river inlet or in the middle channel along the drop-offs. Trolling a worm harness is best for covering large amounts of water in search of the elusive fish.

Anglers should note there are special restrictions on walleye at this lake. Be sure to check the Ontario Fishing Regulations summary for specifics before heading out. Practicing catch and release can also go a long way in helping maintain and even improve the fishing success for this prized sport fish.

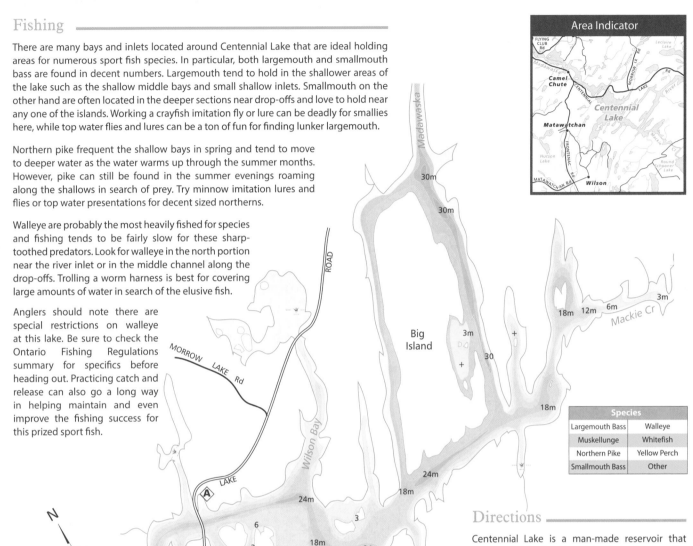

Area Indicator

Species	
Largemouth Bass	Walleye
Muskellunge	Whitefish
Northern Pike	Yellow Perch
Smallmouth Bass	Other

Directions

Centennial Lake is a man-made reservoir that was created by the Mountain Chute Dam on the Madawaska River. To reach Centennial Lake, follow Highway 41 between Highway 7 and Highway 132 to the village of Griffith. Once in town, look for the Matawachan Road near the Rapids End Store. The Matawachan Road travels south along the river eventually reaching the Centennial Lake Road, which branches east. This road skirts the northern shore of the lake and leads to the boat launch that is found across the bridge over the Madawaska River.

Centennial Lake Road can also be picked up from the east off Highway 511 at Calabogie Lake. The road takes you past Calabogie and Black Donald Lakes before eventually reaching the northern shore and boat launch onto Centennial.

Facilities

Along with the boat launch at the north end, there are a number of camps and lodges located around Centennial Lake. For more information on these accommodations it is recommended to inquire locally.

Other Options

There are numerous alternate fishing options found around Centennial Lake. To the south there is a good collection of harder to access lakes such as **Brule Lake, Fortune Lake** and **Mackie Lake**. All three offer different fishing opportunities and are not as heavily fished as their northern neighbour.

Location: 13 km (8 mi) east of Apsley
Elevation: 332 m (1,089 ft)
Surface Area: 1,387 ha (3,427 ac)
Maximum Depth: 45.7 m (150 ft)
Mean Depth: 27.1 m (89 ft)
Way Point: 44° 49' 00" Lat - N, 78° 00' 00" Lon - W

Chandos Lake

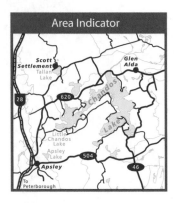

Area Indicator

Fishing

This popular cottage destination lake is regularly fished throughout the season. Bass, both smallmouth and largemouth, seem to be the most readily caught species. Bass average about 0.5-1 kg (1-2 lbs) although can reach up to 1.5+ kg (3.5+ lbs) in size on occasion. The lake is home to a seemingly endless array of small bays that make for prime bass holding areas.

Chandos Lake is also home to a naturally reproducing strain of lake trout. They and are mainly found in the east portion of the lake where the depths offer a much more suitable habitat for lakers. Trolling is the preferred angling method for lake trout, as the finicky trout is best found by covering large tracts of water. For increased lake trout success, locate the anomalies along the lake bottom such as rock shoals where baitfish will normally congregate.

Lake trout remain under heavy angling pressure in Chandos Lake and the practice of catch and release is recommended. Before heading out, be sure to check your regulations for slot size restrictions and sanctuary periods.

Directions

Chandos Lake is found just east of Highway 28 and has several access points. The main public access point is found at the north end of the lake. To find this area, travel north on Highway 28 and take the second Apsley cut-off to County Road 620. Follow this road along the north side of Chandos Lake all the way to the small picnic area and boat launch at the top end of the lake.

Facilities

There are a few small marinas on Chandos Lake along with a public boat launch and picnic area on the north shore. There are also two private tent and trailer parks found off Balmer Road along the south shore. The nearest provincial park is **Silent Lake**, which lies to the north off Highway 28 and is a full facility park complete with showers and flush toilets.

Other Options

To the north of Chandos Lake there are many lakes to choose from, including **Silent Lake** and **Eels Lake**. Silent Lake offers angling for lake trout and bass in a park setting, while Eels Lake provides fishing opportunities for smallmouth bass, walleye and lake trout.

Species
Lake Trout
Largemouth Bass
Northern Pike
Smallmouth Bass
Yellow Perch

N

400m 0 400m 800m 1200m 1600m
Scale

To Hwy 28

Tallan Creek

West Bay

6m
12
12m

Chandos Lake

Scott's Landing

620

Garden Isl

6m

Little Loon Lake

BALMER Rd

South Bay

Standish Isl

30m

6m
12
18m
24
30m
34
37m

To Hwy 62

Winter Bay

WINTERS BAY Rd

46

Paudash Isl

43m

43m

30

Gilmour Bay

21m

18

504

Charleston Lake

Location: 13 km (31 mi) east of Prescott
Elevation: 85 m (278 ft)
Surface Area: 2,518 ha (6,220 ac)
Maximum Depth: 91 m (300 ft)
Mean Depth: 17.4 m (57 ft)
Way Point: 44° 32′ 00″ N, 76° 00′ 00″ W

18 Zone

Fishing

Charleston Lake is a deep lake with an abundance of islands and private bays to explore. Natural limestone helps keep the waters clean and the fish healthy. Fishing in the big lake is fair to good for smallmouth bass and largemouth bass that can reach up to 2 kg (4 lbs) in size. Northern pike and the elusive lake trout are the other popular sportfish found in the lake.

Bass can be found along rocky shore areas, drop-offs and in the many shallow, weedy bays. Fishing success for Charleston Lake's northern pike is regarded as fair to slow, although there are good sized pike caught annually. A hot spot for bass and pike is around the two 3 m (10 ft) shoal humps located in the southern portion of the lake east of Croziers Island. Try trolling along the humps or even casting jigs or spinner baits nearby.

Lake trout are stocked periodically in Charleston Lake, providing decent fishing opportunities throughout the season. The best locations for lake trout are the deeper holes. The area along the western shore can be good at times. Alternatively, try the area south of Croziers Island along the southwest shore

Before you head out on Charleston Lake, be sure to check your regulations. There are specific restrictions on the type of baitfish that are permitted for angling use.

Directions

Located northeast of the town of Gananoque, this big lake is a popular spot during the summer months. Visitors flock to Charleston Lake as it is close to a United States border crossing and the cities of Ottawa and Kingston. The easiest way to find the lake is to travel along Highway 401 to Exit 659 at Prince Reynolds Road (County Road 3). Follow this road north past the village of Lansdowne, where the road name then changes to Outlet Road. From Outlet Road, there are a number of smaller access roads that lead to different shore areas, which includes an access road to Charelston Lake Provincial Park.

Facilities

This large, scenic lake is home to **Charleston Lake Provincial Park** as well as several cottages and tourist operators. The main access area to the lake is via the park but there are public access points also found near the village of Outlet and Charleston. Alternatively, private marinas or tourist lodges offer pay per use launching and mooring facilities.

Charleston Lake Provincial Park encompasses almost three quarters of the shoreline and offers a large full facility campsite. Visitors can enjoy the fantastic hiking trails, the beautiful canoeing opportunities and the nice beaches and picnic areas at the park. It is recommended to make reservations before arrival. For more information on Charleston Lake Provincial Park, call (613) 659-2065 and for reservations, call (888) ONT-PARK.

Charleston Lake
Fish Stocking Data

Year	Species	Number
2011	Lake Trout	4,000
2010	Lake Trout	3,000
2007	Lake Trout	10,000

Area Indicator

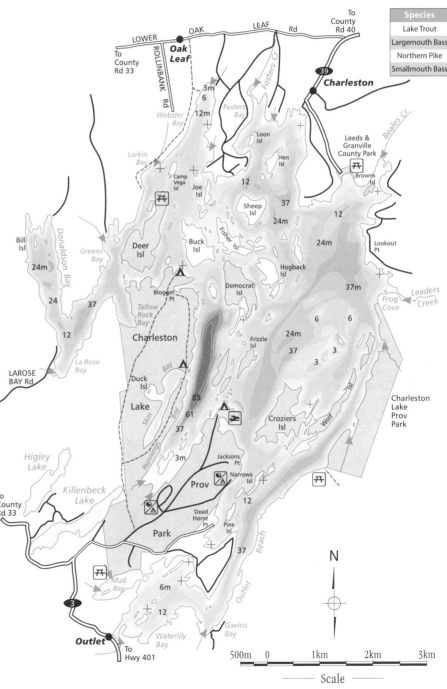

Species
Lake Trout
Largemouth Bass
Northern Pike
Smallmouth Bass

Zone **17**

Location: 15 km (9 mi) north of Peterborough
Elevation: 254 m (833 ft)
Surface Area: 2,280 ha (5,634 ac)
Maximum Depth: 6.7 m (22 ft)
Mean Depth: 3.3 m (10.6 ft)
Way Point: 44° 28′ 57″ N, 78° 20′ 54″ W

Chemong Lake- Upper

Area Indicator

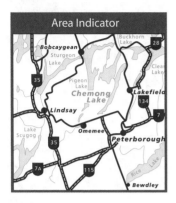

Fishing

Chemong Lake is a popular Kawartha lake and host to several fishing tournaments throughout the open fishing season. It is part of the tri-lake water system consisting of Chemong Lake, Buckhorn Lake and Pigeon Lake and is also part of the Trent-Severn Waterway. Stretching 14 km long and 1 km wide, it is a big lake with plenty of water to explore. Visitors will find a host of species to look for including carp, muskellunge, smallmouth and largemouth bass, walleye and more recently perch. Due to its shallow nature, Chemong Lake is quite weedy providing plenty of superb habitat for all fish species.

Continues>>

Species
Carp
Largemouth Bass
Muskellunge
Smallmouth Bass
Walleye
Yellow Perch

Facilities

The **Selwyn Conservation Area** located along the eastern shore of the lake is a popular summer spot for visitors. The conservation area offers a boat launch, picnic area, beach and trail systems. The park is also available for camping for groups by reservation only. Call (705) 745-5791 for more information.

Along with the conservation area a number of facilities are available on the north end of Chemong Lake. These facilities include a tent and trailer park found on the north shore as well as a bed and breakfast and small marina and boat launch south of the conservation area.

Directions

A popular access spot to Upper Chemong Lake is from the public boat launch at the Selwyn Conservation Area. To find the conservation area, follow County Road 29 north from Peterborough to County Road 23, which is also known as Buckhorn Road. Take County Road 23 northwest all the way to the settlement of Selwyn. At the four-way junction in Selwyn, turn west along Selwyn and then 12th Line Road. Continue west to Birch Island Road, where a right takes you north to the conservation area. If you prefer, there is also another boat access just south of the conservation area that is found at the end of 12th Line Road and Pratts Marina Road.

Other Options

The closest angling alternative to Chemong Lake is the neighboring **Buckhorn Lake**. Buckhorn Lake is connected to the western shore of Chemong Lake and is part of the main Trent Severn Waterway. Regardless of the increased boat activity, Buckhorn Lake offers good angling opportunities for its resident largemouth bass, smallmouth bass, walleye and muskellunge.

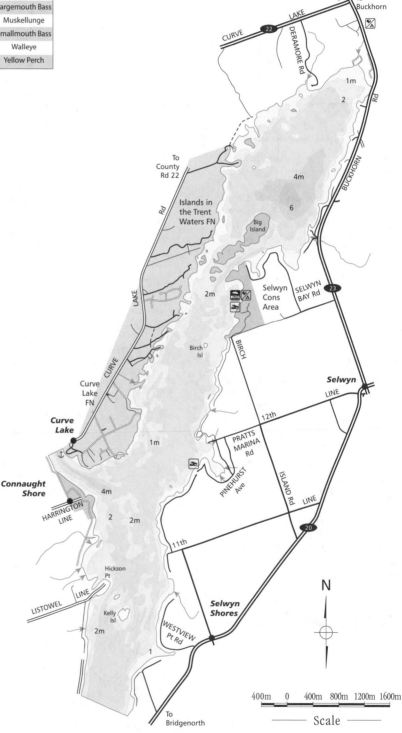

Chemong Lake- Lower

Location: 15 km (9 mi) north of Peterborough
Elevation: 254 m (833 ft)
Surface Area: 2,280 ha (5,634 ac)
Maximum Depth: 6.7 m (22 ft)
Mean Depth: 3.3 m (10.6 ft)
Way Point: 44° 28' 57" N, 78° 20' 54" W

17 Zone

Fishing

Look for weed lines around the lake to help increase your success. A productive method in finding walleye on this lake is to troll along weed lines with a worm harness tipped with a worm. The attractant of the spinners on the lure grab the attention of walleye, while the worm is often the key ingredient to enticing the strike. With all the weed structure it can be difficult at times to know if you have a hit or not. It takes some practice in knowing the difference between a good weed tug and a walleye strike in the Kawartha Lakes.

If you can't get out on a boat, the causeway is a well-known hotspot for walleye. Fishing live bait under floats and casting crankbaits works well during spring.

If you are looking for bass, the best place to start is around the weed lines. Bass will sit along the structure or literally right in the weed cover. Work your presentations along these areas for added success. Weedless lures or jigs are recommended to avoid hook ups.

Musky hunters will also need to be patient on this lake. However, muskellunge are aggressive fish and will often hit any well-presented spoon. The classics are still the Daredevil and the Five of Diamonds size 12–15 cm (4–5 inches).

Anglers looking for a place to fish during winter will be happy to hear Chemong Lake now offers perch and few other panfish. These fish are quite small, but do provide steady action. There is also the chance to catch the bigger species like largemouth bass and muskie through the ice. Most of the action takes place off the causeway in the deeper water away from the weedy shoreline.

Watch for sanctuary areas for the walleye.

Directions

The South End of Chemong Lake lies just to the west of the city of Peterborough. The village of Bridgenorth is a popular access point and can be found via County Road 18 or Chemong Road. You can find County Road 18 by following County Road 1 west from Highway 7 at Fowlers Corner. There are marinas in town but most launch from the site across the Bridge at Youngstown.

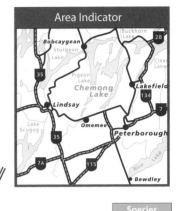

Area Indicator

Species

Species
Largemouth Bass
Muskellunge
Panfish
Smallmouth Bass
Walleye
Yellow Perch

Facilities

Bridgenorth has plenty to offer Chemong lake visitors, including easy access to supplies and other amenities, such as lodging. Marinas can be found in Bridgenorth, near Fife's Bay as well as near the settlement of Youngstown. There is also a boat launch available across the causeway from Bridgenorth on the west side of Chemong Lake.

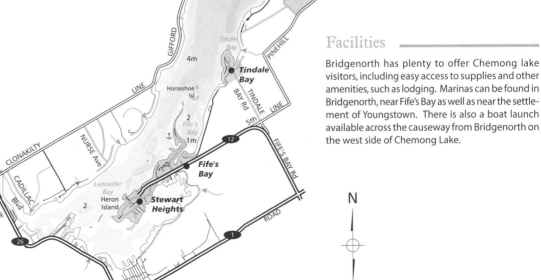

Zone 15

Location: 11 km (6 mi) north of Burleigh Falls
Elevation: 359 m (1,178 ft)
Maximum Depth: 18 m (59 ft)
Mean Depth: 6.8 m (22.5 ft)
Way Point: 44° 40′ 00″ Lat - N, 78° 15′ 00″ Lon - W

Cherry Lake

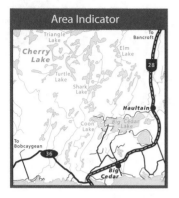

Area Indicator

Species
Lake Trout
Largemouth Bass
Yellow Bass
Yellow Perch

Cherry Lake		
Fish Stocking Data		
Year	Species	Number
2013	Lake Trout	200
2011	Lake Trout	200

Fishing

This scenic backcountry lake is a fantastic location to get away from the hustle and bustle of the urban world. Cherry Lake is part of a collection of interconnecting lakes that offer great canoeing possibilities and the chance to catch that cherished lake trout. To help maintain a decent fishery here, lake trout are stocked on occasion.

The best time to try for these stocked trout, which are actually char, is in the spring just after ice off. At this time, lake trout are readily found near the surface and will aggressively take spoon and spinner presentations. Although trolling along the drop-off areas is the preferred method, when the lakers are hitting at this time of year, it is possible to fish for them from shore. In addition to small spoons and spinners, you may even want to try a simple bobber and a dead minnow. Lakers will often cruise by and pick up any decent looking meal.

As the water warms, lakers will seek the solace of the cooler water in the deeper parts of the lake and they become increasingly difficult to catch. Trolling becomes a necessity and gear to reach the depths of the lake where the trout are is vital to success. Canoe trippers should bring leadcore line to help them find these elusive trout during the dog days of summer. A baited lure with lots of action, like a Flatfish or Kwikfish, trolled just off the bottom will work best.

Directions

Cherry Lake lies within the expanded boundary of the Kawartha Highlands Provincial Park and is part of the Turtle Lake Canoe Route. The lake is only accessible via portage from either Triangle Lake to the north or Turtle Lake to the south.

The main canoe access area for this group of lakes is found at the east end of Long Lake. Long Lake can be reached by travelling north along Highway 28 past Lakefield to Long Lake Road off the west side of the highway. From the highway, it is a short drive to the access point and parking area at Long Lake Lodge. A small fee may apply for parking.

Other Options

There are plenty of other angling options available in the nearby area. **Triangle Lake** to the north of Cherry Lake provides fishing for lake trout, while **Turtle Lake** to the south offers angling for smallmouth bass. Other options in the area also include **Cox Lake** to the north and **Stoplog Lake** to the east. Cox Lake is inhabited by smallmouth bass and stocked lake trout, while Stoplog Lake is home to resident lake trout and both smallmouth and largemouth bass.

Facilities

There is a camping area and other facilities available at **Long Lake Lodge** at the eastern shore of Long Lake. The lodge also hosts a boat launch and parking area for canoeists. Since the paddle to Cherry Lake is at least a day away, there are several established rustic campsites available on all the nearby lakes. Campsites are user maintained and usually only offer a fire pit.

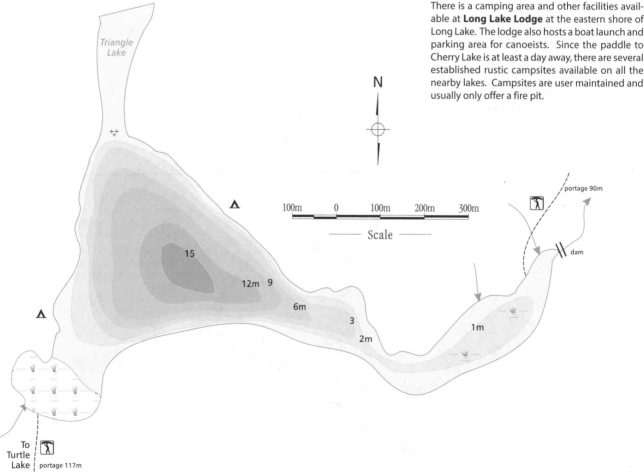

Christie Lake

Location: 16 km (10 mi) west of Perth
Elevation: 155 m (509 ft)
Surface Area: 646 ha (1,596 ac)
Maximum Depth: 18.3 m (60 ft)
Mean Depth: 8.5 m (28 ft)
Way Point: 44° 48'00" N, 76° 26'00" W

18 Zone

Fishing

Anglers to Christie Lake can enjoy fishing for a variety of sportfish such as smallmouth bass, largemouth bass, northern pike and walleye. Bass fishing is quickly becoming popular in the region, although fishing for walleye remains the fish of choice to most anglers.

For both bass species try working shore structure around the many small islands found around the lake. These islands are prime holding areas for big bass. You can also pick up the odd northern pike off any of the islands. Alternatively, working a weedless spinner type lure or jig in the weedy bays at dusk can be very effective for pike.

Walleye anglers will find this species likes to roam around shoals, which are abundant around the lake. A few of the more popular spots are the shoals just off Pickerel Island and to the east of Big Island. Try a white or yellow jig just off the bottom and wait for the walleye to cruise by looking for a meal. Another effective lure is a worm harness. Trolling a worm harness through these shoals can work wonders at times.

Another hot spot for all species is the inlets of the Tay River. The flow of the river is a natural attractant to sportfish since food levels are always higher around river mouths. Predatory fish like pike and walleye love to cruise these feed areas in search of an easy meal.

In order to help walleye stocks, a spring fishing sanctuary has been imposed on the lake. Other regulations include a slot size limit. Be sure to check your Ontario Recreational Fishing Summary before heading out as the regulations are continuously changing.

Other Options

Little Silver Lake is a much smaller lake found to the west of Christie Lake off County Road 36. Look for Little Silver Lake Road off the east side of the main road. The small lake is inhabited by decent sized largemouth and smallmouth bass.

Facilities

There are no public boat launching facilities available at Christie Lake, although there are a few pay for use launches available at a few of the private camps and lodges around the lake. Visitors will also be able to find other rental items such as cabins, canoes or motorboats available. Alternatively, the nearby town of Perth offers full service amenities including hotels, restaurants and grocery stores.

Directions

Christie Lake is located southwest of the town of Perth and is part of the Tay River system. To reach the lake from Perth, follow the Christie Lake Road (County Road 6) west. The road can be found in both Perth or off the south side of Highway 7. As can be expected, Christie Lake Road travels directly to the lake, passing by the southern shoreline.

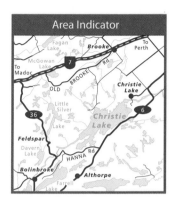

Species
Largemouth Bass
Northern Pike
Smallmouth Bass
Walleye

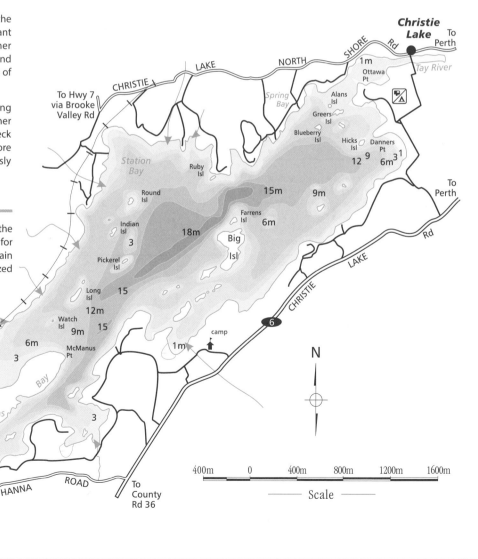

Zone 18

Location: 18 km (11 mi) west of Carleton Place
Elevation: 161 m (528 ft)
Surface Area: 452 ha (1,117 ac)
Maximum Depth: 10.7 m (35.1 ft)
Mean Depth: 3.7 m (12.1 ft)
Way Point: 45° 05′ 00″ N, 76° 10′ 00″ W

Clayton & Taylor Lakes

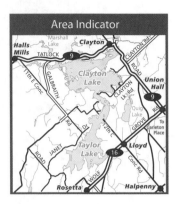

Area Indicator

Species
Largemouth Bass
Northern Pike
Smallmouth Bass
Walleye

Fishing

Taylor Lake flows into Clayton Lake creating a lake perimeter that is roughly 15 kilometres long. With a maximum depth of about 3 metres (10 feet), the lakes are quite shallow and weedy making the ideal habitat for warm water sportfish. While the fishing can be challenging due to the heavy weed areas, if you know how to work through the weeds it can be very good at times for walleye and northern pike as well as smallmouth and largemouth bass.

Although there are numerous cottages on the two lakes, the fishing has actually been improving recently. Fishing can be fair to good for bass and decent for walleye through most of the season. In general, the water quality in Clayton Lake and Taylor Lake is improving due to reduction in phosphates from direct dumping into the lake from old cottage drainage systems. With continued improvements, the lakes should see a steady increase in water quality and hence fishing quality.

Topwater presentations can be a lot fun much of the year for both species of bass, while trolling a weedless chartreuse or fire tiger coloured worm harness with a worm can be deadly for walleye. Other options include weedless frog or even a weedless jig to work into the heavy weed cover found in many areas of both lakes.

There is a sunken floating bridge at the narrows between Clayton and Taylor Lakes that was wiped out by hurricane Connie in 1964 and many of the logs can be seen on the bottom on the lake and provide great structure for smallmouth and other species. Try working jigs along the logs or weedless presentations to find a lunker.

Directions

From Ottawa or Toronto you follow Highway 7 (west form Ottawa and east from Toronto) to Tatlock Road or County Road 9, just west of the village of Carleton Place. Head north on Tatlock Road for approximately 20 km to the north shore of Clayton Lake. Private pay for access can be found from Clayton Lakeside Cottages on the west shore, while a rougher public launch is located along the northernmost shore of Clayton Lake. You can access Taylor Lake from Clayton Lake via water.

Facilities

The town of Carleton Place has every amenity to offer travelers. From fast food, to groceries to fishing gear, all can be found in this quiet town. Those looking to overnight in the area can find cottages for rent through local postings or the internet. **Clayton Lakeside Cottages** is one alternative on the western shore that a small marina, convenience store and boat rentals.

Other Options

If the fishing is slow in these lakes or if you just would like to try something different, you can always head to the town of Carleton Place and put your boat in **Mississippi Lake**. There is a public boat launch right in town (look for signs) and the fishing can be decent on the off days at Clayton and Taylor. Mississippi is a popular lake for boating and makes an interesting day trip to explore the area further. You can travel the lake for several kilometres and view some fantastic cottages along the lakeshore.

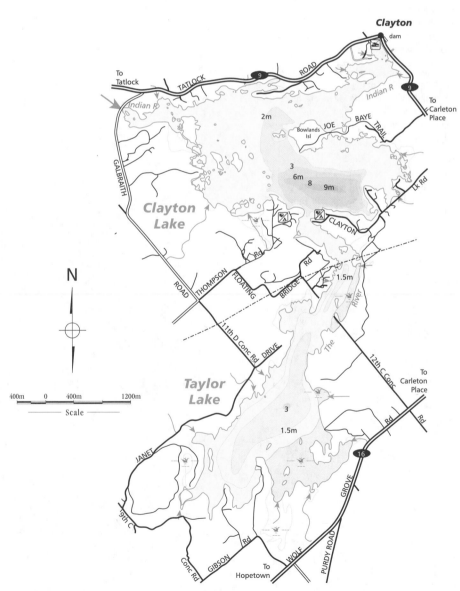

Clear Lake

Location: 5 km (3 mi) south of Westport
Surface Area: 172 ha (425 ac)
Maximum Depth: 33 m (108 ft)
Mean Depth: 16.1 m (53 ft)
Way Point: 44° 36′ 00″ N, 76° 18′ 00″ W

18 Zone

Fishing

As a part of the Rideau Canal, Clear Lake does experience significant boating traffic throughout the summer months. As a result, the lake is heavily fished but still remains a relatively good angling option.

The main sportfish species are smallmouth bass, largemouth bass, northern pike and walleye. Both bass species are the easiest to find, as they will hide near any sort of structure, either manmade or natural. Try working spinners or jigs around cottage docks to see if you can lure a bass from the shadows. Some of the biggest bass are caught right below the docks.

A good area for both bass and northern pike is the western end of the lake. This region is home to weedy bays, which make up prime habitat for ambush ready bass and pike. Weedless type spinners or top water lures can be quite productive in these areas, especially during overcast periods or at dusk.

Walleye in Clear Lake are definitely the hardest sportfish to find on a consistent basis. The best way to locate these predators is to sit off one of the many shoal humps found around the lake and jig not far off bottom. The shoal area located in the eastern middle of the lake is a good spot to try to find cruising walleye. The shoal is shallow enough to provide weed growth, which enhances baitfish activity and eventually brings in predatory fish like walleye. Many anglers looking for walleye do not even go out onto the lake during the summer until almost dark. As with most walleye producing lakes, this species is almost nocturnal in nature and increases feeding as evening sets in.

Directions

Clear Lake is part of the Rideau Canal waterway and is located between Indian Lake to the south and Newboro Lake to the north. The quickest route to the lake by vehicle is by taking Highway 15 to Chaffey's Lock Road (County Road 9). Follow Chaffey's Lock Road southwest and look for Garrett Road off the north side. After a short trek north, you will pass Clear Lake Road, which heads west to the shoreline of Clear Lake.

Travellers that wish to reach Scott Island on the west side of Clear Lake can take a short ferry across the inlet between Indian Lake and Clear Lake.

Other Options

Via the Rideau Canal, visitors to Clear Lake can access **Newboro Lake** to the north and **Indian Lake** to the south. If your luck is slow on Clear Lake, it is a short ride to either of these great Eastern Ontario fishing lakes. Visitors to Indian Lake can fish for smallmouth bass, largemouth bass, northern pike and stocked splake. Both bass species along with walleye and northern pike inhabit Newboro Lake. Be sure to check the depth chart and details found on these lakes later in the book.

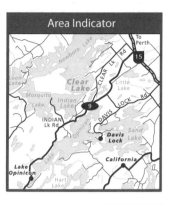

Area Indicator

Species
Largemouth Bass
Northern Pike
Smallmouth Bass
Walleye

N

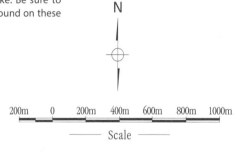

| 200m | 0 | 200m | 400m | 600m | 800m | 1000m |

Scale

Facilities

There are several cottages and lodges along Clear Lake, many of which can be rented during the summer. Inquire locally for rental opportunities. For basic supplies, the village of Newboro is located to the north of Clear Lake off County Road 36.

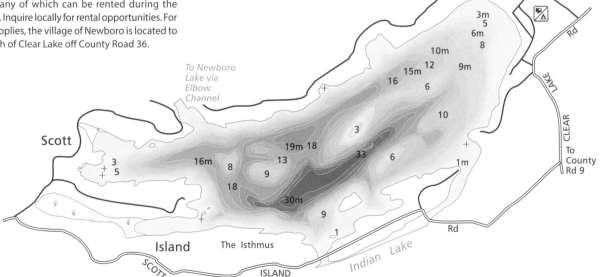

© Backroad Mapbooks

Location: 11 km (7 mi) northeast of Apsley
Elevation: 327 m (1,073 ft)
Maximum Depth: 3 m (10 ft)
Mean Depth: 2 m (6.5 ft)
Way Point: 44° 50' 00" Lat - N, 78° 01' 00" Lon - W

Clydesdale Lake

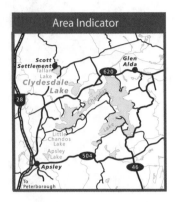

Area Indicator

Species
Largemouth Bass
Smallmouth Bass

Fishing

Both largemouth and smallmouth bass inhabit Clydesdale Lake. Fishing for bass can be fair at times and is most productive during overcast periods or at dusk. Clydesdale Lake is a shallow body of water with and average depth of only about 2 m (6.5 ft). The shallow nature of the lake helps create the perfect conditions for weed growth that provide cover for bass. Look for bass along weed lines or even underneath weed cover. In heavy weeds, a jig type lure can be worked through the cover and provide fewer snags than spinner type lures. The regions off either one of the small islands are sure to be a holding area for bass.

When the weather is unstable, when the water is cold, or when the bass are lethargic use slower, vertical presentations. This is best in early spring and again in fall. Jigs are the most common, and soft plastic-bodied jigs are preferred by many anglers, as they deliver life-like action. Injecting it with salt or scent further enhances its fish-catching ability. Soft plastics come in hundreds of different shapes, sizes, and colours, but baitfish and crayfish are the two most common, as these are commonly eaten by smallmouth.

When the weather is unstable, when the water is cold, or when the bass are lethargic use slower, vertical presentations. This is best in early spring and again in fall. Jigs are the most common, and soft plastic-bodied jigs are preferred by many anglers, as they deliver life-like action. Injecting it with salt or scent further enhances its fish-catching ability. Soft plastics come in hundreds of different shapes, sizes, and colours, but baitfish and crayfish are the two most common, as these are commonly eaten by smallmouth.

Directions

Clydesdale Lake is settled in the rolling hill area north of the town of Apsley. The lake can be reached by following Highway 28 north to County Road 620 at the town of Apsley. Follow County Road 620 northeast all the way to the lake. A few access roads, including Richmond Road, jut off the north side of County Road 620 and lead to Clydesdale Lake. Watch for private property.

Facilities

There are really no facilities available at Clydesdale Lake, although supplies and accommodations can be found in and around the town of Apsley. For overnight camping, there are two tent and trailer parks on the southern shore of Chandos Lake that are within a short drive from Clydesdale Lake. If you prefer, **Silent Lake Provincial Park** is a little further away, although it can be reached via Highway 28 just north of Apsley.

Other Options

Chandos Lake is located just south of Clydesdale Lake. There is an access area to Chandos Lake off the south side of County Road 620 east of Clydesdale Lake. Chandos Lake offers fishing opportunities for largemouth bass, smallmouth bass, northern pike and lake trout. Please practice catch and release whenever possible.

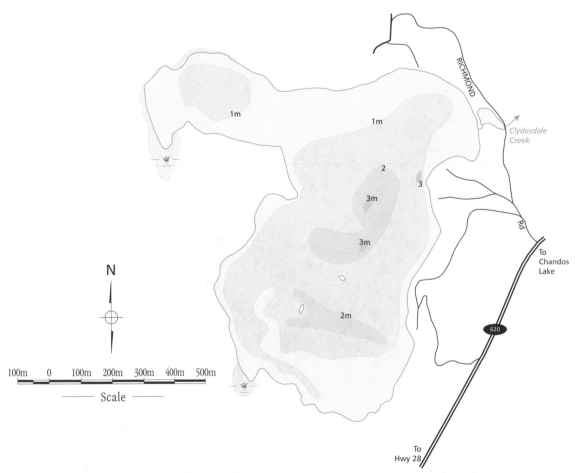

Collins Lake

Location: 10 km (6 mi) north of Kingston
Surface Area: 326 ha (806 ac)
Maximum Depth: 9.1 m (30 ft)
Mean Depth: 4.7 m (15.4 ft)
Way Point: 44° 22' 00" N, 76° 28' 00" W

Fishing

This popular lake receives a lot of angling pressure throughout the year due to its close proximity to the city of Kingston. However, the nutrient rich, weedy nature of the lake has enabled the lake to continue to produce decent fishing results over the years. Collins Lake is inhabited by mainly smallmouth and largemouth bass but there is also a fair population of muskellunge.

Fishing success is best for bass and with the ample vegetation found around the lake fishing can be decent at times. Try working a jig in and out of the pockets of weeds or try working a weedless spinner bait right through the vegetation. Bass will be found cruising in and out of the weed lines most of the time. The southern portion of the lake is known as a good holding area for bass.

Fishing for muskellunge is a true test of skills, as the finicky predator can frustrate even the most ardent of anglers. Musky cruise weed lines in search of food, especially during overcast and dusk periods. If you do the same, you may just get lucky. Try using large plugs and crank baits or trolling a long Bucktail streamer to produce results on occasion.

Directions

North of Kingston, you can find Collins Lake by following the old Perth Road (County Road 10) north. About 13 km (8 mi) north of Highway 401 look for the Sunbury Road (County Road 12) off the east side. It is a short drive east along the Sunbury Road until you will pass by the northern end of Collins Lake.

Facilities

Collins Lake has a tent and trailer park located on the northeast shore that offers pay per use access to the lake. The city of Kingston is also found merely minutes away to the south. The big city has plenty to offer visitors, including all range of accommodations, restaurants as well as bait and tackle shops.

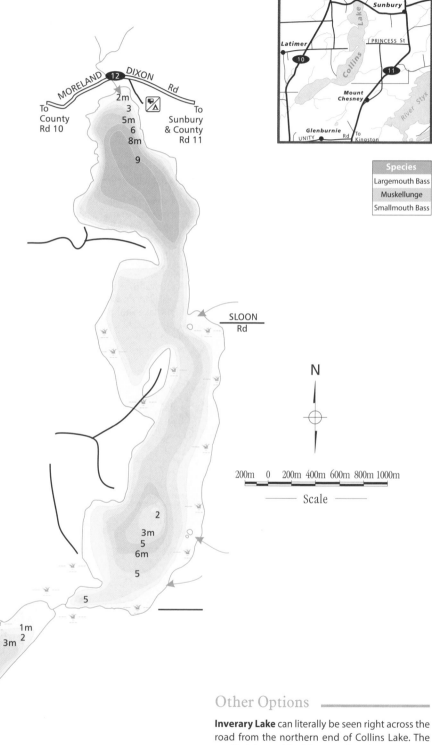

Area Indicator

Species
Largemouth Bass
Muskellunge
Smallmouth Bass

Other Options

Inverary Lake can literally be seen right across the road from the northern end of Collins Lake. The smaller lake provides fair to good results on occasion for smallmouth and largemouth bass. Similar to Collins Lake, bass in Inverary Lake average about 0.5-1 kg (1-2 lbs) although can be found larger on occasion. A small population of muskellunge is also rumoured to exist in Inverary Lake.

Location: 19 km (11 mi) south of Trenton
Elevation: 79 m (258 ft)
Surface Area: 600 ha (1483 ac)
Maximum Depth: 16.7 m (55 ft)
Mean Depth: 7 m (23 ft)
Way Point: 44° 00′ 00″ Lat - N, 77° 27′ 00″ Lon - W

Consecon Lake

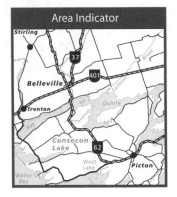

Area Indicator

Species

Species
Largemouth Bass
Northern Pike
Smallmouth Bass
Walleye
Yellow Perch

Fishing

Consecon is derived from the Indian word "Knan Nokjarm" which means an opening, and "con con" which means pickerel. Needless to say, there are walleye in the lake. Anglers will also find smallmouth and largemouth bass, northern pike and yellow perch. For something different, there are even Gar pike found in the lake.

Gar pike are an odd looking fish that some compare to small alligators. Some anglers like to fly fish for these creatures, while others snare them using a steel leader and a minnow. When they hit the minnow, you pull and the leader gets caught between their teeth. They are big fish and landing anything over a metre long is definitely a thrill. They seem to school together.

Northern pike and walleye are the more likely target of most anglers. The area just west of the Melville Creek can be a fair holding area during the early part of the open water season. Trolling a worm harness can be an effective method at times. Try to troll along weed lines for increased success.

Smallmouth and largemouth can be found throughout the lake, including in the shallow western portion of the lake west of the rail tracks. The lake has a number of established weed areas that also make for prime holding areas for largemouth and the odd smallmouth bass.

Directions

Prince Edward County is famous for beautiful countryside, spectacular sunsets and miles of rugged shoreline. Consecon Lake lies in the heart of the county to the south of Trenton. To reach the lake, follow Highway 401 to County Road 33 also known as the Loyalist Parkway. Follow this road south past the west arm of the Bay of Quinte eventually reaching the small settlement of Consecon and Consecon Lake.

Facilities

The Loyalist Parkway, the main route to the town of Consecon, offers a wide choice of accommodation and sightseeing attractions. Beaches, wineries, quaint villages, boutique shopping, art galleries and at least 125 notable heritage buildings lie adjacent to the Parkway. Consecon offers retail facilities, while a resort with camping and cabins is found along the northern shore of Consecon Lake via Lakeside Drive.

Other Options

The two closest and most popular fishing destinations in the area are **Lake Ontario** and the **Bay of Quinte.** There are several boat launch areas onto both waterbodies or if you require a guide, there are numerous outfitters that will take you out for a day of fishing for a nominal fee. Fishing in Lake Ontario is mainly for big salmon, rainbow trout and the odd lake trout. The Bay of Quinte is famous for its walleye; however, numerous other species can be caught in the bay. Bass and pike can be found in both waters, generally closer to land where shore structure is found.

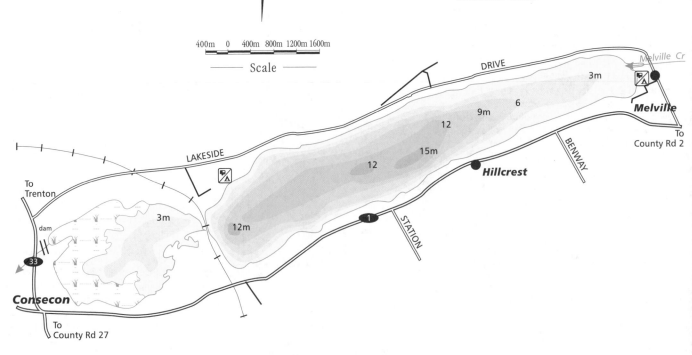

Constance Lake

Location: 5 km (9 mi) north of Kanata
Elevation: 58 m (190 ft)
Surface Area: 132 ha (325 ac)
Maximum Depth: 3.4 m (11 ft)
Mean Depth: 1.9 m (6.2 ft)
Way Point: 45° 24′ 00″ N, 75° 59′ 00″ W

Fishing

This shallow, weedy lake is a regularly fished lake due to its close proximity to the city of Ottawa. Anglers visiting Constance Lake for the first time will be surprised with the number of northern pike resident in the lake. Most lakes in the region are inhabited with healthy populations of bass, although Constance Lake provides its best fishing opportunities for pike. Smallmouth and largemouth bass in the 0.5-1 kg (1-2 lb) range as well as a limited number of walleye are also found in the warm water lake.

Pike can be found by trolling spoons, flipping jigs or casting spinner baits along the weedy areas. Look for bass in weedy areas or along any type of shore structure. The small point off the eastern end of the lake tends to be a good holding area for these aggressive fish. The rocky underwater structure attracts bass and a number of fish can often be caught off the point. Walleye fishing is usually quite slow with ice fishing being the most productive method of luring the prized sportfish.

Area Indicator

Species
Largemouth Bass
Northern Pike
Smallmouth Bass
Walleye

Directions

Constance Lake is located northwest of the Ottawa suburb of Nepean. To reach the lake, follow Highway 417 to Nepean and take the 138 exit north. You should now be on County Road 49, which eventually connects to County Road 9 (Dunrobin Road). About 2 km (1.2 mi) along Dunrobin Road, look for River Road off the east side. Take River Road to the intersection with the Berry Side Road, which accesses a launching area for Constance Lake.

Facilities

A small, fee based launching facility is available at the eastern end of the lake. The nearby town of Carp or the Ottawa suburb of Nepean offers all the main amenities, including hotels, groceries and other supplies.

Other Options

Within minutes of Constance Lake, you can find the mighty **Ottawa River**. Boat access to the river is readily available in several areas. The large river provides a good variety of fish for anglers to try their luck at. Smallmouth bass are quite abundant and are often found throughout the river while largemouth bass can also be found in certain areas. Northern pike and muskellunge are the largest fish and these predators can be easily found exceeding 6 kg (13 lbs) in size. Walleye remain the main sportfish targeted by anglers and fishing can be good on occasion. Other species that can be a lot of fun catching in the Ottawa River include sturgeon, whitefish and panfish, such as perch.

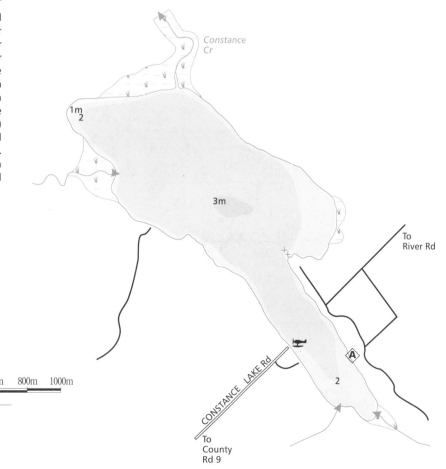

N

| 200m | 0 | 200m | 400m | 600m | 800m | 1000m |

Scale

Zone 15

Location: 5 km (3 mi) west of Haultain
Mean Depth: 6.8 m (22.5 ft)
Maximum Depth: 15.2 m (50 ft)
Way Point: 44° 37′ 00″ Lat - N, 78° 12′ 00″ Lon - W

Coon Lake

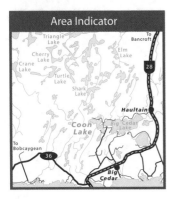

Area Indicator

Species
Largemouth Bass
Muskellunge
Smallmouth Bass

Fishing

Coon Lake is home to a number of cottages but the lake seems to avoid the summer vacation rush. Fishing in the lake is regarded as generally fair for its resident smallmouth and largemouth bass. There are a few weedy patches found around the lake that make for good hiding areas for ambush ready largemouth bass. Smallmouth bass can be found in weed cover but also off rocky drop-off around the shoreline. Top water presentations can be effective at times, but spinner baits and jigs seem to be a more productive lure for the bass of Coon Lake.

A population of muskellunge also inhabit the lake and fishing can be fair at times. Seasoned musky anglers will often find that Coon Lake can be a productive muskellunge fishery. Similar to most musky lakes, the action is often best in the late summer to fall period.

Directions

Coon Lake is found not far from Highway 28 north of Lakefield. To reach the smaller lake, follow Highway 28 north from Lakefield to the settlement of Burleigh Falls. Just north of Burleigh Falls you can find Coon Lake Road off the north side of Highway 28. Follow Coon Lake Road around the east end of Coon Lake to the boat launch area on the east shore.

Facilities

Along with the boat launch, Coon Lake is part of a fantastic canoe route. Coon Lake is sometimes used as the southern access point to the chain or as the first lake in the route beginning from Big Cedar Lake to the east.

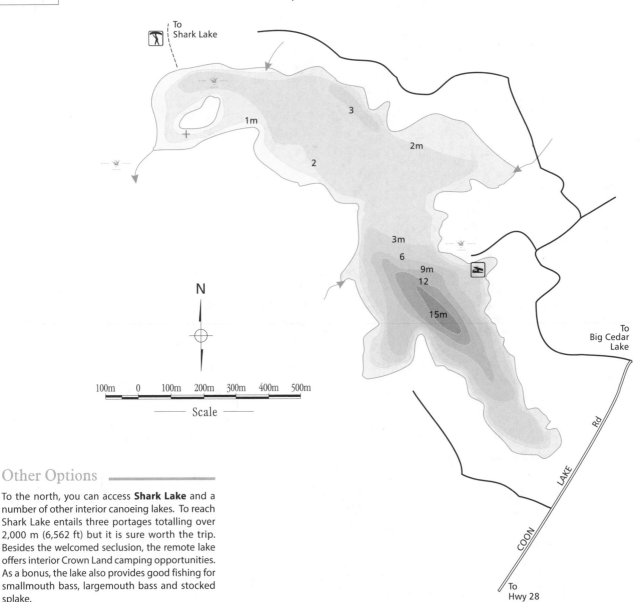

Other Options

To the north, you can access **Shark Lake** and a number of other interior canoeing lakes. To reach Shark Lake entails three portages totalling over 2,000 m (6,562 ft) but it is sure worth the trip. Besides the welcomed seclusion, the remote lake offers interior Crown Land camping opportunities. As a bonus, the lake also provides good fishing for smallmouth bass, largemouth bass and stocked splake.

Copper Lake

Location: 9 km (5 mi) north of Apsley
Maximum Depth: 5.4 m (18 ft)
Mean Depth: 4 m (13.1 ft)
Way Point: 44° 47′ 00″ N, 78° 10′ 00″ W

Zone 15

Fishing

Since access to Copper Lake is more challenging, the fishing remains decent. As is often the case, the few portages keep the bulk of anglers out of a lake.

Fishing in Copper Lake is known to be good at times for nice sized largemouth bass. The shallow nature of the lake makes for ideal bass habitat and there is plenty of weed growth found around the lake. For fly anglers, top water poppers or even a floating Muddler Minnow can create a real frenzy of action on the lake.

Copper Lake is also inhabited by a marginal population of walleye. Some claim the fishing for walleye can be good, while others have had little or no luck at all for the sharp toothed predator.

Facilities

Copper Lake is a Crown Land lake that has become a part of the **Kawartha Highlands Provincial Park** expansion. The park was established to help preserve much of the remote access parts of the region. Currently, Copper Lake offers visitors a few rustic user maintained campsites. The campsites are usually clean and very tranquil. Please be sure to carry any garbage out after your visit to help keep them that way.

The nearest development is on Anstruther Lake. The bigger lake is home to several cottages and a marina. Basic supplies can also be picked up in the town of Apsley.

Directions

This backcountry fishing lake can be accessed by canoe and a series of portages. To begin the long journey in, you will need to access Anstruther Lake to the south and then Rathburn Lake to the west.

From Highway 28 just south of the cut-off to the town of Apsley, look for the Anstruther Lake Road. Follow this road past a marina before reaching the public access area to Anstruther Lake. There is a canoe put in at the access area, as well as free parking. From the north end of Anstruther Lake a short 162 m (530 ft) portage leads to Rathburn Lake. Paddle to the eastern shore of Rathburn and the mouth of Anstruther Creek. From here you will need to portage and paddle up the creek, eventually meeting the isolated Copper Lake.

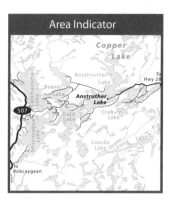

Species
Largemouth Bass
Walleye

Other Options

To access Copper Lake, you must first travel across **Rathburn Lake**. Rathburn Lake is an interior lake that is home to user maintained Crown Land campsites and fishing opportunities for smallmouth bass, largemouth bass, walleye and stocked lake trout.

Location: 30 km (18 mi) northeast of Havelock
Max Depth: 15 m (49 ft)
Mean Depth: 4.6 m (15 ft)
Way Point: 44° 35' 00" Lat - N, 77° 50' 00" Lon - W

Cordova Lake

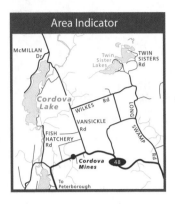

Area Indicator

Species
Northern Pike
Smallmouth Bass
Walleye
Yellow Perch

Directions

Cordova Lake is a popular recreational lake that is frequented by anglers and canoeists. To find the lake, travel east from the city of Peterborough on Highway 7 to the town of Havelock. Just to the east of town, take County Road 48 northeast past Freeman Corners and Cordova Mines. Look for Vansickle Road off the north side of the 48 and follow this road for about 6 km to the north end of the lake and the boat launch at Cordova Lake Campground.

Facilities

Cordova Lake Campground provides camping, bait and a boat launch at the north end of the lake. For those willing to brave bush roads, there is also another launch located at south end off of Fire Route 18. It is about 3 km north of Preston Road to the lake. Be careful if you plan to haul a boat on this rough backroad.

Fishing

The history of Cordova Mines and area is rich with stories of the gold rush years. Although the gold mining days are now gone, anglers will find their own treasures in the tea-stained waters of Cordova Lake. From smallmouth and largemouth bass to walleye and pike, fishing can be quite productive here. There are also a few muskellunge as well as abundant rock bass and perch if you prefer fast action for panfish.

The most plentiful species are smallmouth bass, which average over 1 kg (2 lbs) and occasionally reach 2.5 kg (5 lbs). Anything that resembles the baitfish common in the lake is a good bet. As an added bonus you may also catch walleye and northern pike in these same areas.

The most challenging aspect to fishing Cordova Lake has to be deciding what and where to fish. There are several well marked rock shoals around the lake that make great places to start. Try working spinners, jigs and crankbaits along the structure areas and if fishing is slow, slow the retrieve down significantly. Another spot to try is the expansive weed bed that extends the width of the lake opposite of where the Crowe River enters the lake. Try weedless lures worked slowly throughout this weed bed. Early in the season, walleye like to hold near the inlet of the river.

Other Options

Belmont Lake to the south is another fantastic Kawartha Lake that is a great summer vacationing location. Smallmouth bass and largemouth bass make up the majority of the angling success on Belmont Lake. Northern pike and walleye also inhabit the lake.

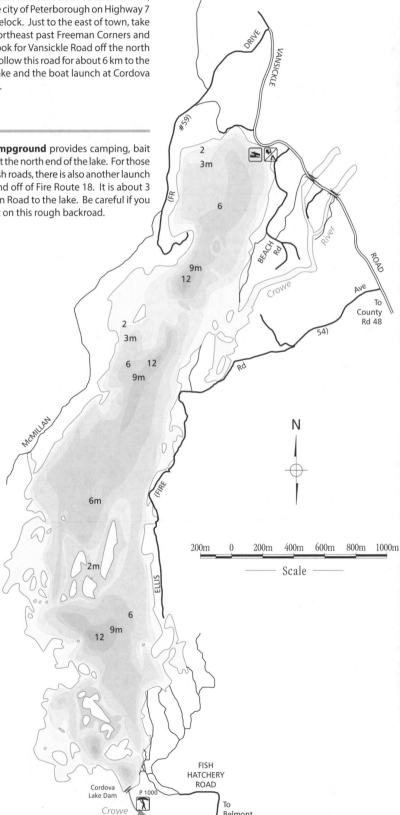

Crab Lake

Location: 10 km (6 mi) west of Apsley
Maximum Depth: 6.7 m (22 ft)
Mean Depth: 3 m (9.8 ft)
Way Point: 43° 44′ 00″ Lat - N, 78° 12′ 00″ Lon - W

Fishing

Crab Lake is an isolated waterbody that consists of five bays that head off in all directions. Locally known as Star Lake, it is much larger than it first appears. Each inlet provides its own unique character and the potential to find some of the nice sized smallmouth bass that roam the lake.

Smallmouth can be readily found throughout the lake, however steady producing areas can be found off the two small islands in the middle of the lake. One spot that should definitely be tried is the 3 metre (10 ft) hump in the middle of the northeast portion of the lake. This abnormal structure area is a good attractant for smallmouth. Try working spinners, jigs and crankbaits along the structure areas. Some specific lures that work well are small Black Fury spinners, Zara Puppies, Yamamoto Smoke grubs, black and chartreuse jigs or pumpkin coloured tube jigs.

Directions

Found on the Wolf Lake Canoe Route, Crab Lake is best accessed by boat. The access point to Wolf Lake is found off Anstruther Lake Road, about 5 km west of Highway 28. Once on Wolf Lake, it is a short paddle west to the 107 metre portage to Crab Lake.

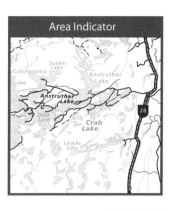

Area Indicator

Species
Smallmouth Bass
Yellow Perch

Facilities

Crab Lake is home to several user maintained, rustic campsites. The campsites are usually made up of a small cleared area and a fire pit and can be found down any of the bays that make up Crab Lake. The nice sites are great for a mid-week camping vacation but can be a little busy on weekends.

Other Options

Some other fishing options in the area include **Wolf Lake** and **Loon Call Lake** to the north and east of Crab Lake. Alternatively the much larger **Anstruther Lake** to the west is another good bass fishing option. Anstruther Lake also has a small lake trout population, while Loon Call Lake is stocked with splake periodically. Musky hunters may find the odd muskellunge in Wolf Lake.

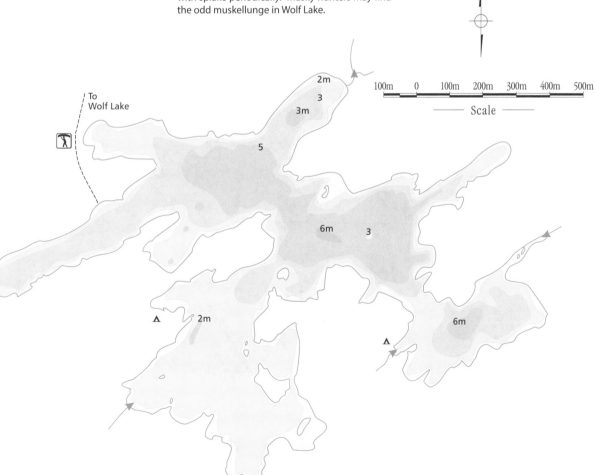

Location: 28 km (17.4 mi) northeast of Kingston
Elevation: 98 m (332 ft)
Surface Area: 650 ha (1606 ac)
Max Depth: 5.5 m (18 ft)
Mean Depth: 2.6 m (8.5 ft)
Way Point: 44° 26′00″ N, 76° 18′00″ W

Cranberry Lake

Area Indicator

Species
Largemouth Bass
Northern Pike
Smallmouth Bass

Fishing

The many bays and coves of this shapely lake have plenty to offer anglers, including fishing opportunities for smallmouth bass, largemouth bass and northern pike. The numerous islands and underwater rock structures have created excellent smallmouth bass habitat. Fishing for smallies is fair to good at times. Look for smallmouth off any sort of shoreline structure, especially the smaller islands. The shallower shoal areas scattered around the lake also provide great holding areas for bigger smallmouth.

For largemouth bass and northern pike, the shallower, weedy bays are usually the best areas to concentrate efforts. Try working top water lures such as a floating Rapala or popper for some exciting action. During the summer, largemouth bass will often be holed up in the bays all day long. On the other hand, northern pike like to cruise into the bays in search of easy meals at dusk and during overcast periods.

Directions

Cranberry Lake is a manmade lake created by British Army engineers during the construction of the Rideau Canal. The lake can be found north of Highway 401 and Kingston not far off Highway 15. From the 401, take Exit 623 north along Highway 15. Continue north past Joyceville and County Road 12 and you should see signs to Cranberry Lake off the west side of the highway.

Facilities

As a part of the **Rideau Canal system**, Cranberry Lake is well developed with cottages and tourist type lodges and resorts for visitors to enjoy. Boat access to the lake is either by paying a fee to launch at a lakeside lodge or by boat along the Rideau waterway. For camping enthusiasts, there are also a few tent and trailer parks on the lake. Alternatively, the nearby city of Kingston offers all amenities including hotels, restaurants and groceries.

Other Options

To the east of Cranberry Lake, **South Lake** offers a good fishing alternative in the area. To reach the lake, continue along Highway 15 north until you reach County Road 32. From Highway 15 it is a short drive south along County Road 32 to the eastern shore of the lake. South Lake is best fished for its smallmouth and largemouth bass, although a small population of northern pike also inhabit the lake. Try jigs and top water lures for all three species.

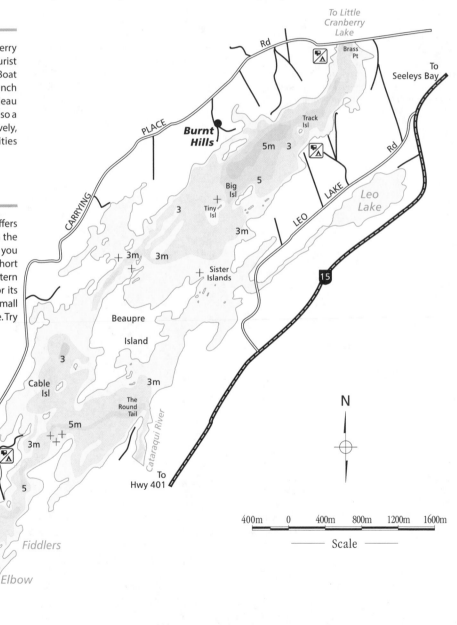

Crosby Lake

Location: 2 km (1.2 mi) southeast of Althorpe
Elevation: 313 m (1,027 ft)
Surface Area: 263 ha (650 ac)
Maximum Depth: 17.7 m (58 ft)
Mean Depth: 8.2 m (27 ft)
Way Point: 44° 45′00″ N, 76° 26′00″ W

Fishing

This popular cottage destination lake offers fishing opportunities for smallmouth bass, largemouth bass, northern pike and walleye. Bass are the most active sportfish found in the lake and provide most of the action. Fishing for bass is fair to good at times for bass that can reach up to 1.5 kg (3.5 lbs) in size. The shallower, weedy sections of the lake are the best areas to find largemouth bass, while smallmouth can often be found near any of the small islands found around the lake.

For walleye, there are a number of shoals around the lake that can attract this aggressive predator. One particular hot spot is found around the two shoal humps located in the southern dip in the lake. Trolling a worm harness or still jigging with coloured jigs along these shoals can pick up the odd walleye.

Northern pike also roam the shore areas of Crosby Lake and can often be caught using attractor type lures. Try using a spinner bait or silver spoon.

Directions

Crosby Lake lies to the northwest of the town of Westport. The easiest way to access the lake is to travel along Highway 7 to County Road 36 just east of Silver Lake Provincial Park. Follow County Road 36 south past Boilingbroke to the Althorpe Road (County Road 6) or further south to the Big Crosby Road. Both roads branch off the east side of County Road 36 and provide access to Crosby Lake.

Facilities

There are no established public launching areas on Crosby Lake. However there are some road allowances that run next to the lake where a small craft such as a canoe can be launched. For basic supplies, such as restaurants and other retailers, the town of Westport can be found within a short drive south along County Road 36.

Other Options

To the east of Crosby Lake, you can find **Little Crosby Lake** via a short portage or by the Scotch Line (County Road 10). Little Crosby Lake is about one quarter of the size of the larger Crosby Lake and offers fishing opportunities for smallmouth bass, largemouth bass, northern pike and walleye. Similar to Crosby Lake, bass provide the bulk of the action on the lake, although the odd pike and walleye can be picked up on occasion.

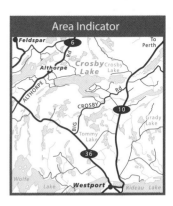

Area Indicator

Species
Largemouth Bass
Northern Pike
Smallmouth Bass
Walleye

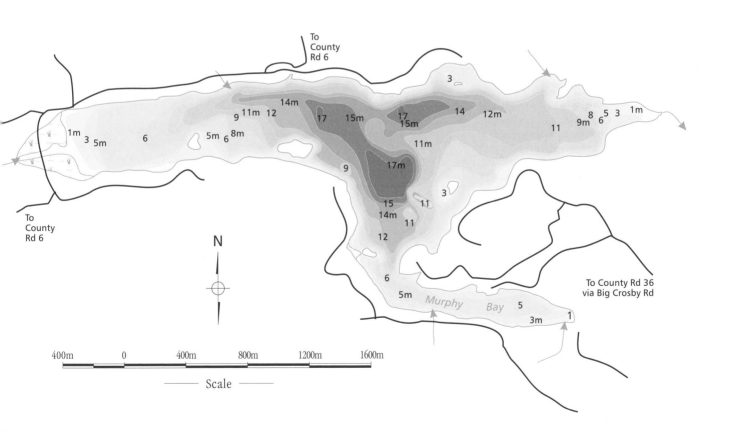

© Backroad Mapbooks

Location: 7 km (4 mi) southeast of Ompah
Elevation: 240 m (787 ft)
Surface Area: 1,678 ha (4,145 ac)
Maximum Depth: 31.1 m (102 ft)
Mean Depth: 8.4 m (27.6 ft)
Way Point: 44° 55'00"N, 76° 48'00"W

Crotch Lake

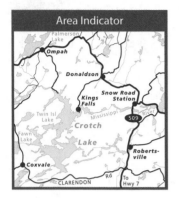

Area Indicator

Species

| Largemouth Bass |
| Northern Pike |
| Smallmouth Bass |
| Walleye |

Directions

Crotch Lake is one of the largest lakes in the region and is located northwest of Sharbot Lake. To find the lake, follow Highway 7 to Highway 509 and head north. After about 9 km along Highway 509, look for the Clarendon Road off the west side. Travel west along the Clarendon Road approximately 8 km to the southern shore of Crotch Lake.

To access Crotch Lake from the north, follow Highway 509 to the village of Ompah and look for the South Bush Road. The South Bush Road is one of the rough 2wd roads that wind their way to the northern end of the lake.

Fishing

Crotch Lake is a popular summer destination lake that provides good fishing. As a result, fishing pressure in the lake is heavy for its resident largemouth bass, smallmouth bass, northern pike and walleye. The beautiful lake has many bays and islands along with good weed cover that create good holding areas for sportfish.

A hot spot for all species is around the inflow and outflow areas of the Mississippi River. Anchor just back from these areas and cast lures such as jigs, crankbaits and spinners. Another recommended hot spot is the 3 m (10 ft) shoal area found in the northern middle section of the lake. The area usually sports plenty of weed growth and has some rock structure as well. Bass hold in the area regularly and both walleye and northern pike will cruise the region during dusk and overcast periods.

Largemouth bass also like to hide in the shallower sections of the lake in any sort of weed cover. There are dozens of quiet bays around the lake that can provide consistent action for bass. For smallmouth bass, working near any of the islands with deeper presentations can be good. Anglers looking to catch northern pike and walleye are best to troll slowly along weed lines during dusk or overcast periods. For walleye a worm harness is effective, while pike can be enticed to chase after flashy spoons periodically. During the winter, ice fishing can be productive for walleye, northern pike and other pan fish. Try jigging a small spoon or a white jig tipped with a worm.

To help pressured walleye stocks, a special slot size regulation is in place for walleye. Consult your regulations for specific restrictions annually.

Facilities

Two public boat launches are found on Crotch Lake, one on the northern shore and the other on the southern shore. Along with these launch areas are a few cottages and lodges.

An alluring feature of Crosby Lake is the ample Crown Land campsites found around the lake. The sites are scenic, user maintained areas providing basic amenities such as a fire pit and privy. Before arriving at Crotch Lake, obtain permits for overnight camping, road use and parking in the nearby town of Plevna.

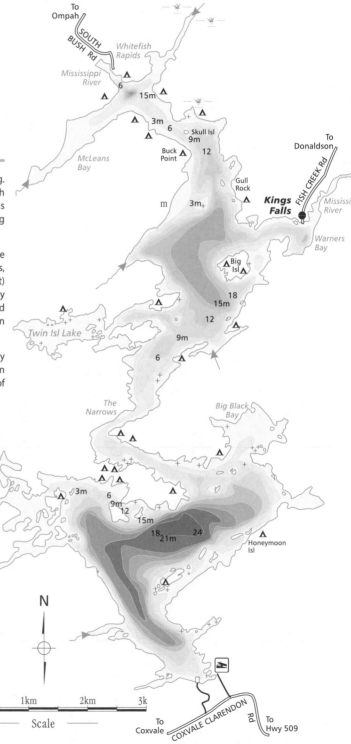

Crow Lake

Location: 13 km (8 mi) southeast of Sharbot Lake
Elevation: 259 m (559 ft)
Surface Area: 436 ha (1,078 ac)
Maximum Depth: 38.1 m (125 ft)
Mean Depth: 14.5 m (47.7 ft)
Way Point: 44° 36′00″ N, 76° 25′00″ W

18 Zone

Species	
Lake Trout	Walleye
Largemouth Bass	Whitefish
Northern Pike	Yellow Perch
Smallmouth Bass	

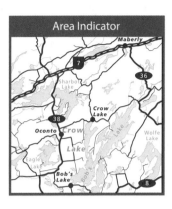

Area Indicator

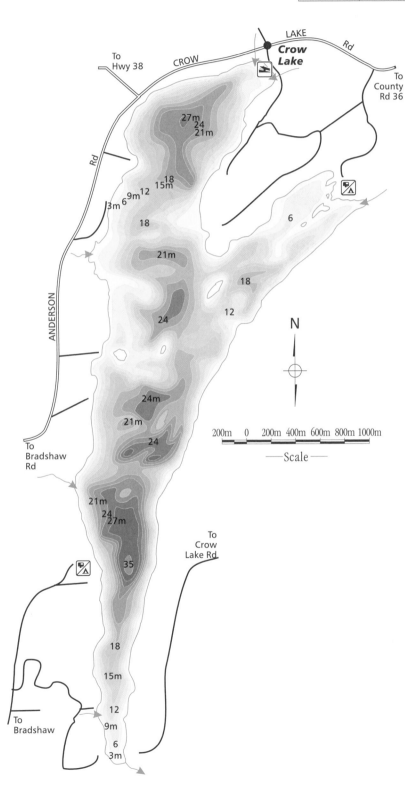

Fishing

The sportfish present in Crow Lake are smallmouth bass, largemouth bass, walleye, northern pike and lake trout. Fishing success is best for bass, although northern pike can be quite active on occasion.

Look for smallmouth off any rocky area, especially off the small islands found in the northern end of the lake. The shallower shoals in the 9 m (30 ft) range around the lake are also good holding areas for both bass and northern pike. Along these shoals, you will often find bass, while the pike action increases during overcast periods and at dusk. A jig worked off the bottom or a crayfish imitation fly or lure can be effective.

For walleye, it is best to troll along drop-offs and shoals that sport some weed growth. Success for walleye in Crow Lake can be quite slow at times and as a result, trolling is recommended to cover as much water as possible.

For lake trout, it is best to try to get out on the lake right after the season opens in spring when the water temperature is still cool near the surface. Trolling a spoon in the middle to upper layer of the lake during this time can be effective. During the summer months, a downrigger is required to reach the deep holes around the lake where lake trout hide to escape the summer heat.

Directions

Crow Lake is located south of the small town of Sharbot Lake not far from the Trans Canada Highway (Highway 7). To reach the lake, follow Highway 7 to the junction with Highway 38 and head south. Follow the highway south through the town of Sharbot Lake and look for Crow Lake Road off the east side of the road. It is a short drive east to the northern shore of Crow Lake.

Facilities

Along with a number of cottages, a few tent and trailer parks are established on Crow Lake. Boat access to the lake is limited to pay per use at one of the trailer parks. Visitors can find all the basic amenities, including a small grocery store, in the nearby town of Sharbot Lake.

Location: 2 km (1.2 mi) west of Marmora
Elevation: 228 m (748 ft)
Surface Area: 875 ha (2,162 ac)
Maximum Depth: 15.8 m (52 ft)
Mean Depth: 5.6 m (18.3 ft)
Way Point: 44° 29' 00" Lat - N, 77° 44' 00" Lon - W

Crowe Lake

Area Indicator

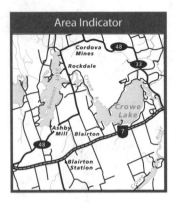

Fishing

Crowe Lake is a very interesting lake to fish due to the unique contours of the lake bottom. The weedy nature of the lake provides a multitude of structure for walleye, bass and other sportfish. Walleye fishing certainly draws the most anglers and can be productive at times, especially since the lake has recently been stocked to aid this fishery. The deeper holes where the depth changes dramatically around the lake are prime holding areas. Try trolling or jigging off one of the surrounding shoals to attract walleye and other predatory fish.

Anglers looking for smallmouth or largemouth bass should note that the shoreline area is filled with weed growth and bass sit ambush ready for passing lures. All the typical bass lures will produce on Crowe Lake but, similar to any lake, productivity can definitely be affected by variables such as weather patterns.

One of the largest sportfish on the lake is muskellunge. These predators can take some patience but may yield the catch of a lifetime. Alternatively, perch and black crappie are a lot easier to catch as these small fish run in schools and are easily enticed with small lures or a bobber and bait.

Species	
Black Crappie	Smallmouth Bass
Lake Trout	Walleye
Largemouth Bass	Yellow Perch
Muskellunge	Other

Facilities

The town of Marmora has plenty of retail options for visitors, including a grocery store and a hardware store for various supplies. The town can be a bustle of activity during the summer months as cottagers flock to the area in search of their summer solace. For overnight camping, there are four tent and trailer parks available on Crowe Lake. Alternatively, there are a few motels off Highway 7 near the town of Marmora.

Directions

This popular cottage destination lake lies just outside of the town of Marmora. From Highway 7, turn north at the lights onto County Road 33. County Road 33 parallels the east side of the Crowe River and leads directly to Crowe Lake. To reach Marmora, follow Highway 7 east from the city of Peterborough past the town of Havelock.

Watch for special size restrictions on muskellunge on Crowe Lake

Crowe Lake		
Fish Stocking Data		
Year	Species	Number
2013	Walleye	22,774
2011	Walleye	24,736

Crystal Lake

Location: 20 km (12 mi) north of Bobcaygeon
Maximum Depth: 33 m (108 ft)
Mean Depth: 19.2 m (63 ft)
Way Point: 44° 46'00" Lat - N, 78° 29'00" Lon - W

Fishing

Crystal Lake is home to several camps and cottages and is regularly fished throughout the year. Smallmouth bass provide the most action on the lake and fishing for the feisty sport fish is generally fair. Look for smallies near cottage dock structures or off any of the small rocky islands found around the lake.

Crystal Lake is also inhabited by natural populations of walleye and lake trout. Fishing for these prized species is fair at best. Walleye anglers should look to shoal areas around the lake to help increase angling success. One spot in particular is the shoal hump found just to the north of the deep 33 m (108 ft) hole located in the middle of the lake.

To help aid the lake trout fishery, the lake is now stocked. This, along with the special restrictions such as slot size limits, should help these fragile sportfish. Anglers looking for lakers will find better success in the spring or fall when they are closer to the surface. During summer, lead line or a downrigger is recommended to get deeper where the trout like to hold.

Area Indicator

Directions

The southern access route to Crystal Lake begins in the town of Fenelon Falls. To reach Fenelon Falls, follow Highway 35 north of Lindsay to County Road 8. County Road 8 travels east from Highway 35 to Fenelon Falls. Follow the road through the town to County Road 121. If you follow County Road 121 north it will eventually meet Crystal Lake Road. Crystal Lake Road (also known as 11th Concession Road) is a rough 2wd access road that traverses directly to the southern shore of Crystal Lake.

Facilities

Crystal Lake offers a boat launch area located along the southern shore off the Crystal Lake Road. Supplies can be found in the town of Fenelon Falls or alternatively in the town of Lindsay. There are a few campgrounds near Fenelon Falls or if you don't mind a longer drive, **Balsam Lake Provincial Park** lies within minutes west of Fenelon Falls.

Crystal Lake		
Fish Stocking Data		
Year	Species	Number
2013	Lake Trout	1,200
2011	Lake Trout	1,200
2009	Lake Trout	2,000

Species
Lake Trout
Smallmouth Bass
Walleye
Whitefish
Yellow Perch

Other Options

A few good fishing alternatives can be found south of Crystal Lake via the Forest Access Road. The Forest Access Road can be quite rough in sections and requires a high clearance vehicle. Both **Otter Lake** and **Loom Lake** are found next to the logging road and offer Crown Land camping opportunities and fishing for smallmouth bass. Otter Lake is also inhabited by a population of muskellunge, while Loom Lake supports a small largemouth bass fishery.

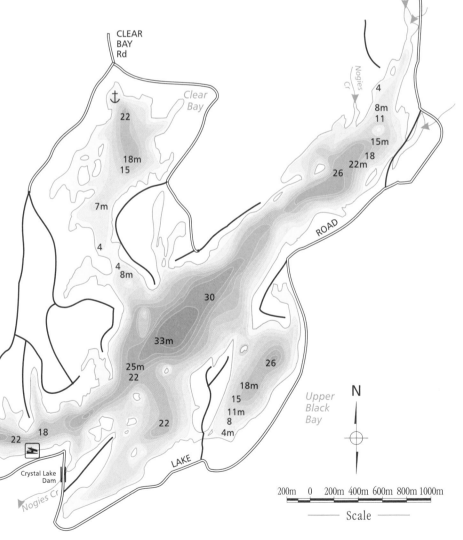

Location: 19 km (11.8 mi) north of Maberly
Elevation: 156 m (513 ft)
Surface Area: 603 ha (1490 ac)
Maximum Depth: 16.8 m (55.1 ft)
Mean Depth: 5.2 m (17.7 ft)
Way Point: 44° 58′ 00″ N, 76° 34′ 00″ W

Dalhousie Lake

Area Indicator

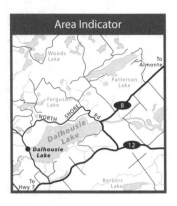

Species	
Black Crappie	Smallmouth Bass
Brook Trout	Walleye
Largemouth Bass	Whitefish
Northern Pike	Yellow Perch

Fishing

Over the past decade, Dalhousie Lake has become increasingly popular as a summer vacation lake. As a result, fishing pressure in the lake is steady. However, anglers can still have decent success throughout the year. Dalhousie Lake is a weedy lake providing good cover for all of its resident sportfish.

The most active species found in the lake are smallmouth and largemouth bass. Look for bass to hide in the shallower sections of the lake in any sort of weed cover. Anglers looking to catch northern pike and walleye are best to troll slowly along weed lines. The best time for both species is during dusk or overcast periods, when the predators cruise into the shallower sections of the lake in search of food. Jigging off drop-off areas is another highly used method for walleye. The recommended lure for walleye is a worm harness or white jig, while pike can be enticed to chase after flashy spoons on occasion.

A known hot spot for all species is around Geddes Rapids, where the Mississippi River flows into Dalhousie Lake. Work just off the rapids, casting into the flow. This area often holds a number of fish and is best just after walleye season opens in the spring or in the late fall. When fishing this area, be sure to consult your annual regulations for restrictions. There is a special sanctuary around the Mississippi River where it enters Dalhousie Lake to help protect walleye stocks.

During the winter, there is currently a two month ice fishing season that enables anglers to try their luck through the ice for walleye, northern pike and other pan fish. For walleye or pike, try jigging a white jig tipped with a worm or even a small spoon.

Directions

Dalhousie Lake is found north of the Trans Canada Highway (Highway 7) along the Mississippi River system. To find the lake, follow Highway 7 to Maberly Elphin Road (County Road 36) east of Sharbot Lake. Head north along this road to the junction with Corners Road (County Road 12). Corners Road travels east, passing by a number of local access roads including The Lake Road, which passes by the southwest shore of Dalhousie Lake.

Facilities

Although the shoreline is well developed with cottages and camps, you can easily launch a canoe from the access roads at the eastern and western ends of Dalhousie Lake. The private tent and trailer park is located along the Mississippi River near the eastern part of the lake and may offer camping and boat launching facilities.

Other Options

A good nearby angling alternative to Dalhousie Lake is Stump Lake, which is located just west of Dalhousie Lake. **Stump Lake** was created by the hydro dam on the Mississippi River and is accessible via County Road 36. Sportfish resident in the smaller lake include smallmouth bass, largemouth bass, northern pike and walleye. Fishing is best for bass, although anglers are occasionally surprised by a good sized walleye or northern pike.

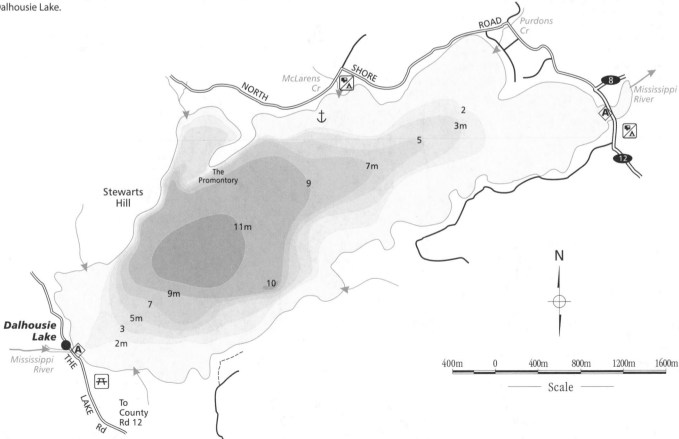

Dalrymple Lake

Location: 28 km (17 mi) east of Orillia
Maximum Depth: 9 m (29.5 ft)
Mean Depth: 7 m (23 ft)
Way Point: 44° 38' 00" Lat - N, 79° 07' 00" Lon - W

17 Zone

Fishing

Due mainly to the easy access and close proximity to the urban development of Toronto, Dalrymple Lake is a heavily fished lake. The lake was once home to a quality fishery, although with the surrounding development the fishing quality has decreased significantly. Smallmouth and largemouth bass are the two most productive sport fish, while angling success for walleye and northern pike is very slow at times. Similar to most other Kawartha Lakes, muskellunge once inhabited Dalrymple Lake. With the past introduction of northern pike, muskellunge are now thought to be near extinction. There are also rumours of tiger pike, the northern pike, muskellunge hybrid in Dalrymple, although this report has never been officially verified.

Dalrymple Lake is divided into two halves by County Road 6. Upper Dalrymple Lake is actually the southern portion, while Lower Dalrymple Lake is the northern half of the lake. Upper Dalrymple is very shallow and almost swamp-like in several areas and fishing is often slow. Lower Dalrymple Lake has definitive weed lines that can be easily located. Fishing along these weed lines by trolling or jigging can produce results for all sport fish species.

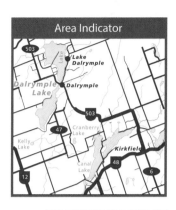

Area Indicator

Species	
Black Crappie	Smallmouth Bass
Largemouth Bass	Walleye
Muskellunge	Yellow Perch
Northern Pike	Other

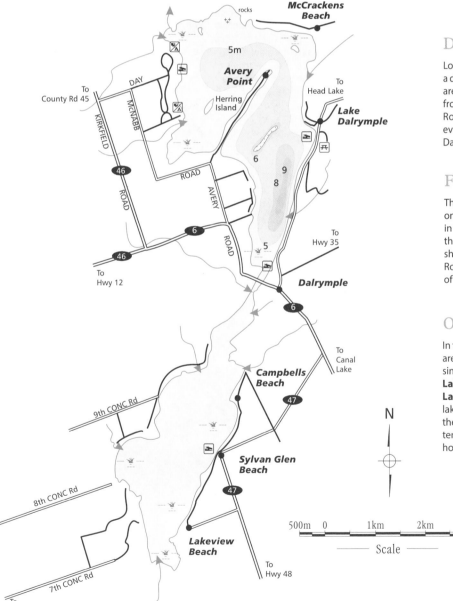

Directions

Located east of the town of Orillia, Dalrymple Lake is a developed lake that can be accessed from several areas. To reach the lake, follow Highway 12 east from Orillia to County Road 46 (Lake Dalrymple Road). Head northeast along the county road eventually meeting County Road 6, which leads to Dalrymple Lake.

Facilities

There are four established boat launch areas located on Dalrymple Lake, with three of the launches found in the northern end. Along with the boat launches, there are two tent and trailer parks found along the shoreline of Lower Dalrymple Lake (northern end). Roofed accommodations can be found in the town of Orillia to the west.

Other Options

In the nearby area, there are several other lakes that are easily accessible and offer angling opportunities similar or even better than Dalrymple Lake. **Young Lake** to the north is a smaller fishing lake, whereas **Lake Couchiching** to the west is a much larger lake and is part of the Trent Severn waterway. To the north of Dalrymple Lake past Young Lake the terrain begins to change to more rolling hills and is home to hundreds of fishing lakes to be explored.

Zone 18

Location: 17 km (10 mi) northwest of Verona
Surface Area: 23 ha (56 ac)
Maximum Depth: 12.5 m (41 ft)
Mean Depth: 8.6 m (28.2 ft)
Way Point: 44° 30′ 00″ N, 76° 45′ 00″ W

Depot Lake- 1st

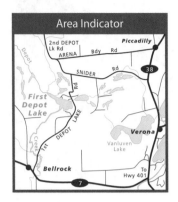

Area Indicator

Species
Largemouth Bass
Northern Pike
Smallmouth Bass
Walleye

Other Options

You can find **Hambly Lake** just to the east of the junction between Highway 38 and Bellrock Road (County Road 7). The small lake has a few cottages along its shoreline and offers fishing opportunities for mainly smallmouth and largemouth bass. A small population of northern pike and walleye does exist in the lake, although fishing is quite slow for both species.

Fishing

The First Depot Lake is not a part of the Depot Lakes Conservation Area and is therefore home to a few scenic cottages. Fishing is often fair for smallmouth bass and largemouth bass in the 0.5-1 kg (1-2 lb) range. Although fishing is slower for the bigger northern pike and walleye, most anglers to the lake will spend their time searching for these elusive predators.

Bass are best caught by using spinner baits or jigs along structured areas such as weed beds or rocky drop-offs. The inflow and outflow areas of Depot Creek are also good holding areas for both bass species.

Persistent anglers can find regular success for northern pike and walleye, especially during dusk when both predators cruise the shallows in search of food. Casting jigs, crankbaits or other attractor type lures can create a flurry of action for both species. On occasion top water flies and lures can be a lot of fund for northern pike and bass.

Directions

The Depot Lakes are a series of popular lakes found between Highway 401 and the Trans Canada Highway (Highway 7). The easiest way to access the First Depot Lake is to take Highway 401 to Exit 611 near Kingston. Head north along Highway 38 past the town of Harrowsmith and look for the Bellrock Road (County Road 7) off the west side of the road. Travel west along the Bellrock Road past the Bellrock Mill Dam to the First Depot Lake Road. Take the First Depot Lake Road north to the eastern shore of the lake.

Facilities

There are no facilities available at the First Depot Lake, although there are basic amenities available in the town of Harrowsmith to the south. Alternatively, the city of Kingston has plenty to offer visitors, such as hotels, restaurants and a good variety of retailers. For overnight camping, the **Depot Lakes Conservation area** found to the north of the First Depot Lake offers interior and drive-in camping. Call (613) 374-2940 for more information.

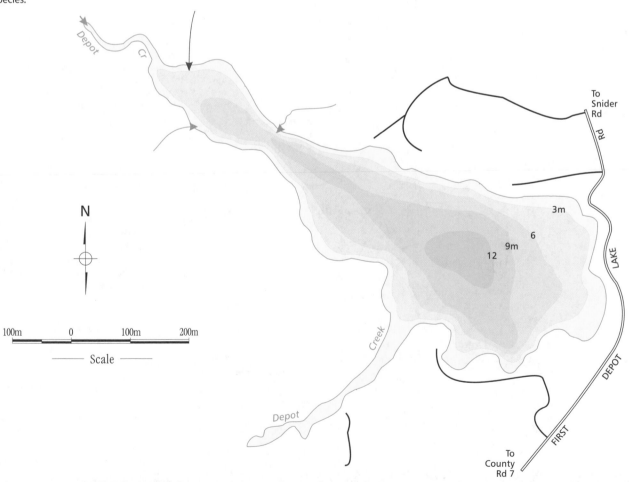

N

100m   0   100m   200m

Scale

Depot Lake- 2nd

Location: 24 km (15 mi) northwest of Verona
Surface Area: 160 ha (394 ac)
Maximum Depth: 27 m (88.6 ft)
Mean Depth: 14.5 m (47.9 ft)
Way Point: 44° 33′00″ N, 76°45′00″ W

18 Zone

Fishing

The Second Depot Lake is the focus lake for the Depot Lakes Conservation Area. Angling success in the Second Depot Lake can be slower than in the Third or Fourth Depot Lake, although anglers can expect fair to good success for smallmouth bass and largemouth bass up to 1.5 kg (3.5 lbs) in size. Look for the rocky outcrops near the many islands around the lake for added success.

Small numbers of walleye and northern pike exist in the lake; however, fishing is usually much slower than for bass. The best time for success for northern pike and walleye is at dusk when the predators cruise into the shallows in search of food.

Facilities

The Second Depot Lake is part of the **Depot Lakes Conservation Area**, which is home to many vehicle and water accessible campsites. Visitors will also find launching facilities available along the southern shore of the lake. For those anglers wishing to stretch their legs, the conservation area has over 9 km (5.5 mi) of hiking/biking trails to enjoy. For more information and rates for camping call (613) 374-2940. For supplies, the nearby villages of Harrowsmith and Sydenham have a number of retailers available including a bank and a general store.

Directions

The Depot Lakes are a series of popular lakes found between Highway 401 and the Trans-Canada Highway (Highway 7). To find the Second Depot Lake, follow Highway 38 north from the 401 at Exit 611 west of Kingston. Highway 38 leads to the Snider Road north of the hamlet of Verona. Take Snider Road west to the 2nd Lake Road and turn north. At the 'T' junction on the 2nd Lake Road, turn west. This branch leads to the southern shore of the Second Depot Lake.

Other Options

The **Third Depot Lake** is found immediately to the north of the Second Depot Lake. In addition to drive in and water accessible campsites, fishing can be rewarding. Smallmouth bass, largemouth bass, walleye and northern pike are all available in varying quantities.

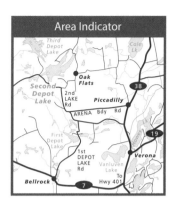

Area Indicator

Species
Largemouth Bass
Northern Pike
Smallmouth Bass
Walleye

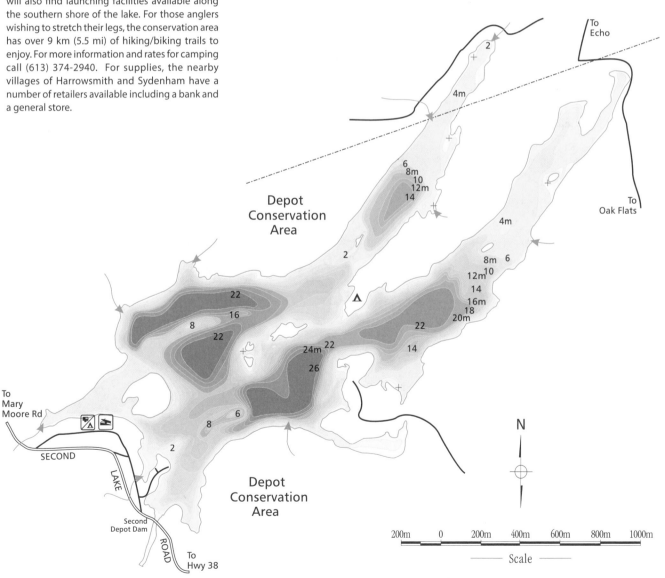

Zone 18

Location: 40 km (24.8 mi) north of Kingston
Elevation: 135 m (444 ft)
Surface Area: 382 ha (944 ac)
Maximum Depth: 68.3 m (224 ft)
Mean Depth: 22.4 m (73.5 ft)
Geographic: 44° 32' 00" N, 76° 35' 00" W

Desert Lake

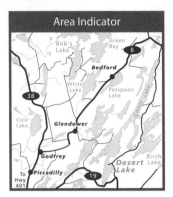

Area Indicator

Species
Lake Trout
Largemouth Bass
Northern Pike
Smallmouth Bass

Other Options

Two very close fishing alternatives to Desert Lake are **Thirteen Island Lake** and **Sand Lake**. Sand Lake is a small lake found to the north of Desert Lake and offers fishing for smallmouth bass, largemouth bass and the occasional walleye. Thirteen Island Lake lies due west of Desert Lake and can be reached off the Beyos Road north from Desert Lake Road. The scenic lake is home to resident populations of smallmouth bass, largemouth bass, northern pike and walleye.

Fishing

Desert Lake is a southern Canadian Shield Lake that is made up of rocky shorelines surrounded by rolling hills. The lake is home to a good population of smallmouth and largemouth bass, which make up the bulk of the action on the lake. Look for bass near the many drop-offs found around the lake or in the shallow weedy bays. Northern pike can also be found in the weedy bays where they cruise for baitfish.

The most sought after species in Desert Lake is the prized lake trout. The lake is home to a naturally reproducing strain of lake trout, which is a rare commodity in southern Ontario. The extreme depths of the lake have helped the lake trout survive development around the lake. Unfortunately for anglers, the deep nature of the lake also allows lakers to retreat to the depths of the lake and fishing can be slow, even throughout the cooler late spring and fall periods. The only way to find lake trout in this lake is to troll. If you do catch a lake trout in Desert Lake, please help preserve this rare natural strain and practice catch and release.

Directions

Anglers will find Desert Lake just to the west of Frontenac Provincial Park. Follow Highway 401 to Kingston and take exit 611 north along Highway 38. Shortly after passing through the town of Harrowsmith, look for the small village of Verona and the Desert Lake Road off the east side of the county road. Follow Desert Lake Road east to the southern shore of the lake.

Facilities

A number of cottages and a few private lodges are found around Desert Lake. For a small fee, visitors can launch a boat at the tent and trailer park on the southern end of the lake. Otherwise, a canoe can be launched into the lake off the side of the road. Basic supplies can be picked up in nearby Verona or Harrowsmith. Alternatively, the city of Kingston, to the south, offers all amenities including hotels and restaurants.

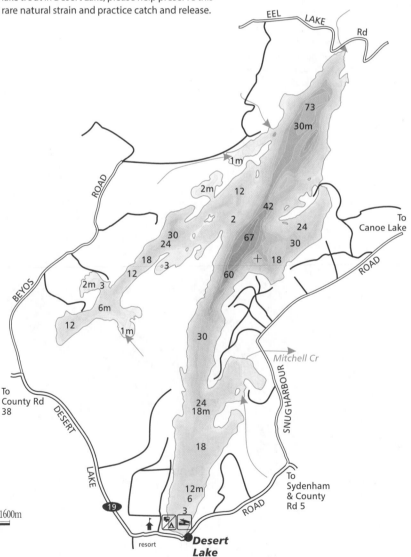

N

400m   0   400m   800m   1200m   1600m

— Scale —

Devil Lake

Location: 9 km (5.5 mi) south of Westport
Elevation: 131 m (430 ft)
Surface Area: 1,062 ha (2,623 ac)
Maximum Depth: 44.5 m (146 ft)
Mean Depth: 14.4 m (47.1 ft)
Way Point: 44° 35'00" N, 76° 27'00" W

18 Zone

Fishing

The main sportfish found in Devil Lake are smallmouth bass, largemouth bass, northern pike and a rare naturally reproducing strain of lake trout. The lake is riddled with islands and is home to numerous back bays and pockets, which provide fantastic holding areas for species such as bass and northern pike.

Smallmouth bass can be found in the 1.5 kg (3.5 lb) range and will often ambush attractor type lures and flies such as spinners or streamers. Look for smallmouth near rocky shoreline structures or underwater rock gardens. When fishing success for bass is slow, try flipping a jig off the bottom of these holding areas. Bass will often suck the bait in as it passes by providing for a fantastic fight.

Largemouth bass can be found around the shoreline and structure areas of the lake, although they most predominantly frequent the shallower, weedy bays. Working a weedless spinner bait or jig through this structure can provide good results at times. On occasion, anglers fishing these weed lines will hook into a cruising pike, especially during dusk. Pike in Devil Lake are usually small, although the odd 4 kg (9 lb) northern is caught annually.

The most prized sportfish found in Devil Lake is lake trout. Lakers can be found closer to the surface just after the season opens but only for a short period. As soon as the heat of summer sets in, lake trout retreat to the depth of the lake and can only be found by trolling with down rigging equipment.

Please practice catch and release to aid all species in Devil Lake.

Directions

Devil Lake is one of the larger lakes in the area and borders the popular Frontenac Provincial Park. To reach Devil Lake, travel along Highway 401 to Kingston and take Exit 617. From the exit, head north along the Perth Road (County Road 10). Perth Road travels past a number of scenic lakes, including Buck Lake, before traversing along the eastern shore of Devil Lake.

Facilities

For boat access to Devil Lake, visitors are recommended to use one of the pay per use facilities available at the tent and trailer parks resident on the lake. Alternatively, it is possible to launch a canoe into the lake off Perth Road. Camping enthusiasts can enjoy one of the ten interior **Frontenac Provincial Park** campsites available on the lake. For a more refined overnight option, all amenities including hotels are available in the city of Kingston to the south. For more information on Frontenac Provincial Park call (613) 376-3489 or for campsite reservations call 888-ONT-PARK.

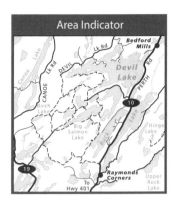

Species
Lake Trout
Largemouth Bass
Northern Pike
Smallmouth Bass

Other Options

Adventure seekers may be interested in exploring the nearby **Moulton Lake** and **Tetsmine Lake** in Frontenac Provincial Park. Both lakes can be reached by short trail/portage from the western end of Devil Lake. The small lakes are stocked annually with brook trout, which provide for good fishing in the spring for fish in the 25-30 cm (10-12 in) range.

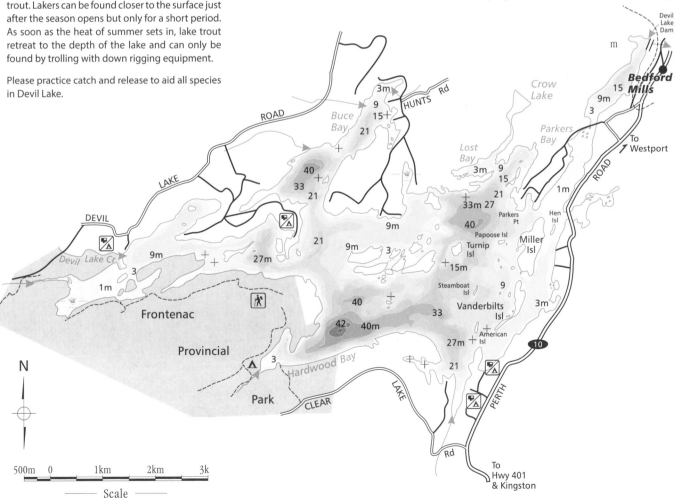

Location: 9 km (5.5mi) south of Coe Hill
Maximum Depth: 42.7 m (140 ft)
Mean Depth: 18.3 m (60 ft)
Way Point: 44° 47′ 00″ Lat - N, 77° 44′ 00″ Lon - W

Dickey Lake

Area Indicator

Species
Lake Trout
Largemouth Bass
Smallmouth Bass

Fishing

There are a number of cottages and camps along the shore of Dickey Lake. However, the lake can be a peaceful lake to fish even during the busiest times of the summer cottage rush. Fishing in the lake is best for smallmouth and largemouth bass, which can be found throughout the lake along shore structure areas. There are a few weedier parts of the lake where you can find largemouth bass, while smallmouth are often found near rocky shoreline structures. It is also recommended to try near man-made shore structures such as docks. Bass can sometimes be found hiding in the shade of the wharf.

A natural population of lake trout also inhabits the lake but fishing is often slow. Ice fishing in the winter is a productive method for lake trout, while trolling silver spoons in spring can also provide results. To help protect lake trout stocks, there are special ice fishing and slot size restrictions in place. As a fragile species, it is recommended to practice catch and release for lake trout whenever possible.

Directions

Dickey Lake is located in a more remote region of the Kawarthas in the expanse of land found between Highway 28 and Highway 62. The easiest way to reach the lake is to travel north along Highway 62 and turn west onto Steenburg Lake Road North. Along Steenburg Lake Road North, you will pass Steenburg Lake then the small settlement of Murphy Corners before reaching Dickey Lake. Look for signs off Steenburg Lake Road North marking the access road to Dickey Lake. There is a rough boat launch and parking area along the north shore.

Facilities

The boat launch is the main facility found on Dickey Lake. Rustic Crown Land camping opportunities can be found south of Dickey Lake at Freen Lake, although a portage is required to access the lake. Your best bet for accommodations and supplies is either the town of Bancroft to the north or the town of Madoc to the south.

Other Options

Freen Lake and **Lake of Islands** are very close by. Lake of Islands is accessible by boat from the southern end of Dickey Lake, while Freen Lake is accessible by a rough portage from Lake of Islands. Both lakes offer angling opportunities for largemouth and smallmouth bass.

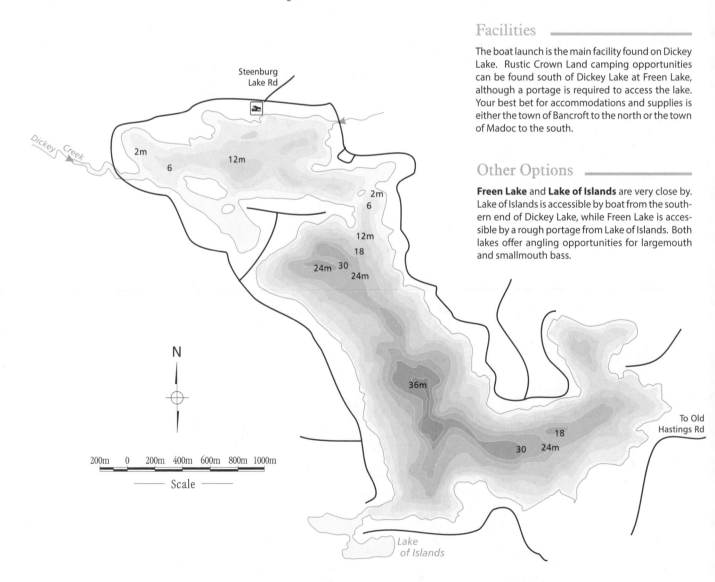

Dog Lake

Location: 28 km (17.4 mi) north of Kingston
Elevation: 98 m (322 ft)
Surface Area: 441 ha (1089 ac)
Maximum Depth: 49.7 m (163 ft)
Mean Depth: 5.7 m (18.7 ft)
Way Point: 44° 26′ 00″ N, 76° 20′ 00″ W

Directions

Dog Lake lies northeast of Kingston just off Highway 15. To reach Highway 15, follow Highway 401 to Kingston and take Exit 623 north. Highway 15 will take you past Joyceville and eventually to Sunbury Road (County Road 12). Travel west along Sunbury Road to the southern end of Dog Lake. The northern end of the lake can be found off the access road to the village of Burnt Hills.

Facilities

A number of cottages and resorts are located along the shores of Dog Lake. The better boat access areas are found at any one of these private lodges or tent and trailer parks. Amenities, such as groceries and overnight accommodations, are available in Kingston to the south.

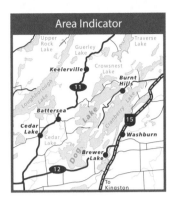

Dog Lake			
Fish Stocking Data			
Year	Species	Number	Life Stage
2010	Splake	7,000	Fry
2009	Splake	14,726	Fry
2008	Splake	8,000	Fall Fry

Species

Lake Trout
Largemouth Bass
Northern Pike
Smallmouth Bass
Splake

Fishing

As a part of the Rideau Canal system, Dog Lake receives a good share of angling pressure throughout the season. However, the lake continues to produce well, especially for bass. Other sportfish include the feisty northern pike and stocked splake.

Both smallmouth and largemouth bass are found in the lake and fishing can be good at times for bass up to 2 kg (4.5 lbs) in size. Look for smallmouth off rocky drop-off areas and near islands. Largemouth are found mostly in the shallower bays of the lake. Bass can be caught on a variety of lures, with spinners and jigs working consistently.

The shallow bays of Dog Lake, especially at the southern end, provide prime habitat for northern pike and other weed loving species such as largemouth bass and perch. Look for weed lines and other structure for pike, which tend to roam these areas more frequently during dusk. Try spinner baits, jigs or top water flies and lures for this aggressive predator.

Lake trout were once a natural element found in Dog Lake but over fishing has resulted in extinction of the species. Today, the brook trout/lake trout hybrid, splake, is stocked annually and provides for fair fishing throughout the summer and winter months. The best location on Dog Lake to find splake is the deeper northern end of the lake. Trolling with a downrigger is the most effective fishing method for these elusive fish during summer.

Location: 37 km (23 mi) northeast of Peterborough
Surface Area: 176 ha (435 ac)
Maximum Depth: 7 m (23 t)
Mean Depth: 3 m (9.8 ft)
Way Point: 44° 32' 00" Lat - N, 78° 06' 00" Lon - W

Dummer [White] Lake

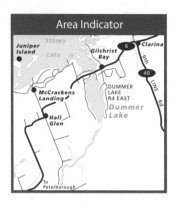

Area Indicator

Species	
Black Crappie	Smallmouth Bass
Largemouth Bass	Walleye
Muskellunge	Yellow Perch

Fishing

Dummer Lake remains a popular Kawartha cottage destination lake and anglers benefit from the high nutrient base that most of the Kawartha Lakes boast. Fishing in the lake is generally fair for nice sized smallmouth and largemouth bass. Walleye are the other main sport fish but fishing is slow to fair at times for walleye that average about 0.5-1 kg (1-2 lbs) in size. Look for walleye along weed lines and along the drop-off located in at southern end of the lake. The underwater point found in the middle of the lake is also known to hold greater concentrations of walleye at times. Trolling over this area with a worm harness can be an effective angling method. Smallmouth bass can also often be picked up closer to shore off the southern drop-off area.

Directions

Dummer Lake is located just south of the much larger Stoney Lake. To find the lakes, follow Highway 7 east from Peterborough to Highway 134. Travel north along Highway 134 to the Highway 28 junction. Look for County Road 6 (Stoney Lake Road) leading east from Highway 28. A marina on Dummer Lake is accessible off a small access road off the south side of County Road 6.

Facilities

Other than the marina, there are no facilities available on Dummer Lake. There are tent and trailer parks in the area on Stoney Lake and Buckhorn Lake near Burleigh Falls. Otherwise, roofed accommodations, such as motels, are available in the town of Lakefield or the city of Peterborough to the south.

Other Options

Neighbouring **Stoney Lake** is all but attached to Dummer Lake. Stoney Lake offers fishing opportunities for bass, walleye and muskellunge. If you prefer smaller lakes, by following Highway 28 north past Burleigh Falls, you will enter more rolling terrain that is home to countless lakes that offer fishing opportunities. There are many lakes, such as **Eels Lake** and **Silent Lake**, which are accessible via roads not far from Highway 28. There are also several hike or paddle-in lakes in this area.

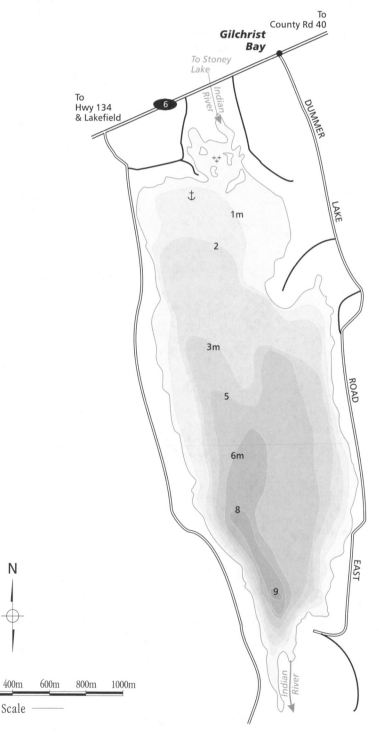

200m 0 200m 400m 600m 800m 1000m

Scale

Eagle Lake

Location: 10 km (6.2 mi) south of Sharbot Lake
Elevation: 198 m (650 ft)
Surface Area: 661 ha (1633 ac)
Maximum Depth: 35.4 m (116 ft)
Mean Depth: 12.2 m (40.2 ft)
Way Point: 44° 41′ 00″ N, 76° 42′ 00″ W

Fishing

Eagle Lake has dark green coloured water and is inhabited by smallmouth bass, largemouth bass, northern pike and lake trout. Fishing for bass is fair to good at times for bass that average around 0.5-1 kg (1-2 lbs) in size. A good way to find smallmouth bass in Eagle Lake is to locate underwater rock structures. From the depth chart, you can find the location of these structures to help increase your chances at finding fish. Largemouth bass tend to stay in the shallow bays around the lake. Look for any sort of weed cover or underwater structure and you should be able to find some largemouth.

Northern pike can be found almost anywhere in the lake but the best time and place to fish for northerns is during overcast or dusk periods in the shallow bays. Trolling a flashy spoon can be productive but for some real fun, try working a top water fly or lure across the surface.

Lake trout continue to maintain a natural population in Eagle Lake despite the heavy angling pressure on the species. By the time the season opens, lakers are usually in deeper water, therefore, trolling the deeper holes is the best method for success. As the heat of summer sets in, downriggers are required to reach deep holding lake trout.

Directions

You can find Eagle Lake south of the town of Sharbot Lake near the village of Parham. To reach the lake, follow Highway 7 to the junction with Highway 38 and head south. Just south of the village of Oconto, there are a number of different access roads that branch west off Highway 38 to Eagle Lake.

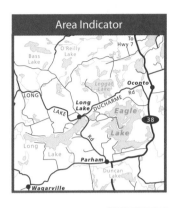

Area Indicator

Species
Lake Trout
Largemouth Bass
Northern Pike
Smallmouth Bass
Whitefish
Yellow Perch

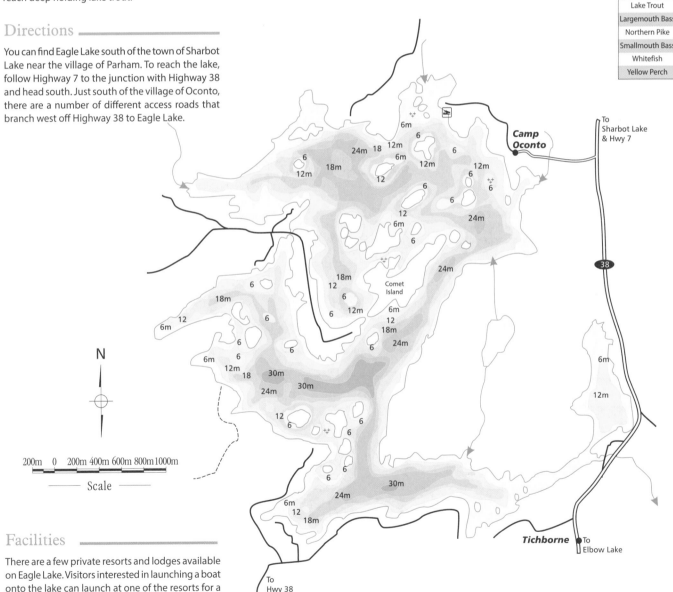

Facilities

There are a few private resorts and lodges available on Eagle Lake. Visitors interested in launching a boat onto the lake can launch at one of the resorts for a small fee. Basic supplies can be found in the village of Parham, while other services such as a grocery store and bank can be found in the town of Sharbot Lake to the north.

Location: 12 km (7.5 mi) south of Maberly
Elevation: 177 m (576 ft)
Surface Area: 172 ha (425 ac)
Maximum Depth: 21.3 m (70 ft)
Mean Depth: 8.3 m (27.3 ft)
Way Point: 44° 46′ 00″ N, 76° 30′ 00″ W

Farren Lake

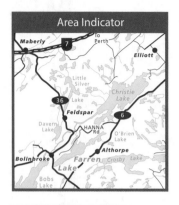

Area Indicator

Species	
Largemouth Bass	Splake
Rainbow Trout	Yellow Perch
Smallmouth Bass	Other

Farren Lake		
Fish Stocking Data		
Year	Species	Number
2011	Splake	30,000
2009	Splake	28,500
2008	Splake	3,500

Facilities

Since most of the shoreline on Farren Lake is privately owned, there is no public boat launching facility available. It is possible to launch a small boat or canoe from alongside County Road 36. For supplies and something a little different, visitors can explore the scenic lakeside town of Westport to the south. Westport is home to a unique downtown retail area and has a few great restaurants available for hungry travellers.

Other Options

Crosby Lake lies to the southeast of Farren Lake and is accessible just off the Althorpe Road (County Road 6). Fishing in the lake is fair to good at times for decent sized smallmouth and largemouth bass. Walleye and northern pike are also found in the lake, although fishing success for both species can be slow. Alternatively, **Little Crosby Lake** is found further east and provides similar or better action than Crosby Lake.

Fishing

Farren Lake sits in relative seclusion on the northern tip of the massive Bob's Lake and its thousands of coves, inlets bays and islands. You will find the smaller lake south of the townships of Feldspar, Bolingbroke and Althorpe. Rainbow trout were once regularly stocked with some success in Farren Lake but today splake are stocked in the lake regularly. Alternatively, bass, perch and other panfish offer good fishing at times.

Smallmouth and largemouth bass, along with perch, make up a good portion of the action on Farren Lake during the summer months. The two bass species are not usually very big but they are aggressive and can be found in good numbers in areas. Look for bass around the shoals in the 3 metre (10 foot) range. Try working a jig or tube bait off the bottom for success. Another good method is working a crayfish fly or lure imitation near the bottom. Largemouth bass tend to stay in the shallow bays year round. Weedless lures, live bait, and topwaters work the best.

During early spring, late fall and winter splake can be found just about anywhere in the lake. Try fishing with small spoons, jigs tipped with soft plastics or live bait, and small crankbaits. For smallmouth bass try fishing fallen trees, inlets, and back bays in the spring and islands, weedlines, shoals, and rocky drop offs with crawfish imitators, live bait, jigs, crankbaits, and spinners. During summer, the hybrid fish reverts to the deeper portion of the lake and persistent anglers using downrigging equipment can find some success though you are going to have to use downriggers or lead core line to get your flashy spoons down deep enough in the deep hole.

Directions

Located north of the town of Westport, you can find Farren Lake from two directions. From the north, follow Highway 7 to the junction with County Road 36 near the village of Maberly. From the highway travel south along County Road 36 past the hamlet of Feldspar to eventually reach the western shore of the lake.

From the south, follow Highway 15 north from Highway 401 to County Road 36 near Crosby. Head west then north along County Road 36 past the towns of Newboro and Westport. Continue north on County Road 36, past Althorpe Road (County Road 6) and you will soon come to the western shore of Farren Lake.

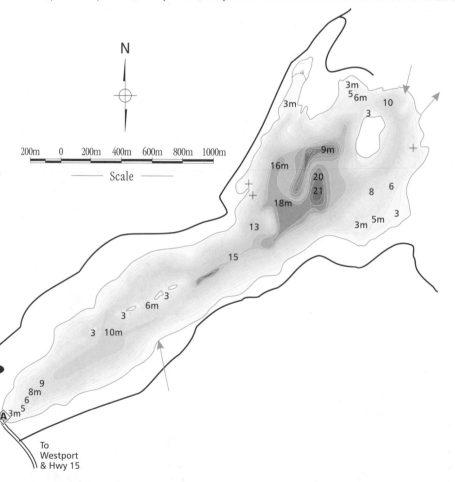

Fortescue Lake

Location: 13 km (8 mi) southwest of Gooderham
Maximum Depth: 27.4 m (90 ft)
Mean Depth: 15 m (49.2 ft)
Way Point: 44° 50' 00" Lat - N, 78° 26' 00" Lon - W

Fishing

The main sport fish in Fortescue Lake is smallmouth bass. Smallmouth bass can reach good sizes in the lake and can be found mainly along shore structure. Cottage docks and rocky shoreline areas are good holding areas for smallmouth. For the larger smallies, try closer to the bottom off one of the small islands around the lake or a little ways back from one of the rocky points around the lake. A crayfish imitation fly or lure can work exceptionally well on this lake. Work the crayfish along the bottom in a short jerk type fashion to entice even lethargic bass into striking.

Adding to the bass fishery are stocked lake trout as well as the odd muskellunge. In the spring, lake trout are found in the shallower water near shore, and can even sometimes be caught using topwater lures. However, as the weather warms up, lake trout head for deeper waters, usually the very deepest areas of the lake. The only way to get a lure down that deep is to either use a downrigger or a very long line jig.

Muskie are mainly picked up later in the fall. You can catch muskie using bucktails, deep running crankbaits or spinnerbaits like the Mepps' Giant Killer. However, Muskies can be frustratingly difficult to find, and depending on the time of year and their particular mood, they can be found in holding over reefs, in the weeds, near the surface or down on the bottom.

Directions

The western access route to Fortescue Lake begins along County Road 45. To reach County Road 45, take Highway 35 north to the town of Norland. At Norland, you will find County Road 45 off the east side of the highway. Follow County Road 45 to the town of Kinmount where County Road 45 essentially changes to County Road 503. Travel east along County Road 503 to White Lake Road. Take White Lake Road east to the settlement of Fortescue located near the northwest shore of Fortescue Lake.

Facilities

There are no facilities available on Fortescue Lake, although supplies and other essentials are available in the towns of Kinmount or Norland. For overnight accommodation, there is a private tent and trailer park south of Norland. Alternatively, **Balsam Lake Provincial Park** can be reached within minutes of Norland. The park provides a number of amenities including showers and flush toilets. Call (888) ONT-PARK for reservations, as the park can be quite busy during the summer months.

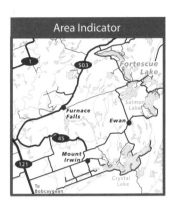

Area Indicator

Species
Lake Trout
Muskellunge
Smallmouth Bass

Other Options

On your way to Fortescue Lake, via White Lake Road, you will pass the southern end of **Salerno Lake** approximately 2 km west of Fortescue Lake. Salerno Lake is a cottage destination lake that offers decent fishing for mainly smallmouth bass. There are reports of catches of largemouth bass and walleye and muskellunge also inhabit Salerno Lake. The larger predators are often the main sport fish sought after by anglers on the lake.

Fortescue Lake		
Fish Stocking Data		
Year	Species	Number
2012	Lake Trout	600
2010	Lake Trout	600
2009	Lake Trout	300

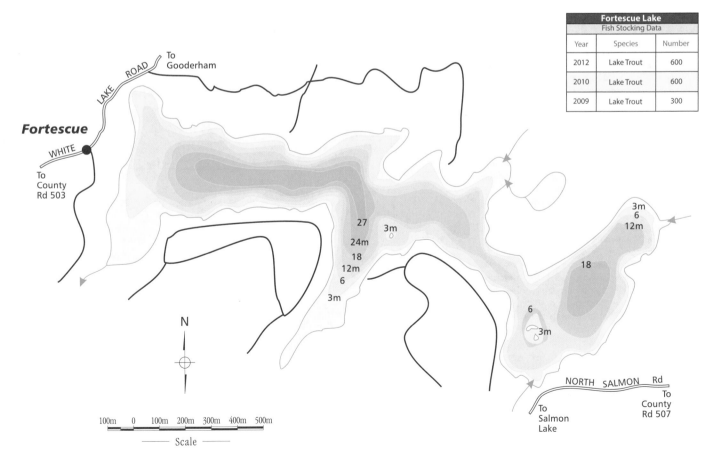

Location: 4 km (2.4 mi) north of Coboconk
Elevation: 270 m (885 ft)
Surface Area: 786 ha (1,943 ac)
Maximum Depth: 18.3 m (60 ft)
Mean Depth: 10.8 m (35.4 ft)
Way Point: 44° 41'00" Lat - N, 78° 45'00" Lon - W

Four Mile Lake

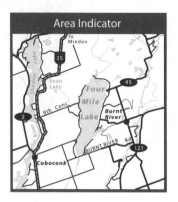

Area Indicator

Fishing

This scenic Kawartha area lake is home to numerous cottages and camps and offers fishing opportunities for smallmouth bass, largemouth bass, walleye and muskellunge. Success for bass and walleye is regarded as fair but some nice sized fish are caught every year. The northern portion of the lake is a productive area for bass, as largemouth bass utilize the weed growth in the region for cover. Top water flies and lures can create some decent action in this area, mainly at dusk.

A good area to look for walleye on Four Mile Lake is off the large shoal point located in the northwest end of the lake. A shoal is an underwater structure that naturally attracts walleye and even muskellunge on occasion. If you can also locate weed growth in the area, your chances of success are sure to increase. Trolling worm harnesses or still jigging are both effective methods for walleye on Four Mile Lake.

Directions

You will find this medium sized Kawartha Lake east of the village of Coboconk. Coboconk is easily reached via Highway 35 north of Lindsay. From Coboconk, travel east along the 7th Concession Road to Boundary Road. Follow Boundary Road south to Burnt River Road and head east. Burnt River Road travels past the south side of Four Mile Lake. To reach the boat launch, travel further west to County Road 121 and head north. Look for Hillside Drive to the west and follow this road to the western shore of the lake and the boat launch area.

Facilities

The small boat launch provides the main access to Four Mile Lake. You can find all the essential supplies, such as food, fuel and lodging in and around Coboconk. For the campers at heart, **Balsam Lake Provincial Park** is located west of Coboconk via County Road 48. The park is a full service park complete with showers and flush toilets. For reservations call (888) ONT-PARK.

Other Options

The **Burnt River** lies just to the east of Four Mile Lake and is accessible by 2wd roads from several areas. Despite the fact there is good smallmouth and largemouth bass fishing, anglers often overlook the river. The bass are not overly big compared to the nearby lakes, although they can reach some impressive sizes on occasion. The river also plays a vital role as a spawning channel for both walleye and muskellunge from Cameron Lake. Both species can be found in the river in sporadic numbers just after their respective season opens. The stretches of the river from Kinmount south are your best bet for some productive fishing action. Watch for fish sanctuaries on some portions of this river.

Species
Largemouth Bass
Muskellunge
Smallmouth Bass
Walleye

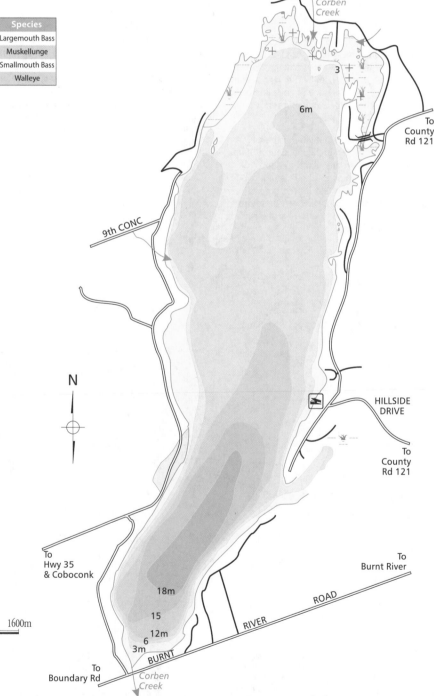

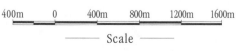

Scale

400m   0   400m   800m   1200m   1600m

Gananoque Lake

Location: 13km (8 mi) north of Gananoque
Elevation: 91 m (300 ft)
Surface Area: 616 ha (1522 ac)
Maximum Depth: 23.7 m (78 ft)
Mean Depth: 7 m (22.8 ft)
Geographic: 44° 27′ 00″ N, 76° 09′ 00″ W

Area Indicator

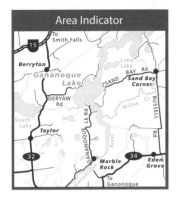

Species

Largemouth Bass
Northern Pike
Smallmouth Bass

Fishing

The geographical nature of the Gananoque Lake forms prime fish habitat. From weedy bays to rocky shorelines, there are plenty of areas for anglers to explore. Largemouth bass and northern pike are the two dominant species found in the lake, although smallmouth bass do exist in marginal numbers.

With the ample weedy bays and other structured areas, largemouth bass and pike provide for fair to good fishing at times. Bass can be found on occasion in the 2 kg (4.5 lb) range, while pike can grow to 4 kg (9 lbs). In addition to the weedy bays, other good holding areas can be found off the shoals and islands around the lake. Casting a tube jig or streamer fly can produce consistent results for both species. Alternatively, follow Highway 401 further east to Exit 659 and County Road 3. Follow County Road 3 north past the community of Dulcemain and look for the Sand Bay Road heading west. Sand Bay Road leads to the eastern shore of Gananoque Lake.

Directions

Gananoque Lake is a popular recreational lake formed by the damming of the Gananoque River. It is home to a few cottages and private resort style camps. To reach the lake, follow Highway 401 to the town of Gananoque and take Exit 648 north. Just off the exit, you will be travelling along County Road 2 towards the hamlet of Legge. Turn north at Legge onto County Road 34 and follow County Road 34 to the village of Emery. At Emery, look for the Gananoque Lake Road and follow it north. The Gananoque Lake Road travels to the southern end of the lake.

Alternatively, follow Highway 401 further east to Exit 659 and County Road 3. Follow County Road 3 north past the community of Dulcemain and look for the Sand Bay Road heading west. Sand Bay Road leads to the eastern shore of Gananoque Lake.

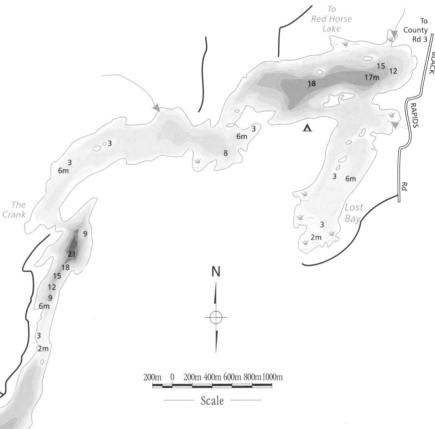

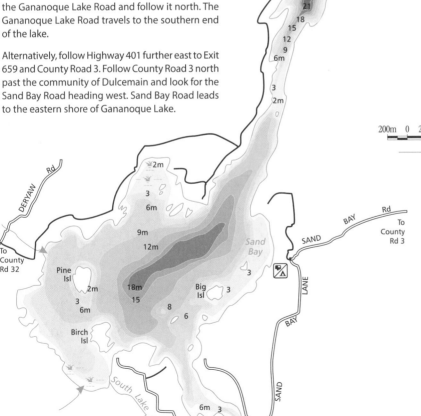

Facilities

Access directly onto Gananoque Lake is limited to the few private lodges located on the lake., which offer accommodations and boat rentals. Alternatively, a small boat or canoe can be launched in the Gananoque River south of the lake near Emery. The river soon widens significantly providing access to the southern end of the lake.

One of the other main recreation opportunities on Gananoque Lake is the **Charleston Lake/ Gananoque Lake Canoe Route**. The route travels across Gananoque Lake via Wiltse Creek to the south and forms a loop with Charleston Lake. Paddlers have established a few Crown Land campsites en route. On Gananoque Lake, the two main camping areas are found along the eastern shore and near Lost Bay.

Fishing

The Ganaraska River is a fabled Southern Ontario fishing river that provides some quality rainbow trout and Chinook salmon fishing opportunities. The river has been researched extensively and written about perhaps even more extensively, dating back to over a century or more.

The river originally was a brook trout stream that provided spawning opportunities for Atlantic salmon (it is still debated if and where Atlantics spawned centuries ago). Today, the river is home to a thriving rainbow trout or steelhead population that was introduced from British Columbia in the west. The Ganaraska steelhead fishery opens the 4th weekend in April with many anglers fishing the dawn hours and even prior for a chance to catch that big steelhead.

Brook trout can still be found throughout the river, but mainly in the upper feeder streams and the north arm of the river. Brown trout have also established themselves well in this system and can be found to good sizes, especially for river brown trout.

In the fall introduced Chinook salmon begin their spawning run and provide a great chance to catch some huge fish. You may also come across Coho salmon and migratory brown trout at this time.

In the summer, trout fishing can be slow; however, smallmouth bass, pike, walleye, perch, catfish, carp, and freshwater drum (sheephead) can all be found around the mouth of the river and in the harbour. Shore fishing the Ganaraska is open all year from the Canadian National Railway bridge south to Lake Ontario just adding to your Ganaraska fishing possibilities.

Outside of the main river it is recommended to head north to the many feeder streams of the Ganaraska. There are some steelhead runs that can travel quite a distance and the odd feeder stream can provide some great action. In the summer and fall, these feeders also hold resident rainbow, brook trout and the odd brown trout making for a ton of fun on lighter gear.

Directions

From Toronto you take Highway 401 east to the town of Port Hope. There are two cut off ramps to Port Hope with the second one or Exit 464 leading to the Ontario Street or County Road 28 in Port Hope. From here there are several access points to the Ganaraska River. If you travel south towards downtown Port Hope you can access the river right in town. There is plenty of parking around the river crossings including near the LCBO and near the Ministry of Transportation building. Further towards Lake Ontario you will find parking opportunities near the river as well.

Heading north along County Road 28 offers additional access opportunities. The first is a small parking area off the west side of the highway that provides access to the Ganaraska Region Conservation Authority (GRCA) property. You can also park further north right at the GRCA headquarters and head out from there.

Other popular access points include the crossing of the river along Highway 2 just west of the 28 and also at the Sylvain Glen Conservation Area site. Essentially wherever the river crosses the road there is access, but please be aware of private property.

Facilities

Overnight travellers to Port Hope have plenty of options for accommodations including a full service hotel right at the County Road 28 and Highway 401 interchange. Additionally, there are plenty of restaurants and other stores in the town for all your travelling needs.

Species		
Brook Trout	Northern Pike	Walleye
Brown Trout	Rainbow Trout	Yellow Perch
Chinook	Smallmouth Bass	Other
Coho	Steelhead	

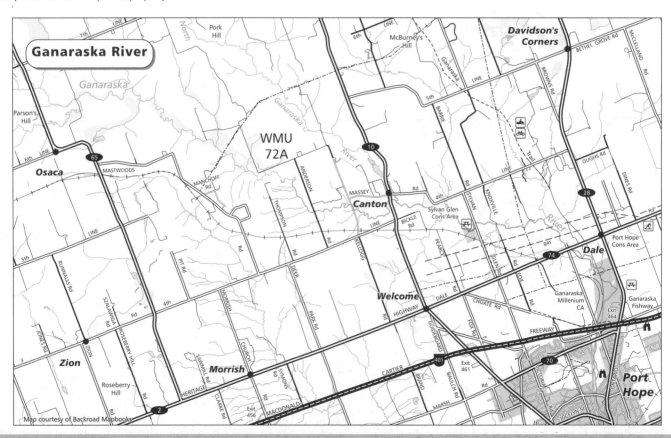

Map courtesy of Backroad Mapbooks

Gold Lake

Location: 12 km (7.5 mi) east of Catchacoma
Maximum Depth: 14.3 m (47 ft)
Mean Depth: 22.2 m (72.7 ft)
Way Point: 44° 43′ 00″ Lat - N, 78° 17′ 00″ Long - W

15 Zone

Fishing

Fishing in Gold Lake can be good at times for small-mouth and largemouth bass. The bass populations in the lake continue to maintain themselves despite some increased fishing pressure throughout the past decade or so. The rocky shoreline characteristic of the lake is ideal habitat for lunker smallmouth, whereas there are several quiet weedy bays around the lake that are suitable for largemouth bass. Anglers should also try near cottage docks. Both bass species can be found hunkered underneath various docks and there are a number of docks around the lake that are certainly bass worthy.

The other main sport fish species found in Gold Lake is lake trout. Lake trout once were abundant in this Kawartha Lake, although similar to a majority of the developed lakes in Ontario, the species are in rapid decline due to over fishing and lake development. Fishing for lakers in Gold Lake is currently quite slow. Gold Lake is part of the winter/spring fishing sanctuary to help the ailing lake trout stocks.

Directions

To find Gold Lake follow County Road 36 north of the town of Buckhorn to Flynn's Turn and head north along County Road 507. Just north of Mississauga Lake, look for Beaver Lake Road. Follow Beaver Lake Road east to the boat launch onto the north end of Gold Lake.

Facilities

Other than the boat launch located on the north end of the lake, there are no facilities available on Gold Lake. There is a private tent and trailer park available on Catchacoma Lake near the junction of County Road 507 and Beaver Lake Road, otherwise the town of Buckhorn to the south has plenty of various accommodations available. The town is also home to numerous retail operations offering supplies to help make your fishing trip in the area a success.

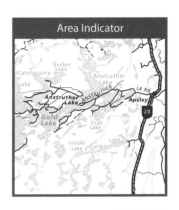

Area Indicator

Species
Black Crappie
Lake Trout
Largemouth Bass
Smallmouth Bass

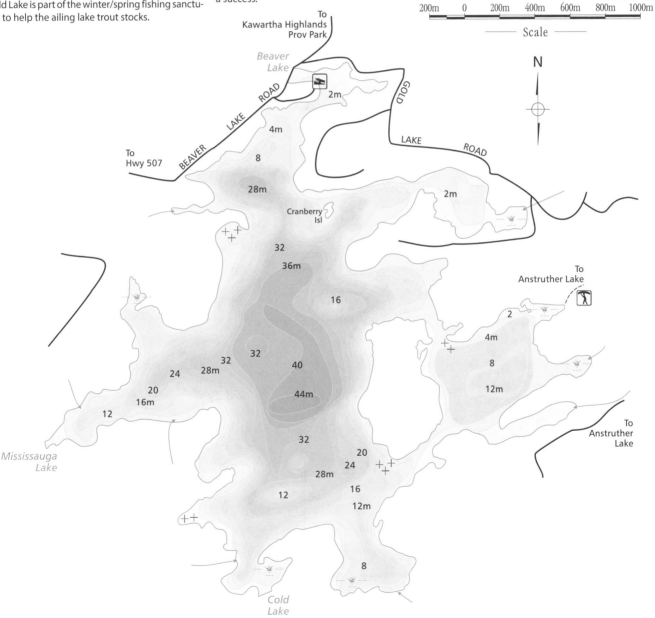

Location: 9 km (5.5 mi) northeast of Sydenham
Elevation: 140 m (460 ft)
Surface Area: 221 ha (546 ac)
Maximum Depth: 61.6 m (202 ft)
Mean Depth: 18 m (59 ft)
Way Point: 44° 28′ 00″ N, 76° 35′ 00″ W

Gould Lake

Fishing

Visitors to Gould Lake will enjoy the scenic nature of the area along with good fishing at times, especially for its resident bass. Smallmouth and largemouth bass are found in the lake in fair numbers and average about 0.5-1 kg (1-2 lbs) in size. A good area to find bass is in any of the smaller bays or near one of the islands. Locating weed lines and other structure greatly increases success. Try yellow or white jigs or even tube jigs along bottom structure.

A natural population of lake trout once thrived in Gould Lake, however, over the years, fishing pressure has reduced the population dramatically. Most lake trout action occurs in the spring, just after the season opens. If you do happen to be lucky enough to hook into a laker, please be sure to practice catch and release to help maintain the future viability of the species.

Area Indicator

Species	
Black Crappie	Smallmouth Bass
Lake Trout	Yellow Perch
Largemouth Bass	

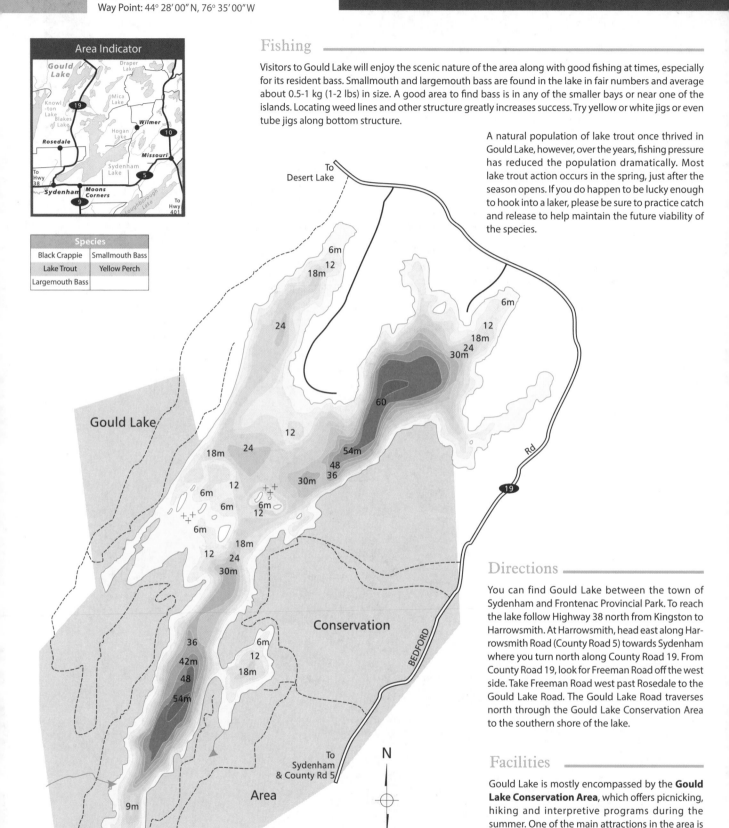

Directions

You can find Gould Lake between the town of Sydenham and Frontenac Provincial Park. To reach the lake follow Highway 38 north from Kingston to Harrowsmith. At Harrowsmith, head east along Harrowsmith Road (County Road 5) towards Sydenham where you turn north along County Road 19. From County Road 19, look for Freeman Road off the west side. Take Freeman Road west past Rosedale to the Gould Lake Road. The Gould Lake Road traverses north through the Gould Lake Conservation Area to the southern shore of the lake.

Facilities

Gould Lake is mostly encompassed by the **Gould Lake Conservation Area**, which offers picnicking, hiking and interpretive programs during the summer. One of the main attractions in the area is the Rideau Trail, which passes by the western end of the lake. A rough boat launch suitable for car top boats and canoes is also available. A small fee is required to access the lake and conservation area. For more information call (613) 546-4228.

Graham Lake

Location: 30.6 km (19 mi) west of Brockville
Elevation: 107 m (351 ft)
Surface Area: 265 ha (655 ac)
Max Depth: 4.5 m (15 ft)
Mean Depth: 2 m (6.5 ft)
Way Point: 44° 34′ 00″ N, 75° 53′ 00″ W

Fishing

Graham Lake is a scenic Eastern Ontario lake that offers fair fishing for smallmouth and largemouth bass in the 0.5-1 kg (1-2 lb) range. Smallmouth bass are hard to find at times due mainly to the shallow nature of the lake that better suits largemouth bass. Largemouth can be found almost anywhere, although locating weed structure is the key to finding bass consistently.

Northern pike are also found in the lake and can reach up to 3.5 kg (8 lbs) in size. Similar to largemouth bass, pike can almost be found anywhere in the lake and can be very exciting to catch. Both largemouth bass and northern pike will hit similar presentations, such as top water flies or lures. Other lures that work well are jigs and top water baits like the rapala. For fly anglers, try poppers or even colourful weed less streamers.

Adding to the fishery are black crappie and yellow perch. These panfish are typically easy to catch by using a typical bait and bobber set up.

Directions

Northwest of the city of Brockville, visitors can find Graham Lake by following Highway 401 to Exit 695 near Mallorytown. Head north from the exit to County Road 2. Take a short jaunt east along County Road 2 to the junction with County Road 5. County Road 5 continues north passing by Caintown before reaching the western end of Graham Lake. Access to Graham Lake can be found at one of the tent and trailer parks or lodges located along the southern shore of the lake. Look for these tent and trailer parks off Lake Street.

Area Indicator

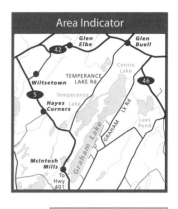

Species	
Black Crappie	Smallmouth Bass
Largemouth Bass	Yellow Perch
Northern Pike	

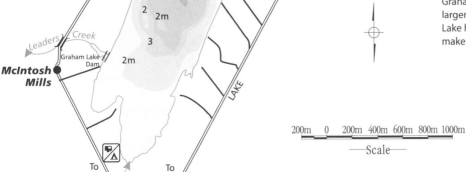

Facilities

Along with the tent and trailer parks there are a few cottages and camps scattered around Graham Lake. Travellers looking for supplies will find the city of Belleville is not far away to the south. Belleville is home to numerous hotels, restaurants and retail stores.

Other Options

Two nearby lakes that provide a decent fishing alternative are **Centre Lake** and **Temperance Lake**. Centre Lake is connected to Graham Lake via a dam at the northern end of Graham Lake. Temperance Lake is located near the northwest end of Graham Lake. Both lakes are inhabited by mainly largemouth bass and northern pike. If Graham Lake happens to be slow, either one of these lakes makes a fine alternative.

200m 0 200m 400m 600m 800m 1000m
— Scale —

Zone 18

Location: 20 km (12 mi) west of Ompah
Elevation: 370 m (1,214 ft)
Surface Area: 164 ha (406 ac)
Max Depth: 20 m (65.6 ft)
Mean Depth: 10.7 m (35.1 ft)
Way Point: 45° 01′ 00″ N, 76° 57′ 00″ W

Grindstone Lake

Area Indicator

Species	
Black Crappie	Splake
Largemouth Bass	Yellow Perch
Smallmouth Bass	

Grindstone Lake Fish Stocking Data		
Year	Species	Number
2012	Splake	6,500
2010	Splake	9,500

Fishing

Grindstone Lake is a small spring fed lake northeast of Plevna, in the Madawaska Highlands. It is 2.6 km long and has 5 major bays off of the main body. With over 17 km of shoreline there is plenty of structure to hide the bass, black crappie, perch and splake that reside here. Although splake are stocked here, visitors should note that the local cottage association maintains the access road in winter and does not permit public access at that time.

Recent reports indicate that the primary catch in Grindstone Lake is smallmouth bass. The two best spots on the lake for smallmouth are the rocky shoal areas found in the southeast end and the middle of the lake. The rocky underwater structure is a magnet for smallmouth and if they are biting, you should easily be able to find some good action. Try working tube jigs or crayfish imitation flies or lures along these shoals.

Other popular lures include tube bodies, twister-tail grubs, spider grubs, and tiny finesse worms. All work well under most conditions, but a 4-inch tube jig seems to be most popular. Colour choices range from natural, translucent tubes, to earth tones (greens and browns), white, smoke, and chartreuse, sprinkled with metal flakes.

Stocked every other year, splake provide a good alternative to the bass and panfish. Splake are fast growing, good fighting fish that are best caught in the spring just after ice off. Once the ice retreats, not only are the splake hungry, the oxygen content of the lake allows them to feed near the surface. As the summer approaches, splake will act less like brook trout and more like lake trout and revert to the deeper sections of the lake.

Directions

Grindstone Lake is another one of those out of the way lakes that are found in the Madawaska Highlands northwest of Bon Echo Provincial Park. To find the lake, begin by travelling along Highway 7 to the junction with Highway 509 just north of Sharbot Lake. Travel north along the small highway past the villages of Donaldson and Ompah. Just before the highway veers south again, look for Mountain Road off the north side of the highway. If you reach Plevna, you have gone too far. Follow Mountain Road north to Grindstone Lake Road and turn east. The Grindstone Lake Road heads northeast all the way to the southern shore of the lake.

Highway 509 can also be reached from the west via Highways 506 and 41 north of Kaladar and Highway 7. Once on Highway 509, continue north past Plevna to Mountain Road. It is advised to carry along a copy of the Backroad Mapbook for Eastern Ontario. In addition to detailed maps, this book is filled with valuable information on all sorts of outdoor activities like camping areas, paddling routes and other fishing holes.

Facilities

There are several cottages located along the southern shore of Grindstone Lake, although the northern portion of the lake remains Crown land. Visitors will also find a public boat launch area suitable for smaller boats available along the south shore. For campers, a couple of water access only campsites have been established along the northern shore of the lake. These sites are quite basic and are user maintained; therefore, please pack out any garbage you find or bring to the lake. For basic supplies, the nearby village of Plevna is home to a general store.

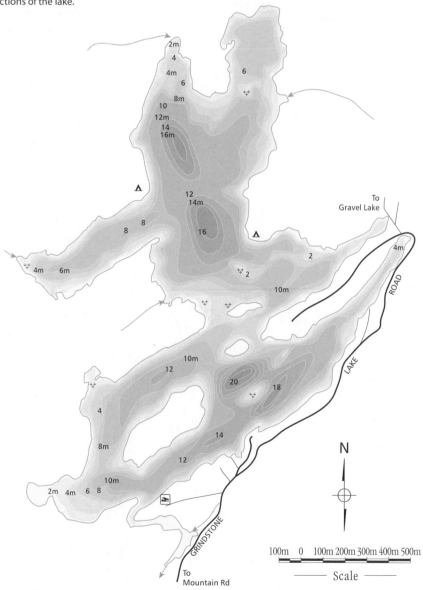

Grippen Lake

Location: 9 km (5.5 mi) southwest of Lyndhurst
Elevation: 90 m (295 ft)
Surface Area: 191 ha (472 ac)
Maximum Depth: 16 m (52.5 ft)
Mean Depth: 11.5 m (37.8 ft)
Way Point: 44° 30′ 00″ N, 76° 09′ 00″ W

Fishing

Grippen Lake offers fair fishing for smallmouth and largemouth bass up to 1.5 kg (3.5 lbs) in size. Largemouth are the dominant bass species found in the lake and make up the bulk of the action. In addition to weedy areas, largemouth can also be found near the island and off either one of the points along the southern shore. Jigs, spinners and top water flies and lures can all produce results.

Northern pike are also found in Grippen Lake and provide for fair to slow fishing for pike that average about 2 kg (4.5 lbs) in size. For consistent pike success, try trolling a flashy spoon. During the dawn and dusk periods, pike are more aggressive and can be taken off the surface with a top water fly or lure.

Facilities

A public beach and car top boat launch area are available at the northern end of Grippen Lake. For supplies and accommodations, the city of Kingston is found to the south. Alternatively, campers will find **Charleston Lake Provincial Park** is a short drive east. The popular park offers full facilities and is often busy during the summer months. It is recommended to make reservations before arrival by calling (888) ONT-PARK. For more information about Charleston Lake Provincial Park, please call (613) 659-2065.

Directions

Grippen Lake is found to the west of the popular Charleston Lake Park, not far from Highway 15. From the south, follow Highway 401 east of Kingston to Exit 623. Turn north on Highway 15 towards Seeley's Bay. Just past Seeley's Bay, look for Lyndhurst Road (County Road 33) off the east side of the highway. Follow Lyndhurst Road east to the northern access point to the lake.

Other Options

Singleton Lake lies to the east of Grippen Lake and is accessible via Outlet Road (County Road 3). The lake is part of the Gananoque River system and is inhabited by smallmouth bass, largemouth bass and northern pike. Fishing is best for bass, although a nice sized pike can surprise anglers from time to time. Bass in the lake can be found in the 1 kg (2 lb) range.

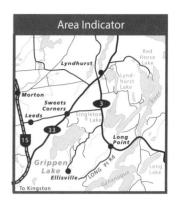

Species	
Black Crappie	Rainbow Trout
Largemouth Bass	Smallmouth Bass
Northern Pike	Yellow Perch

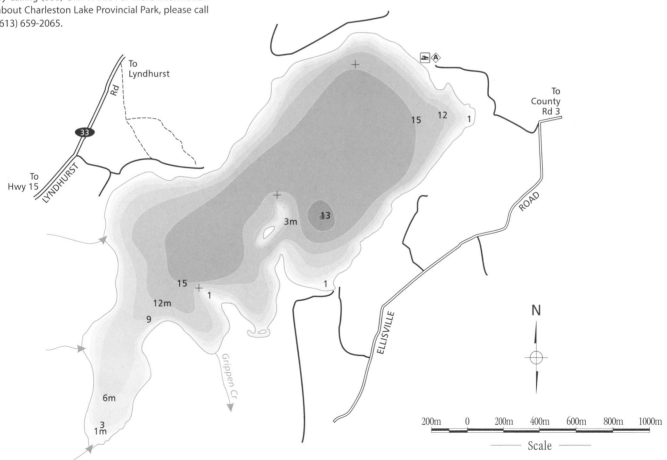

Zone **15**

Location: 9 km (5.5 mi) west of Norland
Max Depth: 7 m (23 ft)
Mean Depth: 4.2 m (14 ft)
Way Point: 44° 43'00" Lat - N, 78° 56'00" Long - W

Head Lake

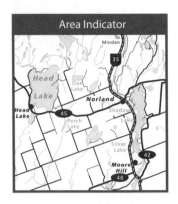

Area Indicator

Species	
Black Crappie	Smallmouth Bass
Largemouth Bass	Walleye
Muskellunge	

Directions

You can reach Head Lake by first following Highway 35 north from Lindsay to the town of Norland. At Norland, turn west onto County Road 45. County Road 45 will lead you past the southern shore of Head Lake to two boat launch areas.

Other Options

If you continue north along Highway 35 past Norland, the geography of the area begins to change from the low lying region of the south to a more rolling hills formation characteristic of the Canadian Shield. Around the town of Minden, there are countless lakes to be explored. Some are accessible via established roads, while others can only be found via canoe.

Fishing

Head Lake has a very interesting bottom structure and is made up of many shoal humps and rock piles. Smallmouth bass often congregate around these 2-3 m (4-7 ft) humps and can be readily taken with a jig worked off the bottom. At times smallmouth can be a fickle sport fish and it may be required to slow your lure presentation down in order to entice strikes. Working the jig in an up and down fashion gives the bass time to slowly view the bait. With this type of presentation bass will usually suck the lure in on the down swing, making strikes a little more challenging to detect than normal.

A fair population of muskellunge are also found in Head Lake and the lake has developed a good reputation among musky hunters. Trolling the larger type musky lures off shoal areas in fall can provide results. Although bass anglers working spinner baits or other similar lures catch the odd musky occasionally, musky fishing is a completely different form of angling and takes plenty of experience to achieve results regularly. Some good-sized musky are caught and released in Head Lake each year.

Adding to the fishery are black crappie and small populations of largemouth bass and walleye.

Facilities

There are two boat launches onto Head Lake. The first launch is located near the corner of the 5th Concession Road and County Road 45, while the second launch area is found to the west via a short road just east of the junction of Suter Drive and County Road 45. There is a small picnic area at the first boat launch. Along County Road 45, you will also find two tent and trailer parks.

Alternatively, Balsam lake Provincial Park is located south of Head Lake off County Road 48 west of the town of Coboconk. **Balsam Lake Provincial Park** is a full facility park, offering various amenities such as flush toilets and showers. Call (888) ONT-PARK for reservations.

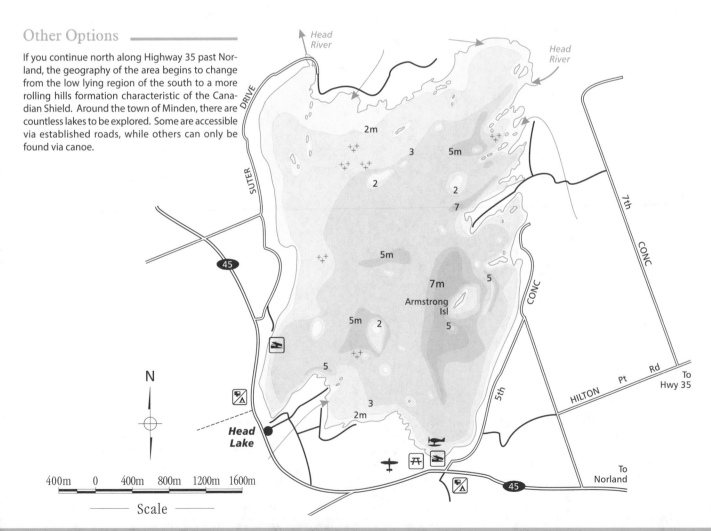

Indian Lake

Location: 14 km (8.5 mi) west of Elgin
Elevation: 122 m (400 ft)
Surface Area: 266 ha (658 ac)
Max Depth: 26 m (85 ft)
Mean Depth: 10 m (33 ft)
Way Point: 44° 36′ 00″ N, 76° 20′ 00″ W

Fishing

As part of the Rideau Canal Waterway, Indian Lake can be busy during the summer months. Regardless of the boating activity, fishing in this scenic lake can be steady for warm water species such as smallmouth bass, largemouth bass and pan fish. Northern pike also reside in the lake but fishing is usually a little slower. Bass average around 0.5-1 kg (1-2 lbs) in size and are best found near any of the islands. Largemouth bass are usually much easier to find than smallmouth. Try using a yellow or white coloured jig or even a spinner bait. A few hot spots to try are near any of the underwater rock formations marked on the depth chart. These areas make fantastic structure for both bass species.

Splake are the cold water species in the lake and are stocked annually. The hybrid fish provide for fair fishing throughout the winter months or in the spring just after ice off. During winter, try working small spoons or jigs aside drop-off areas or shoals. In the spring, trolling silver or gold spoons are the most effective angling method.

Directions

Indian Lake is located between Kingston and Smiths Falls along the renowned Rideau Canal. To reach the lake by vehicle, follow Highway 15 north from Highway 401 or south from Smiths Falls to Opinicon Road (County Road 9) in Crosby. Continue southwest along Opinicon Road to Chaffey's Lock and the launch at the federal docks.

Alternatively, Indian Lake can be accessed via the canal waterway. It is linked to Mosquito Lake and Clear Lake to the north or Opinicon Lake to the south.

Facilities

Chaffey's Lock is home to one of the many Rideau Canal system of locks. Over the years, the area has become a popular tourist destination for people travelling by either boat or in a vehicle. The area hosts a number of lodges and motels all catering to visitors needs. **Dorothy's Fishing Lodge** offers accomodations and meals and can be reached at info@dorothysfishing.com.

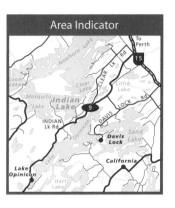

Area Indicator

Species	
Largemouth Bass	Splake
Northern Pike	Walleye
Panfish	Whitefish
Smallmouth Bass	Yellow Perch

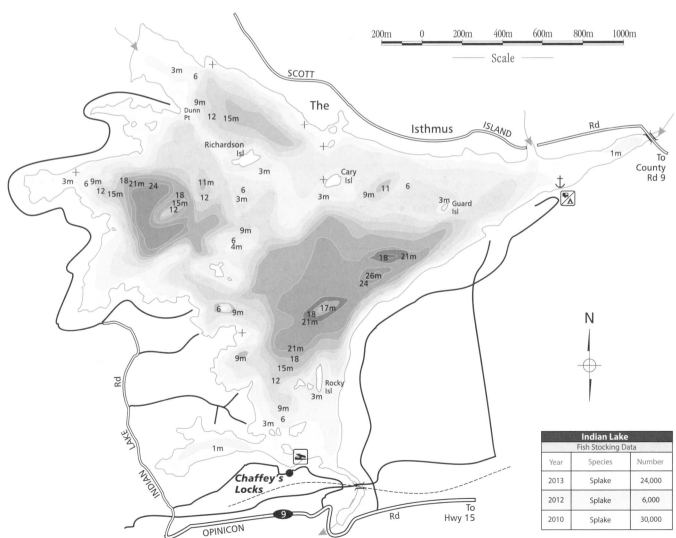

Indian Lake		
Fish Stocking Data		
Year	Species	Number
2013	Splake	24,000
2012	Splake	6,000
2010	Splake	30,000

Location: 6 km (3.7 mi) south of Apsley
Elevation: 278 m (912 ft)
Surface Area: 1,221 ha (3,013 ac)
Maximum Depth: 42.7 m (140 ft)
Mean Depth: 8.4 m (27.5 ft)
Way Point: 44° 37′ 00″ Lat - N, 78° 02′ 00″ Lon - W

Jack Lake

Area Indicator

Directions

Jack Lake lies northeast of the city of Peterborough about 2.5 hours from Toronto. To find the lake, follow Highway 28 north from Peterborough to the village of Apsley. Take Highway 504 east past Apsley and look for the familiar blue boat launch sign. This marks Jack Lake Road, which is found off the south side of Highway 504 just outside of town. Also known as County Road 52, Jack Lake Road travels south to a boat launch found at the northwest corner of the lake. Branching from Jack Lake Road are several side roads including countless fire access roads that can lead to more secluded bays on the lake.

Facilities

The main access to the lake is at the public boat launch at the northwest corner of Jack Lake. Also in this area are a couple resorts offering cottage rentals, camping and boat rentals. Both **Jack's Lake Lodge** and **Miller's Timber Sands** also offer a few last minute supplies and local knowledge on where and how to fish the big lake. For supplies such as gas and groceries, the village of Apsley lies minutes to the north. There is also information on private cottages for rent in town or by inquiring locally with the Kawartha Lakes Chamber of Commerce.

Backcountry or Crown land camping is also possible. With most of the lake protected by the Peterborough Crown Game Preserve, this beautiful lake has numerous small bays and islands from which to base camp. There are several user maintained sites scattered around the lake. Please pack out what you pack in to help maintain the natural beauty of the lake and surrounding area.

Other Options

While there are many smaller lakes found in the immediate area that provide fishing opportunities, two more notable destinations are **Chandos Lake** and **Kashabog Lake**. Chandos Lake lies to the north of Jack's Lake while Kashabog Lake lies to the southeast. Both lakes offer fishing opportunities for smallmouth and largemouth bass. Chandos Lake also supports a population of lake trout and northern pike, while Kashabog Lake is home to muskellunge and walleye.

Fishing

Officially named Jack Lake, the lake is locally known as Jack's Lake. Some believe the name is derived from the local native chief sarcastically called "Handsome Jack", who died in 1835. Adding to the history of the lake, the waterbody was actually known as White Lake in the latter half of the 19th century.

Found with in the northern portion of the Kawartha Lakes region, the clean freshwater lake is protected by the Peterborough Crown Game Preserve around most of the shoreline. The irregular shaped lake is dominated by three main bays with numerous smaller bays and a myriad of islands scattered throughout. The largest bay is Sharpe Bay on the western end of the lake, while Brooks Bay at the northwest end is the most developed.

The water levels on Jack Lake are maintained by the double-sluice, 200 metre (650 foot) concrete dam at the south end of the lake. The reservoir helps feed the popular Trent Severn Waterway.

Jack Lake has a long tradition of welcoming anglers from around the world. It was originally home to bass and lake trout, but fish species such as muskellunge, walleye and more recently black crappie have been introduced into the lake. Fishing is considered good for bass, walleye and muskie, while lake trout anglers will have to be more patient. Alternatively, crappie fishing is very good throughout the year and in winter for this small, but nice eating fish.

This beautiful lake is riddled with dozens of small bays and islands making for prime habitat for sportfish such as bass and walleye. Smallmouth and largemouth bass provide for the bulk of the angling action and average about 1 kg (2 lbs) in size, although they can be found larger on occasion. Top water action can be a lot of fun during summer evening just before the sunsets. Work a popper fly or lure along shore structure for those exciting top water strikes. When the lake is too choppy or it is too bright for the fish, a good alternative is suspended jerkbait. These minnow-shaped plugs are weighted so that they hover in place when stopped. Ideal lure length is between 10 cm and 25 cm (3–7 inches). Soft plastic jerkbaits, which flutter and glide like an injured baitfish can be irresistible to smallmouth.

Typical of the area, despite smaller numbers of fish, walleye seem to get most of the attention on this lake. Fishing for average sized fish can be slow at times. To find more consistent fishing, it is recommended to try working off points and shoals as well as near weed lines. Walleye will cruise these areas in search of baitfish, especially as evening approaches. A good example of a decent point to try off is Hurricane Point in the southwest end of the lake.

Muskellunge hunters will also find a decent number of muskie in the big lake. Fishing for these big predators is best in the fall. Casting lures such as a Mepps Black Fury or Five of Diamonds spoons from the deeper water towards the weedbeds around the islands can entice the big aggressive fish into a strike. Fish over 90 cm (35 inches) are not uncommon on Jack Lake. Remember muskie are very sensitive to sound, and scatter when they hear a boat approaching or a lot of noise from careless anglers.

Although fishing for lake trout is considered slow on Jack Lake, lakers are still there and can still offer a lot of fun in a day. In the spring, lake trout are found in the shallower water near shore, and can even sometimes be caught using topwater lures. However, as the weather warms up, lake trout head for deeper waters, usually the very deepest areas of the lake. The only way to get a lure down that deep is to either use a downrigger or a very long line jig.

Anglers will also find that there is good crappie fishing near the shoreline where there is cover such as sunken logs or bushes. Crappie are shy fish so your bait will need to be placed close to their home. Small minnows suspended under a float as well as tiny white or chartreuse jigs tipped with bait can create a frenzy of action. These prized fish are considered excellent table fair and up the bulk of the action on Jack Lake during winter.

Jack Lake

Location: 6 km (3.7 mi) south of Apsley
Elevation: 278 m (912 ft)
Surface Area: 1,221 ha (3,013 ac)
Maximum Depth: 42.7 m (140 ft)
Mean Depth: 8.4 m (27.5 ft)
Way Point: 44° 37' 00" Lat - N, 78° 02' 00" Lon - W

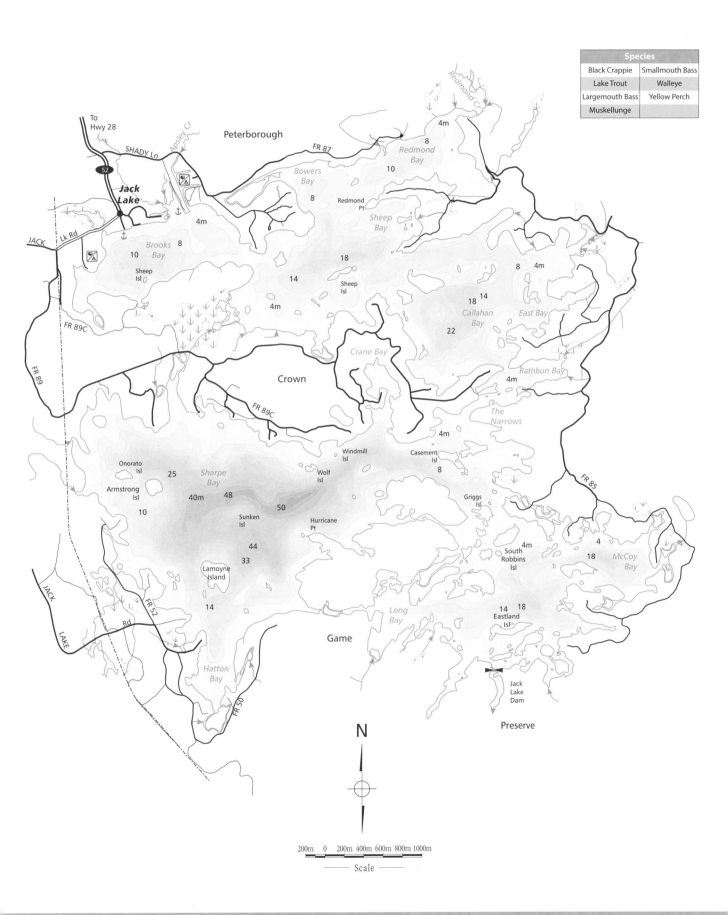

Species	
Black Crappie	Smallmouth Bass
Lake Trout	Walleye
Largemouth Bass	Yellow Perch
Muskellunge	

To Hwy 28
SHADY Ln
Apsley Cr
Peterborough
FR 87
Redmond Cr
52
Jack Lake
JACK Lk Rd
Brooks Bay
Sheep Isl
Bowers Bay
Redmond Pt
Redmond Bay
Sheep Bay
Sheep Isl
Callahan Bay
East Bay
Rathbun Bay
Crane Bay
The Narrows
Crown
FR 89C
FR 89
FR 89C
Windmill Isl
Wolf Isl
Casement Isl
Onorato Isl
Sharpe Bay
Armstrong Isl
Sunken Isl
Hurricane Pt
Griggs Isl
FR 85
Lamoyne Island
South Robbins Isl
McCoy Bay
JACK LAKE Rd
FR 52
Long Bay
Eastland Isl
Game
Hatton Bay
FR 50
Jack Lake Dam
Preserve

4m, 8, 10, 8, 18, 14, 4m, 8, 14, 18, 8, 4m, 22, 4m, 4m, 8, 25, 40m, 48, 50, 10, 44, 33, 14, 4m, 4, 18, 14, 18

N

200m 0 200m 400m 600m 800m 1000m
— Scale —

Location: 7 km (4.3 mi) northeast of Burleigh Falls
Elevation: 259 m (850 ft)
Perimeter: 4.2 km (2.6 mi)
Maximum Depth: 13 m (42.6 ft)
Mean Depth: 8.8 m (28.9 ft)
Way Point: 44° 36′ 40″ Lat - N, 78° 09′ 45″ Lon - W

Julian Lake

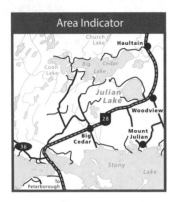

Area Indicator

Species
Muskellunge
Smallmouth Bass
Yellow Perch

Fishing

Smallmouth bass provide the mainstay of the sport fishery and can be found throughout the lake. A few of the more popular areas to fish are over one of the 1-3 m (2-7 ft) shoal humps that can be found in the lake. Just off the small island can also be a decent holding area for smallmouth bass. Try working a jig near the bottom off these shoals to find those lunker smallmouth. Some nice sized bass are caught in Julian Lake annually.

A population of muskellunge also inhabits the lake. The size of these large fish can be quite a sight when compared to the size of the lake. Muskellunge fishing is best in the fall when musky generally move closer to shore structure as the cool temperatures arrive. Trolling the deeper areas of the lake is recommended during the summer months.

Directions

Follow Highway 28 north from Lakefield past the settlement of Burleigh Falls. Not far past Burleigh Falls, you can find Julian Lake Road off the west side of the highway. Although the lake is very close to Highway 28, Julian Lake is not readily noticeable and offers some seclusion from the busy roadway.

Facilities

Near the southern end of Julian Lake there is a tent and trailer park available for overnight accommodations. Further to the west along Julian Lake Road, there is another tent and trailer park available on Big Cedar Lake. For roofed accommodation, the town of Lakefield is merely minutes away offering various motels and bed and breakfasts.

Other Options

North of Julian Lake there are a multitude of different lakes available for fishing. There is a whole series of interconnected lakes north of **Big Cedar Lake** that are all accessible via canoe and a series of portages. These lakes offer fishing opportunities from lake trout to bass and provide real seclusion from the hustle and bustle of urban life. You can also try a few of the easier accessible lakes to the north off Highway 28, such as **Silent Lake, Eels Lake** or **Paudash Lake**. All three lakes have plenty to offer anglers.

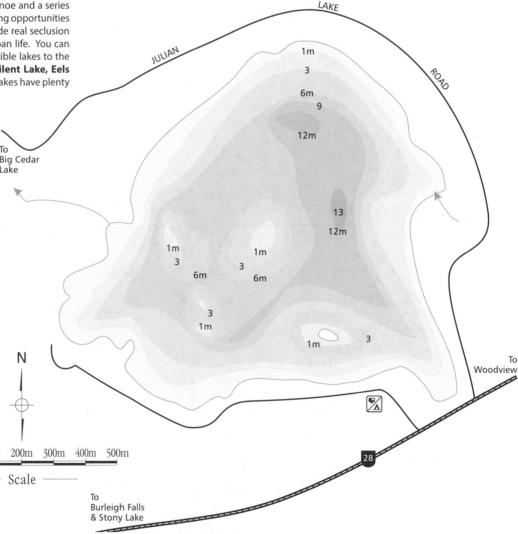

Kasshabog Lake

Location: Kasshabog Lake
Elevation: 262 m (859 ft)
Surface Area: 810 ha (2,002 ac)
Maximum Depth: 24.3 m (80 ft)
Mean Depth: 13.7 m (45 ft)
Way Point: 44° 38′ 00″ Lat - N, 77° 58′ 00″ Long - W

15 Zone

Fishing

Kasshabog Lake has seen its once productive walleye fishery suffer recently. However, the lake is now stocked in hopes of bringing it back to its glory days. While worm harnesses and jigs are the mainstay for most anglers when fishing for walleye, be sure not to overlook minnow type crankbaits and lures like the classic Rapala or even Shad Rap or X-Rap. During the summer, look for walleye to be cruising along the drop-off areas and along any deep weed lines. Trolling along these areas with a worm harness, crankbaits or spinners that resemble baitfish in summer can produce decent results.

The lake is part of the water control system for the Trent Severn Waterway and is dammed at the mouth of the North River along the southern shore. The countless bays, inlets and islands around the lake make for great bass habitat. Fishing for both smallmouth and largemouth bass is fair to good at times for some nice sized bass. There is also a small population of muskellunge resident in Kasshabog Lake.

Facilities

There are a few small marinas located on Kasshabog Lake, most notably near Stony Lake Bay. Other than the marina access points, there is a public boat launch onto MacDonald Bay on the northeast end and onto Stony Lake Bay on the southwest end.

Accommodations are available at the towns of Havelock or Norwood to the south of Kasshabog Lake. There is also a tent and trailer park to the south off County Road 6 on Stony Lake.

Species	
Largemouth Bass	Walleye
Muskellunge	Yellow Perch
Smallmouth Bass	

Directions

Kasshabog Lake lies to the east of Petroglyphs Provincial Park and is accessible from the east or west. From the east, the lake can be reached by following County Road 6 past Stoney Lake to West Kosh Drive. From the west, the lake can be found by following Highway 7 east to County Road 46 just outside of Havelock. County Road 46 can be followed north all the way to the lake.

Other Options

Two more out of the way lakes that can provide for some productive sport fishing are **West Twin Lake** and **Sandy Lake**. These two lakes lie to the east of Kasshabog Lake and are inhabited by smallmouth bass and muskellunge. West Twin Lake also boasts a healthy population of largemouth bass. The lakes are much smaller than Kasshabog, although the fishing productivity can make them good alternate choices.

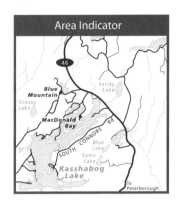

Area Indicator

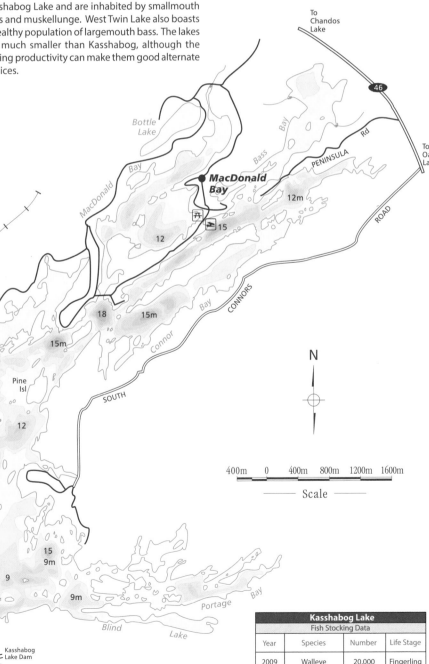

Kasshabog Lake			
Fish Stocking Data			
Year	Species	Number	Life Stage
2009	Walleye	20,000	Fingerling

Location: 4 km (2.4 mi) south of Fernleigh
Elevation: 260 m (850 ft)
Surface Area: 116 ha (286 ac)
Maximum Depth: 21.3 m (70 ft)
Mean Depth: 12.2 m (40 ft)
Way Point: 44° 50' 00" N, 77° 04' 00" W

Kashawakamak Lake

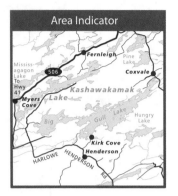

Area Indicator

Species	
Burbot	Walleye
Largemouth Bass	Whitefish
Northern Pike	Yellow Perch
Smallmouth Bass	Other

Fishing

This large lake is part of the Mississippi River system and is part of the Mazinaw/Mississippi Canoe Route. Fishing in the lake is good at times for smallmouth and largemouth bass to 1.5 kg (3.5 lbs), while northern pike and walleye success is a little slower. The structure found around the lake is ideal for bass. There are countless shallow bays, drop-offs and underwater rock piles all waiting to be fished. Working a jig or crayfish imitation fly or lure can be productive. Another lure that can work consistently is the spinner. Try casting spinners from a boat or canoe towards shore structure or near underwater rock structures.

While fishing for bass, anglers will often be surprised by aggressive northern pike, especially during the evening periods. Top water flies and lures can also have decent success during the evening for both bass and pike. Cast along weed lines or even right into the weeds for some top water action fun.

Walleye fishing in Kashawakamak Lake is definitely slower than for the other species. The prized walleye tend to cruise shoals, especially during the evening period. Trolling a worm harness slowly along weed lines or still jigging off a shoal can be effective at times.

Facilities

Visitors to Kashawakamak Lake can access the lake at several maintained launch sites. Most of the sites are found along the southwestern shore of the lake via Myers Cave Road and Kashawakamak Road. The northern shore access point can be reached via an access road off Highway 506. Camping enthusiasts can enjoy the many crown land campsites that have been formed by **Mazinaw/Mississippi Canoe Route** paddlers around the lake. All sites are user maintained, therefore, be sure to pack out all of your garbage. Alternatively, there are a few lodges on Kashawakamak Lake for visitors to stay under a roof while the village of Cloyne to the west offers a small grocery store.

Directions

For obvious reasons, Kashawakamak Lake is sometimes referred to as Long Lake. Visitors can find the big lake north of Highway 7. At the village of Kaladar, turn north on Highway 41 and follow this highway to the rustic Highway 506 south of Cloyne. Follow Highway 506 east to Myers Cave where you will reach the northwest shore of the long lake. There are a number of public access points scattered around the lake.

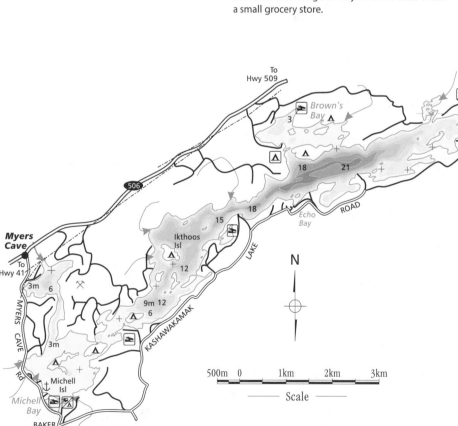

Other Options

Mannerheim Lake and **Shoepack Lake** are two small lakes that can be found just to the south of Kashawakamak Lake. Shoepack Lake is accessible by the Kashawakamak Road and rumoured to be inhabited by brook trout. Mannerheim Lake is a more remote option that requires a rough portage from the southeastern shore of Kashawakamak Lake. The lake receives little angling pressure and is inhabited by a population of smallmouth bass.

Katchewanooka Lake

Location: Lakefield
Surface Area: 351 ha (867 ac)
Maximum Depth: 10.1 m (33.1 ft)
Mean Depth: 2.2 m (7.2 ft)
Way Point: 44° 27' 00" Lat - N, 78° 16' 00" Long - W

Fishing

Similar to several of the Trent Severn lakes, Katchewanooka Lake is a shallow water body. Fishing in the lake is best for largemouth and smallmouth bass, as the aggressive sport fish can literally be found almost anywhere in the lake. The ample weed structure in the lake provides prime holding areas for both bass species. Many nice sized bass have been found off Second or Third Islands or even near Hills Island.

Walleye and muskellunge can be found in Katchewanooka Lake in fair numbers and are often the focus of anglers visiting the lake. Both predators like to cruise weed lines and shoal structure in search of baitfish. Trolling is a great way to cover water to help increase your success rate. For walleye, a worm harness trolled along weed beds can be particularly effective on this lake.

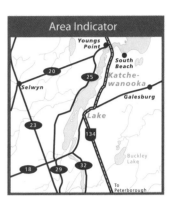

Area Indicator

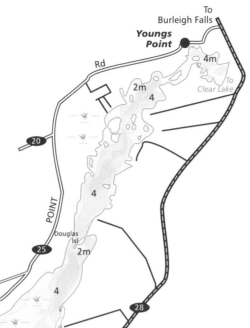

Species

Largemouth Bass
Muskellunge
Smallmouth Bass
Walleye
Yellow Perch

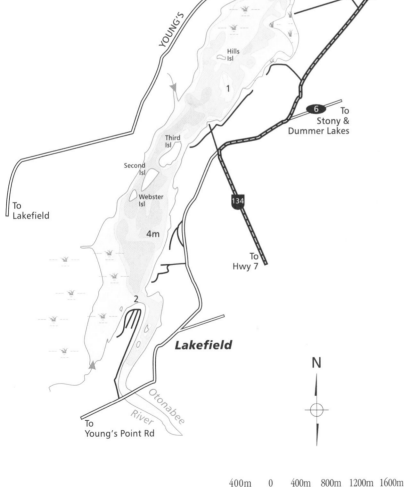

Directions

This Trent Severn Waterway lake is the picturesque backdrop to the north portion of the town of Lakefield. The lake was created by the damming of the Otonabee River and is the first in a large chain of lakes stretching to the Georgian Bay. The main access area to the lake is from the town of Lakefield, which is found north of Peterborough and Highway 7. From Highway 7 follow Highway 134 north to where the highway turns into Highway 28. You can find a boat launch to the lake along the southern shore not far off Bridge Street (Highway 28).

Facilities

Lakefield has plenty to offer visitors; including an entire downtown retail area, several restaurants and accommodations. The town is very scenic and is a fine place to spend summer holidays. The main access area to Katchewanooka Lake is the boat launch found in the town park north off Bridge Street. There is also a small marina found along the south side of the lake accessible from Lakefield.

Other Options

If you are travelling along the Trent Severn Waterway, the **Otonabee River** to the south of Katchewanooka Lake offers fishing opportunities for a variety of sport fish. The main sport fish found in the river is bass, although you can find the odd walleye and muskellunge on occasion. The river is a great spot for kids to fish since it is full of various pan fish such as rock bass, crappie and perch.

400m   0   400m   800m   1200m   1600m

— Scale —

Location: 12 km (7.5 mi) northeast of Kaladar
Elevation: 194 m (636 ft)
Surface Area: 546 ha (1,349 ac)
Maximum Depth: 27 m (88.5 ft)
Mean Depth: 7.9 m (26 ft)
Way Point: 44° 44' 00" N, 76° 58' 00" W

Kennebec Lake

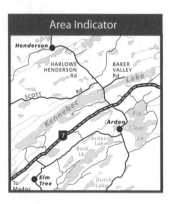

Area Indicator

Species
Largemouth Bass
Northern Pike
Smallmouth Bass
Walleye
Yellow Perch

Kennebec Lake			
Fish Stocking Data			
Year	Species	Number	Life Stage
2010	Rainbow Trout	4,000	Fry
2009	Rainbow Trout	4,000	Fry
2008	Rainbow Trout	4,000	Fall Fry

Fishing

This murky lake is inhabited by a number of warm water sportfish species including smallmouth bass, largemouth bass, northern pike and walleye. Fishing is fair for smallmouth and largemouth bass that can reach up to 1.5 kg (3.5 lbs) in size. Smallmouth are best found along rock walls and off any of the small islands around the lake. The 10 m (32 ft) shoal area located in the middle of the western end of the lake is a good holding area for smallmouth. Working a jig along the bottom in this area can also pick up the odd walleye and northern pike on occasion. Largemouth bass are mostly found in the shallower more weedy areas of the lake, especially in the western end of the lake.

Fishing success for northern pike and walleye is much slower than for bass. Pike are best found in the shallower sections of the lake, in particular the narrows between the east and west end of the lake is productive at times. Trolling a spoon or casting spinner baits along structure areas can entice pike strikes.

Recently Kennebec Lake has been stocked with rainbow trout. The popular sportfish can be caught using small spoons and spinners; however, fly-fishing can be even better. Fly anglers should try streamer type patterns such as a leech or dragonfly nymph to find these acrobatic trout.

Directions

This long, narrow lake is located east of the village of Kaladar not far off Highway 7. To reach the lake follow Highway 7 to the flashing yellow light at the turn off to the town of Arden. Head north off the highway along the Harlowe Henderson Road. Kennebec Lake is only a short distance along this road. A small boat or canoe can be launched from the side of the road.

Facilities

There are a few cottages along the shoreline of Kennebec Lake as well as a tent and trailer park for visitors. The nearby town of Arden is home to a general store with basic supplies, while groceries and other amenities can be found in the town of Sharbot Lake to the east.

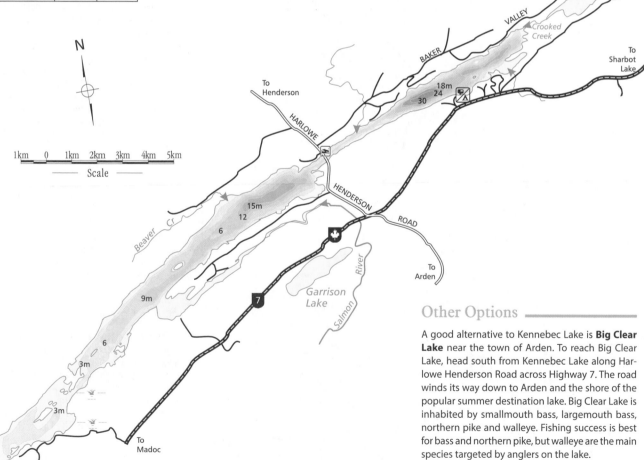

Other Options

A good alternative to Kennebec Lake is **Big Clear Lake** near the town of Arden. To reach Big Clear Lake, head south from Kennebec Lake along Harlowe Henderson Road across Highway 7. The road winds its way down to Arden and the shore of the popular summer destination lake. Big Clear Lake is inhabited by smallmouth bass, largemouth bass, northern pike and walleye. Fishing success is best for bass and northern pike, but walleye are the main species targeted by anglers on the lake.

Leggat Lake

Location: 15 km (9 mi) south of Sharbot Lake
Elevation: 208 m (682 ft)
Surface Area: 183 ha (452 ac)
Maximum Depth: 18 m (59 ft)
Mean Depth: 2.8 m (9.2 ft)
Way Point: 44° 43′00″N, 76° 43′00″W

18 Zone

Fishing

Smallmouth and largemouth bass are the two main sportfish found in Leggat Lake. Fishing success for bass is fair to good for bronze backs that can reach up to 1.5 kg (3.5 lb) in size. A small population of northern pike remains in the lake; however, fishing is usually slow.

The best area to find bass in this lake is along shoreline structure. Look for fallen trees, rocky outcrops or weeds along shoreline areas. One particular hot spot is around the small island found in the south end of the lake. The island structure tends to be an attractant for both bass species and can provide consistent success at times. Try casting spinners or jigs along the shoreline areas.

Facilities

The public access area to Leggat Lake lies along the southwest shore and is suitable for car top boats and small trailers. For supplies, Sharbot Lake to the north is home to a bank, grocery store and a few other retailers. Campers can stay at nearby **Sharbot Lake Provincial Park**, which is found along Highway 7 west of Sharbot Lake.

Directions

Leggat Lake is located southwest of the town of Sharbot Lake. To find the lake, follow Highway 7 to the junction with Highway 38 just north of Sharbot Lake. Head south along the quiet highway and look for Ducharme Road off the west side of the highway just past the hamlet of Oconto. After a few minutes along Ducharme Road, you will pass by the southern end of Leggat Lake. Once you see the southern shore of Leggat, look for the Leggat Lake Road, which should be the second road that branches north. The Leggat Lake Road looks like a cottage access road but it does lead to the public access area along the western shore.

Other Options

En route to Leggat Lake you will pass by the eastern shore of the small **Oconto Lake**. Fishing in Oconto Lake is fair for largemouth and smallmouth bass. A small population of northern pike is also known to be in the lake.

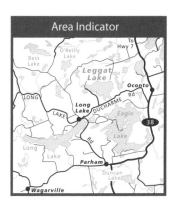

Area Indicator

Species
Largemouth Bass
Northern Pike
Smallmouth Bass

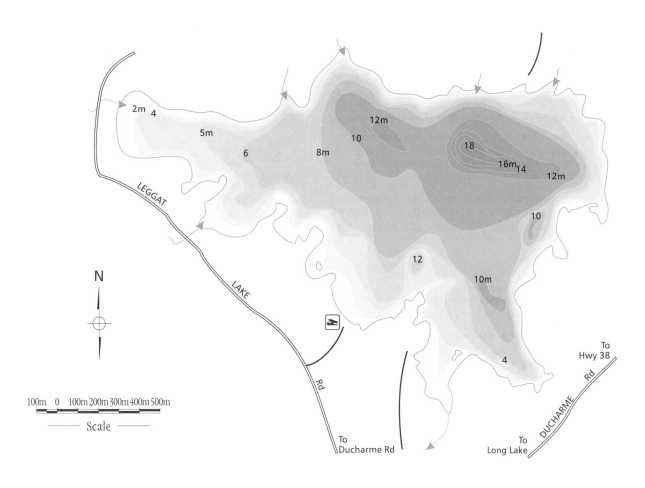

N

100m 0 100m 200m 300m 400m 500m

Scale

Zone 20

Location: Hamilton to Kingston
Elevation: 219 m (719 ft)
Surface Area: 1,896,000 ha (4,685,118 ac)
Maximum Depth: 244 m (800 ft)
Mean Depth: 86 m (282 ft)
Way Point: 43° 56' 42" Lat - N, 78° 10' 05" Long - W

Lake Ontario

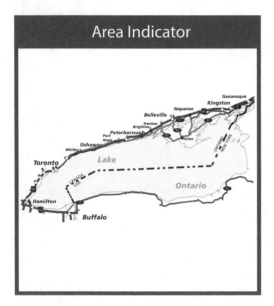

Area Indicator

Directions

Forming the southern boundary of Ontario, there is virtually unlimited access to this Great Lake. From Hamilton to Toronto, access is best off xxx highway. Further east, Highway 401 provides good access from Whitby through to Belleville. It is also possible to access the river from Prince Edward County south of the 401 and Kingston.

Facilities

There are literally thousands of places to stay when visiting Lake Ontario, but listing all the camping, RV, hotel, motel, motor home and resorts on or close to the shores of the Great Lake would take a whole book. Here are the various provincial parks to visit:

Presqu'ile Provincial Park is south of Brighton along Route 66 and has plenty of facilities for the avid fisherman to set camp. There are 160 campsites available, including 27 electrical sites and 14 backcountry water access sites. This site has a boat launch for easy access to the lake, picnic tables and toilet facilities.

North Beach Provincial Park is located just south of Trenton, this day-use park is 89 hectares (219 acres) in size and protects 1.2 kilometre stretch of sandbar along the northern shores of Lake Ontario. There are all the usual park amenities while popular activities include windsurfing, boating and swimming.

Sandbanks Provincial Park is a 1,509 hectare (3,728 acre) reserve found just south of Wellington off Highway 33. There are numerous campgrounds throughout the park with a total of 549 campsites, including 140 electrical sites. There are also several boat launches throughout the park that access Lake Ontario along with toilet facilities, picnic tables, showers, a general store and laundry facilities. The beaches along this stretch of the lake are arguably some of the best in Ontario with the towering sand dunes and warm summer waters.

Fishing

Lake Ontario is one of the five Great Lakes of North America. In the Wyandot (Huron) language, ontario means "Lake of Shining Waters". It is the 14th largest lake in the world and when its islands are included, the lake has a shoreline that is 1,146 kilometres (712 miles) long. Its length is 311 kilometres (193 miles) and its width is 85 km (46 miles). Adding to the lakes mass, it has an average depth of 86 metres (282 feet) and a maximum depth approximately 244 metres (800 feet). Lake Ontario's primary source is the Niagara River, draining Lake Erie, with the St. Lawrence River serving as the outlet into the Atlantic Ocean.

With incursions of warm air from the southwest, the lakes open waters rarely freeze in winter. From November to May, the main body is well mixed at a uniform temperature while from June through October the waters are stratified with a warm upper layer approximately 10–20 metres (32–66 feet) deep, a cooler secondary layer until 100 metres (328 feet) and the depths below this are always less than 5C (41F).

Lake Ontario is famous for its fantastic salmon fishing, with Chinook the kings of the waters; many topping the scales at over 14 kilograms (30 pounds). Other species of salmon in the big lake include Coho, pink and Atlantic salmon. Most salmon congregate off shore in the spring, feeding on smelt and alewifes before retreating to deeper water in the summer. Trolling with a variety of spoons using downriggers is the most common way of fishing salmon on Lake Ontario. Good spoons to use are Williams, nasty boys and northern kings. Pier fishing and shore angling can also produce great results. Casting spoons, like cleos and pixies, on windy days or at dusk and dawn can produce some excellent fishing.

Not to be outdone, there are numerous trout species that inhabit Lake Ontario. Average lake trout in the big lake range between 3 and 4 kilograms (6–8 pounds), although trophy lakers at over 9 kg (20 lbs) are not uncommon. Brook trout, on the other hand, are usually much smaller averaging 1–3 kg (2–6.6 lbs) and found closer to shore. Open water fishing techniques are the same for lake trout as salmon since the trout stay inland in the spring and fall and move deeper in the summer months. Shore anglers should focus around river mouths during the spring and fall. Casting spoons or spinners at these river mouths is extremely effective.

Adding to the mix, anglers will find some decent sized walleye, northern pike and muskellunge in Lake Ontario. Walleye average around 1 kilogram (2.2 pounds) but 1.8–2.2 kg (4–5 lb) pickerel can be plucked at any time of the day or season. Some walleye trophies have come in at over 4.5 kilograms (10 pounds) in the big lake. Pike average approximately 1.3–2.7 kg (3–6 lbs) and top out around 6.8 kg (15 lbs). The bigger muskellunge average between 2.3 and 16.3 kg (5–36 lbs) in Lake Ontario, but some reports have trophies being caught weighing around the 25 kilogram (55 pound) mark.

Bass are often overlooked by anglers on the big lake and there are many parts of the lake where smallmouth and largemouth bass can be found. There are regular reports of big bucket mouths over 2.5 kg (5 lbs) being pulled from the shallower regions of the lake. Smallmouth prefer to swim in schools and once hooked, provide some of the best fight pound for pound than any other freshwater fish. The odd smallmouth reaches 1.8 kg (4 lbs) in size in Lake Ontario.

Hotspots in and around Lake Ontario include Big Bay, Long Reach, Prince Edward Bay, Wellington Bay and Adolphus Reach to name just a few. Ontario is home to an astounding 160 of Canada's 228 species of freshwater fish. Here are some of the species you can find in Lake Ontario waters.

Lake Ontario

Location: Hamilton to Kingston
Elevation: 219 m (719 ft)
Surface Area: 1,896,000 ha (4,685,118 ac)
Maximum Depth: 244 m (800 ft)
Mean Depth: 86 m (282 ft)
Way Point: 43° 56′ 42″ Lat - N, 78° 10′ 05″ Long - W

16 Zone

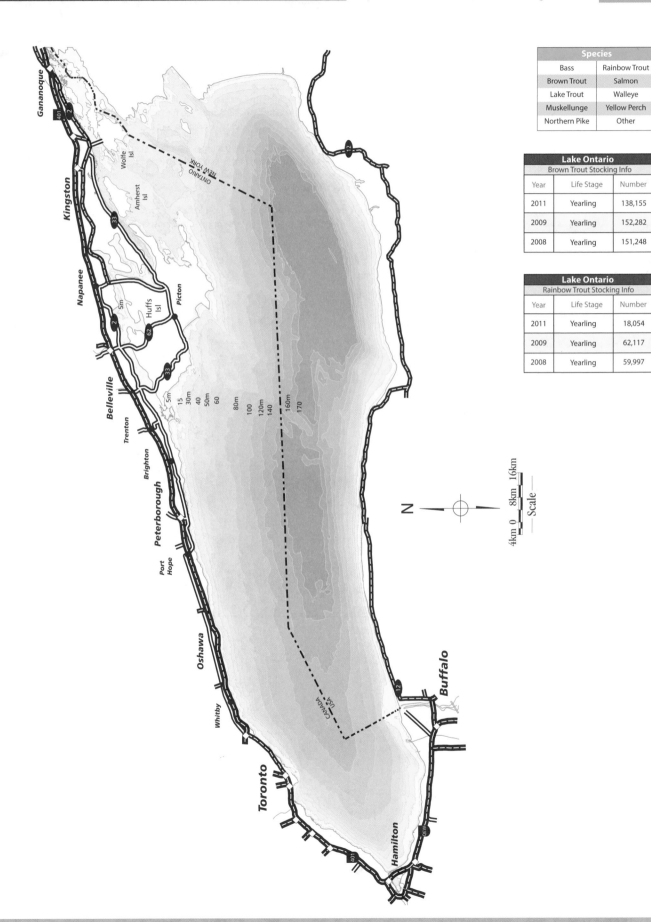

Species	
Bass	Rainbow Trout
Brown Trout	Salmon
Lake Trout	Walleye
Muskellunge	Yellow Perch
Northern Pike	Other

Lake Ontario		
Brown Trout Stocking Info		
Year	Life Stage	Number
2011	Yearling	138,155
2009	Yearling	152,282
2008	Yearling	151,248

Lake Ontario		
Rainbow Trout Stocking Info		
Year	Life Stage	Number
2011	Yearling	18,054
2009	Yearling	62,117
2008	Yearling	59,997

Location: 40 km (24.8 mi) north of Kingston
Elevation: 119 m (389 ft)
Surface Area: 785 ha (1940 ac)
Maximum Depth: 10.7 m (35 ft)
Mean Depth: 2.5 m (8.3 ft)
Way Point: 44° 34' 00" N, 76° 19' 00" W

Lake Opinicon

Area Indicator

Fishing

This popular summer cottage lake is part of the Rideau Canal Waterway and offers fair to good fishing at times for smallmouth and largemouth bass in the 1 kg (2 lb) range. There are plenty of prime holding areas for both bass species. Coupled with the ample weed structure and you have the makings for some productive bass waters. Try casting jigs and spinners along drop-offs or weed beds for ambush ready bass. During dusk and overcast periods bass can be enticed to hit top water flies and lures. Colourful popper flies can be exciting, while spincasters should try a floating Rapala.

Northern pike also inhabit the lake, although fishing is generally slow. Similar to bass fishing, try casting spinner baits or jigs along shore structure and near islands. The best time to try for northern pike is during the evening when pike cruise into shallower areas in search of food. There is the odd big northern that can surprise unsuspecting anglers.

There are two all year fish sanctuary areas on Opinicon Lake, one at the northern end and one at the southern end of the lake. Be sure to check your regulations for the specific sanctuary areas.

Species	
Black Crappie	Smallmouth Bass
Largemouth Bass	Yellow Perch
Northern Pike	Other

Directions

East of Frontenac Provincial Park, Opinicon Lake is part of the popular Rideau Canal Waterway. By vehicle, the lake is best accessed from just north of Kingston. Follow Highway 401 to Exit 617 and head north along Perth Road (County Road 10). Continue north along the Perth Road to Raymond's Corners and the junction with the Opinicon Road (County Road 9). The Opinicon Road traverses northeast eventually passing by the northern shore of the lake. To reach Opinicon Lake by vehicle from the north, follow Highway 15 south from Smith's Falls to Opinicon Road (County Road 9).

Boaters can access Opinicon Lake via the Rideau Canal from Sand Lake to the east or Indian Lake to the north.

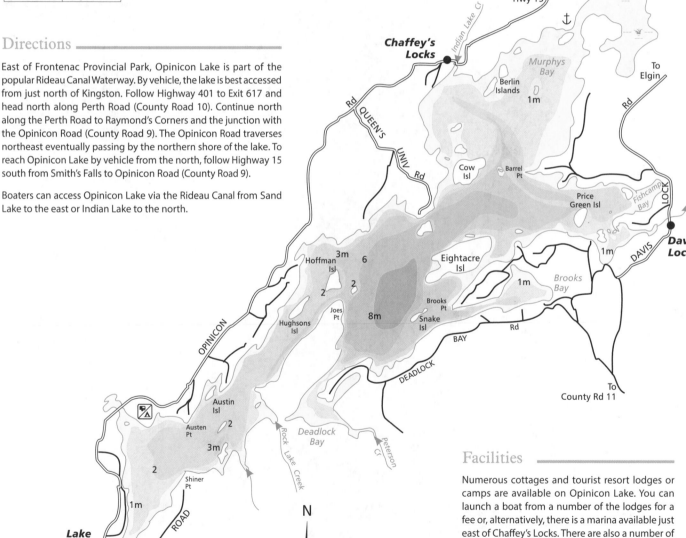

Facilities

Numerous cottages and tourist resort lodges or camps are available on Opinicon Lake. You can launch a boat from a number of the lodges for a fee or, alternatively, there is a marina available just east of Chaffey's Locks. There are also a number of motels, cabins and lodges available in and around Chaffey's Locks for visitors. The nearby towns of Newboro and Westport to the north are home to a number of retailers and restaurants and are within a short drive of Opinicon Lake.

Lake St. John

Location: 17 km (10 mi) northeast of Orillia
Elevation: 219 m (720 ft)
Surface Area: 619 ha (1,530 ac)
Maximum Depth: 7.6 m (25 ft)
Mean Depth: 4.3 m (14.2 ft)
Way Point: 44° 41'00" Lat - N, 79° 19'00" Lon - W

Fishing

Due to the close proximity to urban development and major highways, Lake St. John is a heavily fished lake. Thankfully, with the increase practice of catch and release, the lake continues to support a decent sport fish fishery for a variety of species.

Fishing is best for smallmouth and largemouth bass, as bass can be found virtually anywhere along the shore structure of the lake. Bass are also readily found off any of the small islands or around the 3 m (7 ft) shoal humps. The western region of the lake is known to be the main producing area for walleye, especially along the drop-off. Many anglers simply troll a rapala or worm harness along the drop off in search of walleye. Smallmouth bass can also be caught using this method. One particularly productive area of the lake for northern pike is the large bay found near the airport. This shallow, weedy bay often holds fair numbers of northern pike and largemouth bass. At dusk, try top water flies or lures for both species in this bay.

Directions

Lake St. John is located to the east of the much larger Lake Couchiching. From the town of Orillia, follow Highway 12 east to County Road 44. Take County Road 44 north to Lake St. John. Look for signs to the village of Langford and follow the road to the village and the marina on Lake St. John.

Facilities

Along the northwest shore of the lake, there is a tent and trailer park available for overnight use. The marina on the southwest shore is the only other facility on the lake. For roofed accommodations, the town of Orillia to the south has plenty to offer. Orillia is also and ideal location to stock up on supplies to make your outdoor adventure a success.

Other Options

Lake Couchiching is part of the Trent Severn Waterway and offers fishing opportunities for smallmouth bass, largemouth bass, northern pike and walleye. If your luck happens to be slow for the main sport fish, try working closer to shore for any one of the many panfish that can be readily caught in Lake Couchiching.

Area Indicator

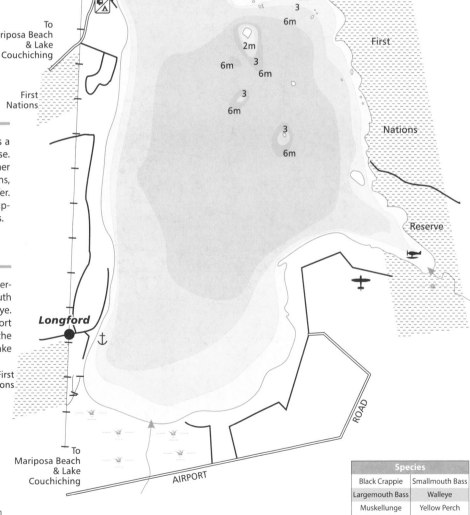

N

200m 0 200m 400m 600m 800m 1000m

— Scale —

Species	
Black Crappie	Smallmouth Bass
Largemouth Bass	Walleye
Muskellunge	Yellow Perch
Northern Pike	Other

Location: Port Perry
Elevation: 250 m (820 ft)
Surface Area: 8,255 ha (20,399 ac)
Max Depth: 7.6 m (25 ft)
Mean Depth: 1.4 m (4.5 ft)
Way Point: 44° 09′ 00″ Lat - N, 78° 54′ 00″ Long - W

Lake Scugog

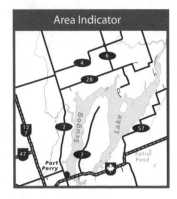

Area Indicator

Species	
Black Crappie	Walleye
Largemouth Bass	Yellow Perch
Muskellunge	Other
Smallmouth Bass	

Fishing

Lake Scugog continues to be a decent provider of sport fishing opportunities regardless of the pressure the lake continues to experience. The low-lying, weedy nature of the lake makes for lush habitat for all the sport fish that inhabit its waters. Smallmouth and largemouth bass can be found almost anywhere around the lake; although predominantly around weed cover.

Similar to other Kawartha Lakes, walleye and muskellunge are the main attraction for anglers and fishing for both species can be good at times. For both predators, look for weed areas with an abundance of baitfish. Trolling or drifting along weed lines with a worm harness can be quite effective on this lake for walleye. Muskellunge can be picked up on occasion with the larger spinner baits or crank baits. Still jigging along the drop offs near the deeper portions of the lake is also a proven method in finding walleye. Try off Lakeside Beach, Caeserea or Scugog Point for a better chance at success.

Directions

You will find Lake Scugog in the midst of a low-lying wetland region. The lake is considered as one of the main Kawartha Lakes; although unlike the other lakes, Scugog is not a part of the Trent Severn Waterway. The lake is easily found by following Highway 7A to the town of Port Perry. Port Perry is situated along the southwest shore of the lake and is the main access area to Lake Scugog. There are several other marinas and access points around the lake.

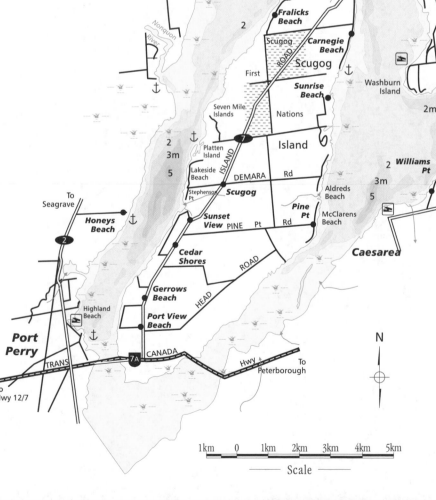

Facilities

Port Perry is a scenic lakeside community offering all the essentials, such as motels, groceries and other supplies. The town is regarded as the main access area to the lake, although there are several other boat launches and marinas that can be found around the lake. One of the unique features to the lake is that it is home to a charity casino. If fishing is slow, you can always head down Island Road on Scugog Island to the casino to try your luck.

Other Options

An often overlooked alternative to Lake Scugog is the **Scugog River**. The Scugog River is home to a productive sport fishery for bass, although walleye and the odd muskellunge lurk in the depths. Watch for sanctuary areas and special restrictions on the river.

Lasswade Lake

Location: 20 km (12 mi) east of Apsley
Elevation: 333 m (1,093 ft)
Surface Area: 29 ha (71 ac)
Maximum Depth: 9 m (30 ft)
Mean Depth: 5 m (16.4 ft)
Way Point: 44° 41' 00" Lat - N, 78° 45' 00" Lon - W

15 Zone

Fishing

When you visit Lasswade Lake, you will find a few cottages on the eastern end of the lake, although the lake is not overly developed. There is a good population of smallmouth and largemouth bass in the lake and they provide for the majority of the angling action. The shallow east end is a favourite holding area for largemouth bass, while you can find largemouth in the western portion of the lake generally closer to shore. If you are looking for smallmouth bass, try off the west side of the long point or the west side of the island.

Lasswade Lake is also stocked periodically with rainbow trout. Rainbow fishing was good at times, although has decreased over the past few years, probably due to the lower number of trout that have been stocked into the lake. Fly fishing can be an exciting way to entice trout into biting. The best time of the year for rainbow is during the spring or fall periods.

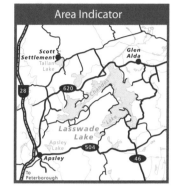

Area Indicator

Species
Largemouth Bass
Rainbow Trout
Smallmouth Bass

Directions

To reach Lasswade Lake, follow Highway 28 north from the town of Lakefield to the cut-off to County Road 504. Follow County Road 504 east past the town of Apsley to McCauley's Road. Take McCauley's Road north to the eastern shore of Lasswade Lake. You can see the access area from the road.

Facilities

There is a rustic boat launch found on the southern shore of Lasswade Lake. Supplies can be picked up in the town of Apsley, which is located minutes to the east of the lake. For overnight accommodations, there are a few motels off Highway 28 south of Apsley. There is also a few tent and trailer parks in the area on Chandos Lake to the north and Jack Lake to the south.

Other Options

The South Bay of **Chandos Lake** is located to the north of Lasswade Lake and can be accessed off County Road 504. Chandos Lake is a popular cottage destination lake that provides angling opportunities for smallmouth bass, largemouth bass, walleye, northern pike and lake trout.

Lasswade Lake			
Fish Stocking Data			
Year	Species	Number	Life Stage
2010	Rainbow Trout	1,900	Fry
2009	Rainbow Trout	1,900	Fry
2008	Rainbow Trout	1,000	Fry

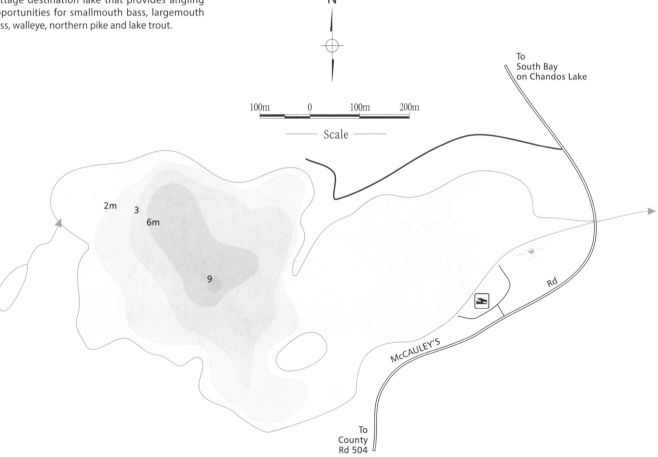

Location: 8 km (5 mi) north of St Ola
Elevation: 313 m (1,027 ft)
Surface Area: 830 ha (2,051 ac)
Maximum Depth: 27.4 m (90 ft)
Mean Depth: 13.7 m (45 ft)
Way Point: 44° 53' 00" Lat - N, 77° 37' 00" Lon - W

Limerick Lake

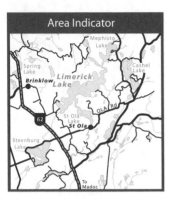

Area Indicator

Species	
Lake Trout	Whitefish
Largemouth Bass	Yellow Perch
Smallmouth Bass	

Directions

Limerick Lake can be found by travelling east on Highway 7 to the junction with Highway 62 at the town of Madoc. Take Highway 62 north past the villages of Eldorado and Bannockburn to Limerick Lake Road. The road is well signed on the highway and should not be difficult to find. Follow Limerick Lake Road east for approximately 3 km to Martins Landing and a small marina on the southern shore of Limerick Lake.

Fishing

Nestled in the rocky rolling hills of the lower Madawaska Highlands, Limerick Lake is a scenic lake characterize by a rocky shoreline. The lake is home to several camps and cottages and the fishing quality of the lake remain fairly steady despite its development.

Fishing is best for smallmouth and largemouth bass, which can be found to 2 kg (4.5 lbs) in size on occasion The average sized bass in Limerick Lake remains around 0.5-1 kg (1-2 lbs). Look for smallmouth bass off an of the rocky drop-off areas around the lake as well as just off the two small islands. Largemouth are primaril found in the weedier shallow bays of the lake.

The other main sport fish resident in Limerick Lake is a natural population of lake trout. As with most develope lakes in Ontario, the lake trout stocks are under extreme angling pressure. This is certainly true on Limerick Lak as recent regulation changes have been enacted to help support the ailing lake trout stocks. If you do pla to fish for lake trout, the practice of catch and release will go a long way in helping sustain this great specie through the 21st Century. Special restrictions on Limerick Lake include lake trout slot sizes and only one lin permitted during ice fishing season.

Facilities

Other than the marina at Martins Landing, there are no other facilities on Limerick Lake. The lake is part of a short canoe route that begins to the north on Mephisto Lake and ends to the south at a take out area off the Highway 62 crossing of the Beaver Creek.

For overnight accommodations, there is a tent and trailer park available on St. Ola Lake to the south of Limerick Lake. If you prefer, the town of Bancroft to the north is merely minutes away and has plenty to offer the outdoor traveller. The towns of Bannockburn, Eldorado and Gilmour south of Limerick Lake are each home to a general store where basic supplies can be obtained for your outing.

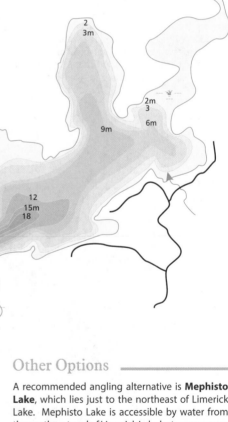

Other Options

A recommended angling alternative is **Mephisto Lake**, which lies just to the northeast of Limerick Lake. Mephisto Lake is accessible by water from the northeast end of Limerick Lake but a canoe may be required to navigate the channel. Alternatively, Mephisto Lake is accessible via a boat launch area along its eastern shore. The access area can be reached by taking Weslemkoon Lake Road to the Egan Creek Access Trail Road. Mephisto Lake offers fishing for smallmouth bass, largemouth bass and the occasional natural lake trout.

Lingham Lake

Location: 56 km (34 mi) north of Madoc
Elevation: 290 m (950 ft)
Surface Area: 722 ha (1,784 ac)
Max Depth: 5.5 m (18 ft)
Mean Depth: 2.5 m (8.1 ft)
Way Point: 44° 46′00″ N, 77° 25′00″ W

Fishing

Lingham Lake is a man-made lake, which was formed by the damming of the Black River in 1925. The lake is inhabited by largemouth and smallmouth bass and was once considered as one of the best bass fishing destinations in Eastern Ontario. Not even a decade ago, it was difficult to find another person on Lingham Lake any time of the year. The fishing was fast and the fish were big. Anglers expected to catch plenty of bass in the 2+ kg (4.5+ lb) range.

Today, after bass season opens, the lake becomes flooded with anglers, especially on weekends. Due to over harvesting, bass in the 2 kg (4.5 lb) range are a rarity and the fishing success rate has dropped dramatically. It is still a scenic lake to visit and fishing can be good on occasion.

To help maintain the bass fishery in Lingham Lake, the lake is now part of a late fall to summer fishing sanctuary. Please do your part to enhance the future of Lingham Lake's bass fishery by practicing catch and release as much as possible.

Directions

There are two access routes to Lingham Lake, one from the south and one from the north. Both options require you to follow Highway 62, which is found north of Highway 7 at Madoc. The southern access starts at the village of Bannockburn. Head east along the Bannockburn Road, which changes to the Lingham Lake Road at the settlement of Cooper. Lingham Lake Road begins to follow the Black River before there is a branch north that heads towards the southern shore of the lake. The final access road into the lake is very rough in sections and a 4wd vehicle is recommended.

The northern access to Lingham Lake is a preferred access for the more adventurous traveller. From Highway 62, continue north of Bannockburn to the Weslemkoon Lake Road. Head east along the Weslemkoon Lake Road past the settlement of Gilmour and veer east off the road along a rougher access road just before Wadsworth Lake. After approximately 4 km (2.5 mi) along this road, look for an even rougher southern branch road. This road winds its way southeast for over 15 km (9 mi) to the northern access. Look for a clearing where an old hunting cabin used to sit. This is the main parking area. From here, it is a short portage to the Black River, which flows slowly south to Lingham Lake.

Facilities

General stores are located in Bannockburn and Gilmour offering opportunities to stock up on basic camping supplies. A parking area and rough boat launch is located at the southern access to Lingham Lake. At the northern access, motorized vehicles are not permitted on the portage and boats that are cached along the river are removed annually.

Lingham Lake is part of a newly established conservation reserve, which helps protect the natural environment of the lake and its shoreline. While it is part of a reserve, there is no maintenance done to any campsites other than what users do themselves. Unfortunately, many of the sites are beginning to show signs of heavy use and abuse. Please help preserve this unique experience by cleaning up after your visit and packing out any garbage from the area.

Area Indicator

Species
Largemouth Bass
Smallmouth Bass
Yellow Perch

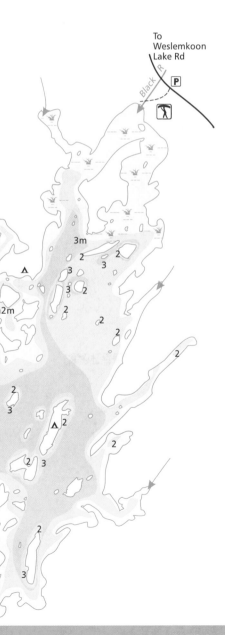

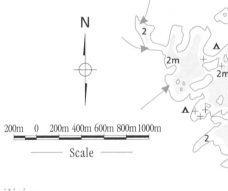

Zone **15**

Location: 10km (6mi) north of Apsley
Maximum Depth: 18 m (59 ft)
Mean Depth: 7.8 m (25.7 ft)
Way Point: 44° 49′ 00″ Lat - N, 78° 09′ 00″ Lon - W

Little Anstruther Lake

Area Indicator

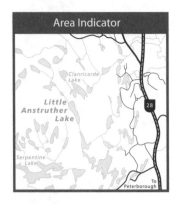

Species
Lake Trout
Largemouth Bass
Smallmouth Bass

Directions

Set amid the rolling hills northwest of the village of Apsley, Little Anstruther Lake is a backcountry lake that is mainly visited during the winter. There are no well-established trails or roads to the lake; therefore, summer access would have to be on foot by bushwhacking. In the winter, ice anglers frequent the lake and there is often an established snowmobile trail that can be picked up from the logging road located north of the lake or branch trails off the 108 Snowmobile Trail to the southeast.

Facilities

Little Anstruther Lake is a remote lake that offers no facilities. For experienced backcountry travellers, rustic Crown land camping is certainly possible. Basic supplies can be found in the village of Apsley to the south of the lake, off the east side of Highway 28.

Other Options

Clanricarde Lake can be accessed by rough portage from Little Anstruther Lake and offers a similar rustic backcountry experience. The lake offers fishing opportunities for smallmouth bass that rarely see a lure.

Fishing

Little Anstruther Lake is stocked almost annually with lake trout, which provide for productive fishing mainly in the winter through the ice. The lake trout in the lake are generally small but they can be a lot of fun to catch on a sunny winter day. Try jigging a small spoon or even a white jig at the north end of the lake closer to the Camp Creek inflow. Adding bait will often entice even the most lethargic laker into striking.

Both smallmouth and largemouth bass also inhabit the lake and fishing can be fair to good during the summer months if you can get into the lake. Look for lunker smallmouth off the deep drop-off found along the west side of the lake. Smallmouth bass love structure and will gravitate to anything that they can use as cover. To locate these sportfish look for underwater drop offs, rocky shoals or shorelines. While typical largemouth bass lures will work for smallmouth, including topwater presentations, underwater presentations (spinners, jigs and crank-baits) are regularly more effective. If fishing is slow, slow the retrieve down significantly.

Little Anstruther Lake		
Fish Stocking Data		
Year	Species	Number
2012	Lake Trout	200
2010	Lake Trout	200

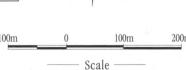

N

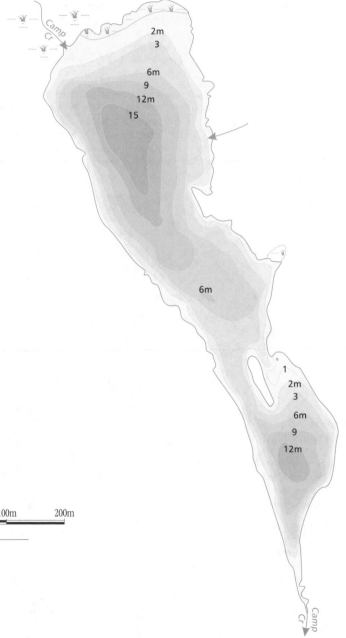

100m   0   100m   200m
— Scale —

Little Clear Lake

Location: 32 km (19 mi) north of Sydenham
Elevation: 175 m (575 ft)
Surface Area: 55 ha (136 ac)
Maximum Depth: 39.6 m (130 ft)
Mean Depth: 17.5 m (57.5 ft)
Way Point: 44° 33′ 00″ N, 76° 30′ 00″ W

Fishing

As a canoe access lake, Little Clear Lake not only offers solitude but it also offers better fishing than most lakes that are easily accessible by roads. The lake is inhabited by smallmouth and largemouth bass but the most prized sportfish found are lake trout and more recently stocked brook trout.

Lake trout were originally introduced in Little Clear Lake in 1968 and the species quickly adapted to the deep lake. The species is now a naturally reproducing strain. Fishing for lake trout is best in the early part of the season when they are closer to the surface. Trolling silver and gold spoons is the most effective angling method, although spinners also work at times. The small shoal area found near the northeastern side of the lake is a good holding area for lakers in the spring. During summer, fishing slows as the fish revert to the many deep holes around the lake.

Smallmouth and largemouth bass are found along the shoreline areas of Little Clear Lake. Casting along rocky drop-off areas with jigs or spinners is always effective. For bass anglers, perhaps the best spot on Little Clear is the large 1.5-3 m (5-10 ft) shoal located at the northeastern end. Try working jigs or streamer flies along the shoal for ambush ready bass.

Directions

Set in the heart of the majestic Frontenac Provincial Park, Clear Lake is accessible via the Clear Lake Road. The road beyond Big Clear Lake is gated but there is a good trail and portage system for anglers to use throughout the park. To find the Clear Lake Road, travel north along the Perth Road (County Road 10) from Kingston and just past Buck Lake, look for the Clear Lake Road off the west side. You can put in a canoe off the side of the road along the northern shore of Big Clear Lake. From Big Clear Lake, it is a 666 m (2,185 ft) portage to Black Lake and after a short paddle across Black Lake it is a 503 m (1,650 ft) portage to Little Clear Lake.

Facilities

Little Clear Lake is part of **Frontenac Provincial Park** and is home to four rustic interior campsites. The campsites are basic, made up of a fire ring and privy. For more information on Frontenac Provincial Park call (613) 376-3489 or for campsite reservations call (888) ONT-PARK or visit www.ontarioparks.com .

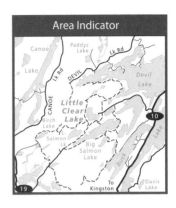

Area Indicator

Species	
Lake Trout	Smallmouth Bass
Largemouth Bass	Yellow Perch

Little Clear Lake			
Fish Stocking Data			
Year	Species	Number	Life Stage
2009	Brook Trout	800	Fry

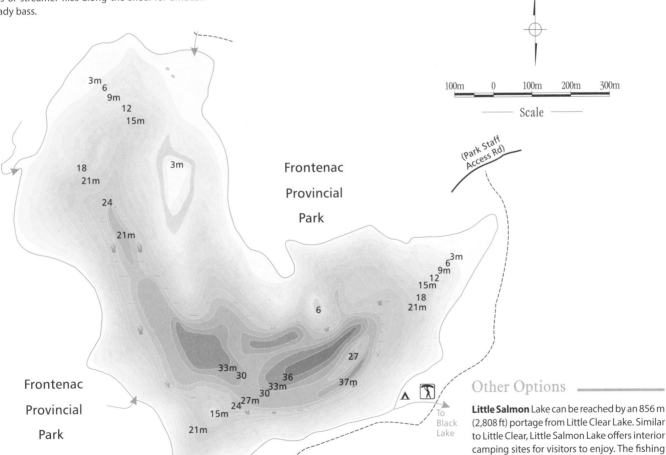

Other Options

Little Salmon Lake can be reached by an 856 m (2,808 ft) portage from Little Clear Lake. Similar to Little Clear, Little Salmon Lake offers interior camping sites for visitors to enjoy. The fishing in the lake is fair to good for smallmouth bass, largemouth bass and lake trout.

Location: 33 km (20 mi) north of Kingston
Elevation: 145 m (475 ft)
Surface Area: 38 ha (94 ac)
Maximum Depth: 43.9 m (144 ft)
Mean Depth: 16.7 m (54.7 ft)
Way Point: 44° 32' 00" N, 76° 31' 00" W

Little Salmon Lake

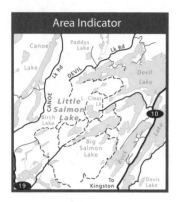

Area Indicator

Species
Lake Trout
Largemouth Bass
Yellow Perch

Fishing

As an interior access Frontenac Provincial Park lake, Little Salmon Lake has plenty to offer visitors that are willing to work to reach the lake. The lake is home to populations of largemouth bass and lake trout. Largemouth are best found along shoreline areas, especially near weed lines and other structure such as deadfalls. Try working jigs, spinners, streamer flies and poppers along shoreline areas for aggressive bass. Casting along rocky drop-offs with jigs or spinners can also be effective

Lake trout were originally introduced in Little Salmon Lake in 1968 and the species quickly adapted to the deep lake. The species is now a naturally reproducing strain. Fishing for lake trout is best in the early part of the season. The small shoal area found near the north side of the lake is a good holding area at this time. Trolling spoons like a Little Cleo is the most effective angling method for lakers, although spinners can work at times.

Directions

Little Salmon Lake is part of the series of lakes that help make Frontenac Provincial Park such a wonderful destination. The best way to access the lake is via portage or trail from Big Salmon Lake. To reach Big Salmon Lake, follow Highway 38 north from Highway 401 to the village of Harrowsmith. Head east at Harrowsmith along the Harrowsmith Road (County Road 5) to the town of Sydenham. Turn north along County Road 19 from Sydenham and follow this road to the Salmon Lake Road. Travelling east along the Salmon Lake Road will lead you directly into Frontenac Provincial Park and the eastern shore of Big Salmon Lake.

From Big Salmon Lake, paddle east along the lake or follow the park trails to Little Salmon Lake. The portage to Little Salmon Lake from Big Salmon Lake is located about half way along the northern shore of Big Salmon Lake. The portage is 923 m (3,028 ft) over generally flat terrain.

Facilities

Little Salmon Lake is part of **Frontenac Provincial Park** and is home to four interior campsites. The campsites lie along the northeastern shore of the lake and are basic, made up of a fire ring and privy. Other than the rustic campsites, there are no other facilities at Big Clear Lake. For more information on Frontenac Provincial Park call (613) 376-3489 or for campsite reservations call (888) ONT-PARK or visit www.ontarioparks.com.

Other Options

Little Clear Lake can be found via an 856 m (2,808 ft) portage from the eastern shore of Little Salmon Lake. Little Clear Lake is home to a few Frontenac interior camp sites and offers fair to good for smallmouth bass, largemouth bass and lake trout. Similar to Little Salmon Lake, lake trout were introduced into Little Clear Lake in the late 1960's. The trout have established naturally reproducing success and are best caught in the early part of the season by trolling.

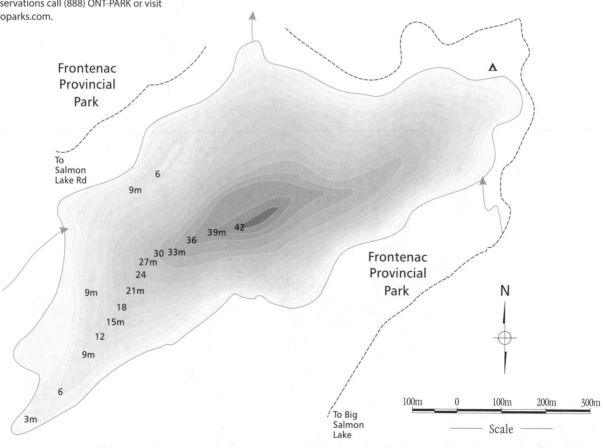

Long Lake

Location: 13 km (8 mi) south of Sharbot Lake
Elevation: 164 m (538 ft)
Surface Area: 301 ha (744 ac)
Maximum Depth: 13.4 m (44 ft)
Mean Depth: 6.1 m (20.2 ft)
Way Point: 44° 40′ 00″ N, 76° 46′ 00″ W

Fishing

Due to the easy access and number of cabins on the lake, the summer months can be busy. As a result, the angling pressure can be heavy. Regardless, anglers can still expect to have some success for resident smallmouth and largemouth bass, which can reach up to 1.5 kg (3.5 lbs) in size. The other sportfish found in Long Lake are northern pike and walleye.

Smallmouth are the more prevalent bass species found in the lake. They are best found along rocky shore structure, near islands or even over the 3 m (10 ft) shoal area located in the middle of the lake. Working a tube jig or other type of jig off the bottom can produce some exciting action at times.

Fishing success for northern pike is better than for walleye, although success for both species is generally fair to slow. Jigging or trolling a worm harness can work for walleye, while northern pike are often caught by accident when fishing for bass.

Facilities

Long Lake is a scenic lake with a number of cottages and camps scattered around the shoreline. There is a boat launch area with a small dock and beach area available along the eastern shore of the lake. For basic supplies and groceries, the nearby town of Sharbot Lake is the closest option.

Directions

Southwest of Sharbot Lake, Long Lake is a scenic lake easily found to the west of Highway 38. Highway 38 connects the two major highways in the area, Highway 7 to the north and Highway 401 to the south. Depending on which major highway you use, you will need to follow the smaller Highway 38 north or south to the village of Parham. At Parham, continue west along the Wagarville Road for a short distance to the junction with Long Lake Road. Head north along the Long Lake Road as it winds its way past the eastern shore of the lake. A boat launch and dock area are located just off the Long Lake Road.

Other Options

Eagle Lake lies to the east of Long Lake not far from the village of Parham. Eagle Lake is quite a bit bigger than Long Lake and offers fishing opportunities for smallmouth bass, largemouth bass, northern pike and a naturally reproducing strain of lake trout. Fishing is best for smallmouth and largemouth bass, although at times northern pike can be active. This is a popular summer destination lake, therefore, fishing can be challenging at times.

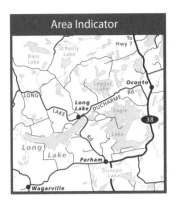

Area Indicator

Species
Largemouth Bass
Northern Pike
Smallmouth Bass
Walleye

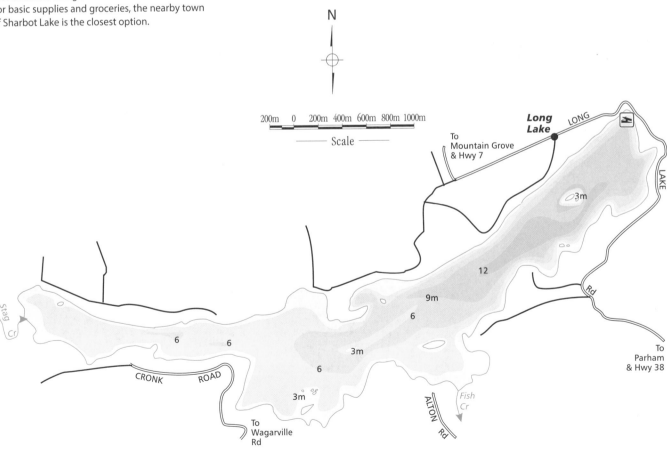

Zone 18

Location: 21.5 km (13.4 mi) north of Kingston
Elevation: 124 m (408 ft)
Surface Area: 1,065 ha (2,632 ac)
Maximum Depth: 6.1 m (20 ft)
Mean Depth: 2.1 m (6.8 ft)
Way Point: 44° 27′00″ N, 76° 25′00″W

Loughborough Lake- East

Fishing

Loughborough Lake is a popular vacationing destination for locals and distant visitors alike. The close proximity of the lake to the city of Kingston makes it an ideal summer destination. Although the lake is quite busy, the fishing success in both portions of the lake remains steady.

Loughborough Lake once supported a natural lake trout fishery. However, as the popularity of the lake increased, over time the lake trout stocks have decreased. Today, the lake is part of a stocking program that places over 35,000 lake trout in the lake annually. Fishing success for these stocked lakers is consistent with trout in the 3+ kg (6.5 + lb) range caught annually. Lake trout fishing is best at the beginning of the season when water temperatures are still cooler. Trolling for lake trout, especially on this larger lake, is your best bet for success.

Unknown to many, a number of years ago, the lake was once a part of a splake stocking program. Unfortunately, there have not been any recent reports of splake remaining in the lake. Loughborough Lake also holds fair numbers of smallmouth bass and largemouth bass in the 0.5-1 kg (1-2 lb) range. Northern pike are the other sportfish resident in the lake, although they are bigger, they are much more difficult to find compared to bass. The East Basin of Loughborough Lake is quite shallow compared to the West Basin. Visitors will find the lake riddled with islands both big and small. The shallow nature of the lake makes prime habitat for bass, northern pike and pan fish. There are literally dozens of underwater rock gardens, shallow, lily padded bays and weed beds to explore for both species. Lake trout are rarely, if ever caught in this section of the lake.

The East Basin of Loughborough Lake is quite shallow compared to the West Basin. Visitors will find the lake riddled with islands both big and small. The shallow nature of the lake makes prime habitat for bass, northern pike and pan fish. There are literally dozens of underwater rock gardens, shallow, lily padded bays and weed beds to explore for both species. Lake trout are rarely, if ever caught in this section of the lake.

Directions

Loughborough Lake is a beautiful lake found north of Kingston, not far from Frontenac Provincial Park. The main access area to the East Basin of the lake is near the village of Battersea. Battersea is about 24 km (15 mi) from Highway 401 near Kingston. To reach Battersea, take Exit 619 off the 401 and head north along the Battersea Road (County Road 11). Just past Cedar Lake, you will reach the village of Battersea and the southeast shore of Loughborough Lake. There is a boat launch and marina available.

Species	
Lake Trout	Smallmouth Bass
Largemouth Bass	Splake
Northern Pike	Yellow Perch

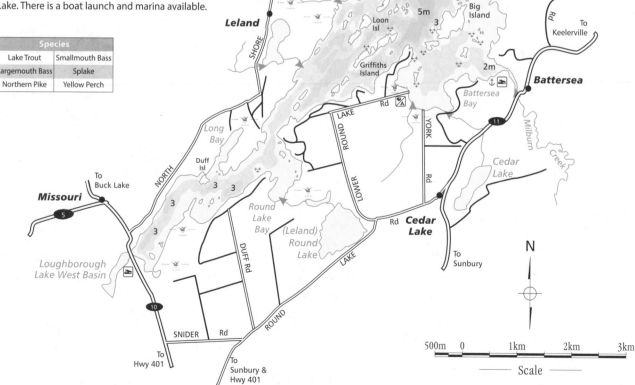

Loughborough Lake- West

Location: 21.5 km (13.4 mi) north of Kingston
Elevation: 124 m (408 ft)
Surface Area: 739 ha (1,824 ac)
Maximum Depth: 38.4 m (126 ft)
Mean Depth: 8.7 m (28.7 ft)
Way Point: 44° 27′ 00″ N, 76° 25′ 00″W

18 Zone

Fishing

Unlike the East Basin, the West Basin of Loughborough Lake is very deep in sections; reaching up to 38 m (126 ft) in the southern end of the lake Today, the lake is part of a regular stocking program. The deep nature of this section makes for suitable habitat for lake trout and rainbow trout. A prime hot spot for lakers is the 11 m (36 ft) shoal located in the northwest section of the lake. Many lake trout have been hooked by trolling past this shoal area. The shoal attracts baitfish, which in turn attracts hungry lakers.

For northern pike and largemouth bass, the shallow Harper Bay and the northwest bay can be good for both species. In addition, smallmouth and largemouth bass can also be found hanging around the 3 m (10 ft) shoal located along the northeast shore of the West Basin.

Facilities

On top of a few lodges, there are tent and trailer parks that have been established along both portions of Loughborough Lake. These private establishments are good places to base your activities around the popular lake.

Directions

To access the West Basin of Loughborough Lake take Exit 617 off Highway 401 near Kingston and travel north along the Perth Road (County Road 11). North of the village of Inverary, the Perth Road passes between the East and West Basins of Loughborough Lake. There is access to both sections of the lake at the public boat launch next to the bridge.

Other Options

Lacey Lake and **Fishing Lake** are two small lakes that lie north of the East Basin of Loughborough Lake. Lacey Lake can be found via the North Shore Road, while Fishing Lake can be accessed via Fishing Lake Road. Fishing Lake offers a little better fishing for both smallmouth and largemouth bass than Lacey Lake. Fishing Lake is also home to a small population of northern pike.

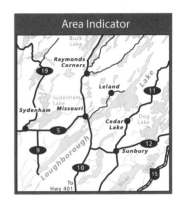
Area Indicator

Loughborough Lake (West Basin)		
Fish Stocking Data		
Year	Species	Number
2013	Lake Trout	15,000
2012	Lake Trout	8,000
2010	Lake Trout	8,000

Species	
Black Crappie	Northern Pike
Lake Trout	Rainbow Trout
Largemouth Bass	Yellow Perch

Location: 4 km (2.4 mi) west of Apsley
Elevation: 351 m (1,150 ft)
Maximum Depth: 16.4 m (54 ft)
Mean Depth: 7.7 m (25.5 ft)
Way Point: 44° 44' 00" Lat - N, 78° 09' 00" Lon - W

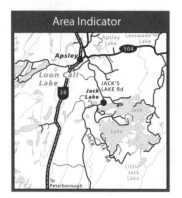

Area Indicator

Fishing

Some cottages dot the shoreline of Loon Call Lake but the lake can be quite peaceful, even in the middle of the summer cottage rush. The lake is a long shaped lake that has rocky shoreline areas suitable for its resident smallmouth bass. Largemouth bass are also found in the lake and can usually be found closer to shore hunkered around weed structure or even cottage docks. Fishing for bass remains fair for average sized bass.

The lake is also stocked with the hybrid trout species, splake. Splake can reach good sizes in Loon Call Lake. The most productive time to try for splake is during the winter through the ice. Try jigging a spoon or even a white jig along the shoal areas beside the deeper portions of the lake.

Directions

To reach Loon Call Lake, follow Highway 28 north from Lakefield past Burleigh Falls to Anstruther Lake Road. Following Anstruther Lake Road west will take you right past the boat access to Loon Call Lake. From the highway to the boat access on Loon Call Lake, it is approximately 3 km.

Other Options

Fortunately, if your luck is slow on Loon Call Lake, there are plenty of fine fishing alternatives nearby. The two closest lakes are **Wolf Lake** and **Crab Lake**. Wolf Lake provides fishing for smallmouth bass and muskellunge, while Crab Lake offers fishing for smallmouth bass.

Species	
Largemouth Bass	Splake
Northern Pike	Walleye
Smallmouth Bass	

Loon Call Lake		
Fish Stocking Data		
Year	Species	Number
2013	Splake	2,100
2011	Splake	2,100

Facilities

Other than the boat launch located on the eastern shore of Loon Call Lake, there are no other facilities. However, the village of Apsley is merely minutes away to the east. All the basic supplies for a fantastic outing can be obtained there.

100m 0 100m 200m 300m 400m 500m

Scale

Lower Beverley Lake

Location: 10 km (6.2 mi) north of Lyndhurst
Elevation: 91 m (300 ft)
Surface Area: 767 ha (1,894 ac)
Maximum Depth: 23 m (75.4 ft)
Mean Depth: 17.5 m (57.4 ft)
Way Point: 44° 36′ 00″N, 76° 08′ 00″W

Fishing

Lower Beverley Lake is a popular summer destination lake that offers fair to good fishing for largemouth bass in the 1+ kg (2+ lb) range. Smallmouth bass are also present in the lake, although in much smaller numbers. Largemouth bass are best found in the shallower sections of the lake, like the back bays, where weed growth is most prevalent. Two good areas for largemouth are Welly's Bay and Oak Bay along the southwestern end of the lake. Jigs, spinners and top water flies and lures can all produce well for largemouth.

Northern pike also inhabit Lower Beverley Lake in fair numbers and can be found up to 3 kg (6.5 lbs). Similar to largemouth bass, northerns frequent the shallows, especially during the evening periods. Northern pike usually will not hit the surface flies and lures as much as bass, although periodically they are aggressive enough to pull down top water presentations. Streamer type flies, spoons, jigs and spinner baits can all work well for pike.

Facilities

In the town of Delta off County Road 42, there is a local tent and trailer park that offers boat launching for a small fee. Other accommodations and services are available in town or in the nearby towns of Lyndhurst or Athens. For campers, **Charleston Lake Provincial Park** is only minutes to the east of Lower Beverly Lake.

Directions

Northwest of Charleston Lake Provincial Park, Lower Beverley Lake is part of the Gananoque River system. You can reach the lake by travelling along Highway 401 to Exit 623 at Kingston. Head north from the exit along Highway 15 to the Lyndhurst Road (County Road 33) just north of Seeley's Bay. The Lyndhurst Road traverses northeast to the junction with County Road 42. County Road 42 then travels northwest to the village of Delta, which lies along the eastern shore of the lake.

Other Options

South of Lower Beverly Lake, via the Gananoque River system, you can find **Lyndhurst Lake.** Similar to Lower Beverley Lake, Lyndhurst Lake is inhabited by mainly largemouth bass and northern pike, with the odd smallmouth bass here and there. Fishing in Lyndhurst Lake is generally fair.

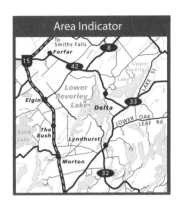

Area Indicator

Species	
Black Crappie	Smallmouth Bass
Largemouth Bass	Splake
Northern Pike	Yellow Perch

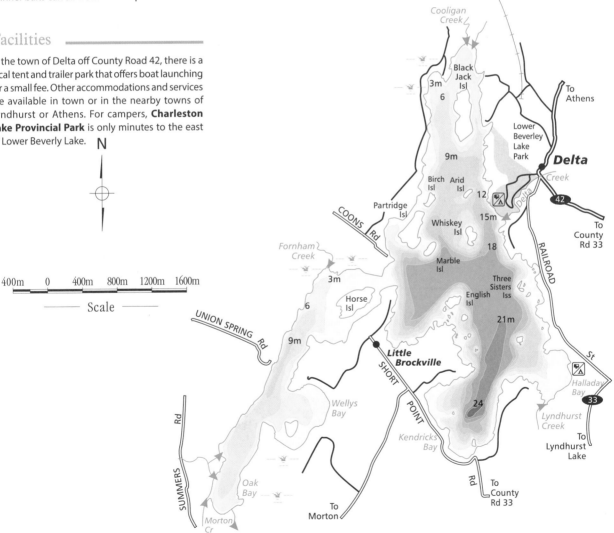

Zone 17

Location: Burleigh Falls
Maximum Depth: 15 m (49.2 ft)
Mean Depth: 6 m (19.7 ft)
Way Point: 44° 29′ 00″ Lat - N, 78° 23′ 00″ Lon - W

Lower Buckhorn Lake

Fishing

As part of the Trent-Severn Waterway, the lake experiences significant angling pressure throughout the season. However, characteristic to other Kawartha Lakes, the Buckhorn Lakes are nutrient rich due to the low-lying terrain and support a productive fishery.

Anglers will find success is often best for largemouth and smallmouth bass, as the many bays and islands make for prime bass habitat. Bass can be found almost anywhere in the lake. The key is to find weed beds and other structure where bass hold out in the greatest numbers. When fishing, one thing to take into account is that due to heavy boater traffic on the lake, bass can be quite spooky at times. If the bass are lethargic, try slower presentations such as a tube jig or crayfish imitation type lure worked off bottom.

As is common in the area, walleye are the most popular sport fish and fishing is generally fair for decent sized walleye. Deer Bay is a known holding area for these feisty predators. The area just off Black Point is also considered a decent holding area during portions of the season. The key to finding them is to locate structure such as weed lines.

Muskellunge are not as popular as walleye, although musky anglers from around the province visit the Buckhorn Lakes annually in search of big musky. Since this is a heavily fished lake, the practice of catch and release will go a long ways to help maintain the fishery.

Area Indicator

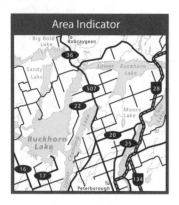

Species	
Black Crappie	Smallmouth Bass
Largemouth Bass	Walleye
Muskellunge	Yellow Perch

Directions

Lower Buckhorn Lake is actually the more northern portion of the great Buckhorn Lake that is commonly known as Lovesick Lake. This section of the big lake is easily accessed from the village of Burleigh Falls. To reach Burleigh Falls, travel north along Highway 28 from the town of Lakefield. Highway 28 passes right between Lower Buckhorn Lake to the west and Stoney Lake to the east. There is a boat launch along the southeast shore of Lower Buckhorn off the west side of the highway.

Facilities

The focal point of the facilities for Lower Buckhorn Lake is the village of Burleigh Falls. The village and area is home to a motel and a few general stores as well as a tent and trailer park. There are also a few other tent and trailer parks that can be found along the southern shore of the lake. Two marinas, one near Davis Point and another near Victoria Springs, provide boat access and mooring as well.

Wolf Island Provincial Park protects Wolf Island and a portion of the northern shore of Lower Buckhorn Lake. The park is a day-use only park offering access to a short series of user maintained hiking trails.

Other Options

The Buckhorn Lakes lie amid a chain of Kawartha Lakes that all offer similar angling opportunities. You can further explore **Buckhorn Lake** (formerly Upper Buckhorn Lake) by boat to the west, while **Stoney Lake** lies to the east. Each of these lakes is inhabited by decent populations of bass and is home to resident muskellunge and walleye.

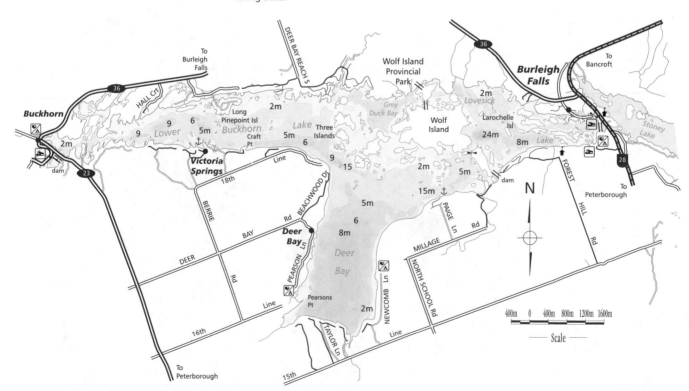

Lower Rideau Lake

Location: Smiths Falls
Maximum Depth: 18 m (59 ft)
Mean Depth: 9.4 m (31.1 ft)
Way Point: 44° 36' 00" N, 76° 08' 00" W

Fishing

This beautiful lake is very popular during the year, especially during the summer months. Nonetheless the fishing success remains consistent and anglers can expect fair to good fishing at times for smallmouth bass in the 0.5-1.5 kg (1-3.5 lb) range. Northern pike, walleye and lake trout round out the sportfish pursued in Lower Rideau Lake.

The shallow nature of the lake makes for prime bass habitat. There is plenty of weed growth around the lake, which provides excellent cover. Look for bass along weed lines or right in the weeds. Try using weedless type presentations such as a weedless spinner bait or tube jig. Often, when angling for bass, you will hook into a northern pike or walleye.

Fishing success for both northern pike and walleye is slower than for bass, although both species do frequent the lake in fair numbers. One area to try for larger pike and walleye is along the weed lines located next to the deep hole in the southeastern part of the lake. The bigger fish will often sit in the deeper water and cruise into the adjacent shallows in search of food. Try using a minnow imitation lure or a jig along the drop-off area for some nice sized fish.

Lake Trout are stocked in nearby Big Rideau Lake annually and there are reports of catches on occasion in Lower Rideau Lake. The shallow nature of Lower Rideau makes it unsuitable for lake trout during the summer, although you may get lucky in the early part of the season when out for one of the other sportfish species.

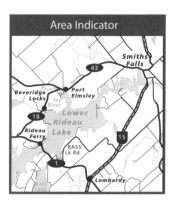

Area Indicator

Species	
Black Crappie	Smallmouth Bass
Lake Trout	Walleye
Largemouth Bass	Whitefish
Northern Pike	Yellow Perch

Directions

Located just outside of Smiths Falls, Lower Rideau Lake is a popular destination for locals and visitors alike. The lake is the last large water body when approaching Ottawa along the Rideau Canal. Alternatively, the lake can be accessed by vehicle via Rideau Ferry Road (County Road 1) south from the town of Perth or via Highway 15 at the town of Smiths Falls.

Facilities

The **108 Resort** is a Best Western Hotel situated on the shores of the lake. The resort is considered more of a golf and Nordic ski resort than a fishing camp. For anglers looking for something a little more intimate, there are a number of Bed and Breakfasts within the area.

Other Options

The **Tay River** flows into the northern end of Lower Rideau Lake and is often overlooked as an angling alternative to Lower Rideau Lake. The river flows from Bob's Lake to the west and offers fishing opportunities for mainly largemouth bass and smallmouth bass, although the odd walleye and northern pike can be found on occasion. When fishing this river, be sure to check your regulations for specifics on sanctuary areas and other restrictions.

Zone 18

Location: Lyndhurst
Elevation: 90 m (295 ft)
Surface Area: 28 ha (69 ac)
Maximum Depth: 11 m (36 ft)
Mean Depth: 3.6 m (11.8 ft)
Way Point: 44° 33′ 00″ N, 76° 07′ 00″ W

Lyndhurst Lake

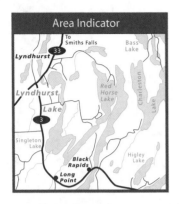

Area Indicator

Species	
Black Crappie	Smallmouth Bass
Largemouth Bass	Yellow Perch
Northern Pike	

Facilities

A small access area can be found in the village of Lyndhurst at the small park off Oakel Street. There is also a general store in the village but for more amenities the towns of Delta to the north or the town of Lansdowne to the south offer a few more retailers.

Fishing

Lyndhurst Lake receives significant angling pressure throughout the open water season, however, anglers can still have success on this shallow lake. Fishing is best for the lake's resident smallmouth and largemouth bass, which average 0.5-1 kg (1-2 lbs) in size. Due to the shallow nature of the lake, largemouth bass are the more dominant species. Largemouth can be found anywhere there is weed structure. Working a tube jig or other type of deep weed lure can be quite effective at times.

The other sportfish found in Lyndhurst Lake is northern pike. Fishing success for northerns is generally fair for smaller sized pike. While northern pike are often caught by accident when fishing for bass, ripping large spinner baits along weed lines can target the predator. The aggressive sportfish often chases down fast, big presentations and the pike of Lyndhurst Lake are no exception.

Directions

Anglers can find this lake west of Charleston Lake at the village of Lyndhurst. The most direct route to the lake is to follow Highway 401 to Exit 659. At the exit, head north along Reynolds Road (County Road 3) past Lansdowne where the road changes to Outlet Road. Continue north along Outlet Road past Singleton Lake to the junction with Lyndhurst Road (County Road 33). Travel east along Lyndhurst Road to the village of Lyndhurst, where you will find the northern shore of Lyndhurst Lake.

Other Options

Located due south of Lyndhurst Lake is **Singleton Lake**. Singleton Lake is accessible via Outlet Road (County Road 3) and offers fishing opportunities for smallmouth and largemouth bass over 1 kg (2 lbs). A small population of northern pike is also found in the lake.

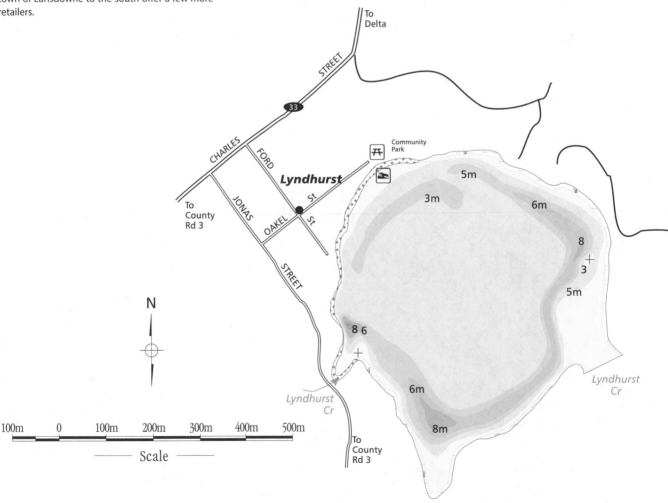

Mackie Lake

Location: 25 km (15 mi) northwest of Ompah
Elevation: 256 m (841 ft)
Surface Area: 157 ha (387 ac)
Maximum Depth: 22.8 m (75 ft)
Mean Depth: 8.5 m (28.1 ft)
Way Point: 45° 05′ 00″ N, 76° 59′ 00″ W

18 Zone

Fishing

The sportfish found in Mackie Lake are smallmouth bass, largemouth bass, northern pike and lake trout. Fishing success is best for smallmouth bass, although northern pike can be quite active on occasion. Look for smallmouth off any rocky areas around the lake, especially off any of the small islands. A jig worked off the bottom or even a crayfish imitation fly or lure can be effective.

Lake trout are stocked in the lake annually and success for lakers can be good at times, especially through the ice and in early spring. Throughout the spring and summer months, trolling allows you to cover as much water as possible. Trolling a spoon in the middle to upper layer of the lake in spring can be effective. Another good holding area at this time is around the 6 m (19 ft) shoal located in the middle of the lake. During the summer months, a downrigger is required to reach the deep holes around the lake where lake trout like to hide to escape the summer heat.

Directions

Mackie Lake is part of a series of remote lakes located north of the small village of Plevna. To find the lake, begin by travelling along Highway 7 to the junction with Highway 509 just north of Sharbot Lake. Follow Highway 509 north past the Mississippi River and the village of Donaldson. The highway will soon veer west towards the village of Ompah. Minutes west of Ompah look for Mountain Road off the north side of the highway. Follow Mountain Road north to the Mackie Lake Road, which leads to the southern shore of the lake. There is a car top boat launch at this end of the lake and a bigger launch at the north end of the lake. You will need to follow the Fortune/Schooner Lake Access Road past Fortune and the Portage Lakes to access the north end of Mackie Lake.

Area Indicator

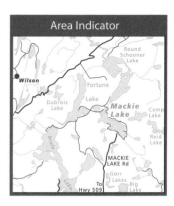

Species	
Lake Trout	Smallmouth Bass
Largemouth Bass	Whitefish
Northern Pike	Yellow Perch

Facilities

Mackie Lake is home to a few cottages and camps as well as tracts of Crown Land. A public access point suitable for smaller trailers is located along the southern shore of Mackie Lake. Another boat launch can be found at the northern end of the lake.

Other Options

Camp Lake and **Reid Lake** are two smaller lakes that lie to the east of Mackie Lake. Both lakes are interior access lakes and require a rough portage or hike to access. Both lakes offer good fishing for nice sized smallmouth bass and are stocked every few years with lake trout. Fishing for lakers is fair through the ice in winter and during the early spring just after ice off.

Mackie Lake			
Fish Stocking Data			
Year	Species	Number	Life Stage
2010	Lake Trout	500	Fry
2009	Lake Trout	500	Fry
2008	Lake Trout	500	Fry

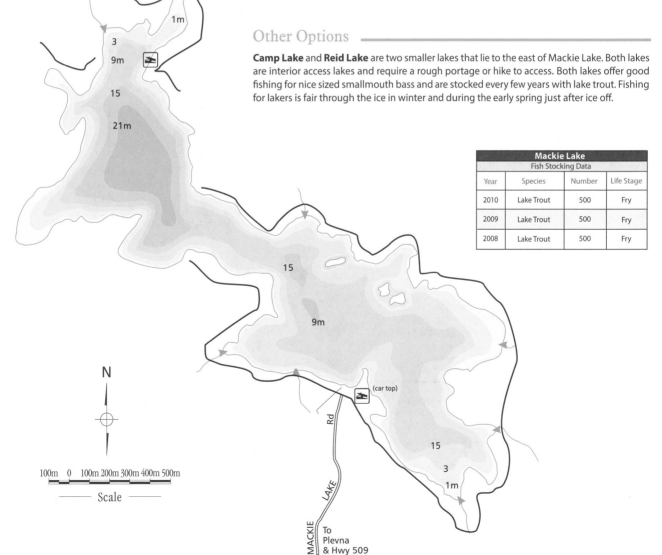

Location: 25 km (15.5 mi) north of Kaladar
Elevation: 268 m (880 ft)
Surface Area: 1,591 ha (3,930 ac)
Maximum Depth: 137 m (450 ft)
Mean Depth: 41.2 m (135.1 ft)
Way Point: 44° 50' 00" N, 77° 12' 00" W

Mazinaw Lake

Area Indicator

Directions

Mazinaw Lake is a beautifully scenic lake that is located next to Highway 41. The narrows between the upper and lower sections of the lake make up a portion of Bon Echo Provincial Park. Access is easily found by following the main highways, Highway 7 or Highway 401, to the smaller Highway 41. Once on Highway 41, head north past Kaladar and the villages of Northbrook then Cloyne. North of Cloyne, Mazinaw Lake soon unfolds along the eastern side of the highway. The main geographical feature of Mazinaw Lake is the large rock, Mazinaw Rock, which lies along the eastern shore of the upper portion of the lake. This towering rock was the historic meeting place for local native tribes. Mazinaw Lake is named after this meeting place, as 'Mazinaw' is known in many native dialects as the word for 'meeting place'. For the adventurous and historic at heart, visitors can view the fascinating ancient native paintings or 'pictographs' located at water level along the large rock wall of Mazinaw Rock.

Fishing

Mazinaw Lake has a maximum depth of 137 m (450 ft) and is one of the deepest inland lakes in Ontario. Fishing in the deep lake is slow to fair for smallmouth bass and largemouth bass that can reach up to 1.5 kg (3.5 lbs). Northern pike and walleye are the other warm water species, while lake trout are the main cold water species found in the lake.

Bass are mainly found along the many rocky drop-off areas around the lake. Try a jig, tube jig or crayfish fly or lure imitation to antagonize lethargic bass. Fishing success for walleye and northern pike is generally slow, although there are good sized walleye and pike caught in Mazinaw Lake annually. Trolling is best for both predators. Try working a worm harness along drop-offs. Alternatively, trolling a good sized spoon should entice northern pike strikes. A good hot spot for for all the species is around the 2 m (6 ft) shoal hump located along the southeast shore of the lower part of the lake.

A natural population of lake trout remains in Mazinaw Lake and with the deep nature of the lake, lake trout should continue to survive. Due to the depths, the only real way to have success for lakers is when they are closer to the surface of the lake. In winter, jigging a small spoon or white jig through the ice can work at times. In the early spring, trolling a spoon is best. In the summer, lakers in Mazinaw Lake can be very hard to find and down rigging equipment is required to reach the depths of where lake trout hold.

As with all lake trout populations in Southern Ontario, special regulations have been imposed to ensure the future viability of the species. Special ice fishing and slot size restrictions are in place to aid lake trout stocks. Be sure to check your regulations before heading out on Mazinaw Lake..

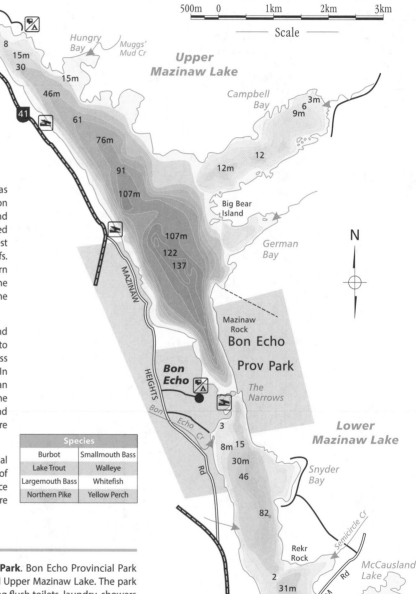

Species	
Burbot	Smallmouth Bass
Lake Trout	Walleye
Largemouth Bass	Whitefish
Northern Pike	Yellow Perch

Facilities

The main feature of Mazinaw Lake is **Bon Echo Provincial Park**. Bon Echo Provincial Park encompasses a good portion of land between the Lower and Upper Mazinaw Lake. The park is a full facility provincial park, providing all amenities including flush toilets, laundry, showers and electrical services. The park is home to 528 campsites, including a number of interior access tenting sites, and a public boat launch. The park is quite popular during the summer months, especially on weekends, therefore, it is highly recommended to make reservations at (888) ONT-PARK before arrival. For more information on Bon Echo Provincial Park, call (613) 336-2228.

There is also a marina as well as several tent and trailer parks around Mazinaw Lake that provide good access to the lake. For supplies, the small village of Cloyne to the south offers a few retailers. Further south, Northbrook is home to a grocery store and a few restaurants.

McGee Lake

Location: 13 km (8 mi) north of Burleigh Falls
Max Depth: 28.3 m (93 ft)
Mean Depth: 13.7 m (44.9 ft)
Way Point: 44° 38' 00" Lat - N, 78° 10' 00" Lon - W

Fishing

McGee Lake is stocked about every two years with lake trout, which provide for decent action mainly in the winter through the ice. Look for lakers along shoal areas near the deeper holes of the lake. Jigging small silver spoons can be effective but some anglers swear that white jigs are the only lure to use in the winter. If fishing is slow, try adding bait and slowing the retrieve down. Often this is all it takes to entice a laker into biting. The lake trout are not very big in McGee Lake but they can be a lot of fun to catch during the winter.

Getting into McGee during the spring is a challenge, but the odd angler does make their way in. Lake trout are also quite active just after ice off when they are found closer to the surface. Anglers will find success by trolling silver or gold spoons or larger streamer type flies that imitate baitfish. For trolling, the Little Cleo or Diamond King are good bets, while fly fishers should try a grey and white streamer with some crystal flash.

Watch for special restrictions on the lake.

Facilities

This secluded Crown land lake offers the opportunity for rustic backcountry camping along its shores or on the large island. Supplies and other necessities can be found via Highway 28 in Burleigh Falls to the south or Apsley to the north.

Directions

McGee Lake is a remote access lake that does not have any established roads or trails accessing it. The main method of access to the lake is via snowmobile during the winter. The lake is frequented by anglers during the winter so you may be able to find an established snowmobile route leading from Highway 28 to the lake.

Other Options

To the west of McGee Lake lies a fantastic chain of backcountry access lakes. The closest lakes are Vixen and Shark Lakes. The lakes can be reached by canoe and portage during the summer or by snowmobile in the winter. **Vixen Lake** offers fishing for smallmouth bass, while **Shark Lake** offers angling opportunities for smallmouth bass, largemouth bass and stocked splake.

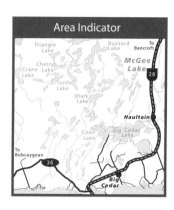

Area Indicator

Species
Lake Trout
Yellow Perch

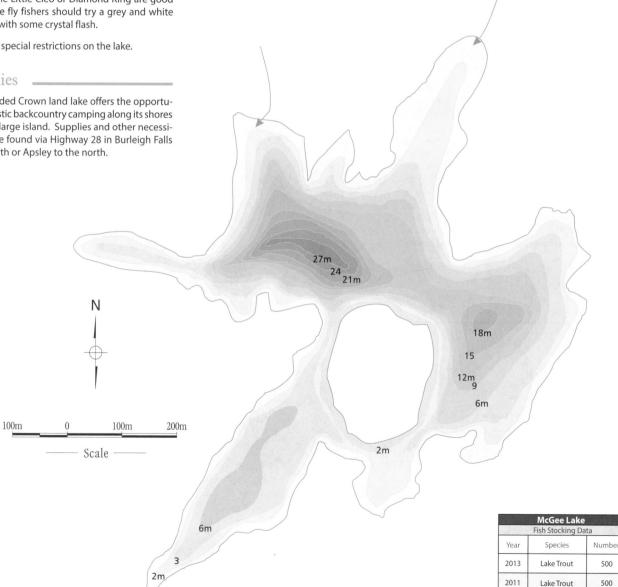

N

100m 0 100m 200m
Scale

27m
24
21m

18m

15

12m
9

6m

2m

6m

3
2m

McGee Lake		
Fish Stocking Data		
Year	Species	Number
2013	Lake Trout	500
2011	Lake Trout	500

Zone **15**

Location: 9 km (5.5 mi) northeast of St Ola
Elevation: 274 m (900 ft)
Perimeter: 7.7 km (4.7 mi)
Maximum Depth: 42 m (137.8 ft)
Mean Depth: 21.7 m (71.3 ft)
Way Point: 44° 43′ 00″ Lat - N, 77° 55′ 00″ Lon - W

Mephisto Lake

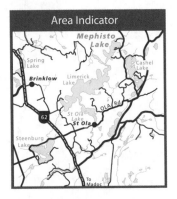

Area Indicator

Directions

Mephisto Lake is part of a series of lakes found north-west of Highway 62 and the settlement of Gilmour. From Highway 62, look for the Weslemkoon Lake Road on the east side of the highway. Travel east along this road, past Gilmour to the settlement of Gunter. The Egan Creek Access Trail/Road will soon be found heading north. Follow the access road past Cashel Lake to Mephisto Lake. There is a short access road to the boat launch area off the west side of the Egan Creek Trail/Road. Look for signs directing you to the lake.

Facilities

Mephisto Lake is a picturesque backcountry access lake that has a rough boat launch area on the north end of the lake. The lake is also home to a number of established Crown Land campsites. The basic campsites are accessible by boat and usually offer a rough fire pit and possibly a pit toilet. Be sure to carry out any garbage, as the sites are user maintained.

As an added bonus, Mephisto Lake is part of a short canoe route. The canoe route travels south from Mephisto Lake across Limerick Lake and St Ola Lake to Beaver Creek. The route then takes you along the Beaver Creek to Highway 62 and the take out area. The route is ideal for beginners or even for experienced trippers that are looking for an easy day or overnight trip.

Fishing

There are a few cottages on Mephisto Lake but the lake is not overly fished. Smallmouth and largemouth bass provide the mainstay of the angling action. The rocky shoreline found around the lake coupled with a number of weedy quiet bays make for prime small-mouth and largemouth bass habitat. Look for bass along weed lines or off any one of the islands. Casting a jig or spinner towards these structured areas will often provide results for decent sized bass.

A natural population of lake trout also inhabit Mephisto Lake, although success is usually quite slow. Fishing for lakers is best through the ice in winter or by trolling in the spring. Look for lakers along the deeper portions of the lake during winter. In the spring, the uniformity of the lake temperature allows the lake trout to roam freely and they can be literally caught anywhere in the lake. If you do plan to fish for lake trout, the practice of catch and release will go a long way in maintaining these stocks. Be sure to check your regulations before heading out, as there are special restrictions on Mephisto Lake to help protect lake trout populations.

Species	
Burbot	Smallmouth Bass
Lake Trout	Whitefish
Largemouth Bass	Yellow Perch

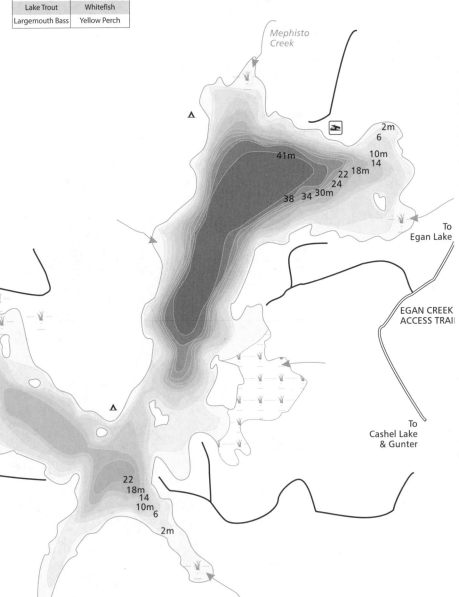

Other Options

Cashel Lake lies to the south of Mephisto Lake and is easily accessible off the Egan Creek Access Trail/Road. There is a rough boat launch onto the lake as well a few user-maintained Crown Land campsites. Fishing in the lake is consistent for largemouth and smallmouth bass. There is also a natural population of lake trout resident in Cashel Lake. Watch for sanctuary periods and special restrictions for lake trout.

Methuen Lake

Location: 22 km (13.5 mi) southeast of Apsley
Elevation: 274 m (900 ft)
Perimeter: 7.7 km (4.8 mi)
Max Depth: 14 m (64 ft)
Mean Depth: 7.1 m (23.3 ft)
Way Point: 44° 43′00″ Lat - N, 77° 55′00″ Lon - W

15 Zone

Fishing

A number of camps and cottages line the shore of Methuen Lake, hence the lake receives regular fishing pressure. Fishing in the lake remains slow to fair for smallmouth and largemouth bass that average 0.5-1 kg (1-2 lbs) in size. A few recommended bass spots are off the two large islands and especially near the small island found in the southern half of the lake. Around the small island, the northern portion is often much more productive than the southern side. Try a jig or even a spinner bait to entice smallmouth strikes.

Unknown to most visitors to Methuen Lake, the lake is also home to muskellunge. Muskellunge are a rare catch in the lake, although ardent musky anglers will often refute this claim.

Facilities

For day visitors, the lake offers a boat launch but not much else. Basic services and supplies can be found in the village of Apsley.

Directions

Travel north along Highway 28 from the town of Lakefield to County Road 504 and the village of Apsley. Follow County Road 504 east to Lasswade and the junction with County Road 46. Take County Road 46 south and just before the road turns west, take the rough access road off the east side of the road. When following the access road, there are a number of offshoot roads leading to cottages. The last offshoot road is the route to the access on Methuen Lake. If you cross the North River, you have gone too far.

Other Options

Imp Lake is a very small out of the way lake that is stocked with splake. The lake lies north of Methuen Lake and is mainly accessed by snowmobile in the winter. Ice fishing on the lake is reportedly good at times for nice sized splake.

Area Indicator

Species

Largemouth Bass
Muskellunge
Smallmouth Bass

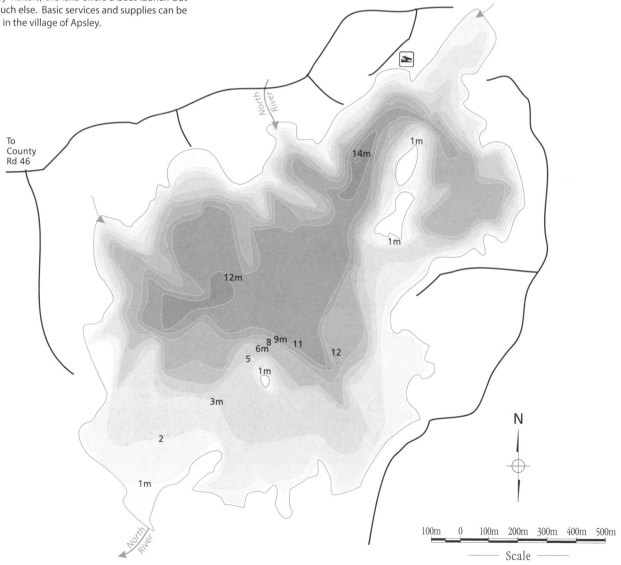

Zone 18

Location: 31 km (19 mi) north of Kaladar
Elevation: 268 m (880 ft)
Surface Area: 508 ha (1,254 ac)
Maximum Depth: 23.7 m (78 ft)
Mean Depth: 9 m (29.8 ft)
Way Point: 44° 52' 00" N, 77° 06' 00" W

Mississagagon Lake

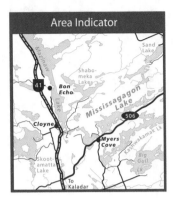

Area Indicator

Fishing

This clear, spring fed lake has plenty to offer anglers, including fishing opportunities for smallmouth bass, largemouth bass, northern pike, perch, walleye and even whitefish. The lake is characterized with islands and underwater rock structures, which create excellent smallmouth bass habitat. Look near any sort of shoreline structure, especially the smaller islands. The shallower shoals scattered around the lake also provide great holding areas for big smallmouth bass that can reach up to 2 kg (4.5 lbs) in size.

For largemouth bass and northern pike, the shallower, weedy bays are good holding areas. Try working top water lures such as a floating Rapala or poppers for some exciting action. Largemouth can be caught all day long, although are most active during overcast periods or at dusk. Most northern pike action is during dusk as they cruise into the bays in search of easy meals.

In the recent past, the natural walleye stocks of Mississagagon Lake suffered dramatically due to over fishing. However, local hatcheries have taken it upon themselves to attempt to re-establish the walleye fishery and now thousands of fingerling walleye are stocked in the lake from time to time.

Directions

Mississagagon Lake is located southeast of Bon Echo Provincial Park, not far from Highway 41. To reach the lake, travel north along Highway 41 from Highway 7 at Kaladar and look for the junction with Highway 506 just south of Cloyne. Highway 506 is a small, sometimes rough highway that travels east soon passing along the southern shore of Mississagagon Lake. There is a public boat launch available on the south shore of the lake. The northern shore remains undeveloped.

The name Mississagagon is derived from native dialect and means 'wide mouth' or 'headwater'. The lake has held the name Mississagagon Lake since as early as 1857.

Species	
Largemouth Bass	Walleye
Northern Pike	Yellow Perch
Smallmouth Bass	Other

Facilities

A public boat launch is available along the southeastern shore of Mississagagon Lake off Highway 506. Along with several cottages, a number of camps and lodges have also been established on the southern shore for visitors to the lake. Alternatively, camping enthusiasts can visit **Bon Echo Provincial Park** to the north off Highway 41. For supplies, the villages of Cloyne and Northbrook have plenty to offer.

Other Options

Just to the west of Mississagagon Lake lies **Marble Lake**. Marble Lake is accessible off Highway 506 and sports a public boat launch along its western shore. Although Marble Lake is much smaller than Mississagagon Lake, fishing in the lake is quite similar. Smallmouth and largemouth bass provide the bulk of the action and success can be good at times. Fishing for walleye and northern pike is slower, although is generally regarded as fair.

Mississagagon Lake			
Fish Stocking Data			
Year	Species	Number	Life Stage
2009	Walleye	11,000	Fingerling
2008	Walleye	7,000	Fingerling

Scale

400m 0 400m 800m 1200m 1600m

Mississagua Lake

Location: Mississagua Landing
Elevation: 294 m (966 ft)
Surface Area: 588 ha (1,452 ac)
Max Depth: 39.6 m (130 ft)
Mean Depth: 17.7 m (58 ft)
Way Point: 44° 42' 00" Lat - N, 78° 19' 00" Lon - W

Fishing

The rocky shoreline around this lake coupled with a number of secluded weedy bays, makes for prime bass habitat. This abundance of habitat translates into good fishing at times for both smallmouth and largemouth bass. Smallies can be found off rocky drop-offs and off any of the islands scattered around the lake. Largemouth bass love to hunker into weed growth and can be found in almost any of the many small weedy bays. One area in particular that is popular for largemouth bass is east of the southern most boat launch. The shallower, weedy area east of the island chain can hold some nice sized largemouth bass.

The other main sport fish found in Mississagua Lake is lake trout. Lake trout in this lake have continued to survive despite the continuously growing pressure on the species. Please help to maintain this species and abide to the winter/spring fishing sanctuary and practice catch and release whenever possible.

Area Indicator

Species

Lake Trout
Largemouth Bass
Smallmouth Bass
Yellow Perch

Directions

Mississagua Lake is part of a series of lakes found northeast of Pigeon Lake and the town of Bobcaygeon. The lake can be reached by first travelling north along Highway 28 from the town of Lakefield to County Road 36. Take County Road 36 west through the village of Buckhorn to Flynn's Turn and the junction with County Road 507. Follow County Road 507 north all the way to Mississagua Lake.

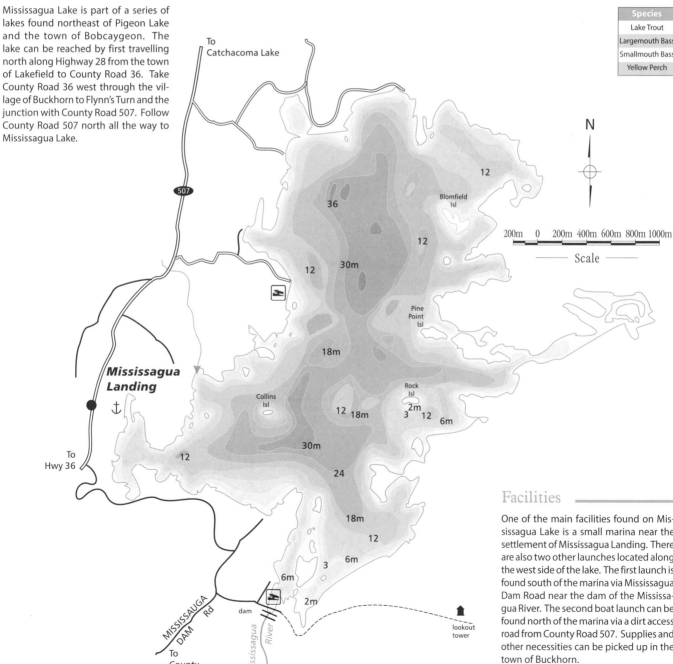

Facilities

One of the main facilities found on Mississagua Lake is a small marina near the settlement of Mississagua Landing. There are also two other launches located along the west side of the lake. The first launch is found south of the marina via Mississagua Dam Road near the dam of the Mississagua River. The second boat launch can be found north of the marina via a dirt access road from County Road 507. Supplies and other necessities can be picked up in the town of Buckhorn.

Zone 18

Location: Carleton Place
Elevation: 134 m (441 ft)
Surface Area: 2,348 ha (5,800 ac)
Maximum Depth: 9.1 m (30 ft)
Mean Depth: 2.7 m (9 ft)
Way Point: 45° 05′ 00″ N, 76° 10′ 00″ W

Mississippi Lake

Area Indicator

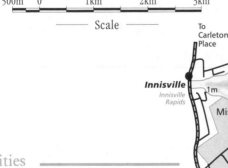

Directions

This large lake lies to the south of Carleton Place, west of Ottawa. The main access to the lake is via Highway 7, as the highway travels right by the southern and northern ends of the lake. Highway 7 can be accessed from Ottawa via Highway 417.

The name 'Mississippi' is another native derivation that means 'Great River'. Ontario's Mississippi River is not as grand as its American counterpart, although the river is quite large by southern Ontario standards.

Species	
Black Crappie	Smallmouth Bass
Burbot	Walleye
Largemouth Bass	Yellow Perch
Northern Pike	Other

Fishing

Anglers to Mississippi Lake can enjoy fishing for smallmouth bass, largemouth bass, northern pike and walleye. Bass fishing is quite popular in the region, although fishing for walleye remains the preferred option for local anglers.

An overall good hot spot for all species is the inlets of the Mississippi River, especially just after the season opens. Other areas include the weedy shore structure and around any of the small islands found around the lake. Bass like to hide around this sort of natural structure. You can also pick up the odd northern pike in the weedy bays. Working a weedless spinner type lure or jig in the weeds can be very effective for pike and largemouth bass at dusk. Fly anglers should try a popper type fly or a weedless Muddler Minnow.

Walleye anglers will find this species prefers to hang around shoal areas. There are a number of shoals found around the lake that can be the hot spot for this roaming predator. A white or yellow jig cast towards shoals or simply jigged in these areas can be good. Another effective lure is a worm harness. Trolling a worm harness through these shoals can also work wonders at times.

In order to help walleye stocks, a spring fishing sanctuary has been imposed on river areas next to Mississippi Lake. Check your regulations for details before you attempt to fish in this large water body.

Facilities

Carleton Place is a small city offering all amenities including hotels, restaurants and numerous retailers. There is a public boat launch to Mississippi Lake found at the municipal park in Carleton Place. Along the east and southeast shore of the lake, there are full service marinas for visitors to use. Alternatively, access and overnight facilities are also available at a number of the local tent and trailer parks or commercial tourist lodges around the lake. For something a little different, why not visit the **Mississippi Lake National Wildlife Area**. It is found along the western shore and open for day-use picnicking and wildlife viewing.

Mitchell Lake

Location: 13 km (8 mi) southwest of Coboconk
Elevation: 159 m (522 ft)
Surface Area: 400 ha (988 ac)
Maximum Depth: 3 m (9.8 ft)
Mean Depth: 0.8 m (2.6 ft)
Way Point: 44° 34' 00" Lat - N, 78° 57' 00" Long - W

17 Zone

Fishing

As a part of the Trent Severn Waterway, Mitchell Lake can be a busy spot at times, especially during the summer. Fishing in the lake is best for smallmouth and largemouth bass, as the shallow weedy lake makes for ideal bass habitat. Since the lake receives heavy boating traffic, the bass can be finicky at times. Despite the traffic, during overcast periods and at dusk, top water lures and flies can create a lot of action. Another proven method of enticing strikes from spooky bass on Mitchell Lake is to work a jig slowly off the bottom. Lift the jig in an up and down fashion to entice covering bass to take a look. It often results in some nice catches.

The two most sought after fish species on Mitchell Lake are walleye and muskellunge. Fishing for both species can be slow at times but there are productive periods for both species. Walleye average about 1 kg (2 lbs) in size, while muskellunge are generally smaller than in the neighbouring Kawartha Lakes of the Trent Severn. Be sure to check your regulations before heading out on this lake.

Facilities

There is a public boat launch available just off County Road 48 onto the south end of the lake. Further to the west, a smaller canoe or car top access can also be found off County Road 48. The other amenities that are offered at Mitchell Lake are two small picnic areas accessible off the main road. For any supplies, Kirkfield has a few retail operations that offer all the basic necessities. For overnight accommodation, **Balsam Lake Provincial Park** is located just minutes away to the east. The park is a full service park complete with showers and flush toilets. For campsite reservations call (888) ONT-PARK.

Directions

This Trent Severn Waterway lake can be found by taking Highway 12 north to County Road 48 and heading east. County Road 48 travels literally right across Mitchell Lake just east of the town of Kirkfield. An alternate route to the lake would be to follow Highway 35 north to the town of Coboconk, then travelling southwest along County Road 48.

Other Options

The two closest fishing alternatives are **Canal Lake** to the west and **Balsam Lake** to the east. Both Lakes are accessible not far from County Road 48 and are inhabited by bass, walleye and muskellunge and make for interesting fishing at times. Since Canal and Balsam Lakes are the larger cousins of Mitchell Lake, they make good nearby alternatives, especially if Mitchell Lake is crowded with boat traffic.

Area Indicator

Species	
Largemouth Bass	Walleye
Muskellunge	Yellow Perch
Smallmouth Bass	Other

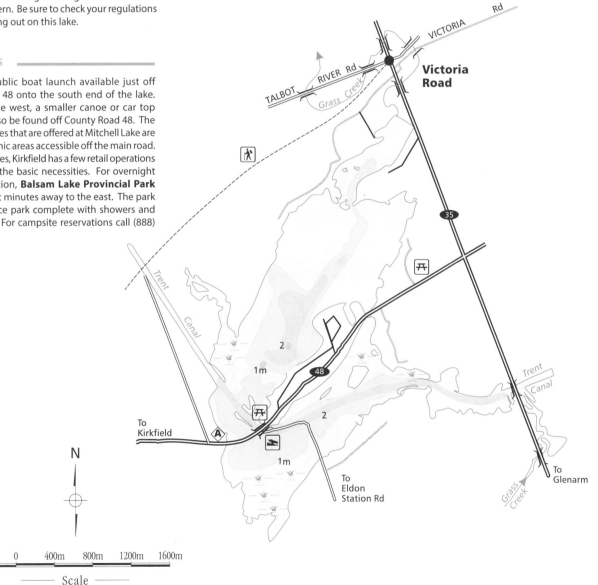

Zone 18

Location: 3 km (2 mi) south of Madoc
Elevation: 155 m (508 ft)
Surface Area: 827 ha (2,043 ac)
Maximum Depth: 11 m (36 ft)
Mean Depth: 4.4 m (14.4 ft)
Way Point: 44° 30' 00" Lat - N, 77° 27' 00" Lon - W

Moira Lake

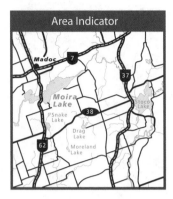

Area Indicator

Fishing

Originally named Hog Lake by settlers, the lake was later renamed after the Earl of Moira, Marquis of Hastings. The lake is one of many popular cottage destination lakes in the region and despite continued fishing pressure, the lake offers a quality fishery. This is due mainly to the fact that the lake sits in a low lying region rich in nutrients.

Fishing in the lake can be good at times for both smallmouth and largemouth bass. Bass average about 0.5-1 kg (1-2 lbs) and can be found much bigger on occasion. Look for bass off either Green Island or Stony Island. The far west side of the lake can also be surprisingly productive at times.

Other sport fish that can be found in the lake include walleye, northern pike and muskellunge. Fishing for walleye and pike can also be good at times, especially during dusk periods. Both predators tend to cruise along the drop-off found around the lake in search of an easy meal. These drop-off areas are often accompanied by good weed growth, which can enhance walleye and pike action. The population of muskellunge may be in slow decline due to competition with pike.

Directions

Located just south of the town of Madoc, Moira Lake is the main geographical feature of the area. Madoc can be reached by travelling east from Peterborough via Highway 7 or by travelling north via Highway 62 from Highway 401 at Belleville. Highway 62 crosses the western portion of Moira Lake. There are also a number of access roads that branch from the highway to the lake. A boat launch can be found off the east side of Highway 62.

Facilities

Along with the boat launch, you can find three separate tent and trailer parks available for overnight camping on the northern shore. For supplies and other items, the town of Madoc has plenty to offer visitors, including restaurants and fast food. For roofed accommodation, various motels can be found in the area off Highway 7 or Highway 62.

Other Options

If you travel north along Highway 62 past Highway 7, you will eventually reach more hilly terrain coupled with numerous lakes for fishing. A few of the more popular lakes found north of Highway 7 are **Jordan Lake, Glanmire Lake** and **Steenburg Lake.** All three lakes offer fishing opportunities for largemouth and smallmouth bass.

Species	
Largemouth Bass	Smallmouth Bass
Muskellunge	Walleye
Northern Pike	Yellow Perch

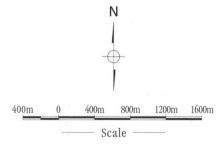

N

400m	0	400m	800m	1200m	1600m

Scale

Mosque Lake

Location: 7 km (4.5 mi) west of Ompah
Elevation: 314 m (1,030 ft)
Surface Area: 104 ha (340 ac)
Maximum Depth: 34.4 m (113 ft)
Mean Depth: 7 m (23.1 ft)
Way Point: 45° 01′00″ N, 76° 55′00″ W

Fishing

Mosque Lake is a rare Eastern Ontario lake that has only cold water species. Rainbow trout are stocked in the lake annually and there is also a natural population of lake trout.

Rainbow provide for fair fishing at times, especially in the spring. This prized sportfish can be caught by using small spoons or spinners, however, fly fishing can be even better. Fly anglers should try streamer type patterns such as a leech or dragonfly nymph to find those big aggressive rainbows. Fishing success for the lake trout is relatively slow. It is recommended to try in the spring as soon as the season opens by trolling small spoons. The lake trout in Mosque Lake are relatively small compared to other lakes in the area.

Mosque Lake is part of a winter/spring fishing sanctuary period in order to help ailing lake trout stocks. Please check you regulations for specific dates before fishing.

Facilities

A rough public boat launch along with a parking area is available along the southern shore of Mosque Lake. Permits are required to use the access road and to park or camp at the lake. Permits can be picked up in the village of Plevna to the west or at the general store in Snow Road Station to the southeast. There are a few user maintained campsites around the lake.

Directions

Mosque Lake is located in the Madawaska Highlands, just west of the small village of Ompah. The lake is found by following Highway 509 north from Highway 7 at Sharbot Lake. Continue on the small highway north past the Mississippi River and the village of Donaldson. The highway will soon veer west towards the village of Ompah. Just west of Ompah, look for the Mosque Lake Road off the north side of the highway. Follow Mosque Lake Road north to the southern shore of the lake. Mosque Lake Road can be rough in sections and a high clearance vehicle is recommended.

Other Options

To the west of Mosque Lake, **Little Mosque Lake** can be reached via a rough portage from along the western shore of Mosque Lake. Little Mosque Lake is stocked every few years with brook trout, which provide for fair to good fishing in the winter or in the early spring..

Area Indicator

Species
Lake Trout
Rainbow Trout

Mosque Lake		
Fish Stocking Data		
Year	Species	Number
2013	Rainbow Trout	7,500
2012	Rainbow Trout	7,500
2011	Rainbow Trout	7,500

N

```
100m    0   100m 200m 300m 400m 500m
```
—— Scale ——

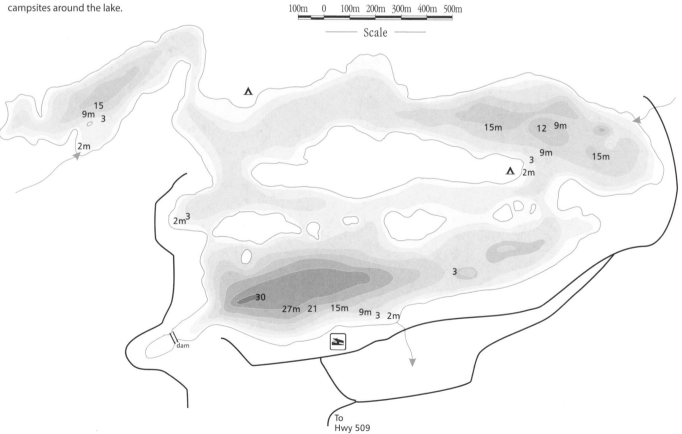

© Backroad Mapbooks

Zone **18**

Location: 18 km (11mi) south of Westport
Elevation: 333 m (1,093 ft)
Surface Area: 205 ha (507 ac)
Maximum Depth: 3 m (10 ft)
Mean Depth: 1.8 m (6 ft)
Way Point: 44° 36′ 00″ N, 76° 22′ 00″ W

Mosquito Lake

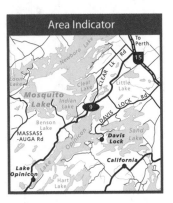

Area Indicator

Species

Largemouth Bass

Northern Pike

Smallmouth Bass

Fishing

Mosquito Lake is a part of the Rideau Canal system and as a result receives plenty of angling pressure throughout the season. However, the lake continues to produce well, especially for bass. Both smallmouth and largemouth bass are resident in the lake and fishing can be fair for bass up to 1.5 kg (3.5 lbs) in size. Try spinner baits, jigs or top water flies and lures for both species. Look for weed lines and try casting lures along these areas to find ambush ready bass. When bass in Mosquito Lake are lethargic and fishing is slow, try working a weedless type fly or lure deep amid the weed structure. A slower presentation can often entice strikes from lazy bass.

The shallow bays of Mosquito Lake also provide prime habitat for northern pike. Pike usually roam these bays during dusk, although they can be found periodically during the day. Most bass type lures will work well for northern pike.

Directions

Mosquito Lake is part of the Rideau Canal Waterway and lies between Benson Lake to the south and Newboro Lake to the north. The easiest way to access Mosquito Lake is by boat from one of the neighbouring lakes.

To find the lake by vehicle, travel north from Kingston or south from Westport along the Perth Road (County Road 10). At the hamlet of Bedford Mills, take the Massassauga Road east. Off the Massassauga Road, a few access roads lead to the western shore of the lake.

Facilities

In addition to a private lodge for visitors to enjoy, there are several cottages along the shore of Mosquito Lake. Although there is no public access, boat launching facilities are available at the lodge for a fee. For supplies and other amenities, the town of Westport to the north has plenty to offer, including restaurants and retailers.

Other Options

Benson Lake is regarded by many as part of Mosquito Lake, although officially the lakes are two distinct water bodies. Fishing in Benson Lake is quite similar to Mosquito Lake as the lake is home to resident smallmouth bass, largemouth bass and northern pike. Look for all species along weed lines and near any other structured areas.

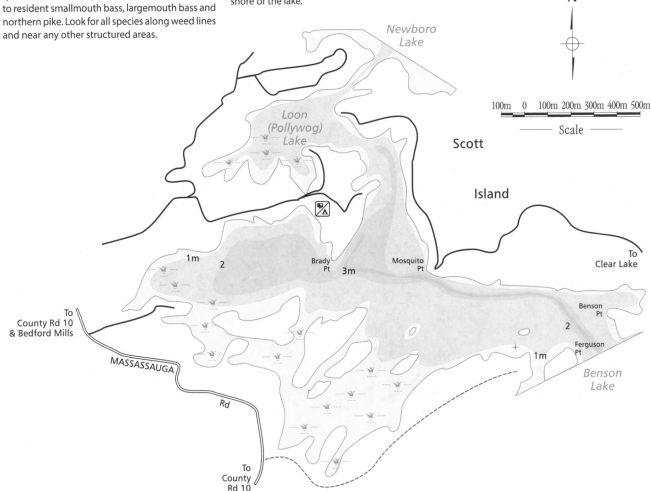

Mud Turtle Lake

Location: 22 km (13.5 mi) north of Havelock
Elevation: 249 m (817 ft)
Maximum Depth: 8 m (26.2 ft)
Mean Depth: 4.2 m (13.7 ft)
Way Point: 44° 38′ 00″ Lat - N, 77° 48′ 00″ Lon - W

18 Zone

Fishing

Mud Turtle Lake is part of the Crowe River system and is a remote access lake. The lake is surrounded by mainly Crown Land and is a very scenic spot. Smallmouth and largemouth bass provide the bulk of the angling action, as fishing can be quite productive at times for decent sized bass. Look for smallmouth over any of the many underwater rock piles. Often a jig worked along the underwater structure will produce some fantastic fighting smallmouth. The numerous weedy bays around the lake make great habitat for largemouth bass. Top water flies and lures can be a blast on Mud Turtle Lake for largemouth.

Smaller populations of walleye and muskellunge also inhabit the lake, although fishing is generally slow to fair. Walleye and musky tend to congregate near the inflow of the Crowe River, especially in spring just after the season opens. There are also minimum length limits in place for the possession of muskellunge.

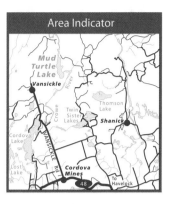
Area Indicator

Species	
Largemouth Bass	Walleye
Muskellunge	Yellow Perch
Smallmouth Bass	Other

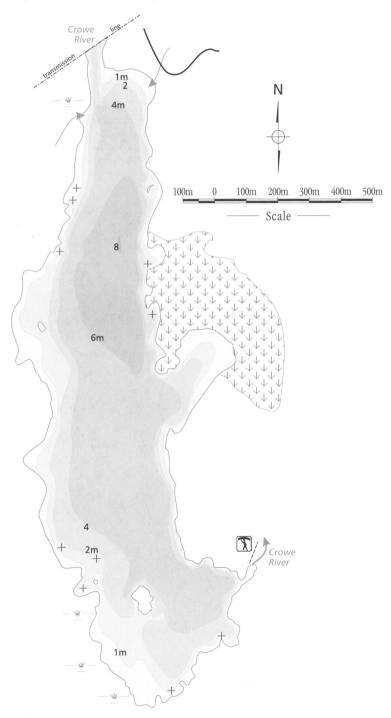

N

Scale
100m   0   100m   200m   300m   400m   500m

Directions

This remote lake is best accessed via canoe down the Crowe River from Whetstone Lake to the north. There is an access point to the canoe route at the end of Tangamong Road, which is found not far off County Road 46 south of Lasswade. Alternatively, the lake can be reached via rough logging roads to its northeastern shore. A good map such as the Backroad Mapbook for Eastern Ontario is essential when finding such hidden lakes.

To access the logging roads, follow Highway 7 to Marmora and head north along County Road 33. Take County Road 33 to Long Swamp Road and continue north. Long Swamp Road will eventually turn into Twin Sisters Road and then Thompson Lake Road. The key is to continue travelling north. As the road gets rougher, the navigation will get even more difficult. Essentially, after you pass Thompson Lake (which is not noticeable from the road) you have to head west. There are a few different road combinations that can get you to the lake. There used to be an old access road to the southern shore of the lake, although there are rumours that parts of the road are washed out.

Facilities

There are no facilities at Mud Turtle Lake but rustic Crown Land camping can certainly be a pleasure. If you do intend to camp, please ensure you leave your campsite clean of any litter when you leave.

Other Options

The area around Mud Turtle Lake is the beginning of a vast area of wetlands. If the fishing is slow on Mud Turtle Lake a very good alternative is **Oak Lake** to the southwest. Oak Lake is quite easy to access as the lake can be reached via County Road 46. The lake offers fishing for smallmouth bass, largemouth bass and the odd muskellunge.

Location: Newboro
Elevation: 122 m (400 ft)
Surface Area: 1,846 ha (4,561 ac)
Maximum Depth: 23.8 m (78 ft)
Mean Depth: 3.2 m (10.4 ft)
Way Point: 44° 38' 00" N, 76° 20' 00" W

Newboro Lake

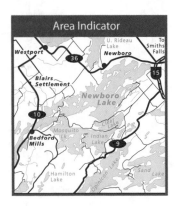

Area Indicator

Species	
Black Crappie	Smallmouth Bass
Largemouth Bass	Walleye
Northern Pike	Yellow Perch

Directions

This Rideau Canal lake is the scenic backdrop for the town of Newboro, which lies along the northern shore. The main access to the lake is found in town. To reach the town, follow Highway 15 to the junction with County Road 42 at the hamlet of Crosby. It is a short trek west along County Road 42 to Newboro.

Other Options

Clear Lake and **Mosquito Lake** are located south of Newboro Lake and can be reached via the Rideau Canal Waterway. The main sportfish found in both lakes are smallmouth bass, largemouth bass and northern pike. Walleye are known to inhabit Clear Lake but are rather scarce in Mosquito Lake. Similar to Newboro Lake, look for weed structure in these lakes to find success for bass and northern pike.

Fishing

Newboro Lake is a popular fishing lake due mainly to being part of the Rideau Canal system. The lake continues to provide decent fishing results with largemouth bass being the dominant species. Smallmouth bass, northern pike and the elusive walleye are also found in the lake.

Bass in the lake are not usually big, but they can be found in good numbers in areas. Look for largemouth around the shallower areas of the lake where weed and other structure can be found. Try working a jig or tube bait off the bottom for success. Another good method is working a crayfish fly or lure imitation near the bottom. This method can be dynamite at times.

Fishing for northern pike is often better than for walleye but is still considered to be fair to slow at times. Pike can be found frequenting the shallower portions of the lake, primarily in the evening. Walleye can also be found in shallower waters on occasion but they usually are found in the 3 m (10 ft) depth range along side weed structures. Jigging and trolling a worm harness in these areas can create a frenzy of action.

Before heading out on Newboro Lake, be sure to check your regulations. There are two sanctuary areas to be aware of.

Facilities

The town and lake of Newboro is one of the many focal points along the Rideau Canal Waterway. All amenities such as resorts, motels and retailers are available in and around town. A public boat launch is also accessible from town. Look for the familiar boat launching signs off County Road 42. Other access facilities are offered at a number of the local lodges or tent and trailer parks located on the lake.

(Map of Newboro Lake with depth markings, islands and bays including Bass Bay, The Bog, Grahams Isl, Wright Isl, Mackay Isl, Long Isl, Lucky Bay, Rosal Isl, Pine Isl, Hungry Bay, Stedmans Island, Topler Isl, McCaskill Isl, Preston Isl, Pritchards Isl, Channel Isl, Sheep Isl, Foley Isl, Bob's Isl, Gibsons Pt, Scott, Lewis Bay, Goat Isl, Lower Bay, Stouts Upper Bay, Iron Mine Bay. Roads to Portland, Crosby, Seeleys Bay, Westport, County Rd 36, County Rd 10, Mosquito Lake, Clear Lake, Hutchings Rd, Crosby Rd)

Scale: 400m 0 400m 800m 1200m 1600m

Nogies Creek

Location: 6 km (3.7 mi) north of Bobcaygeon
Stream Length: 12.5 km (7.7 mi)
Geographic: 44° 35' 16" N, 78° 29' 35" W

15 Zone

Fishing

Nogies Creek is a small stretch of water that flows into Pigeon Lake just outside of the village of Bobcaygeon. This local fishing spot has been one of those secret hot spots for many years and remains a great destination for travelling anglers. The creek is home to panfish, bass and also a population of walleye and muskellunge. Fishing for bass and muskie is best in the spring and fall periods, while smallmouth and largemouth bass along with panfish can be found in the creek year round.

One of the more popular fishing locations is just past the County Road 36 creek crossing, there is a little township park access point and parking area where you can park and fish the creek from shore. If you have a small boat or canoe, it is recommended to launch on the north side of the road and paddle upstream and then proceed to float your way back down to your vehicle. The upper reaches of the creek see way less fishing pressure and the action on some days can be quite good.

A hot lure for both walleye and muskellunge on this system is a perch or similar coloured Rapala. The bigger fish usually feed on the smaller baitfish and will usually strike at a well presented minnow.

One word of caution on this system is that there is a 'No Fishing' sanctuary along the upper reaches. Be aware not to cross into that zone, it is regularly monitored by locals and the Ministry of Natural Resources.

Facilities

The town of Bobcaygeon is the closest option for facilities in this area. The town is home to a small bait and tackle shop, as well as all your basic need amenities such as a grocery store and coffee shop. For accommodations in the area, it is recommended to search the internet for local cottage rentals near Bobcaygeon or on Pigeon Lake nearby.

Other Options

Nogies Creek is a small inflow into the Pigeon River and is a fun destination, although if you get tired or have slow results, there are plenty of immediate nearby opportunities in the area. Most notably, **Pigeon Lake**, as part of the Kawartha Lakes chain is within minutes of Nogies Creek with plenty of public boat access as well. Fishing in Pigeon Lake can be good at times for both bass species and fair to good for walleye and muskellunge.

Species	
Black Crappie	Smallmouth Bass
Largemouth Bass	Walleye
Muskellunge	

Directions

To find this lesser known fishing hot spot, requires working your way to Bobcaygeon. From Toronto, head east along Highway 401 to Highway 115/35, this leads northeast towards Peterborough. Look for the Highway 35 junction that continues north towards Lindsay. At the Highway 7 junction, turn east toward Peterborough and then shortly after, north on Verulam Road or County Road 36 leading to Bobcaygeon. Follow this windy road north all the way through the village of Bobcaygeon and eventually to the crossing of Nogies Creek and the junction of Bass Lake Road.

There is one main access point, which is the public access area off the south side of County Road 36, where parking is offered. There is also an access point on Bass Lake to the north; however, you will need to portage around a small dam and pass through the fishing sanctuary before fishing.

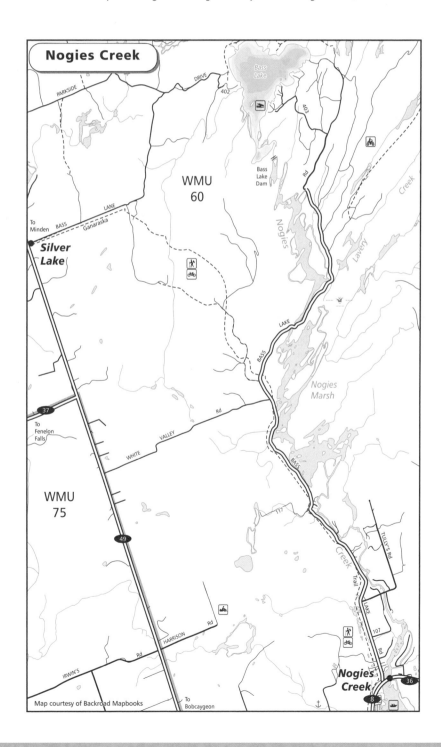

Zone 15

Location: 13 km (8 mi) north of Catchacoma
Elevation: 324 m (1,063 ft)
Maximum Depth: 6 m (19.7 ft)
Mean Depth: 3 m (9.8 ft)
Way Point: 44° 38' 00" Lat - N, 77° 48' 00" Lon - W

Nogies Lake

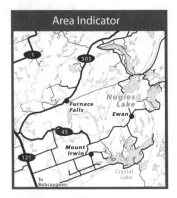

Area Indicator

Species
Largemouth Bass
Smallmouth Bass
Yellow Perch

Fishing

Largemouth and smallmouth bass can be found in Nogies Lake. The shallow nature of the lake makes for ideal bass habitat. Look for weed growth closer to the shoreline to find largemouth bass. There are also numerous underwater rock piles around the lake that are great attractants for smallmouth bass. By locating these rock piles, you are sure to increase your angling success. For slower days, working a jig or other grub type lure off the bottom near structure can be effective. A slower presentation may be needed when bass are being picky.

Panfish, such as yellow perch, can also be found in the shallow lake. These aggressive fish can often be caught using a bobber and bait.

Directions

Nogies Lake is the headwater for Nogies Creek, which runs south out of the lake through a series of small lakes eventually terminating at Pigeon Lake. From the town of Bobcaygeon, follow County Road 49 north to the 13th Concession Road (Galaway Road). Head east along the concession road until it turns into the South Salmon lake Road. Follow South Salmon Lake Road east to Ireland Road. Turn north along Ireland Road and look for the rough access road to Nogies Lake off the west side. A 4wd vehicle may be required to access the lake.

Facilities

There is a rough car top access area along the east side of Nogies Lake that can be reached via a rough 4wd road. Basic supplies and accommodations can be found in the town of Bobcaygeon to the south.

Other Options

Nogies Lake sits in the middle of a cluster of lakes. **Salmon Lake** lies to the east while **White Lake** and **Fortescue Lake** can be found to the north and northeast respectively. All three lakes are accessible via established cottage roads. Bass can be found in all three lakes, while Salmon Lake and Fortescue Lake also host lake trout populations. The odd muskellunge can also be found in Fortescue Lake and White Lake.

N

100m 0 100m 200m 300m

— Scale —

To
Salmon Lake
& Ireland Rd

Nogies Creek

Norcan Lake

Location: 18 km (11 mi) south of Calabogie
Surface Area: 729 ha (1,800 ac)
Maximum Depth: 4.5 m (15 ft)
Mean Depth: 3 m (9.6 ft)
Way Point: 45° 10' 00" N, 76° 52' 00" W

Fishing

This long, narrow lake is part of the Madawaska River system and offers good fishing for smallmouth bass and largemouth bass to 1.5 kg (3.5 lbs) in size. The shallow nature of the lake creates ample habitat for bass and anglers will find plenty of weed area to focus on. Try using weedless type lures such as a spinner bait or tube jig to work through the heavy weed areas to find those bigger bass.

The two other popular sportfish found in Norcan Lake are northern pike and walleye. Fishing can be fair for average sized pike and walleye. Walleye tend to frequent the northern section of the lake closer to the Madawaska River system, while pike can be found literally anywhere in the lake. For walleye, trolling a worm harness along weed areas can be quite effective. Pike can be coaxed into striking at most bass presentations but they prefer to chase down larger lures and flies like a spoon or streamer pattern. For ice fishing, try jigging a white jig or small spoon through the ice for both walleye and northern pike.

Directions

Set amid the scenic hills of the Madawaska Highlands, Norcan Lake is a fantastic destination for a summer fishing adventure. To find the lake from the south, begin by following Highway 7 to the town of Perth. Just west of the main retail strip in Perth, you will find the junction with Highway 511. Travel north along Highway 511 all the way to the village of Calabogie and Calabogie Lake. At Calabogie, Highway 511 meets Highway 508. Head west along Highway 508 (Calabogie Road) and look for the Hydro Dam Road off the south side of the highway. Take the Hydro Dam Road south to the Greens Landing Road. The Greens Landing Road branches off the Hydro Dam Road down to the northern shore of Norcan Lake.

From the north, Highway 508 can be found off Highway 17 east of Renfrew.

Area Indicator

Species
Largemouth Bass
Northern Pike
Smallmouth Bass
Walleye

Facilities

Norcan Lake is a fairly remote lake that is not overdeveloped with cottages and cabins. Visitors will find a few cottages along the northern portion of the lake while the southern end is made up of mainly Crown Land. The allure of Crown Land camping has made Norcan Lake a popular place among backcountry explorers. There are several user maintained campsites on the lake that offer at most a fire pit and privy. Please help maintain the scenic nature of this area and pack out any garbage you may come across.

The main access area to the lake is from the Hydro Dam access found along the northern shore. Small boats and canoes can be launched from roadside. For accommodations and basic supplies, the village of Calabogie is home to a resort, two restaurants and two small general stores. For more amenities, the towns of Renfrew to the north or Perth to the south are each within an hours drive from the lake.

Other Options

Black Donald Lake is located to the northwest of Norcan Lake and can be reached by heading west from **Calabogie Lake** along the Calabogie Road. Black Donald Lake is also known as Centennial Lake and offers fishing opportunities for smallmouth bass, largemouth bass, northern pike and walleye. Similar to Norcan Lake, popular Crown Land campsites are found around the lake.

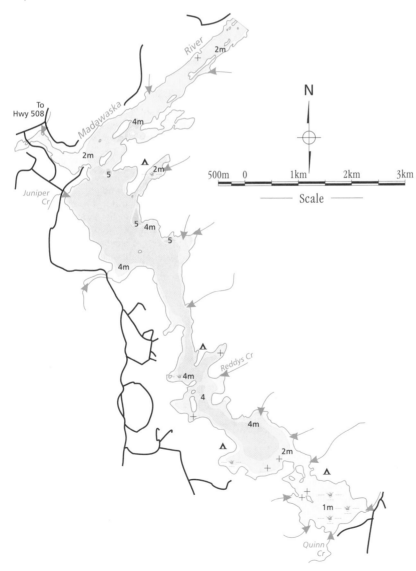

Area Indicator

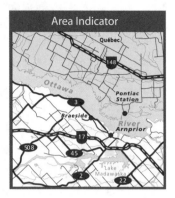

Fishing

Anglers looking for smallmouth bass in this section of the river should attempt to locate one of the many 1-3 m (3-10 ft) shoal humps found around this section. These shoals are magnets for smallmouth and often over a dozen bronze backs will be hanging around one of these humps. Spinners, or on slow days, a tube jig will both work well for smallmouth.

Anglers looking for walleye should jig along the deeper shoal areas in the 5 m (12 ft) range. Also, try to locate any currents along the river near these shoals. Walleye, similar to most species, are attracted to currents and will cruise these areas in search of food. The area just east of Sand Point can be a decent holding area for walleye and other big predators.

For northern pike, Baie Dirty Gut and near Knox Landing are two successful areas. Look for weed structure in these areas for ambush ready northerns.

Fish Species

Smallmouth bass are found all over the river and once you locate a good holding area fishing can be quite good at times.

Northern pike are one of the largest predators in the river and fishing is fair to good at times for pike that can be found exceeding 6kg (13lbs). Look in the slower back bays for cruising northerns.

Walleye fishing in the Ottawa River is generally fair to good for walleye that average 0.5-1.5 kg (1-3.5 lbs). Some walleye are caught annually in the 4 kg (9 lb) range. The prized sportfish travel in loose schools; therefore, still jigging is an effective angling method. Once you find one walleye, you should be able to catch a number of them before they move on.

Muskellunge inhabit the river in several areas and can provide fabulous action for the persistent angler. Most musky are caught incidentally by anglers fishing for other species, although the true muskellunge anglers regard the river as one of the best areas in Southern Ontario.

Several other exciting fish species inhabit the river, including sturgeon, channel catfish and whitefish. Fishing for sturgeon is always slow; however, schools of whitefish can provide nonstop action.

Note: Some areas of the river contain very strong currents and whitewater. It is recommended to consult local outfitters before you venture out on the river. Be sure to check the regulations before fishing.

Directions

The main access area for this portion of the Ottawa River is from the town of Arnprior. Arnprior is located west of Ottawa and can be reached by following Highway 17 to Daniel Street in Arnprior. Daniel Street leads right to the downtown of Arnprior. Look for signs to the local boat launch in the town centre.

Species		
Carp	Muskellunge	Smallmouth Bass
Catfish	Northern Pike	Sturgeon
Gar	Panfish	Walleye
Largemouth Bass	Sauger	Whitefish

Facilities

A small marina complete with a boat launch is available in Arnprior; however, there are also marinas with launches available in Sand Point to the west and Baie Norway in Quebec. The town of Arnprior has plenty to offer visitors, including motels, restaurants and retailers.

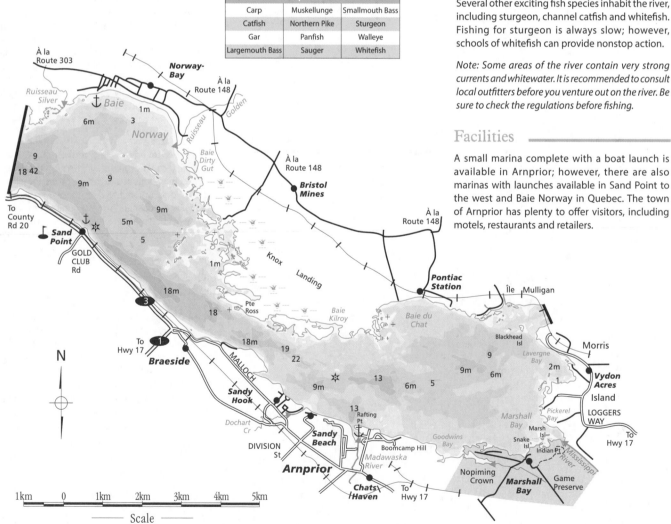

Ottawa River- Constance Bay

Location: 6 km (3.7 mi) north of Kanata
Stream Length: 14 km (8.7 mi)
Geographic: 45° 29′ 12″ N, 76° 04′ 32″ W

18 **Zone**

Fishing

There is plenty of shoreline weed structure along this part of the Ottawa River, which provides hiding areas for bass and northern pike. Many anglers around Constance Bay simply roam around the shallows in search of bass and nice sized pike. Casting weedless type lures like spinner baits and tube jigs can be quite effective for both bass and northern pike. One good hot spot is the 1 m (3 ft) shoal located just north of Buckham's Point. The shoal attracts both bass and pike and can be quite active in the evening.

For walleye, try the 6 m (20 ft) shoal hump found east of Stoney Point. This area is known for cruising walleye and jigging just off the bottom along this shoal can produce nice sized walleye.

Directions

Northwest of Ottawa and Nepean, you can find Constance Bay by following Highway 417 to Exit 138 at Kanata. From the exit, travel northwest along the March Road (County Road 49). Continue northwest along March Road to Dunrobin Road (County Road 9). Follow Dunrobin Road northwest to Constance Bay Road at the town of Constance Bay, which lies along the western shore of the Ottawa River.

Facilities

The town of Constance Bay has plenty to offer visitors, including accommodations and retailers. A boat launch is also located along the eastern shore of Buckham's Bay in town. An alternate boat access can be found near Baskin's Beach, which is accessible near the end of Baskin Beach Road. Baskin Beach Road can be picked up off the east side of Dunrobin Road south of Constance Bay.

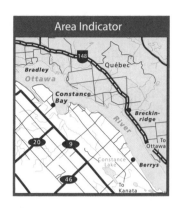

Species		
Carp	Muskellunge	Smallmouth Bass
Catfish	Northern Pike	Sturgeon
Gar	Panfish	Walleye
Largemouth Bass	Sauger	Whitefish

Other Options

Constance Lake is located southeast of Constance Bay and offers consistent fishing for northern pike. Pike are the most dominant sportfish found in the lake, although decent catches of smallmouth bass and largemouth bass can be had. A small number of walleye still exist in the lake, although fishing success can be quite slow at times.

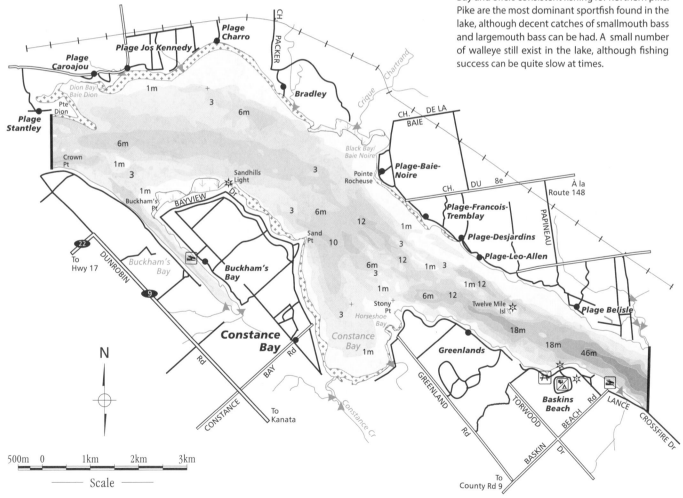

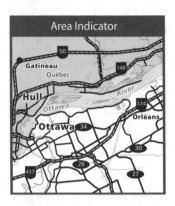

Area Indicator

Species		
Brown Trout	Largemouth Bass	Sauger
Carp	Muskellunge	Smallmouth Bass
Catfish	Northern Pike	Sturgeon
Gar	Panfish	Walleye

Directions

There are several access points to the downtown portion of the Ottawa River. While our map does provide some info, it is recommended to visit www.mnr.gov.on.ca for the specific access points along the river and for especially shore fishing opportunities. There are areas where you can launch a small boat or canoe; however, be sure to research the area you head out to as strong currents are present in many areas and can be dangerous.

Fishing

Even amid the urban sprawl of the city of Ottawa, the Ottawa River is a recreational paradise and is home to a wide variety of sportfish. This portion of the river offers angling opportunities for walleye, smallmouth and largemouth bass, panfish, northern pike and muskellunge. A population of brown trout can also be found in this region.

Smallmouth and largemouth bass are the most popular and regularly caught sportfish along this portion of the river. Try around any drop offs or in or along weed beds. Spinnerbaits and weedless presentations are a good way to locate both species and if the action is slow or tails off, try slowing down your presentations with some jigs or tube jigs. Topwater baits like poppers can be a ton of fun on calmer overcast days.

Like almost all Ontario waterbodies, walleye are perhaps the most sought after fish here. Your best bet for walleye is to locate areas along drop offs or where the current is not slow, but not too strong either. If you can find a decent location, anchor and start jigging with minnows or even just a jig and worm. Walleye fishing has improved over the years in this section, although is still rather slow.

Brown trout were originally introduced into the Ottawa River over twenty years ago. Subsequent additional introductions have had some success and a fly-fishing following the Ottawa browns has developed. The main hotspots for brown trout are in the rapids at Britannia and around the Champlain Bridge. Popular flies are big, olive-coloured woolly buggers or similar streamers.

Other fish species you will find in this massive river include muskellunge, northern pike, sauger (smaller cousin of the walleye), catfish, gar, carp and panfish (including crappie). Panfish are easily found in the shallows throughout almost all areas of this portion of the Ottawa.

Facilities

Travellers to Ottawa have plenty of accommodations and facilities at their fingertips. Countless hotels, motels and shops and restaurants are all at your fingertips. For additional Ottawa fishing info, it is recommended to visit green drake outfitters or any of the local retailers

Other Options

If the Ottawa River is slow, the nearby Rideau River is a close alternative. It flows through the city past several parks where access can be easily obtained. The river is home to all the same species as the Ottawa, with panfish and both bass species being the main sportfish found.

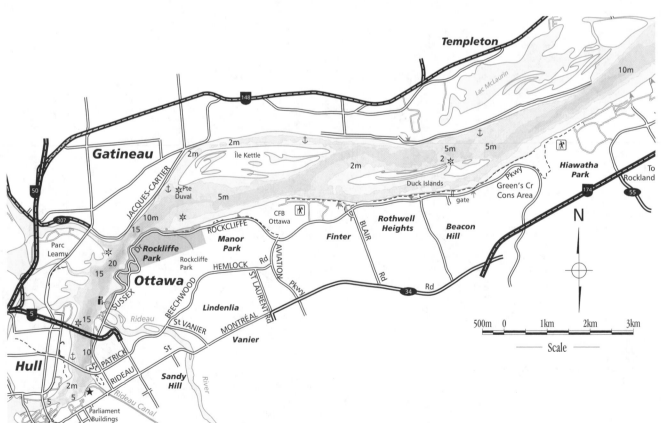

Ottawa River- Petrie Islands

Fishing

Centuries ago, the Ottawa River was perhaps the most important transportation route in all of Canada. The river has played an instrumental role in shaping the development of our country. Today the Ottawa River is a recreational paradise and is home to a wide variety of sportfish. This portion of the river offers angling opportunities for walleye, smallmouth and largemouth bass, northern pike and muskellunge to name a few.

Smallmouth bass are quite prolific throughout the river. Try along any drop offs, points or weed lines. If you are going out for a half day and just looking for some action, smallmouth are your best bet for quantity and a good scrap. Topwater baits like buzzbaits and popper type presentations can be a ton of fun on calmer overcast days, but if the topwater lures are slow, work the deeper areas with jigs or tube plastics.

Largemouth bass are also found in many of the shallower bays and areas of this portion of Ottawa River. Try around any islands or in or along weed beds. Spinnerbaits and weedless presentations are a good way to locate largemouth. If the action is slow or tails off, try slowing down your presentations with some jigs or tube jigs. Largemouth up to 2.5 kg (6 lbs) are not uncommon in the Ottawa.

It is said that the next world record muskellunge is going to be caught in the Georgian Bay, St. Lawrence River or the Ottawa River. Over the past decade or so, new regulations on muskie have greatly increased their population. The population is healthy and muskie up to 13 kg (30 lbs) are possible. Troll weed lines with larger spoons, body baits or bucktail type presentations for the chance at a potential record breaking muskie.

Northern pike are sometimes difficult to avoid in the Ottawa River. Some areas just seem full of small little hammer handles, but there are plenty of 2-4 kg (5-10 lb) pike as well. The big ones go deep in the summer but can be found in the spring and fall right in the calmer bays amid the weeds in search of food.

Like almost all Ontario waterbodies, walleye are perhaps the most sought after fish on this stretch of the river. Your best bet for walleye is to locate areas along drop offs or where the current is decent. If you can find a decent location, anchor and start jigging with minnows or even just a jig and worm.

Other fish species you will find in this massive river include sauger (the smaller cousin of the walleye), catfish, gar, carp and panfish (including crappie). All provide good fishing opportunities for anglers. The gar (sometimes referred to as gar pike) are notoriously difficult to catch as they have a long beak for a mouth that is almost entirely made up of hard bone.

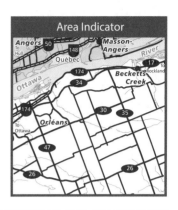

Area Indicator

Species		
Carp	Muskellunge	Smallmouth Bass
Catfish	Northern Pike	Sturgeon
Gar	Panfish	Walleye
Largemouth Bass	Sauger	Whitefish

Directions

There are several access points to this portion of the Ottawa River. The main access area is the boat launch just outside of Cumberland off County Road 174. Baie Clement is just north from the launch across the river and Petrie Islands lie to the west.

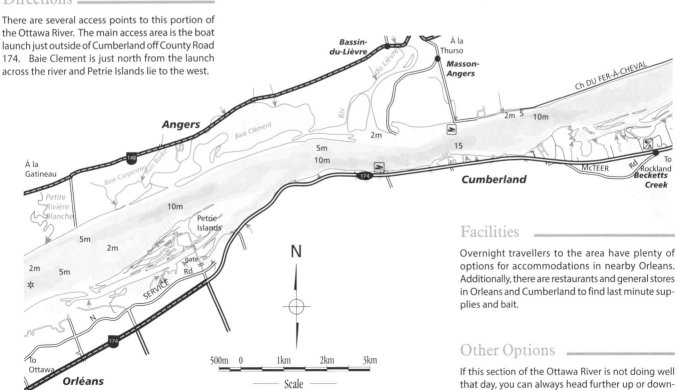

Facilities

Overnight travellers to the area have plenty of options for accommodations in nearby Orleans. Additionally, there are restaurants and general stores in Orleans and Cumberland to find last minute supplies and bait.

Other Options

If this section of the Ottawa River is not doing well that day, you can always head further up or downstream. There are plenty of access points throughout the entire length of the river from Mattawa well past Ottawa.

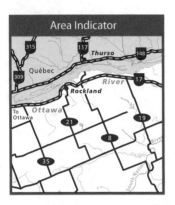

Area Indicator

Species		
Carp	Muskellunge	Smallmouth Bass
Catfish	Northern Pike	Sturgeon
Gar	Panfish	Walleye
Largemouth Bass	Sauger	Whitefish

Fishing

The Lochaber Bay area is a popular area for musky and pike anglers. These big predators will cruise into the shallows at dusk and can be enticed to strike presentations such as bucktails and spinner baits. Smallmouth and walleye can also be found just off the drop offs in the 4 m (13 ft) range.

Another good area for northern pike is the channel along the Gariepy Marsh. Pike often roam along the 1 m (3 ft) channel in search of baitfish and even the odd duckling. Casting a good-sized lure or fly can meet with consistent success at times in this channel.

Facilities

The town of Rockland has plenty to offer visitors including accommodations and a number of retailers, which includes a grocery store. A small marina is also available at the northern end of town and provides a maintained boat launch along the southern shore of the Ottawa River.

Directions

Lochaber Bay, or Baie Lochaber in French, can be accessed by following Highway 174 (Highway 17) east from the city of Ottawa to the town of Rockland. From the 10th Line Road in Orleans east of Ottawa, it is approximately 18 km (11 mi) to the town of Rockland, which lies across from Lochaber Bay of the Ottawa River.

Other Options

The **South Nation River** is the closest angling alternative to the Rockland Area. The South Nation can be reached by following Highway 17 east from Lochaber and remains one of the most important walleye spawning grounds for the Ottawa River. Bass can be found in most of the river, while northern pike and walleye can be found in the sections closer to the Ottawa River. Fishing success for all sportfish can be productive but watch for closures and special restrictions before heading out.

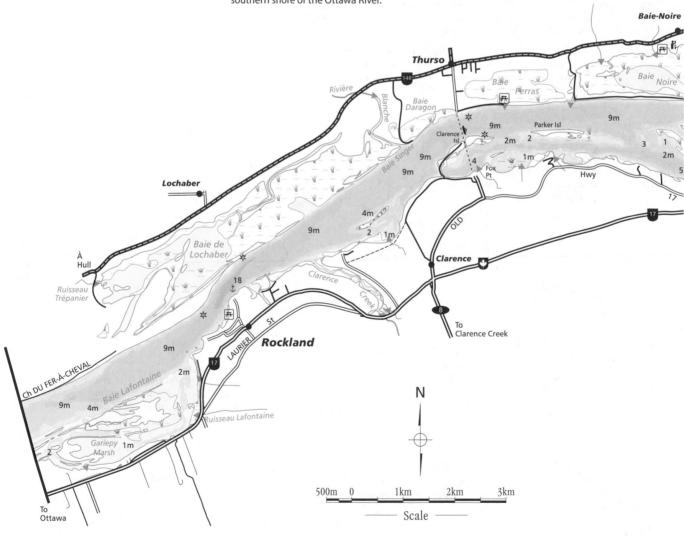

Ottawa River- Wendover

Fishing

There are a number of back bays along this section of the Ottawa River, which are good holding areas for northern pike. Pike anglers should try Baie Noire and Baie Dube near the Quebec side of the river for some big northerns.

For smallmouth and the odd walleye, Baie de la Pentecote is a popular spot. The deeper water coupled with plenty of shoreline structure makes for good bass habitat. Walleye are often caught in this area while they cruise the weed lines for food. The odd northern pike and muskellunge are also hooked in this big bay.

Still jigging along the deeper channel area can be a good method to find walleye consistently. Jigging a worm tipped jig in the 5-10 m (16-32 ft) range off the bottom is a popular and successful angling method used on this part of the river. Locating anomalies like the 5-7 m (16-23 ft) shoal humps should increase your success rate for walleye.

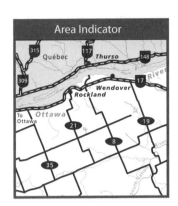

Area Indicator

Directions

The small village of Wendover is the main access point to Baie Noire. Wendover lies to the east of the town of Rockland and is accessible off the north side of Highway 17.

Other Options

Baie de L'Original is located east of Papineauville and can be reached by following Highway 17 to the town of L'Original. The area is actually quite large, almost resembling a lake and is not as heavily fished as the areas closer to Ottawa. Anglers can find good success for smallmouth bass and northern pike, while fishing for walleye and muskellunge is generally fair.

Facilities

The main access points to the Baie Noire area of the Ottawa River are from the village of Wendover and from Jessups Falls. The access at Wendover can be found by taking the 9 Mile Road north off Highway 17. Anglers will find a public boat launch area along the southern end of the river.

To find the Jessups Falls access, continue east along Highway 17 and look for the boat launch area off the north side of the highway before crossing the South Nation River. Along with the boat launch there is a small marina available for visitors. For accommodations and supplies the town of Rockland to the west or Alfred to the east has plenty to offer visitors.

Species		
Carp	Muskellunge	Smallmouth Bass
Catfish	Northern Pike	Sturgeon
Gar	Panfish	Walleye
Largemouth Bass	Sauger	Whitefish

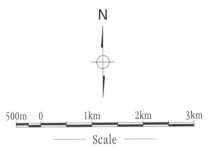

N

500m   0   1km   2km   3km

— Scale —

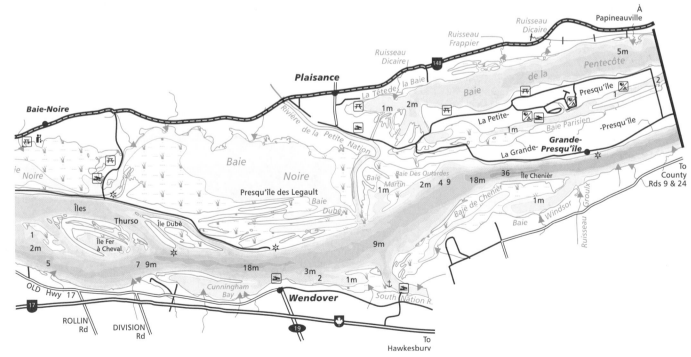

Fishing

The Otonabee River runs through the city of Peterborough and is home to many small city parks and other development. Despite the development around the river, there is plenty of shoreline structure throughout most of its length to provide great cover for all sportfish. You will find a wide variety of fish species in the Otonabee, with the main sportfish species being panfish, smallmouth and largemouth bass, walleye and muskellunge.

Fishing for panfish has become quite popular over the past decade or more with visitors travelling from great distances to give the river a try for perch, crappie and others. These small fish can be quite easy to catch in the stream using bait.

Your best bet for bass and the bigger sportfish is to work the reaches south of Peterborough. There is some amazing shoreline structure in the lower reaches that is literally tangles of shore trees and sunken logs that provide great holding spaces. Work your weedless presentations deep in that structure will often entice smallmouth and largemouth bass out of the weeds. There is also a chance to find walleye the odd northern pike and even the mighty muskellunge. Fishing reports are varied with most success for walleye occurring earlier in the year, pike and bass throughout the warmer months and muskie success usually being better later in the year.

Directions

There are several access points to the Otonabee River. While the main access points can be found around the city of Peterborough at any of the city parks or road crossings. There are also several lesser used access points south of town that can offer a more secluded fishing experience.

To reach the Otonabee from Toronto, take Highway 401 east to Highway 115. Follow Highway 115 northeast all the way to Peterborough and take the Parkway exit to Lansdowne Street. Follow Lansdowne east to George Street and head north to Del Crary Park and the Little Lake access. Alternate access points can be found at the Monaghan Boat Ramp off Monaghan Road south of Lansdowne Street as well as any of the small city parks in the area.

Another popular access point is found at the Squirrel Creek Conservation Area south of town off Wallace Point Road (County Road 21). The conservation area has a rustic cartop and canoe boat launch that provides immediate access to some of the lesser travelled portions of the river.

Facilities

Overnight travellers to the region have plenty to choose from in the city of Peterborough, including hotels, motels, restaurants and even nightclubs and social bars. Tackle is mainly found at the local Canadian Tire or Wal-Mart stores, although outside of town there are roadside stores that offer live bait and a few basic fishing supplies.

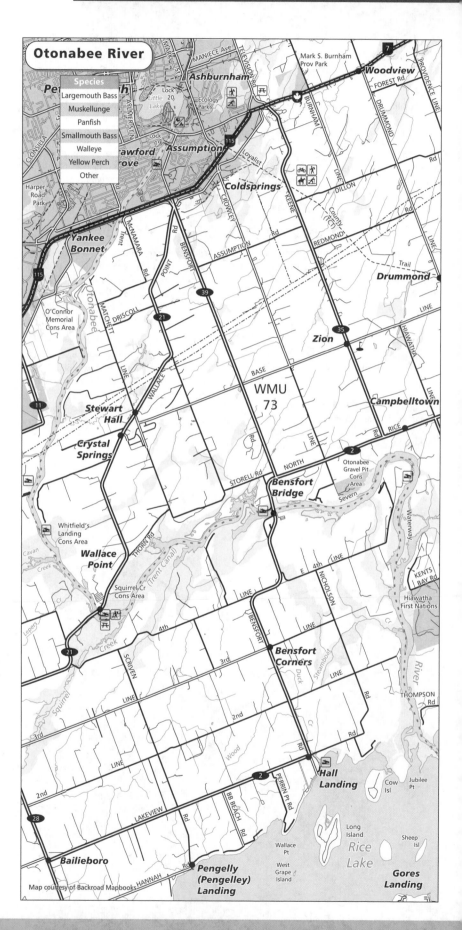

Map courtesy of Backroad Mapbooks

Otter Lake

Location: 14 km (9 mi) south of Perth
Elevation: 124 m (408 ft)
Surface Area: 602 ha (1,488 ac)
Max Depth: 34 m (112 ft)
Mean Depth: 10 m (33 ft)
Way Point: 44° 47′ 00″ N, 76° 07′ 00″ W

Fishing

Otter Lake is deeper than many of the area lakes and as a result holds both warm water and cold water sportfish. Most of the action is a result of the warm water species. Smallmouth and largemouth bass are found in the 0.5-1 kg (1-2 lbs) range, while the odd northern pike can reach larger sizes. Bass are best found along shoreline areas and near shoal areas. The shoreline structure along Otter Lake often sports good weed growth, which are prime holding areas for both smallmouth and largemouth bass. Try casting towards shore structure with spinner baits or jigs. Another prime area for bass and even the odd northern pike is around any of the 2-3 m (6-10 ft) humps found around the lake. Smallmouth love to hang around these shoals and can be very active at times. Fishing for northerns is best along shoals or near shore structure during overcast or dusk periods.

Anglers looking for cold water species will be disappointed to note that the lake trout have been fished out. However, the lake has been stocked in the past with rainbow trout and is now currently stocked with brook trout. Some suggested brook trout spinners are Blue fox, Panther Martin or even various Mepps options.

Area Indicator

Species	
Brook Trout	Smallmouth Bass
Largemouth Bass	Splake
Northern Pike	Yellow Perch
Rainbow Trout	Other

Otter Lake			
Fish Stocking Data			
Year	Species	Number	Life Stage
2010	Brook Trout	400	Fry
2008	Brook Trout	300	Fry

Directions

Approximately 15 km (9mi) south of Smiths Falls, Otter Lake lies just off the west side of Highway 15. Highway 15 travels between Carleton Place to the north and Highway 401 near Kingston to the south. To access the west side of the lake, look for the Otter Lake Road off Highway 15. Otter Lake Road traverses around the lake.

Facilities

Visitors to Otter Lake will find a public boat launch along the southeast shore just off Highway 15. Other pay per use access areas can be found at any of the resident tent and trailer parks found along the lake. Supplies and other amenities are available in Smiths Falls, which is found only minutes to the north.

Other Options

Bass Lake lies just to the north of Otter Lake and is not surprisingly inhabited by smallmouth bass and to a lesser degree largemouth bass. Northern pike are also found in the lake and fishing for can be fair at times. Smallmouth can be especially aggressive during overcast periods. Try working a spinner bait, jig or tube bait for smallmouth.

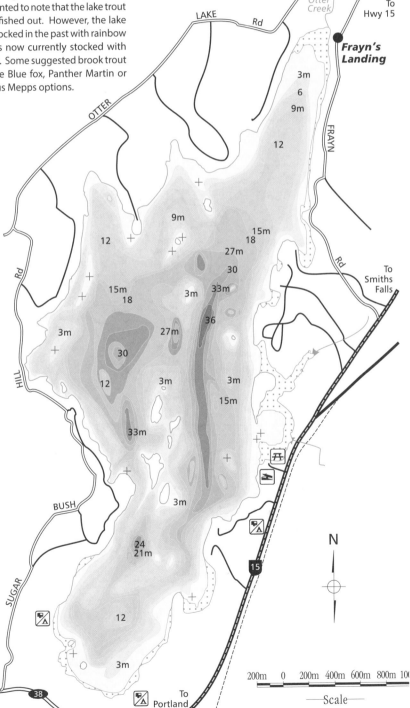

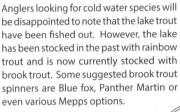

© Backroad Mapbooks

Location: 6 km (3.7 mi) south of Perth
Elevation: 131 m (431 ft)
Surface Area: 625 ha (1,544 ac)
Maximum Depth: 24.4 m (80 ft)
Mean Depth: 9 m (29.8 ft)
Way Point: 44° 51′ 00″ N, 76° 13′ 00″ W

Otty Lake

Area Indicator

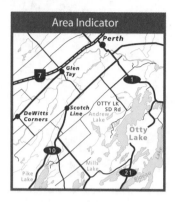

Species	
Black Crappie	Rainbow Trout
Burbot	Smallmouth Bass
Largemouth Bass	Walleye
Northern Pike	Yellow Perch

Fishing

Fishing in Otty Lake can be good for smallmouth and largemouth bass and fair for northern pike. Bass bigger than 1.5 kg (3.5 lbs) are caught annually and rumours have it that there are bass in the 3 kg (6.5 lbs) range in the lake. Bass are best caught by using spinner baits or jigs along structured areas such as weed beds or shoals. A good area for smallmouth is near any of the 6 m (20 ft) humps around the lake. Try a tube jig or even a crayfish fly or lure imitation near the bottom for those lunker bass.

Fishing success for northern pike is much slower than for bass, although persistent anglers can find regular success. Dusk is the best time to look for pike, as they will cruise into the shallows in search of food. Periodically, top water flies and lures can create some exciting action for northern pike and bass.

Directions

History records indicate that Otty Lake was named around 1815 in honour of a local Naval Captain. This scenic Eastern Ontario Lake can be reached by following Rideau Ferry Road (County Road 1) south of the town of Perth. Shortly before Elm Grove Road (County Road 21), there are a number of private access roads that branch off the west side of Rideau Ferry Road. To access the southern shore of Otty Lake, take Elm Grove Road southwest off Rideau Ferry Road..

Facilities

A number of resorts and lodges are located on Otty Lake, as the lake is a popular destination during the summer. Pay per use boat launching facilities are available at most of these private resorts and lodges. For any needed supplies or amenities, the town of Perth to the north of Otty Lake is home to restaurants, motels and other facilities.

Other Options

Andrew Lake is a small lake that lies just to the west of Otty Lake. Fishing in Andrew Lake is slow to fair for generally small northern pike. Try smaller type spoons or Rapalas for cruising pike.

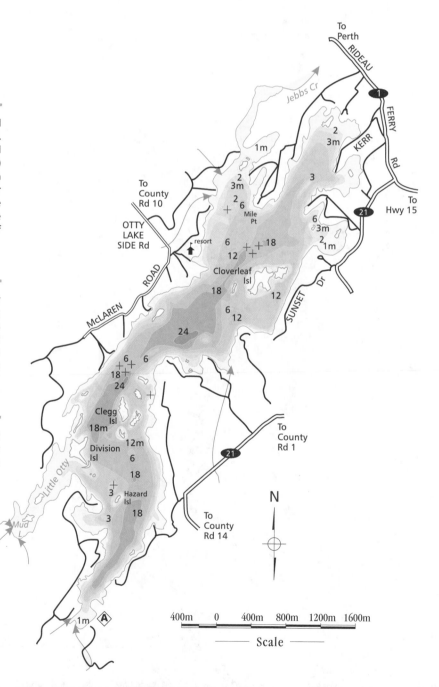

Palmerston Lake

Location: North of Ompah
Elevation: 270 m (885 ft)
Surface Area: 148 ha (365 ac)
Max Depth: 15.8 m (52 ft)
Mean Depth: 4 m (13.3 ft)
Way Point: 45° 00' 49" N, 76° 50' 33" W

Fishing

Palmerston Lake can be found just north of Ompah, which is a gateway to literally hundreds of lakes, rivers and streams in Eastern Ontario. As one of a few clear water spring fed lakes in the area, it is a paradise for swimming, boating and fishing with many coves and bays to explore. Approximately 5 kilometres (3.1 miles) in length, Palmerston has a surface area of 5.39 square kilometres (3.3 miles) and depths ranging from 20–56 meters (65–183 feet). As the summer months approach, average summer water temperatures can get as warm as 24°C (75°F), making for a very enjoyable experience angling in the warm waters.

The most fished species within this lake is the smallmouth (and to a lesser extent largemouth) bass that can occasionally be found in excess of 1.5 kg (3.5 lbs). The best spots are usually along the shorelines amongst the weeds and rocks, areas with big boulders and steep drop-offs. Try using topwater lures and flies and watch the frenzied action. Plastic jigs or any minnow imitation lures or flies can also be very productive.

A natural population of lake trout is also present and stocked from time to time. Fishing for this sportfish is moderate to slow here. This being said however, the ones lurking about have seen a few winters and can be on the larger size if you are a patient angler. Using silver spoons or spinners which imitate the fish's main food source; the minnow, is a great option as lake trout generally stay close to the surface in the early spring and late fall when the water is cold. Alternately, these fish will retreat to the deeper waters in the summer months, so trolling using a downrigger is your best bet. Please try to catch and release the small lake trout for continued population growth as this lake is stocked sporadically at best.

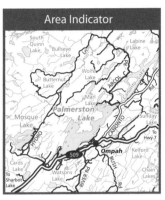

Area Indicator

Species

Lake Trout

Largemouth Bass

Smallmouth Bass

Directions

Palmerston Lake sits on the northern shores of Ompah, Ontario extending north and south for several kilometres in each direction. There a numerous ways to get to the big lake from the town depending on where you are located. To get to Ompah, there are two routes. From the southwest, travel through Fernleigh and Plevna driving north along County Roads 506 and 509 for approximately 30 km. From the east, follow the 509 through Robertsville, Mississippi Station, Snow Road Station and Donaldson before arriving in Ompah.

Facilities

Palmerston/Canonoto Conservation Area is a reserve located between Palmerston and Canonoto Lakes, northeast of Ompah. It is used as a management area for the small dam that lies between the two lakes, as well as a natural reserve for shoreline habitat. There are a few picnic tables as well as boat access to Palmerston Lake.

Summit Lake Provincial General Use Area contains provincially significant upland hardwood forests and waterfowl areas and is home to a variety of fen and marsh habitats. Located in the Township of Canonoto, this protected space is used as for wildlife viewing, hunting and fishing.

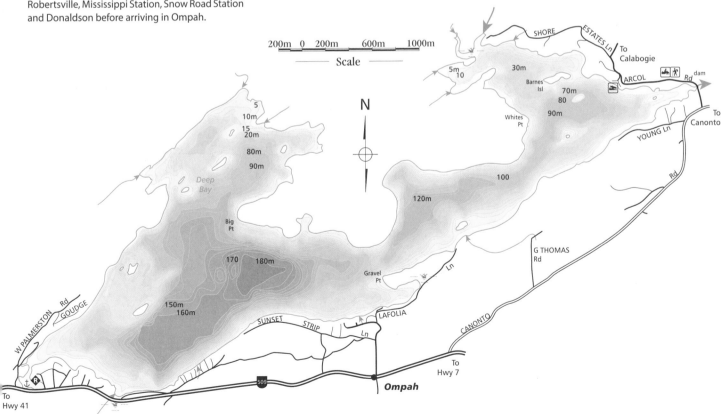

Zone 17

Location: 24 km (15 mi) north of Trenton
Maximum Depth: 6.1 m (20 ft)
Mean Depth: 3.3 m (10.6 ft)
Geographic: 44° 14′ 00″ Lat - N, 77° 47′ 00″ Lon - W

Percy Reach [Trent River]

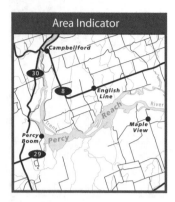

Area Indicator

Species
Largemouth Bass
Northern Pike
Smallmouth Bass
Walleye

Fishing

As a part of the Trent Severn Waterway, Percy Reach can be a busy place during the summer. Regardless of the boating traffic, the region continues to be a favourite area for anglers. The main sportfish species found in the waterbody is largemouth bass, smallmouth bass, walleye and northern pike.

Fishing for bass that average around 0.5-1 kg (1-2 lbs) can be decent at certain times. Largemouth prefer the quiet back bays where plenty of weed growth or shore structure is found. On the other hand, smallmouth prefer underwater drop offs and rocky shoals as cover. The two shoal areas located near Percy Boom are known to be good holding areas for smallmouth as well as walleye and northern pike. Try working a jig over the shoal areas, you are sure to pick up something if you have the patience.

Watch for special regulations in place on Percy Reach.

Directions

The Percy Reach is part of the Trent River found south of the town of Campbellford. The easiest way to find the Percy Reach is by boat on the Trent River system.

By land, follow County Road 30 north from Highway 401 near the town of Brighton. The county road leads to Meyersburg and near Percy Boom, which both lie on Percy Reach. Another possible access is to travel east along County Road 8 from Campbellford. About 9 km along County Road 8 there are a few access roads that branch south off. There are two tent and trailer parks that can be reached by these access roads that offer boat launches onto the Percy Reach.

Facilities

On the Percy Reach itself, there are really no amenities available. In the nearby area there are a few tent and trailer parks that offer overnight camping. For supplies and other amenities, such as motels, the town of Campbellford has plenty to offer and is within minutes of Percy Reach.

Other Options

The entire Trent Severn Waterway offers fishing opportunities for the angler at heart. Closer to Campbellford and the Percy Reach area, the **Trent River** offers smallmouth and largemouth bass and muskellunge. Walleye are also available and mainly caught near the locks at dusk.

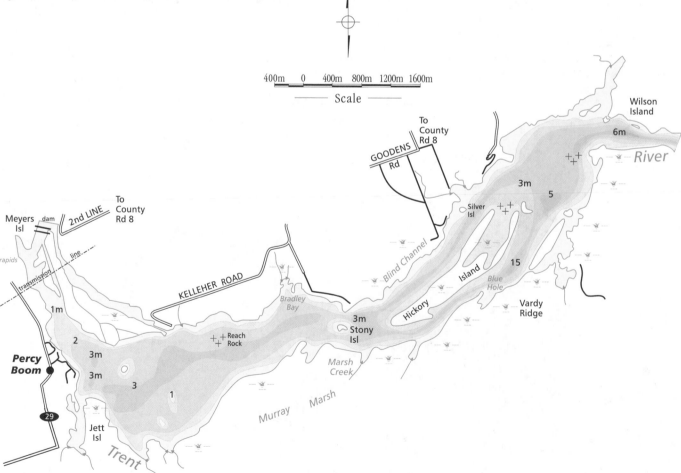

Pike Lake

Location: 11 km (7 mi) north of Westport
Elevation: 145 m (476 ft)
Surface Area: 317 ha (782 ac)
Maximum Depth: 38.4 m (126 ft)
Mean Depth: 8.2 m (27.6 ft)
Way Point: 44° 47′ 00″ N, 76° 21′ 00″ W

18 Zone

Fishing

Pike Lake is a long, narrow lake that is inhabited by smallmouth bass, largemouth bass, northern pike and walleye. There is plenty of bass structure found around the lake, with countless shallow bays and drop-offs for anglers to explore. Smallmouth are the main bass species found in the lake and the feisty fish average around 0.5-1 kg (1-2 lbs) in size. Working a jig or crayfish imitation fly or lure can be rewarding. Another lure that can work consistently is the spinner. Try casting spinners from a boat or canoe towards shore structure.

While fishing for bass, anglers will often be surprised by a northern pike strike, especially during the evening periods. For added fun, top water flies and lures can create some exciting action during the evening for both species. Cast along weed lines or even right in weed structure for top water success.

Walleye fishing in Pike Lake is definitely slower than success for bass or northern pike, although it is the preferred sportfish of most anglers. Walleye tend to cruise shoal areas, especially during the evening period. Trolling a worm harness slowly along weed lines or still jigging off a shoal can be effective. To help enhance the walleye fishery and reduce angling pressure, special slot size restrictions for harvesting have been imposed. Please check your regulations for specifics before heading out.

Other Options

A decent alternative to Pike Lake is **Little Crosby Lake** located to the southwest. Little Crosby Lake offers fair to good fishing at times for average sized smallmouth and largemouth bass. A few northern pike and walleye also exist in the lake; however, success is slow compared to fishing for bass.

Directions

Located between the towns of Perth to the north and Westport to the south, Pike Lake is easily accessible via the Scotch Line (County Road 10). Near Perth, the Scotch Line can be found just south of town off the Rideau Ferry Road (County Road 1). At Westport, the Scotch Line is located near the north end of town where a bridge crosses over a dam along the west end of Upper Rideau Lake.

Facilities

A public boat launch is located off the Scotch Line along the northwest shore of Pike Lake. For more launching services, such as fuel and supplies, a marina is located along the southwest shore. Camping enthusiasts will find tent and trailer parks on the lake.

Species	
Burbot	Smallmouth Bass
Largemouth Bass	Walleye
Northern Pike	Yellow Perch

Zone 17

Location: Bobcaygeon
Elevation: 253 m (830 ft)
Surface Area: 5,344 ha (13,205 ac)
Maximum Depth: 17.4 m (57 ft)
Mean Depth: 3 m (9.8 ft)
Way Point: 44° 27′ 00″ Lat - N, 78° 30′ 00″ Long - W

Pigeon Lake

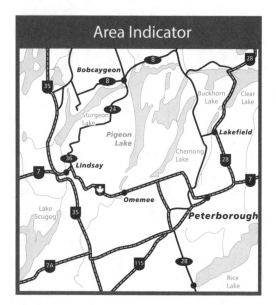

Area Indicator

Species		
Black Crappie	Largemouth Bass	Smallmouth Bass
Brook trout	Muskellunge	Walleye
Burbot	Northern Pike	Yellow Perch

Facilities

Pigeon Lake is home to a number of marinas and settlements along both the east and west sides of the lake that can be used to access the lake from. Bobcaygeon in the north and Omemee in the south are the two biggest centres and most supplies and necessities can be picked up in the villages. A favourite boat launch area of anglers is the access found in Omemee. Boaters will also find good anchoring points at the north end of Big Island well away from the hustle and bustle that Bobcaygeon can be during the peak of summer.

For those looking to stay around the lake will find **Camp Fisherman** and **Pigeon Lake Resort** offer cottages and/or camping. Alternatively, **Emily Provincial Park** located just north of Omemee along the eastern shoreline is a full service campsite with beaches, trails and even boat rentals. It is a popular summer destination and reservations are recommended. Call (888) ONT-PARK or visit www.ontarioparks.com.

Directions

Similar to the southern portion of Pigeon Lake, a small town is the focal point to access. Bobcaygeon is located along the northwest shore of the lake and is generally the main access area to the north part of the lake. To reach Bobcaygeon, follow County Road 36 north from Lindsay. County Road 36 travels right through the heart of Bobcaygeon. Access to the lake can be found in a few areas east of County Road 36.

There are also several marinas with boat launches along the eastern and western shoreline of the lake.

Fishing

Pigeon Lake lies in the heart of the famous Kawartha Lakes chain and is part of the Trent Severn Waterway. It is a long, narrow lake stretching about 27 km (17 miles) in a predominately north-south direction. The big lake is considered one of the best Ontario fishing lakes. It had great habitat with rocky shoals and abundant weed growth to help hide the walleye, muskellunge, smallmouth and largemouth bass and yellow perch that roam the lake.

Most anglers who visit Pigeon Lake fish for walleye. The southwest side of Big Island area and Gannon's Narrows hosts many shoals and weeds which make this lake a prime spot for walleye. Walleye travel in loose schools and once you find them you may be in for some impressive non-stop action so cover the spot thoroughly before leaving.

The narrows connect to Buckhorn Lake and certainly get a lot of attention on opening day in May. The number one choice of lure in this deeper water area is jig and minnow combination, slowly bounced on the bottom. As the water warms up in summer, the walleye will hit faster moving bait, so it's possible to speed up to cover more area. Crankbaits like Shad Raps, Redfins and other hard minnow baits. Drifting works well if the wind is cooperative since there is no engine noise to spook the fish.

If you are looking for a bigger fish to catch, muskellunge is the king of Pigeon Lake. Commonly caught in the 75 cm (30 in) range, they can reach 125 cm (50 in) in size. Needless to say larger spinnerbaits, crankbaits and plugs are needed, although walleye and bass presentations can fool some musky. A few muskie are caught south of Gannon's Narrows, but the northern section is where you will find the structure most often associated with these magnificent game fish. Good areas to try are around the weed lines around Big Island during overcast periods or at dusk. Most muskie are caught later in September and into October.

Smallmouth and largemouth bass can create good action on Pigeon Lake. The heavy weed growth in the southern end of the lake offers good habitat for both bass species, especially for the bigger largemouth bass. In fact, south of Gannon's Narrows is home to some of the biggest largemouth bass in the province, most notably where the lake empties into the Pigeon River. For heavy weeds like these, try working a tube jig or a weedless spinner through the growth.

For smallmouth, look for underwater rock piles or try off rocky island and shore areas. Smallmouth will also hold under other structure types, such as cottage docks or launching areas. All the typical bass lures can be effective on Pigeon Lake. While typical largemouth bass lures will work for smallmouth, including topwater presentations, underwater presentations are regularly more effective. Try working spinners, jigs and crankbaits along the structure areas and if fishing is slow, slow the retrieve down significantly. When smallmouth bass are lethargic, they will often simply suck in the lure or fly as it passes by.

Adding to the mix are panfish, including bluegill, crappie and perch. These fish are a lot of fun to catch from docks using jigs or a bobber and bait set up. Crappie, in particular, like the warm waters of shallow bays, but can be hard to entice out of the cover. Perch will often school up in winter allowing for some good action when you can find them in winter. The key to success at this time is mobility. Drill a few holes, if nothing bites in 15-20 minutes; move on until you locate the schools. Many times when you find green weeds, you will find perch.

Other Options

Any of the nearby Trent Severn Lakes are good alternatives to Pigeon Lake. For a little change from the larger Kawartha Lakes, try venturing north to a few of the more out of the way water bodies. **Bass Lake** offers a little more seclusion and provides fishing opportunities for largemouth bass, smallmouth bass, the odd walleye and muskellunge.

Pigeon Lake

Location: Bobcaygeon
Elevation: 253 m (830 ft)
Surface Area: 5,344 ha (13,205 ac)
Maximum Depth: 13.1 m (43 ft)
Mean Depth: 6.1 m (20.2 ft)
Way Point: 44° 27' 00" Lat - N, 78° 30' 00" Long - W

Species		
Black Crappie	Largemouth Bass	Smallmouth Bass
Brook trout	Muskellunge	Walleye
Burbot	Northern Pike	Yellow Perch

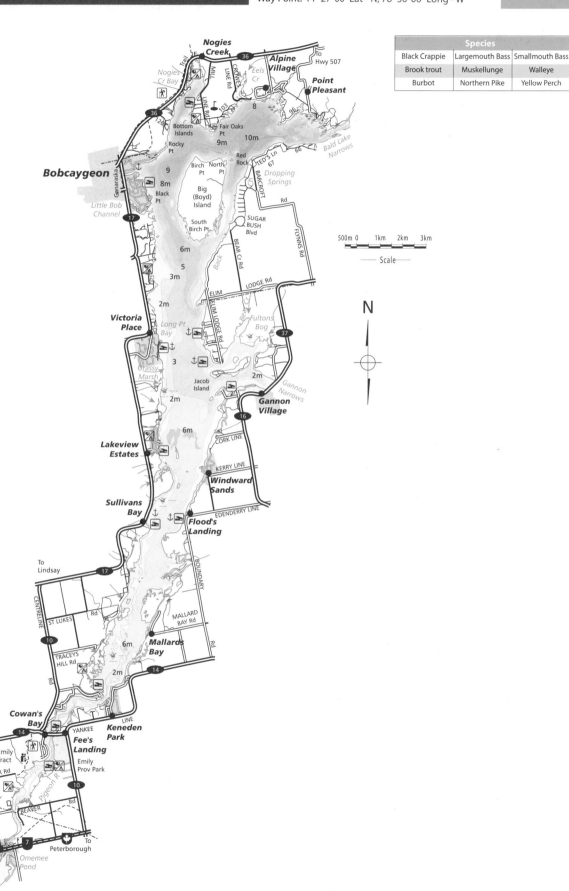

Location: 17 km (10.5 mi) southwest of Westport
Elevation: 183 m (600 ft)
Surface Area: 78 ha (193 ac)
Maximum Depth: 26.8 m (88 ft)
Mean Depth: 9.3 m (30.5 ft)
Way Point: 44° 36'00"N, 76° 35'00"W

Potspoon Lake

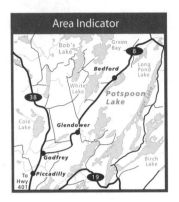

Area Indicator

Species	
Lake Trout	Smallmouth Bass
Largemouth Bass	Yellow Perch
Northern Pike	

Potspoon Lake			
Fish Stocking Data			
Year	Species	Number	Life Stage
2008	Lake Trout	4,000	Fall Fry

Fishing

Visitors to Potspoon Lake will have the opportunity to fish for smallmouth bass, largemouth bass and northern pike. Fishing in Potspoon is regarded as fair for bass, which average about 0.5-1 kg (1-2 lbs) in size. Bass seem to frequent the area around the small island in the northern portion of the lake, although they can also be found along most shoreline areas. Casting a jig or spinner bait towards shore can be effective for both largemouth and smallmouth.

The other main sportfish found in Potspoon Lake is northern pike. Fishing success for northerns is generally slow, although it can pick up on occasion, especially during dusk periods. While pike in Potspoon are usually small, they can put up a good fight when hooked.

Recently, lake trout have been stocked to help aid the natural population found in the lake. Lakers are readily found near the surface in spring and will aggressively take spoon and spinner presentations. Although trolling is the preferred method, when lake trout are hitting at this time of year, it is possible to fish for them from shore. As the waters warm, you will have to fish deeper.

Directions

This small lake lies to the northwest of Frontenac Provincial Park. To find the lake, follow Highway 401 to Highway 38 and head north. Look for Westport Road (County Road 8) off the east side of Highway 38 at Godfrey. Travel east along Westport Road, which eventually changes to Mast Road before passing by the northern shore of Potspoon Lake.

Facilities

There are no facilities available on Potspoon Lake, although you can access the lake by canoe or a small boat off the side of the Westport Road. The towns of Sydenham and Harrowsmith to the south are home to a few retailers offering basic supplies.

Other Options

Garter Lake is a small lake located just to the east of Potspoon Lake and can be reached via an old access road/trail from Potspoon Lake. Garter Lake is stocked annually with lake trout, which provide for fair fishing around the season opener. The lake is also home to a good population of smallmouth bass that average 0.5-1 kg (1-2 lbs) in size.

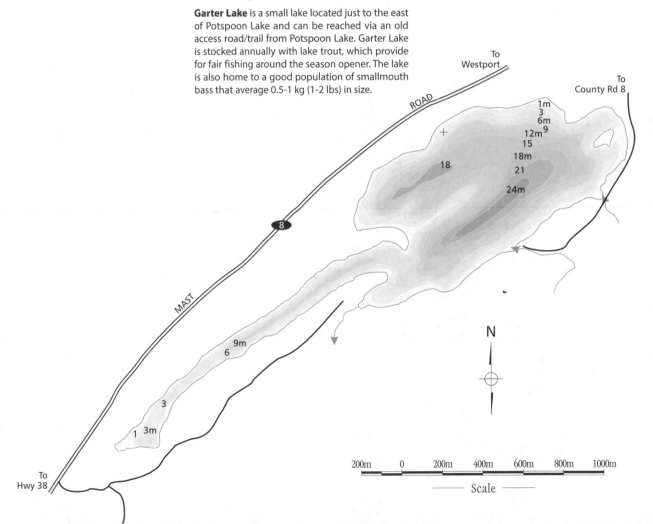

Red Horse Lake

Location: 20 km (12 mi) northeast of Ompah
Elevation: 84 m (276 ft)
Surface Area: 302 ha (746 ac)
Maximum Depth: 37.1 m (122 ft)
Mean Depth: 10.2 m (33.5 ft)
Way Point: 44° 32′00″ N, 76° 05′00″W

Fishing

Due to its close proximity to Kingston, Red Horse Lake can be busy during the summer months. Regardless of the boating activity, fishing in this beautiful lake is good at times for smallmouth and largemouth bass that can reach up to 2 kg (4.5 lbs) in size. Largemouth bass are usually much easier to find than smallmouth bass. Try using a yellow or white coloured jig or even a spinner bait along weed lines. A few hot spots to try for bass are the shallows of Cronin Bay and Washburn Bay.

Northern pike are also found in Red Horse Lake and provide for fair fishing most of the time. Trolling a spoon along shoreline areas can entice strikes but bass anglers looking for lunker bass inadvertently create most of the pike action.

Lake trout are stocked in Red Horse Lake annually and provide for fair fishing just after the season opens. Trolling silver or gold spoons are the most effective angling method for lake trout. During the summer, lakers revert to the depths of the lake and require a downrigger to have any chance at success.

To help maintain the ecological integrity of Red Horse Lake, special live bait restrictions have been imposed. Please check your regulations if you plan to use live bait.

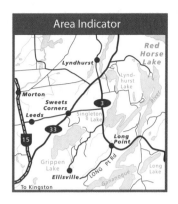

Area Indicator

Directions

Red Horse Lake is part of the Gananoque River system found to the west of the popular Charleston Lake Provincial Park. The name of this lake comes from the blood coloured pictograph of a horse found along one of the rock walls of the lake.

To find the lake, follow Highway 401 to Exit 659 east of Gananoque. From the highway, follow Reynolds Road (County Road 3) north. Reynolds Road crosses over Wiltse Creek before winding its way to the southern shore of Red Horse Lake.

Facilities

Red Horse Lake is surrounded by private land and there is no public access to the lake. Boats can be rented from one of the commercial resorts located along the southern shore of the lake. Pay per use boat launching is also available at the resort.

Red Horse Lake is also part of the **Charleston Lake/ Gananoque Lake Canoe Route**. Paddlers can travel the route in a circle towards Charleston Lake, returning via the Gananoque River to the south.

Other Options

Most of the angling focus in the region around Red Horse Lake is on lakes, however, there are many good sized rivers that have plenty to offer anglers. **Gananoque River** is found to the south and offers good numbers of smallmouth and largemouth bass as well as some northern pike. Bass can be found throughout the entirety of the river, while pike are mainly found in the wider stretches of the river. Casting jigs and spinner baits from shore can be productive for both bass and pike.

Species	
Black Crappie	Northern Pike
Lake Trout	Smallmouth Bass
Largemouth Bass	

Red Horse Lake		
Fish Stocking Data		
Year	Species	Number
2013	Lake Trout	5,000
2012	Lake Trout	5,000
2011	Lake Trout	5,000

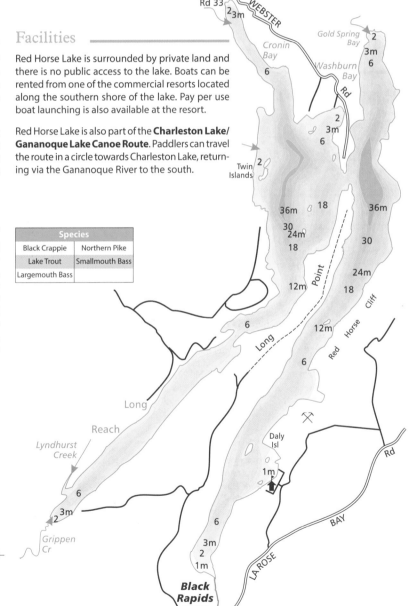

200m 0 200m 400m 600m 800m 1000m

Scale

N

Zone 17

Location: 25 km (15.5 mi) south of Peterborough
Elevation: 338 m (1,109 ft)
Surface Area: 9,156 ha (22,625 ac)
Maximum Depth: 13.4 m (44 ft)
Mean Depth: 2.3 m (7.6 ft)
Way Point: 44° 12′ 00″ Lat - N, 78° 10′ 00″ Long - W

Rice Lake

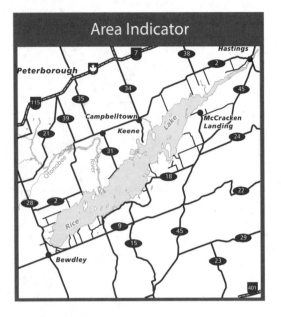

Area Indicator

Species	
Black Crappie	Smallmouth Bass
Largemouth Bass	Walleye
Muskellunge	Yellow Perch
Northern Pike	Other

Directions

Found between Peterborough and Highway 401, this man-made lake is the first in the chain of Kawartha Lakes that stretches west towards Lake Simcoe. Although there are access areas at a few of the small settlements along the southern and northern shores of the lake, the main launching area is found in Bewdley at the west end of the big lake. County Road 28, which runs north from Port Hope and the 401 north to Highway 115 near Peterborough, provides access to Rice Lake Drive. This side road is the main road into Bewdley and the launching site. The busy public boat launch cannot be missed in town.

At the east end of the lake, the town of Hastings is a popular starting point for trips onto Rice Lake and beyond. Hastings actually lies along the Trent River, but provides easy access to the Trent Severn Waterway and Rice Lake to the west. The town can be found by following County Road 45 north from Highway 401 near Cobourg or by travelling south along the same county road from Highway 7 east of Peterborough. Once in town, look for signs to the boat launch area.

Facilities

With 30 resorts and fishing camps to choose from, Rice Lake has no shortage of places from which to get out on the lake from. Most are scattered along the south shore of the lake where there are several boat launches to choose from. However, the main public access is at the west end of the big lake in the village of Bewdley. Home to a couple restaurants and a general store, the town also provides ample parking near the boat launch. Visitors at the east end of Rice Lake will find Hastings the biggest centre to pick up supplies from. The small town is actually found along the Trent River to the east of the big lake.

Serpent Mounds Park is now owned and operated by the Hiawatha First Nation offering camping and a boat launch on the north side of the lake. The **Rice Lake Conservation Area** is a day-use only area that provides a good spot for nature viewing off the southwest end of the lake

Fishing

Once known for its wild rice cultivation, Rice Lake is said to have more fish per acre than any other lake in Ontario. Considering it is 32 km long and 5 km wide, that says a lot. The lake is very shallow and weedbeds and mudflats are abundant creating a very fertile environment for the abundant panfish that help provide food for the highly sought after predatory fish, such as bass, walleye, and muskellunge.

Rice Lake is one of the largest of the Kawartha Lakes and is part of the Trent Severn Waterway, which connects to the lake by the Otonabee and Trent Rivers. Although the lake receives significant angling pressure, fishing remains consistent.

The prized walleye fishing is the main attraction of anglers to the lake. In spring, walleye can be found scattered in the large weed flats around Bewdley or at the mouth of the Otonabee River. Use jigs tipped with worms or minnows, in the deeper holding pools off Jubilee Point. If exploring the Bewdley area, be prepared to cover a lot of water until you find where the fish are hiding.

In summer, the walleye school in the deeper channels on the south end of Rice Lake, just out from Gores Landing. Also fish the waters near Tick Island and the old railway line. Walleye can be difficult to locate in summer but working the weed beds and shoals in these areas can be very rewarding. The key is to find that anomaly in the lake bottom that will attract baitfish. One of the favourite lures or set ups for trolling for walleye is the worm harness. The worm harness is a spinner type lure specifically designed to hold bait and be trolled at various depths and speeds. Walleye on Rice Lake average over 0.5 kg (1-2 lbs), but the odd lunker in the 2.5 kg (5-6 lbs) range is possible.

With so many weeds and shallow areas, it is not a surprise that largemouth bass are quite common in Rice Lake. In fact, tournaments are held yearly for these bucketmouths that can grow as big as 2.5 kg (5-6 lbs). In summer largemouth are concentrated on the weed flats around Bewdley. The trick is to look for pockets in the weeds and cast Texas-rigged worms or plain jigs into these pockets. Cow Island, near the mouth of the Otonabee River, or even further up the river are also good places to try.

Smallmouth bass are not as abundant as their bigger mouthed cousins, but can still be caught in the deeper areas of Rice Lake. One popular holding area is the drop off created by the sunken railroad near Tick Island. Smallmouth are attracted to this area since the many rocks from the old railway attract crayfish, which are smallmouths favourite food.

Rice Lake is also famous for its muskellunge fishing. With the abundance of panfish, these predators can grow over 13 kg (30 lbs), but are usually half that size. The best method to catch muskie on Rice Lake is by trolling. Cover lots of water along the deeper channels on the south end of the lake. Large perch pattern crankbaits are popular, while casting large bucktail flies along weed lines when there is a bit of chop on the lake can also be effective.

A big and growing attraction to Rice Lake is its panfish fishery. In the spring, crappie fishing can be fantastic and you will literally find dozens of people in Bewdley, Hastings and other shallow access points fishing from shore. Crappie in excess of 0.5 kg (1 lb) are quite common and they make excellent table fare. The preferred fishing method is either a worm and float or a small white tube jig and float. Small spinners and even flies can entice strikes. Fishing the edge of the weeds can be very productive, especially when the crappie are schooling. The trick is to get the bait right in close to the often shy fish.

Other Options

The two main fishing alternatives to Rice Lake are the **Trent River** and the **Otonabee River**. Both river systems are part of the Trent Severn Waterway and provide fishing opportunities for bass, muskellunge and the odd walleye. The Otonabee flows into the north part of Rice Lake, while the Trent River flows out of its eastern end.

Rice Lake

Location: Peterborough
Elevation: 338 m (1,109 ft)
Surface Area: 9,156 ha (22,625 ac)
Maximum Depth: 13.4 m (44 ft)
Mean Depth: 2.3 m (7.6 ft)
Way Point: 44° 12′ 00″ Lat - N, 78° 10′ 00″ Long - W

N

1km 0 1km 2km 3km 4km 5km
— Scale —

Species	
Black Crappie	Smallmouth Bass
Largemouth Bass	Walleye
Muskellunge	Yellow Perch
Northern Pike	Other

© Backroad Mapbooks **149**

Zone **18**

Location: 8 km (5 mi) southeast of Perth
Elevation: 124 m (406 ft)
Surface Area: 4,700 ha (11,614 ac)
Maximum Depth: 95 m (312 ft)
Mean Depth: 13.3 m (46.6 ft)
Way Point: 44° 46′ 00″N, 76° 13′ 00″W

Rideau Lake

Area Indicator

Fishing

As the the largest lake along the entire Rideau Canal Waterway, Big Rideau Lake receives a lot of attention with boaters and visitors, especially during the summer months. Although there is heavy fishing pressure on the lake, the angling prospects remain decent and persistent anglers can have success on the lake for northern pike, smallmouth bass and stocked lake trout. There are also walleye, largemouth bass, crappie, rock bass and sunfish found in the lake.

Big Rideau Lake is 32 kilometres (20 miles) long and is 6 kilometres (4 miles) wide. The lake is much narrower at its northeastern end than at its southwestern end. The village of Rideau Ferry is found at the junction between Big Rideau and Lower Rideau Lake at the northeast end, while Narrows Lock links the bigger lake to Upper Rideau Lake at the southwest end. The town of Portland is also found on the southern shore, while hundreds of cottages and homes line the big lake.

Boaters and anglers alike will appreciate the work of the Big Rideau Lake Association who has placed markers on most of the shoals around the lake. Although these are to mark underwater hazards for navigation, they also help point out good fishing holes for smallmouth bass, walleye and northern pike. The odd bass can reach 2 kg (4.5 lbs) in size on the lake. Most walleye and pike caught in the lake are small, but there are definitely some big fish in this lake and every once in a while a big northern catches unsuspecting anglers by surprise.

If you are looking for smallmouth bass or northern pike, the eastern part of the south end of Big Rideau Lake is your best bet. The numerous islands and weed structure make for prime holding areas for both bass and northern pike. Walleye also frequent this area of the lake, although they are usually found in the deeper areas along weed lines. Try working spinners, jigs and crankbaits slowly along the structure areas for all three sportfish.

The northern portion of Big Rideau is quite a bit shallower than the southern section. Anglers will find plenty of weed growth around this part of the lake, which provides excellent cover for warm water sportfish. Look for bass and pike along weed lines or right in the weeds of the many quiet bays. Try using weedless type presentations like a spinner bait or tube jig.

Lake trout are stocked heavily in Big Rideau Lake annually and fishing can be productive just after the season opens. Trolling a flashy spoon as soon as the season opens works best for lakers. As the heat of summer approaches, downrigging equipment will be required to reach the depths where lake trout hang out. Anglers looking for lake trout in Big Rideau Lake have to look no further than the deep channel along the northwest end of the southern portion of the lake. Lake trout are rarely found in the northern section of the lake, but early in the season you can find them in rocky narrows on occasion.

Anglers will also find panfish including crappie, rock bass and sunfish. These small fish are best caught near the shore using a float and work or a small jig tipped with bait.

Before fishing on Big Rideau Lake, be sure to check your regulations. There are special bait restrictions in place as well as a few sanctuary areas on the lake.

Directions

Big Rideau Lake or Rideau Lake is located southwest of the town of Smiths Falls. The main access area to the northern portion of Big Rideau Lake is the marina available at Rideau Ferry. Rideau Ferry is the area where a ferry used to join the southern and northern portions of County Road 1 also known as Rideau Ferry Road. Today, there is a bridge that travels over the lake. To reach Rideau Ferry, follow Highway 15 south form Smiths Falls to County Road 1 at Lombardy. Rideau Ferry is about 5 km northwest of Highway 15.

The main access area to the southern portion of Big Rideau Lake is the town of Portland. Portland is located south of Smiths Falls off Highway 15. Visitors can reach Portland from Highway 401 to the south or from Smiths Falls to the north.

The western shore is also easily accessed off a few county roads. Narrows Lock Road, or County Road 14, leads north from Highway 15 at Crosby and provides access to the Rideau Lake North Shore Road as well as County Road 17 or Lally Road. The later leads to Murphys Point Provincial Park.

Facilities

Big Rideau Lake is the largest lake in the Rideau Canal Waterway. The lake is home to dozens of private lodges and resorts as well as hundreds of cottages. There are several boat access areas onto the lake, including marinas at Rideau Ferry, Portland and along the north shore at Muskrat Hole. The nearby villages of Portland and Newboro have plenty to offer visitors, such as accommodations, restaurants and general retailers. If you prefer a wider array of accommodations and retailers, the town of Smiths Falls is minutes away to the north of the big lake.

Camping enthusiasts can enjoy a stay at one of the tent and trailer parks on the lake or at **Murphy's Point Provincial Park**. Murphy's Point Provincial Park lies along the northwest shore of Big Rideau Lake and is a full facility park complete with flush toilets, a boat launch and showers. There are 160 campsites available at the park, which can be full during summer weekends. To ensure you have a campsite upon arrival, call to reserve your site at (888) ONT-PARK or visit www.ontarioparks.com. For more information on Murphy's Point Provincial Park call (613) 267-5060.

Other Options

Long Lake and **Round Lake** are two small lakes that lie near the northwest shore of Big Rideau Lake near Murphy's Point Provincial Park. Smallmouth and largemouth bass are resident in both lakes and fishing can be productive at times. A portion of Round Lake lies within Murphy's Point Provincial Park and the lake is stocked annually with splake. Fishing can be fair for smaller sized splake, especially in the spring just after ice off.

Rideau Lake

Location: 8 km (5 mi) southeast of Perth
Elevation: 124 m (406 ft)
Surface Area: 4,700 ha (11,614 ac)
Maximum Depth: 95 m (312 ft)
Mean Depth: 13.3 m (46.6 ft)
Way Point: 44° 46′00″N, 76° 13′00″W

18 Zone

Species	
Brook Trout	Smallmouth Bass
Lake Trout	Walleye
Largemouth Bass	Whitefish
Northern Pike	Yellow Perch
Rainbow Trout	Other

N

500m 0 1km 2km 3km
Scale

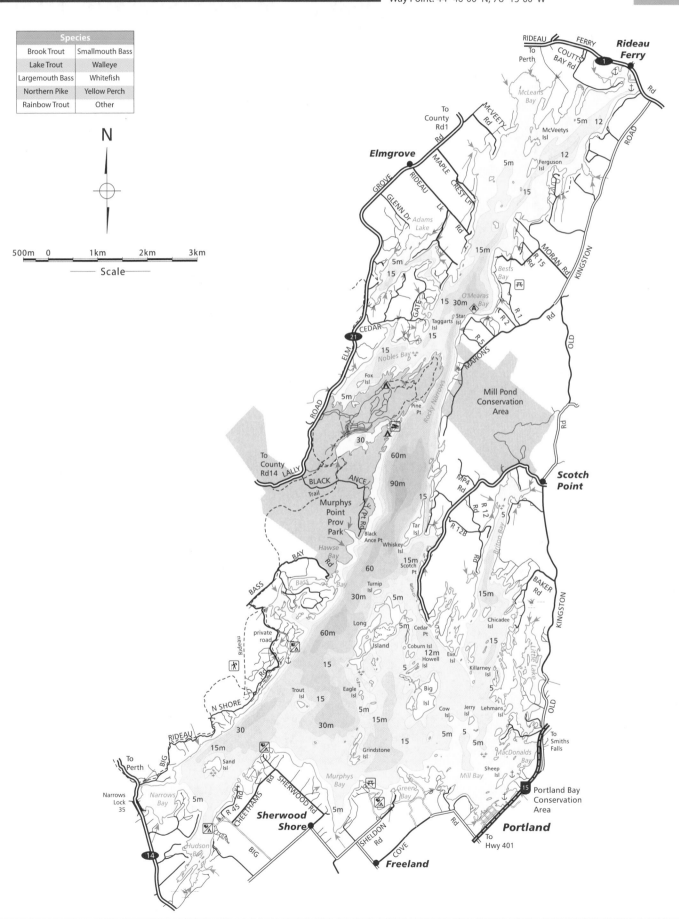

Zone **15**

Location: 42 km (26 mi) south of Bancroft
Elevation: 428 m (1,404 ft)
Surface Area: 29 ha (72 ac)
Mean Depth: 15.5 m (50.7 ft)
Max Depth: 34.7 m (114 ft)
Way Point: 44° 12′ 00″ Lat - N, 78° 10′ 00″ Long - W

Robinson Lake

Area Indicator

Fishing

Robinson Lake is home to a few homes and cottages, but also has a section of Crown land on its northwest side. Stocked every few years with lake trout, fishing for lakers is best in the winter through the ice or during spring; just after ice off. Lake trout are also quite active just after ice off when they are found closer to the surface. Anglers will find success by trolling silver or gold spoons or larger streamer type flies that imitate baitfish. For trolling, the Little Cleo or Diamond King are good bets, while fly fishers should try a grey and white streamer with some crystal flash. In the summer, the lake trout go deep, and you will need a downrigger or lead core line to get to them. A baited lure with lots of action, like a Flatfish or Kwikfish, trolled just off the bottom will work best.

Smallmouth bass are also found in the roadside lake and fishing success is generally fair. A good area to look for smallmouth bass is around the cluster of underwater rock piles that are located near the northeast shore of the lake. Try flipping jigs or other similar type grub baits into the rock area and work it in an up and down jerking fashion. With some patience and a little luck, you should be able to have some decent success in this area.

Species
Lake Trout
Largemouth Bass
Muskellunge
Smallmouth Bass
Yellow Perch

Directions

This small roadside lake is located in the village of Limerick south of the town of Bancroft. You can find the lake by following Highway 62 north from Madoc or south from Bancroft. The lake is easily accessible off the west side of the highway.

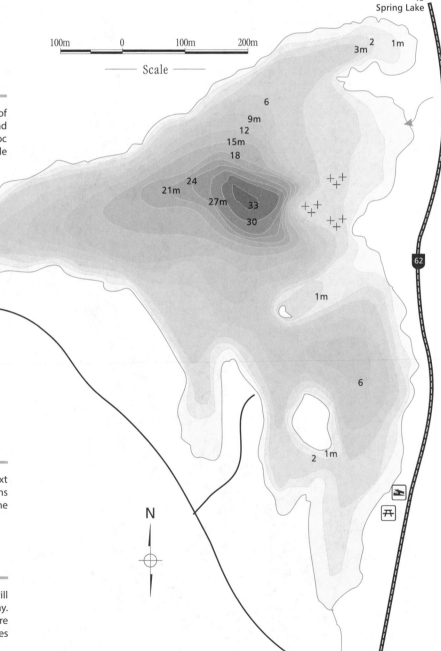

Robinson Lake			
Fish Stocking Data			
Year	Species	Number	Life Stage
2012	Lake Trout	725	Yearling
2010	Lake Trout	300	Yearling
2008	Lake Trout	300	Yearling

Facilities

There is a roadside boat launch and picnic area next to Robinson Lake. Supplies and accommodations can be easily found in the town of Bancroft to the north or the town of Madoc to the south.

Other Options

If you continue north along Highway 62, you will pass a few more lakes off the side of the highway. **Spring Lake** and further north, **L'Amable Lake** are two of the more popular lakes in the area. The lakes offer fishing for bass and trout.

Round Lake

Location: 6 km (3.7 mi) north of Havelock
Surface Area: 568 ha (1,404 ac)
Maximum Depth: 9.8 m (32 ft)
Mean Depth: 4.5 m (14.7 ft)
Way Point: 44° 30' 00" Lat - N, 77° 53' 00" Lon - W

17 Zone

Fishing

As a popular summer destination lake, Round Lake receives significant angling pressure throughout the year; however, the fishing remains fairly steady. The two most abundant sport fish found in the lake are smallmouth and largemouth bass but walleye are the fish of choice of anglers in the area.

Bass can be found throughout the lake and make up the bulk of the fishing activity. A few of the better areas for largemouth bass are around the inflow and outflow areas of the North River. The weedy habitat makes for prime largemouth cover and often largemouth can be caught off the top with popper flies and lures. Smallmouth bass habitat is also in abundance in Round Lake as there are several underwater rock piles around the lake that are favourite holding areas of smallmouth. The 2 m (4.5 ft) shoal hump found in the middle of the lake is worth a try. Work a jig over the hump in an up and down fashion, you may be pleasantly surprised.

Walleye are the most prized sport fish found in Round Lake and they receive heavy fishing pressure throughout the season. Walleye fishing is usually slow, although at times it can pick up. In the early part of the season, look for walleye around the inflow and outflow areas of the North River. As the season progresses, walleye will seek the deeper portions of the lake, but they can be regularly found cruising the shoal areas. The few 5 m (11 ft) shoal humps is a mid season holding area for walleye.

Directions

North of the town of Havelock, you can find Round Lake by travelling north off Highway 7 along County Road 46. County Road 46 traverses past the west side of the lake. The main access is via the tent and trailer park located at the end of a short road that branches off the east side of County Road 46.

Facilities

The only amenity available on Round Lake is the tent and trailer park located along the western shore. For supplies or other trip necessities, the town of Havelock has plenty to offer. Roofed accommodation can be found just outside of town along Highway 7 in either direction.

Other Options

Belmont Lake to the east of Round Lake is the closest angling alternative and is a fine choice. Belmont Lake is accessible via County Road 48 and offers fishing opportunities for smallmouth bass, largemouth bass, walleye and northern pike. Bass fishing is often the most productive sport fishery on the lake.

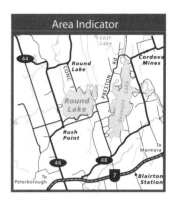

Area Indicator

Species	
Brook Trout	Walleye
Largemouth Bass	Yellow Perch
Muskellunge	Other
Smallmouth Bass	

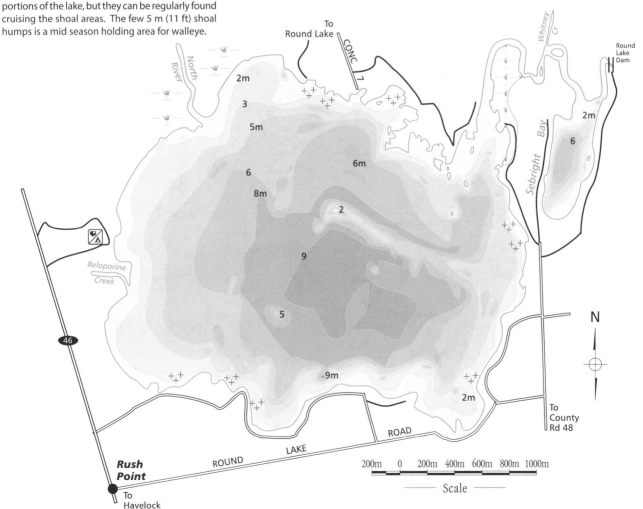

Zone **20**

Location: Brockville
Length: 1,245 km (775 mi)
Geographic: 44° 35′03″N, 75° 41′08″W

Saint Lawrence River-
Rockport to Brockville

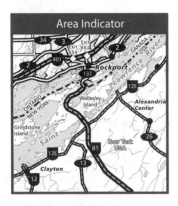

Area Indicator

Species	
Brown Trout	Rainbow Trout
Lake Trout	Salmon
Muskellunge	Walleye
Northern Pike	Yellow Perch
Smallmouth Bass	Other

Fishing

This big and often intimidating river is approximately 1, 250 kilometres (776 miles) long draining the Great Lakes into the Atlantic Ocean in the east. The river has gained even greater notoriety over the last century through the development of the picturesque St. Lawrence Thousand Islands. The geography of the area around the river is spectacular and the rolling forest with picturesque bedrock shorelines often captivates visitors. Today, the river remains busy as a shipping line for all the regions bordering the Great Lakes. The region also doubles as a fantastic outdoor playground with visitors from around the world enjoying the many sites and sounds the area has to offer.

Anglers can expect to have the opportunity to catch some trophy-sized smallmouth bass, northern pike and walleye. Smallmouth bass are found in good numbers over 2 kg (4.5 lbs) in size. Walleye are the main target for most anglers and fishing can be good in the right location and at the right time. Northern pike are sometimes found in abundance to over 5 kg (11 lbs). When angling, be prepared to hook into a wide variety of other species, such as perch, crappie and American eel. A few other sportfish that can be found in this part of the river at times are rainbow trout, brown trout, muskellunge, Atlantic, Coho, pink and Chinook salmon, as well as the odd lake trout and carp. While our depth charts will certainly help you on your fishing adventure, it is recommended to contact a local outfitter or guide for more information on your planned fishing destination. The most popular fishing months are June, July and August.

This portion of the river starts at Brockville and travelling southeast will take you through the Brockville Narrows and the towns of Hillcrest, Butternut Bay, Mallorytown Landing and Rockport along the northern shores of the St. Lawrence and Highway 2. Like almost all of the St. Lawrence, walleye are perhaps the most sought after fish here. Your best bet for walleye is to locate areas along drop-offs or where the current is not slow, but not too strong either. If you can find a decent location, anchor and start jigging with minnows or even just a jig and worm. Walleye fishing has improved over the years in this section, although is still rather slow.

Smallmouth and largemouth bass are also a popular and high population sport fish along this portion of the river around Grenadier Island. There are literally thousands of small islands and underwater shoals that hold dozens of smallmouth. The key is to locate an area and work it with tube jigs or even crayfish imitation flies or lures near the bottom. For northern pike, look in the shallower sections off any of the larger islands. Weed lines are a good sign as to where you can find northern pike. Try trolling a Rapala,

Continued >>

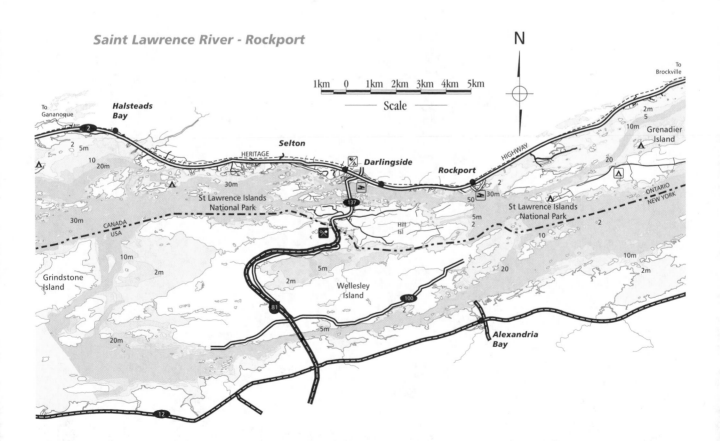

Saint Lawrence River - Rockport

Saint Lawrence River -
Rockport to Brockville

Location: Brockville
Length: 1,245 km (775 mi)
Geographic: 44° 35′ 03″ N, 75° 41′ 08″ W

20 Zone

Fishing

Continued >>

spoon or spinner along these weed areas to entice strikes. Other good places to try are around any drop offs or in or along weed beds. Spinnerbaits and weedless presentations are a good way to locate both species and if the action is slow or tails off, try slowing down your presenta¬tions with some jigs or tube jigs. Topwater baits like poppers can be a ton of fun on calmer overcast days.

A population of brown trout can also be found between Brockville and Rockport. Brown trout were origi-nally introduced into the St. Lawrence over twenty years ago. Subsequent additional introductions have had some success and a fly-fishing following the Ottawa browns has developed. Popular flies are big, olive-coloured woolly buggers or similar streamers. For northern pike, look in the shallower sections off any of the larger islands. Weed lines are a good sign as to where you can find northern pike. Try trolling a Rapala, spoon or spinner along these weed areas to entice strikes. From June to September, this is the best time of the year to pick up trout and salmon in the St. Lawrence River, while muskie are caught in the fall, with October being the best month to fish for these big predators. Anglers should be wary that the river can be a chal¬lenge to fish with strong water currents and many marked and unmarked hazards.

There are also spe¬cial regulations for the St. Lawrence River so make sure you check the updated rules and regulations or check with your local outfitter. Other fish species you will find in this massive river include muskellunge, northern pike, sauger (smaller cousin of the walleye), catfish, gar, carp and panfish (including crappie). Panfish are easily found in the shallows throughout almost all areas of this portion of the Ottawa.

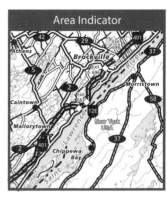

Species	
Brown Trout	Rainbow Trout
Lake Trout	Salmon
Muskellunge	Walleye
Northern Pike	Yellow Perch
Smallmouth Bass	Other

Directions

Getting to this section of the St. Lawrence is acces-sible from Highway 401 to any of the feeder routes to Highway # 2. From Brockville, the coastal town of Hillcrest sits on Anchorage Bay, south you will find Brown's Bay Park between Robinson and Princess Island. More access can be found at Poole's Resort, Rockport and Darlingside. Mountain Road south of Highway 401 will take you to Darlingside, and a little further down at the junction of Highway #2 and #137, you can cross the St. Lawrence and access Hill Island along the Canada United States border. While our map does provide some info, it is recom-mended to visit www.mnr.gov.on.ca for the specific access points along the river and for especially shore fishing opportuni¬ties as this information is invalu-able for areas where you can launch a small boat or canoe. However, be sure to research the area you head out to as strong currents are present in many areas and can be dangerous.

Facilities

Visitors to this region between Brockville and Rockport have plenty of accommoda¬tions and facilities at their fingertips. Countless hotels, motels, shops and restaurants are all at your fingertips.

St. Lawrence Islands National Park if the first Canadian National Park in Canada east of the Rockies, this preserve was established in 1904. St. Lawrence Islands National Park is a group of 20 islands. Accesss is from Mallory Landing and offers a number of amenities for visitors including a beach, picnic area, visitors centre, hiking trails and a boat launch. There is also overnight mooring for passing boaters on a first come, first serve basis. These amenities cover almost all of the islands and most have rustic camping facilities and small trailer/RV lots with outhouses as well.

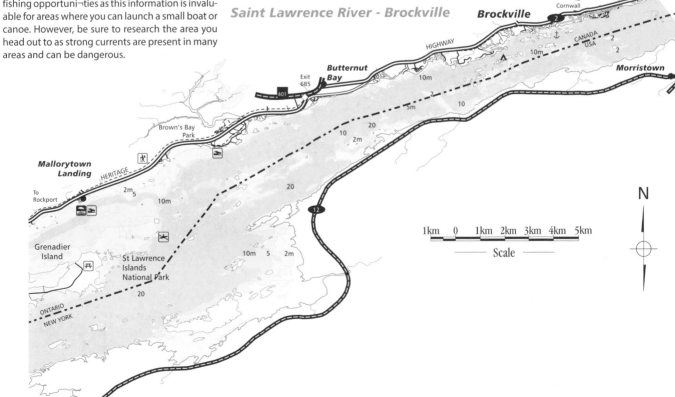

Saint Lawrence River - Brockville

Zone 20

Location: Gananoque
Stream Length: 1,245 km (775 mi)
Geographic: 44°19'56" N, 76°09'40"W

Saint Lawrence River -
Bateau Channel to Gananoque

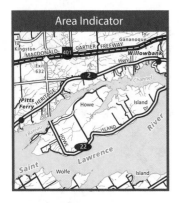

Area Indicator

Species	
Brown Trout	Rainbow Trout
Lake Trout	Salmon
Muskellunge	Walleye
Northern Pike	Yellow Perch
Smallmouth Bass	Other

Fishing

This big and often intimidating river is approximately 1,250 kilometres (776 miles) long draining the Great Lakes into the Atlantic Ocean in the east. The river has gained even greater notoriety over the last century through the development of the picturesque St. Lawrence Thousand Islands. The geography of the area around the river is spectacular and the rolling forest with picturesque bedrock shorelines often captivates visitors. Today, the river remains busy as a shipping line for all the regions bordering the Great Lakes. The region also doubles as a fantastic outdoor playground with visitors from around the world enjoying the many sites and sounds the area has to offer. The historic St. Lawrence River has played an integral role in developing Canada and has been a vital shipping artery since the inception of our nation.

Fishing success in the St. Lawrence River remains among the best in Southern Ontario. Anglers can expect to have the opportunity to catch some trophy-sized smallmouth bass, northern pike and walleye. Smallmouth bass are found in good numbers over 2 kg (4.5 lbs) in size. Walleye are the main target for most anglers and fishing can be good in the right location and at the right time. Northern pike are sometimes found in abundance to over 5 kg (11 lbs). When angling, be prepared to hook into a wide variety of other species, such as perch, crappie and American eel.

Anglers on the St. Lawrence River almost always overlook smallmouth bass and northern pike and the Bateau Channel is no exception. Fishing for both of these sportfish can be quite good at times and there are some big bass and pike caught in the channel annually. Bass are best found near any underwater type structure like a shoal or rock pile, while northern pike are mainly found in the shallow weedy bays. Johnson Bay and the area around Grass Creek are good holding areas for pike. Try working spinner baits or even big attractant flies or lures to find aggressive pike.

The Bateau Channel is known for its quality walleye fishery and anglers flock to the area from around North America as early as May. Perhaps the most effective fishing method is trolling. Try using a worm harness or crankbait next to deeper weed lines. Locating a shoal hump can also dramatically increase your success on the channel. One area in particular that can be productive is around the shoal near Joe Welsh Bay. Some anglers will even anchor near this area and still jig for walleye. Another trick is to try to locate schools of baitfish. The usual predator causing the commotion is smallmouth bass, but you can often catch pike and walleye using this same tactic. Once you locate a walleye, they are often bunched up in schools and you may be in for some impressive non-stop action so cover the spot thoroughly before leaving.

The Thousand Islands area of the St. Lawrence River is also a hot bed for smallmouth bass activity. There are literally thousands of small islands and underwater shoals that hold dozens of smallmouth. The key is to locate an area and work it with tube jigs or even crayfish imitation flies or lures near the bottom. For northern pike, look in the shallower sections off any of the larger islands. Weed lines are a good sign as to where you can find northern pike. Try trolling a Rapala, spoon or spinner along these weed areas to entice strikes.

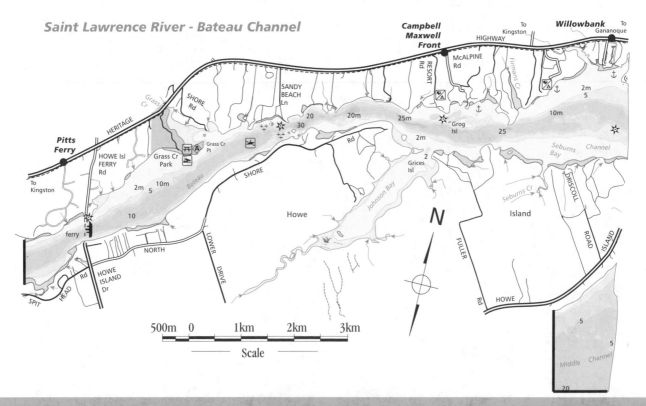

Saint Lawrence River - Bateau Channel

Saint Lawrence River
Bateau Channel to Gananoque

Location: Gananoque
Stream Length: 1,245 km (775 mi)
Geographic: 44°19′56″N, 76°09′40″W

Directions

The Bateau Channel is located east of Kingston and is readily accessible via County Road 2 or the heritage Highway. County Road 2 travels east from Kingston past CFB Kingston and the historic site of Fort Henry. The two main access areas to the Bateau Channel are Campbell Maxwell Front and near Willowbank. Both areas are easily reached via access roads that branch south off County Road 2. An alternate route to Willowbank is to follow Highway 401 to Gananoque. If you follow County Road 32 south from the 401, you will meet County Road 2 in the middle of Gananoque's downtown.

The town of Gananoque is also the main access area for the Thousand Island portion of the St. Lawrence River. To reach Gananoque, follow Highway 401 to Exit 645. Follow County Road 32 south into the town of Gananoque and look for local signs for the marinas and boat launching areas. The Thousand Islands Parkway continues east providing good access to sections further east.

Facilities

The nearby city of Kingston is a fabulous destination near the St. Lawrence River. The city is one of the oldest settlements in Canada and is characterized with cobblestone streets, fantastic restaurants, accommodations and entertainment. Marinas and public launching facilities can be found in several areas in Kingston as well as in nearby Gananoque. North of Kingston and Gananoque, you will find hundreds of fantastic inland lakes to explore, regions such as Frontenac Provincial Park or the Rideau Canal Waterway provide access to some of the best fishing lakes in the region and they are merely minutes to the north of the St. Lawrence River system.

Camping enthusiasts can visit one of the many parks of the St. Lawrence or even the St. Lawrence Islands National Park. For more information on parks of the St. Lawrence, call (800) 437-2233 or visit www.stlawrenceparks.com. Visitors wishing to find out more about the St. Lawrence Islands National Park can call (800) 839-8221.

Area Indicator

Species	
Brown Trout	Rainbow Trout
Lake Trout	Salmon
Muskellunge	Walleye
Northern Pike	Yellow Perch
Smallmouth Bass	Other

Saint Lawrence River - Gananoque

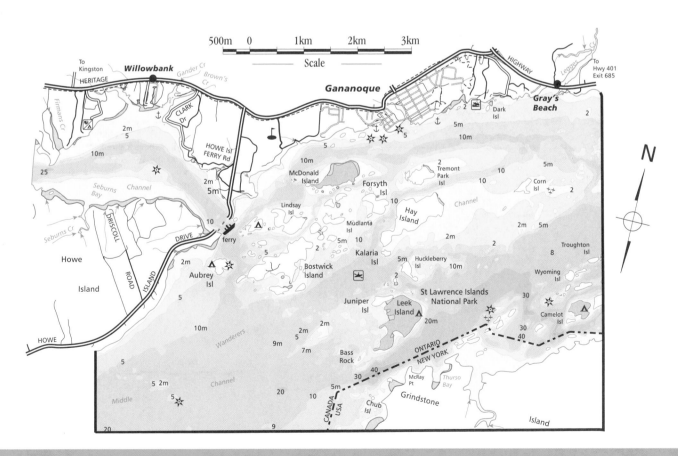

Zone **15**

Location: 24 km (15 mi) southwest of Gooderham
Maximum Depth: 29.2 m (96 ft)
Mean Depth: 15 m (49.2 ft)
Way Point: 44° 49′ 00″ Lat - N, 78° 27′ 00″ Lon - W

Salmon Lake

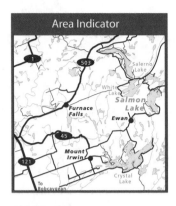
Area Indicator

Species
Lake Trout
Largemouth Bass
Smallmouth Bass
Yellow Perch

Fishing

Smallmouth bass provide the majority of the fishing action on Salmon Lake. Smallmouth can be found throughout the lake near rocky drop-offs along the shore and near the two islands. It is also recommended to also look for smallies around any one of the underwater rock piles found around the lake. An area that is known to hold some lunker smallmouth is the 4 m (9 ft) shoal hump found just north of Eureka Island.

The other main sport fish species is lake trout. Lake trout were stocked in Salmon Lake up until the early 1990's to supplement natural populations. Today, Salmon Lake relies on natural reproduction for its lakers, enhancing the need for catch and release. Be sure to check the regulations before fishing on Salmon Lake, as there are slot size and ice fishing restrictions in place to aid the fragile lake trout stocks.

Directions

Salmon Lake is another fine lake found in the Kawartha Highlands. From the southwest, follow Highway 35 north to the town of Norland. County Road 45 travels east from Norland to the town of Kinmount. At Kinmount, County Road 45 changes to Highway 503. Travel east along Highway 503 to White Lake Road. Take White Lake Road east to the settlement of Fortescue and the junction with the North Salmon Lake Road. Following the North Salmon Lake Road will lead you to Salmon Lake.

North Salmon Lake Road can also be found off Highway 507 to the east.

Facilities

There is a public boat launch located along the northern shore of Salmon Lake that can be reached via an access road off the North Salmon Lake Road. For supplies, the town of Kinmount has plenty to offer.

Other Options

If you take White Lake Road en route to Salmon Lake, you will pass the southern end of **Salerno Lake** approximately 2 km west of North Salmon Lake Road. Salerno Lake is another cottage destination lake in the area that offers decent fishing for visitors. The lake is inhabited by mainly smallmouth bass but there are reports of largemouth bass lurking in the shallower areas. Walleye and muskellunge round out the angling options in Salerno Lake.

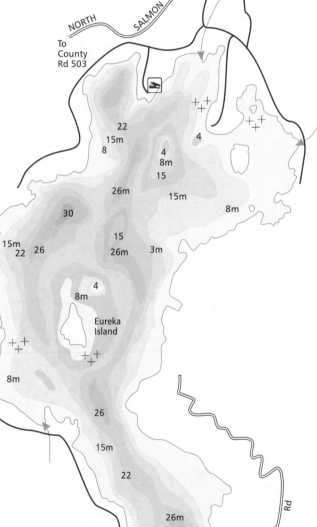

N

100m 0 100m 200m 300m 400m 500m
Scale

Sand Lake - Jones Falls

Location: Jones Falls
Elevation: 116 m (380 ft)
Surface Area: 828 ha (2,046 ac)
Maximum Depth: 14.3 m (47 ft)
Mean Depth: 5.2 m (17 ft)
Way Point: 44° 34′00″N, 76° 16′00″W

Fishing

Sand Lake is a Rideau Canal Waterway lake that is inhabited by a number of warm water sportfish, such as smallmouth bass, largemouth bass, northern pike and walleye. Fishing is usually slow for smallmouth bass, although success for largemouth bass can be fair to good at times. Bass in Sand Lake can reach up to 1.5 kg (3.5 lbs) in size and are mainly found in the shallower, weedy areas of the lake such as in the eastern portion of the lake. In the eastern end of the lake, there are a few 3 m (10 ft) humps that often hold good numbers of bass. Working a jig along the bottom of these shoals can also pick up the odd northern pike.

Anglers looking to find northern pike will find success much slower than for bass. Pike are best found in the shallower sections of the lake and can be caught using bass gear and even top water flies and lures on occasion. Two higher success areas for pike are the two 5 m (15 ft) humps located in the middle and northeastern end of the lake.

A small population of walleye remains in Sand Lake, although fishing success is quite slow. To help with spawning success, there are special annual sanctuary areas in place. Be sure to check your regulations for specifics on these areas.

Area Indicator

Species	
Brook Trout	Walleye
Largemouth Bass	Whitefish
Northern Pike	Yellow Perch
Smallmouth Bass	Other

Directions

Located in between the cities of Smiths Falls to the north and Kingston to the south, Sand Lake can be reached not far off Highway 15. Follow Highway 15 to the County Road 11 and head west. Shortly along the road, you will pass nearby Eel Bay at the southern end of the lake.

Facilities

There are no public boat launching facilities onto Sand Lake, although there are a number of pay per use launching facilities available at private lodges and resorts on the lake. A small marina, located in Eel Bay along the southern shore offers pay per use access to the lake.

For supplies and other amenities, the village of Newboro is located minutes to the north. Alternatively, the cities of Kingston to the south and Smiths Falls to the north are about thirty minutes away by vehicle.

Other Options

Whitefish Lake lies to the south of Sand Lake and is accessible via the Rideau Canal. This popular cottage destination lake offers fair fishing for smallmouth and largemouth bass in the 0.5-1 kg (1-2 lb) range. A small population of northern pike also exists in the lake. There are special sanctuary locations on the lake, therefore, be sure to check the regulations before heading out.

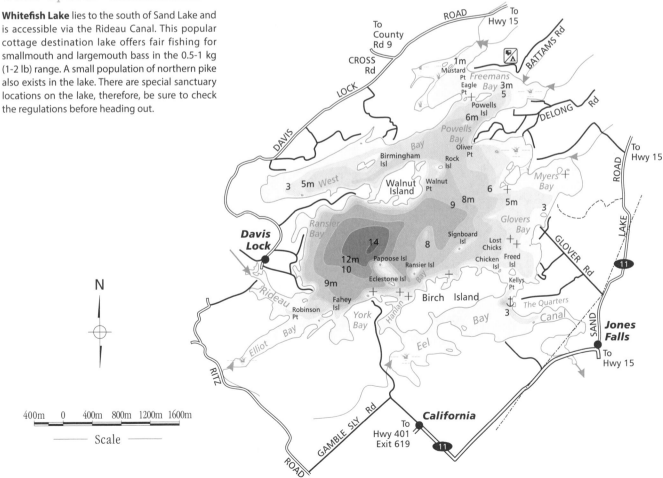

Zone 18

Location: Westport
Surface Area: 157 ha (388 ac)
Maximum Depth: 12.2 m (40 ft)
Mean Depth: 6.8 m (22.3 ft)
Way Point: 44° 41′ 00″ N, 76° 26′ 00″ W

Sand Lake - Westport

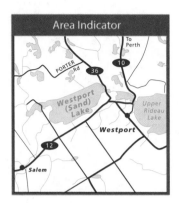

Area Indicator

Species
Largemouth Bass
Northern Pike
Smallmouth Bass
Walleye

Other Options

Tommy Lake is a small lake that lies approximately 5 km (3 mi) to the north of Sand Lake and can be reached via a short access road off County Road 36. Tommy Lake offers fair fishing at times for smallmouth and largemouth bass in the 0.5-1 kg (1-2 lb) range. Some larger bass are caught in the lake annually.

Fishing

As a popular summer destination, Sand Lake receives significant angling pressure. Regardless, anglers can still have a lot of fun on this scenic Eastern Ontario lake. Fishing is fair for smallmouth and largemouth bass, which can reach up to 1.5 kg (3.5 lbs) in size. Bass are best found along the weedy shoreline areas of the lake usually in the 2-4 m (6-13 ft) depth range. Working a tube jig or other type of jig off bottom can be effective during slow periods. When bass are aggressive, most quick presentations like a spinner can create action.

Northern pike and walleye also inhabit Sand Lake, although in smaller numbers than bass. Fishing success for pike is regarded as slow to fair for mainly small northerns. Walleye fishing can be even slower, which is not surprising given the heavy fishing pressure the lake receives. Jigging or trolling a worm harness seems to work for walleye on occasion, while northern pike can be taken on spinner baits, jigs and other faster type presentations.

Be sure to check your regulations for special sanctuary areas on Sand Lake.

Directions

Located just minutes west from downtown Westport, this small lake is a popular summer destination which is often called Westport rather than Sand Lake. To find the lake, follow Highway 15 to Crosby, which lies south of the village of Portland. Head west along County Road 42 and minutes after you pass the village of Newboro you will find Westport, which lies along the western end of Upper Rideau Lake. Sand Lake can be found by following County Road 12 southwest from Westport.

Facilities

There is no boat launch facilities available onto Sand Lake, however, it is possible to launch a canoe from the picnic area off Mountain Road (County Road 36) or from near the Wolfe Lake Dam off the 9th Concession Road.

Cottages line most of the southern and western shore of this lake, many of which can be rented throughout the summer season. Inquire locally in Westport for rental information. Westport also has a number of retailers available as well as restaurants and accommodations for visitors.

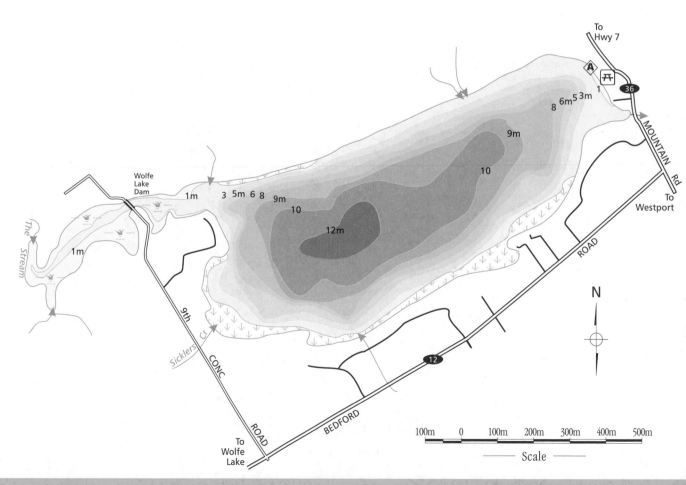

Sandy Lake- Harvey Township

Location: 5 km (3 mi) west of Buckhorn
Maximum Depth: 12.9 m (42.3 ft)
Mean Depth: 6.1m (20.1 ft)
Way Point: 44°32'43" Lat - N, 78°24'19" Long - W

17 Zone

Directions

Sandy Lake is a part of the large chain of Kawartha Lakes that stretches from the Trenton area to Orillia. Since it is not part of the Trent Severn Waterway, Sandy Lake is not as busy as some of the lakes in the area. The lake lies just to the north of Buckhorn Lake and is accessible via cottage roads west of the town of Buckhorn. To reach Buckhorn, take Highway 28 north of Lindsay to Burleigh Falls. At Burleigh falls, follow County Road 36 west all the way to Buckhorn.

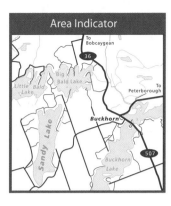

Area Indicator

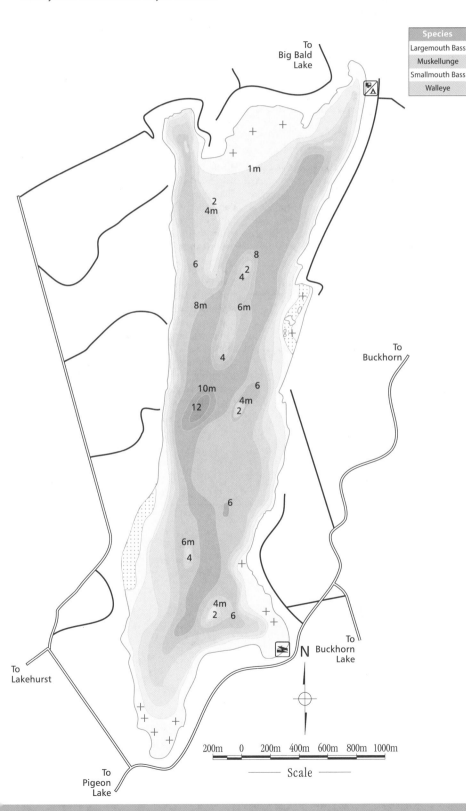

Species
Largemouth Bass
Muskellunge
Smallmouth Bass
Walleye

Fishing

As a more out-of-the-way lake, the fishing in Sandy Lake is said to be better than in the lakes of the Trent Severn Waterway. Sandy Lake is home to several cottages and camps, but still maintains its rough nature lustre. Smallmouth and largemouth bass are the two most abundant sport fish found in the lake and fishing can be good at times. Walleye remain main fishing attraction and can be found in fair to good numbers. Muskellunge round out the large sport fish specimens in Sandy Lake and are available in small to fair numbers.

Sandy Lake is a very unique lake due to the fact that it is spring fed, which is a rarity in this region. The spring fed nature of the lake has resulted in water clarity that is unlike any other Kawartha lake and a water colour that is almost turquoise in nature. The lake also has a very diverse bottom structure. One glance at the depth chart will reveal several 2-4 m (6-13 ft) shoals around the lake. These shoals are ideal holding areas for baitfish and as a result, good locations to try your luck for predators such as walleye or muskellunge. Try stationary jigging or trolling over one of these shoals to target walleye and musky.

Facilities

Along with the numerous cottages and camps, there is a tent and trailer park available on the north eastern shore. Boat access is provided at the tent and trailer park or at the southeast end of the lake. For basic supplies, the town of Buckhorn is not far away or alternatively, you can travel back to Lakefield for more services.

Other Options

Since Sandy Lake lies in the midst of the Trent Severn Kawartha Lakes, there are plenty of accessible angling options close by. **Buckhorn Lake** to the south and the **Bald Lakes** to the north are two fine fishing alternatives. Healthy populations of smallmouth bass, largemouth bass, walleye and muskellunge inhabit both lake systems.

Zone 18

Location: 29 km (18 mi) north of Kaladar
Elevation: 268 m (880 ft)
Surface Area: 268 ha (661 ac)
Maximum Depth: 32 m (105 ft)
Mean Depth: 12.4 m (40.7 ft)
Way Point: 44° 54' 00" N, 77° 08' 00" W

Shabomeka Lake

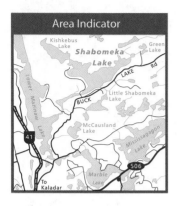

Area Indicator

Species	
Largemouth Bass	Whitefish
Lake Trout	Yellow Perch
Smallmouth Bass	Other

Shabomeka Lake		
Fish Stocking Data		
Year	Species	Number
2013	Lake Trout	2,100
2012	Lake Trout	2,100
2011	Lake Trout	4,100

Fishing

The rugged character of this region makes Shabomeka Lake a scenic lake that offers fishing opportunities for smallmouth bass, largemouth bass and stocked lake trout. Fishing for bass is fair to good at times for nice sized bronze backs. The area around the dam along the southwest shore is a good holding area. In addition, the two small islands and the rocky shoreline of this lake should be explored when looking for lunker bass. Work both tube jigs and crayfish imitations along the bottom. As the bait moves by, bass will often suck it in thinking it is an easy meal.

A natural lake trout population once existed in this lake, although similar to hundreds of other Southern Ontario lakes, the population could not handle excessive fishing pressure. Today, lake trout are stocked in Shabomeka Lake annually and provide for fair fishing through the ice in winter or in the spring just after ice off.

Adding to the mix are panfish like yellow perch, pumpkinseed sunfish and other non-traditional sportfish like whitefish. All are relatively easy to catch and make a fine alternative to the beginner angler.

Directions

Located just outside of Bon Echo Provincial Park, Shabomeka Lake is a picturesque Eastern Ontario lake. To reach the lake, follow Highway 41 north from the village of Kaladar and look for the Buck Lake Road just north of Cloyne. Buck Lake Road is a gravel road that travels east from the highway providing access to the southern shore of the lake.

Other Options

Semicircle Lake is the small lake formed by the dam off the southwest end of Shabomeka Lake. The smaller lake is surrounded by Crown Land and offers fair fishing for smallmouth bass and small northern pike.

Facilities

A rough public boat launch is located off Buck Lake Road along the southern shore of the lake. Shabomeka Lake is also part of the **Kishkebus Canoe Route**, a fantastic canoe route that travels in a circle from Mazinaw Lake. Paddlers have established rustic campsites on the portions of Crown Land that still exist.

If you prefer more established campsites, nearby **Bon Echo Provincial Park** lies off Highway 41. It is a full facility provincial park providing all amenities including flush toilets, laundry, showers and electrical services. The park is home to 528 campsites, including a number of interior access tenting sites. The park is quite popular during the summer months, especially on weekends, therefore, it is highly recommended to make reservations at (888) ONT-PARK before arrival. For more information on Bon Echo Provincial Park, call (613) 336-2228.

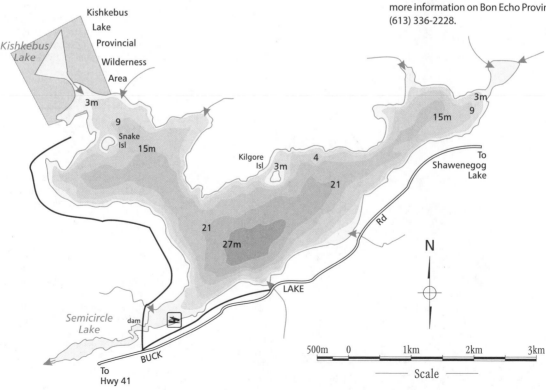

Shadow Lake

Location: Norland
Max Depth: 22 m (72.1 ft)
Mean Depth: 11.5 m (37.9 ft)
Way Point: 44° 43' 00" Lat - N, 78° 48' 00" Long - W

Facilities

There is a main boat launch area in the town of Norland along the northwest side of Shadow Lake. Alternatively, there is a more rustic car top access further down from the boat launch. For overnight accommodations, there are two tent and trailer parks located on the lake. For more established camping, **Balsam Lake Provincial Park** can be found within minutes of Norland to the south off County Road 48. The provincial park offers everything from showers to flush toilets, although can be busy in the summer. Call (888) ONT-PARK for reservations.

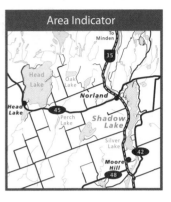

Area Indicator

Species
Largemouth Bass
Muskellunge
Smallmouth Bass
Walleye
Other

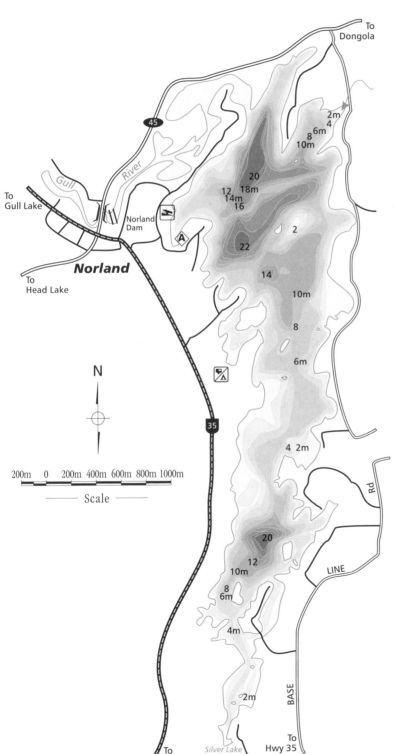

Fishing

Shadow Lake is a well developed cottage destination lake that experiences some significant fishing pressure throughout the year. Fishing is best for smallmouth and largemouth bass. Bass can be found around shore structure such as cottage docks or rocky shoreline. Look for both species off any one of the islands found around the lake.

Walleye are the most heavily fished sport fish species in Shadow Lake and provide for generally fair fishing much of the time. Walleye average about 0.5-1.5 kg (1-3.5 lbs) on the lake. Some recommended walleye holding areas are off any of the large shoal areas found in the middle of the lake or around the 2 m (4 ft) shoal hump in the north end. In both cases, try to locate some weed structure, as walleye will cruise these areas in search of baitfish. In spring, walleye can be found regularly in the shoal areas but in the summer, they tend to frequent the shoals only during the evening or heavy overcast periods.

Muskellunge are also found in Shadow Lake but fishing success is marginal. Anglers who hook into a musky can expect a fish that averages about 3-4 kg (7-9 lbs) in size.

Directions

Shadow Lake is found next to the town of Norland, just off Highway 35. To find the lake, simply follow Highway 35 north from Lindsay to Norland. Look for the signs in town directing you from the highway to the access areas on the lake.

Other Options

To the north of Shadow Lake, the rolling terrain begins to become more rustic compared to the Norland area. This region is home to countless fishing lakes, including **Gull Lake**, which is about found 10 km north of Norland just off the highway. Gull Lake is a large lake that offers fishing opportunities for largemouth bass, smallmouth bass and lake trout.

Zone 18

Location: Sharbot Lake
Elevation: 195 m (639 ft)
Surface Area: 705 ha (1,742 ac)
Maximum Depth: 32 m (105 ft)
Mean Depth: 8.1m (26.5 ft)
Way Point: 44° 46′ 00″ N, 76° 41′ 00″W

Sharbot Lake

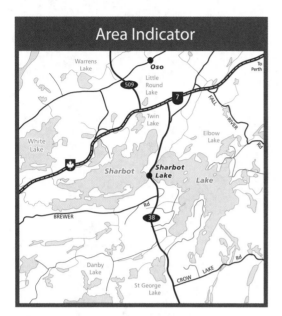

Area Indicator

Directions

Sharbot Lake makes up the scenic backdrop for the village of Sharbot Lake. Both the town and the lake are easily accessible as they lie just off the south side of Highway 7 west of the town of Perth. Boat launches are found at Sharbot Lake Provincial Park off of Highway 7 and in town off of Highway 38. This quieter highway connects Highway 401 in the south near Kingston with Highway 7 in the north and runs right through the lake and village of Sharbot Lake.

Facilities

The village of Sharbot Lake lies between the east and west portions of Sharbot Lake. There is a public boat launch at the bridge separating the two sections of the lake along with a nice beach and play area. The village is home to a grocery store, bank and a few other retailers for all of your fishing supplies. Scattered around town and the lake are a host of inns, lodges and resorts and even private cottage rentals. Inquire locally or simply search the internet to find the location that suites you.

A main attraction to the lake during the summer months is **Sharbot Lake Provincial Park.** Camping enthusiasts can enjoy one of the 194 full service campsites along with beaches, boat rentals, docking and launching facilities. Visitors can also enjoy the nature trails and the paddling opportunities available. For more information on Sharbot Provincial Park call (613) 335-2814 or for campsite reservations call 888-ONT-PARK or visit www.ontarioparks.com.

Other Options

There are dozens if not hundreds of nearby lakes in the Land O' lakes region. One of the closest is **Little Round Lake**. This small lake is located just north of Sharbot Lake at the junction between Highway 7 and Highway 509. The lake is stocked with brook trout every few years, which provide for fair to good fishing through the ice in winter and in the spring just after ice off. While most of the trout caught in the lake are small, the odd brookie can be of good size in this lake.

Fishing

Found 120 km west of Ottawa and 70 km north of Kingston, Sharbot Lake is found in the popular tourist destination of Land O' lakes region because of the numerous lakes in the region. The lake is named after the Mohawk native settler Francis Sharbot. Sharbot built a cabin near the lake in 1826 and a few years later, European settlers arrived and named the lake after Francis. Today, the lake is a popular summer destination lake and receives significant angling pressure throughout the year. The lake is inhabited with smallmouth bass, largemouth bass, northern pike, walleye and a naturally reproducing strain of lake trout. Panfish, such as perch, also provide for steady action for the kids or kid at heart.

The lake itself was created by glaciers and is a deep spring fed that consists of two bodies of water; Upper and Lower Sharbot Lake. There are about 100 islands spread throughout the lake and expansive shallows with weed beds to attract the pike and bass as well as long channels reaching depths over 30 metres (100 feet) that hold lake trout and walleye.

The many islands and numerous back bays provide good holding areas for bass and northern pike. Smallmouth and largemouth bass can be found in the 1.5 kg (3.5 lb) range and will often strike lures and flies like spinners or streamers. Look for smallmouth near rocky shoreline structures or shoal areas in the 3 metre (10 foot) range. Largemouth bass can be found around the shoreline and structure areas of the lake, although they frequent the shallower, weedy areas of the east side of the lake. Try casting a spinner bait or jig through weed patches for ambush ready bucket mouths. When fishing success for bass is slow, try flipping a jig or crayfish imitation off the bottom. Bass anglers will periodically hook into a cruising pike in this weedy area.

Generally, you will find small to medium size pike in the quiet bays, whereas big pike are often found in the areas leading into bays. The larger pike will also hang around rocky points, shoals, islands and other places where there are larger fish that they can feed on. When heading out pike fishing, be sure to have various sizes of the old trusty red and white Daredevil spoon in your box. A few other suggestions include the yellow Five of Diamonds or even bright coloured Rapalas.

The most two most sought after sportfish in Sharbot Lake are walleye and lake trout. Walleye can be found in both the eastern and western sections of Sharbot Lake, while lake trout are mainly located in the western areas. Walleye fishing is usually slow, although it is better than for lake trout. Many anglers prefer to slow troll for walleye with Rapalas or worm harnesses. Dragging the lure along weed lines or drop-off areas is your best bet for success for these elusive sportfish. Jigging off underwater shoal humps or near points is also a popular angling method for walleye.

The lake trout in Sharbot Lake are a naturally reproducing strain of trout, which are becoming increasingly rare in Eastern Ontario. Lake trout are also quite active just after ice off when they are found closer to the surface. Anglers will find success by trolling silver or gold spoons or larger streamer type flies that imitate baitfish. For trolling, the Little Cleo or Diamond King are good bets, while fly fishers should try a grey and white streamer with some crystal flash. In the summer, the lake trout go deep, and you will need a downrigger or lead core line to get to them. A baited lure with lots of action, like a Flatfish or Kwikfish, trolled just off the bottom will work best. If you do happen to catch a laker, please practice catch and release, as these species are quite fragile.

In addition to the bigger fish species described above, Sharbot Lake does hold the ever popular panfish, most notably perch. Perch are feisty fish that can easily be caught from shore using the classic bait and bobber set up. They are also quite active in the winter so if action is slow for lake trout, walleye or pike; turn your attention to perch.

Sharbot Lake

Location: Sharbot Lake
Elevation: 195 m (639 ft)
Surface Area: 705 ha (1,742 ac)
Maximum Depth: 32 m (105 ft)
Mean Depth: 8.1m (26.5 ft)
Way Point: 44° 46' 00" N, 76° 41' 00" W

Species	
Lake Trout	Smallmouth Bass
Largemouth Bass	Walleye
Northern Pike	Whitefish
Panfish	Yellow Perch

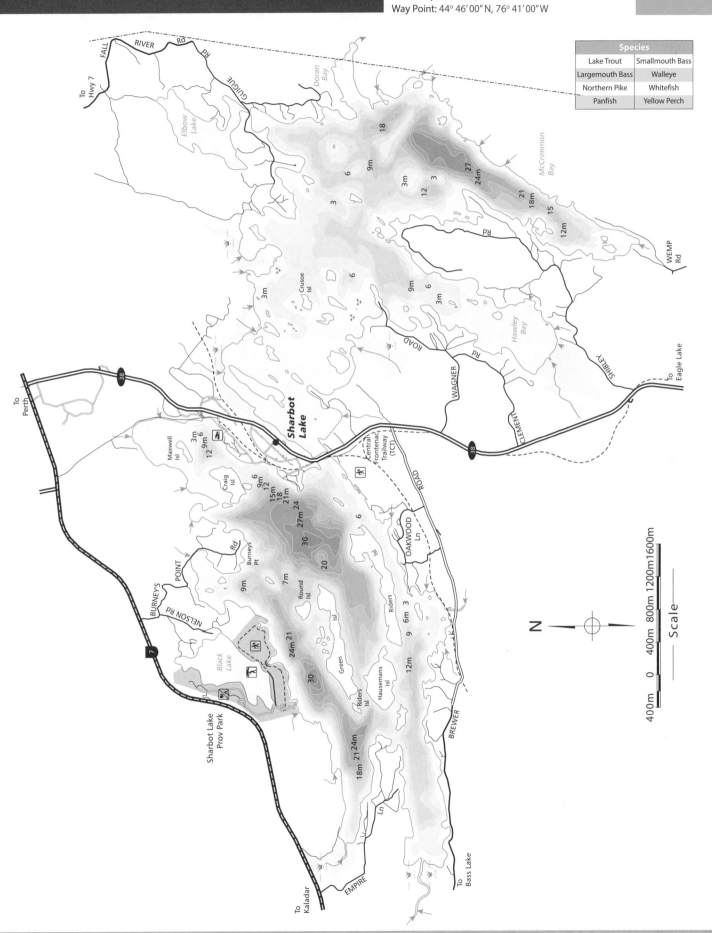

Scale

400m 0 400m 800m 1200m 1600m

N

Location: Norland
Maximum Depth: 22 m (72.1 ft)
Mean Depth: 11.5 m (37.9 ft)
Way Point: 44° 41′00″ Lat - N, 78° 48′00″ Long - W

Silver Lake- Coboconk

Area Indicator

Fishing

The main sport fish that inhabit this warm water lake are bass, walleye and muskellunge. Fishing for bass is best, as smallmouth bass and largemouth bass are both found in the lake in good numbers. Both bass species are mainly located along the shoreline area. Smallmouth can be found deeper than largemouth off rock drop-offs around the lake. The inflow of the Gull River is often a high producing area.

Although they are the preferred species, fishing for walleye and muskellunge is much slower than for bass. Walleye average about 0.5-1.5 kg (1-3.5 lbs) in size and can be found near the Gull River inflow and outflow areas mainly in spring. As the summer sets in, look for walleye off the large shoal area in the eastern portion of the lake. Locating underwater vegetation is essential in producing consistent results for walleye on this lake. Ardent musky anglers will tell you the lake is a pleasure to fish but the average angler may not find too many musky in Silver Lake.

Species	
Black Crappie	Smallmouth Bass
Largemouth Bass	Walleye
Muskellunge	Yellow Perch

Directions

North of the town of Coboconk, Silver Lake can be accessed just off the east side of Highway 35. Although the lake itself can be seen from the highway, the main access is found to the north on Shadow Lake at the town of Norland. In Norland, there are signs on Highway 35 that can easily direct you to the boat launch onto Shadow Lake. From the access area, you must travel south via Shadow Lake then along the meandering Gull River to access Silver Lake.

Facilities

Although Silver Lake is a highly developed lake, there are no immediate amenities found on the lake. Supplies can be picked up in either the town of Norland or Coboconk, while there are a few motels in the area that offer overnight accommodation.

Other Options

Via Highway 35, you can reach a multitude of fishing lakes found north of Silver and Shadow Lakes. Only minutes away, you will pass by **Moore Lake** and **Gull Lake**, both accessible from the highway. Both lakes offer fishing for smallmouth bass, largemouth bass and lake trout. As with most Kawartha area lakes, lake trout populations are quite low.

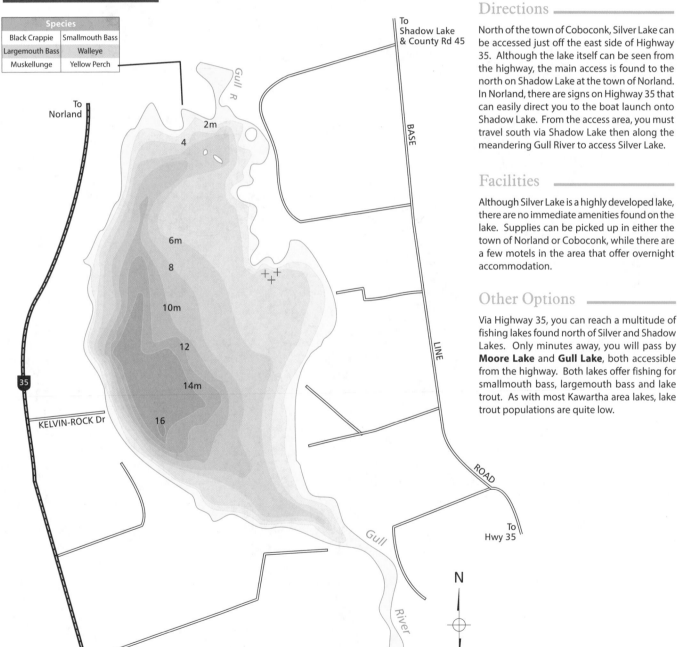

100m   0   100m   200m   300m   400m   500m

— Scale —

Silver Lake- Perth

Location: 5 km (3 mi) north of Sharbot Lake
Elevation: 206 m (675 ft)
Surface Area: 246 ha (608 ac)
Maximum Depth: 24.4 m (80 ft)
Mean Depth: 10.5 m (34.4 ft)
Way Point: 44° 50′ 00″ N, 76° 36′ 00″ W

Fishing

Although Highway 7 flanks the southern shoreline of Silver Lake, the lake remains quite scenic and is home to relatively few cottages. Fishing pressure remains heavy since the lake is easily accessible and there is a popular provincial park on the lake. However, persistent anglers will find smallmouth bass, largemouth bass, northern pike and stocked lake trout.

Smallmouth bass are the most active sportfish and they make up the bulk of action in Silver Lake. Largemouth bass catches are rare. Look for bass along the rocky shoreline areas of the lake. Most anglers will stray away from the highway side of the lake but there is good rock structure here that was created by the road construction. This rock structure attracts bass. Working jigs, spinners and other similar type lures in these areas can be productive. Fly anglers should try crayfish imitation flies or bright streamers. Working streamers in an erratic fashion along the shoreline can create decent action at times.

Silver Lake once supported a natural lake trout fishery, although today, lakers are stocked annually. Fishing is fair for decent sized lake trout and is usually better through the ice and in the spring, just after ice off. While the standard tolling option for lakers is either a silver or gold spoon, some recommended trolling options include most William's spoons, the Little Cleo, Luhr Jensen Diamond King, and even the plastic Apex.

A population of northern pike also exists in the lake. Pike are suckers for a well trolled lure. Other lures that work include a natural colour Rapala Husky Jerk, soft jerkbaits worked slowly over fallen trees, spinnerbaits or natural baits like minnows and worms.

Directions

East of the town of Sharbot Lake, Silver Lake can be found off the north side of Highway 7. Highway 7 travels east to west from the city of Ottawa to Peterborough.

Facilities

Silver Lake Provincial Park lies along the eastern shore of the lake and is home to 148 campsites. Amenities such as a boat launch, rentals and showers are available at the park for visitors to enjoy. The park is quite popular during the summer months, especially on weekends, therefore, it is highly recommended to make reservations at (888) ONT-PARK before arrival. For more specific information on Silver Lake Provincial Park, call (613) 268-2000.

For supplies, the nearby town of Sharbot Lake is home to a grocery store, bank and various other retailers. A small day-use picnicking area is also available along the southwest shore of Silver Lake.

Other Options

About 7 km (4 mi) west of Silver Lake, you can find **Little Round Lake** off the north side of Highway 7. The lake actually lies at the junction of Highway 7 and Highway 509. The lake is stocked annually with brook trout, which provide for fair to good fishing through the ice and in spring just after ice off. Try jigging small spoons through the ice or using small spinners during the spring.

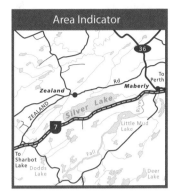

Area Indicator

Species	
Lake Trout	Smallmouth Bass
Largemouth Bass	Splake
Northern Pike	Walleye
Rainbow Trout	Yellow Perch

Silver Lake - Perth		
Fish Stocking Data		
Year	Species	Number
2013	Lake Trout	5,000
2012	Lake Trout	5,000
2011	Lake Trout	5,000

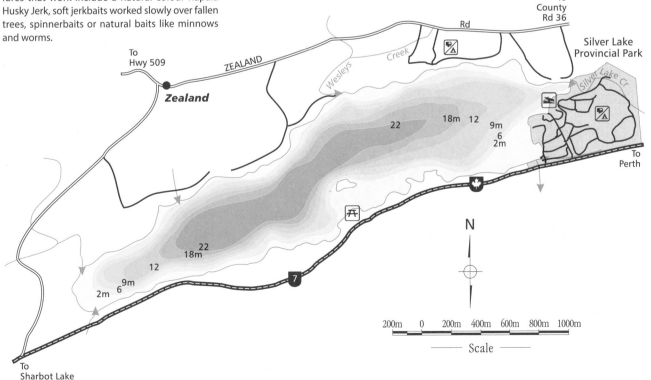

Location: 3 km (1.8 mi) south of Lyndhurst
Elevation: 84 m (276 ft)
Surface Area: 76 ha (188 ac)
Maximum Depth: 13.4 m (44 ft)
Mean Depth: 5.6 m (18.3 ft)
Way Point: 44° 31' 00" N, 76° 07' 00" W

Singleton Lake

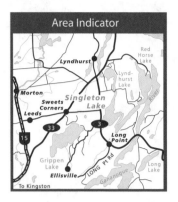

Area Indicator

Species	
Black Crappie	Smallmouth Bass
Largemouth Bass	Yellow Perch
Northern Pike	Other

Fishing

This summer destination lake offers fishing opportunities for smallmouth bass, largemouth bass and northern pike. Fishing for bass is slow to fair for bass to 1 kg (2 lbs). Shoreline structure is the best area to look for bass. Try casting jigs, spinners and streamer type flies towards shore and even cottage docks for ambush ready bass.

A population of northern pike also exists in the lake, although fishing success is usually slow. Northerns can be found along shoreline areas at dusk or during overcast periods. The main hot spots found around Singleton Lake are near any of the small islands or at the mouth of the Lyndhurst Creek. The area around the creek mouth sports good weed growth, creating good habitat for northern pike and bass.

Directions

Singleton Lake lies west of the popular Charleston Lake Provincial Park. One way to find the lake is to take Highway 401 to Exit 659 east of Gananoque. Travel north from Highway 401 along the Prince Reynolds Road (County Road 3). The Prince Reynolds Road passes by the southern shore of Red Horse Lake before reaching the western shore of Singleton Lake.

Facilities

A pay per use boat launch facility is available along the western shore of Singleton Lake at the tent and trailer park. Camping enthusiasts can also stay at **Charleston Lake Provincial Park** located minutes east of Singleton Lake. The park is a full facility park offering all the amenities.

For supplies, Seeley's Bay is located west of the lake and is home to a general store. Alternatively, the village of Delta is minutes north and the town of Gananoque is located not far to the south of Singleton Lake.

Other Options

To the north of Singleton Lake, you can find **Lyndhurst Lake**. The lake can be reached by watercraft from Singleton Lake or by vehicle off County Road 33. Fishing in the lake is fair for largemouth and smallmouth bass in the 0.5-1 kg (1-2 lb) range. Northern pike also inhabit the lake and fishing can be fair at times for generally small northerns.

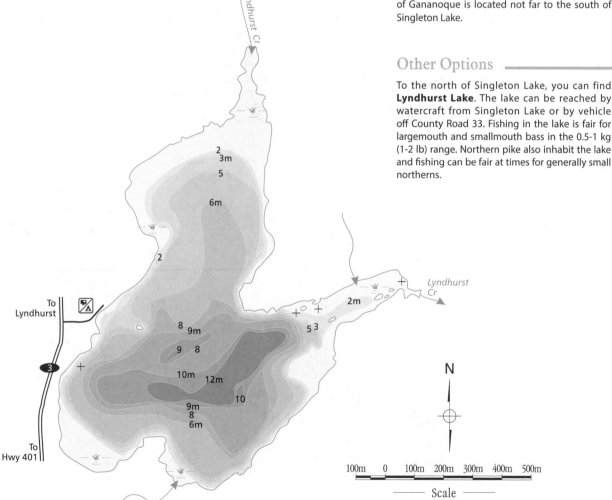

Skootamatta Lake

Location: 3 km (1.8 mi) northwest of Cloyne
Elevation: 305 m (1,000 ft)
Surface Area: 1,287 ha (3,178 ac)
Maximum Depth: 29.2 m (96 ft)
Mean Depth: 8.5 m (27.5 ft)
Way Point: 44° 50′00″N, 77° 16′00″W

Fishing

Skootamatta Lake is an odd shaped lake that offers fair fishing for smallmouth and largemouth bass that can reach up to 2 kg (4.5 lbs) in size. Smallmouth are the dominant bass species found in the lake and make up the majority of the bass action. The rocky shoreline areas around Skootamatta Lake are the prime holding areas for bass. There are also numerous quiet bays that hold good numbers of smallmouth and largemouth bass. In particular, the 2 m (6 ft) hump located east of Big Island is a known hot spot for smallmouth. Tube jigs or crayfish imitation lures or flies can work well along this and other shoal areas.

Anglers on Skootamatta Lake can also expect to have opportunities to catch muskellunge, northern pike, walleye and even whitefish. These predatory fish can be a challenge to find, but trolling a flashy spoon around the lake during the dawn and dusk periods can reap benefits. A few hot spots for walleye and northern pike include the two 6–9 metre (20–30 foot) shoals located just west of Big Island.

Directions

South of Bon Echo Provincial Park, the damming of the Skootamatta River formed this large man-made lake. To find the lake from the south, head north along Highway 41 from Highway 7 at the village of Kaladar. Just past Cloyne, look for Addington Road off the west side of the highway. Addington Road leads northwest to Trails End Road. Turn west along Trails End Road to reach Skootamatta Lake. From Addington Road, there are a few other branch roads that provide access to various other areas of Skootamatta Lake.

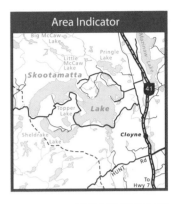

Area Indicator

Species	
Largemouth Bass	Smallmouth Bass
Muskellunge	Walleye
Northern Pike	Whitefish

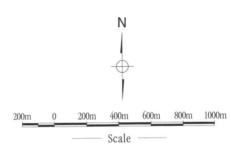

N

200m   0   200m   400m   600m   800m   1000m

Scale

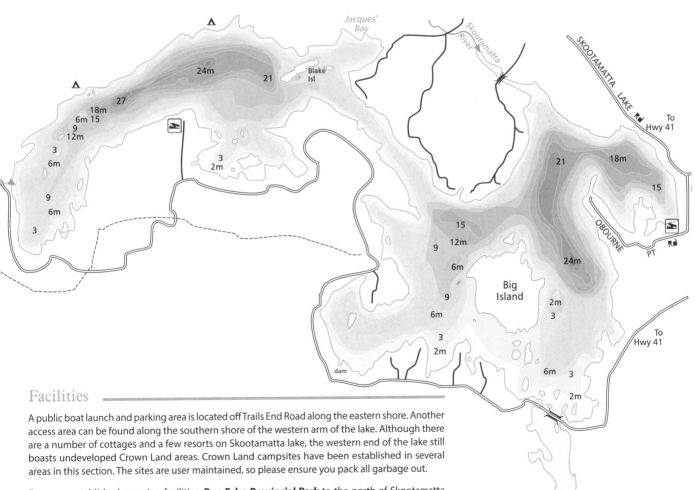

Facilities

A public boat launch and parking area is located off Trails End Road along the eastern shore. Another access area can be found along the southern shore of the western arm of the lake. Although there are a number of cottages and a few resorts on Skootamatta lake, the western end of the lake still boasts undeveloped Crown Land areas. Crown Land campsites have been established in several areas in this section. The sites are user maintained, so please ensure you pack all garbage out.

For more established camping facilities, **Bon Echo Provincial Park** to the north of Skootamatta Lake is home to over 500 campsites. The park also offers full amenities such as flush toilets and showers for visitors to enjoy.

Location: 10 km (6 mi) northwest of Gananoque
Elevation: 99 m (325 ft)
Surface Area: 220 ha (543 ac)
Maximum Depth: 14.6 m (48 ft)
Mean Depth: 5.3 m (17.5 ft)
Way Point: 44° 26′ 00″ N, 76° 13′ 00″ W

South Lake

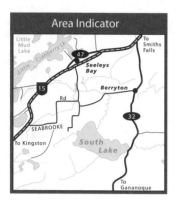

Area Indicator

Species
Largemouth Bass
Northern Pike
Smallmouth Bass

Fishing

Anglers visiting South Lake can expect to find fair fishing for smallmouth and largemouth bass in the 0.5-1 kg (1-2 lb) range. There are plenty of good holding areas as there is ample weed structure throughout the shallow lake. Try casting jigs and spinners along weed beds for ambush ready bass. During dusk and overcast periods bass can often be enticed to hit top water flies and lures. Green or yellow popper flies can be a lot of fun. Spincasters will find the floating Rapala can create exciting top water strikes during these darker periods.

Northern pike also inhabit South Lake, although fishing is generally slow. The best time to try for pike is during the evening when pike cruise into shallower areas in search of food. Try casting spinner baits or jigs along shore structure and near islands. Good sized northern pike have been known to surprise the odd angler in South Lake.

Directions

South Lake lies north of the town of Gananoque. From Gananoque, it is a short drive north along County Road 32 to the eastern shore of the lake. County Road 32 can also be picked up off Highway 15 just west of Seeley's Bay.

Facilities

Private residents surround the access roads to South Lake and as a result there is no official public access to the lake. Visitors with a canoe or small boat can put in at the bridge over South Lake Creek off County Road 32. For supplies and other amenities like motels, the town of Gananoque to the south has plenty to offer.

Other Options

Gananoque Lake is located just east of South Lake and provides good fishing at times for nice sized largemouth and smallmouth bass. Northern pike are also found in the lake in fair numbers and can be found up to 4 kg (9 lbs) in size. Although Gananoque Lake is quite close to the city of Kingston, the lake remains a quality fishery.

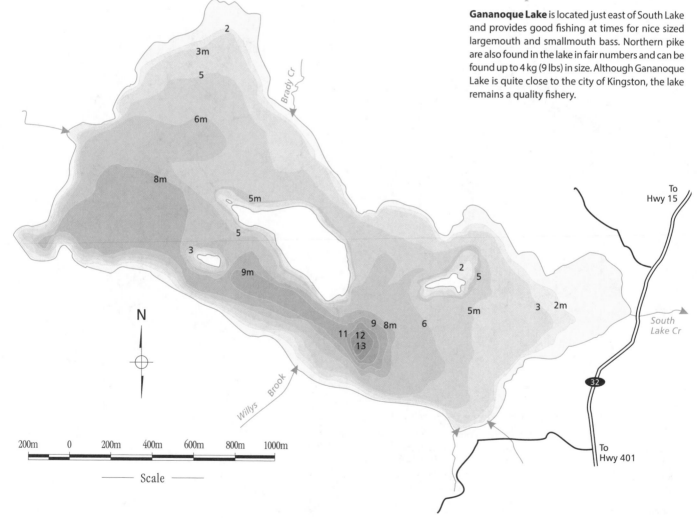

Spring Lake

Location: 41 km (25 mi) south of Bancroft
Maximum Depth: 9 m (30 ft)
Mean Depth: 4.8 m (16 ft)
Way Point: 44° 53′00″ Lat - N, 77° 43′00″ Lon - W

Fishing

Even though Spring Lake lies along Highway 62, the lake is not heavily fished. The lake is currently being stocked with splake to add an alternate fishery to the smallmouth bass that seem to thrive here.

Smallmouth bass are best located along weed lines or off the main island. Smallmouth bass love structure and will gravitate to anything that they can use as cover. To locate these sportfish look for underwater drop offs, rocky shoals or shorelines. While typical largemouth bass lures will work for smallmouth, including topwater presentations, underwater presentations are regularly more effective. Try working spinners, jigs and crankbaits along the structure areas and if fishing is slow, slow the retrieve down significantly. When smallmouth bass are lethargic, they will often simply suck in the lure or fly as it passes by.

When the weather is unstable, when the water is cold, or when the bass are lethargic use slower, vertical presentations. This is best in early spring and again in fall. Jigs are the most common, and soft plastic bodied jigs are preferred by many anglers, as they deliver life-like action. Injecting it with salt or scent further enhances its fish-catching ability. Soft plastics come in hundreds of different shapes, sizes, and colours, but baitfish and crayfish are the two most common, as these are commonly eaten by smallmouth.

Splake are most active in the winter or early spring. Some of the best fishing is found in spring, just after ice off, when this hybrid brook trout/lake trout species can be found near the surface feeding on larvae and smaller baitfish. Small silver spoons or spinners can be effective at this time.

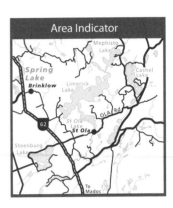

Area Indicator

Species
Burbot
Largemouth Bass
Smallmouth Bass
Yellow Perch

Directions

You can find this small lake off the east side of Highway 62 south of the town of Bancroft. An informal public access is found off the highway.

Facilities

Along with the access along the western shore of the lake, the Hastings Heritage Trail passes along the eastern shore. The trail is a terrific multi-purpose recreation route that is quite popular in the winter with snowmobilers. The trail was originally a rail line and currently stretches from near Algonquin Park south all the way to the town of Trenton.

Other Options

A very close by alternative fishing lake is Robinson Lake to the southwest. **Robinson Lake** is also accessible off Highway 62 and provides steady fishing for smallmouth bass and the odd stocked lake trout.

Spring Lake		
Fish Stocking Data		
Year	Species	Number
2013	Splake	550
2011	Splake	550

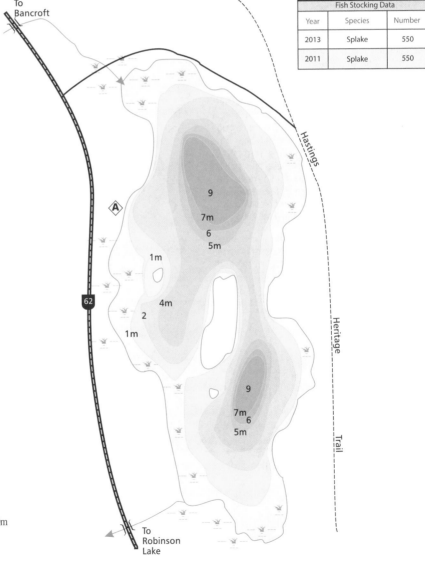

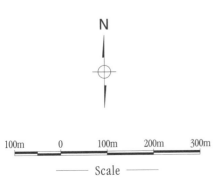

N

100m	0	100m	200m	300m

— Scale —

Zone 15

Location: 46 km (28.6 mi) north of Madoc
Maximum Depth: 3.6 m (12 ft)
Mean Depth: 3 m (9.8 ft)
Way Point: 44° 52′ 00″ Lat - N, 77° 37′ 00″ Long - W

St. Ola Lake

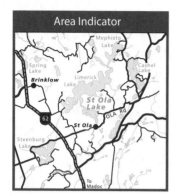

Area Indicator

Species
Largemouth Bass
Smallmouth Bass
Yellow Perch
Other

Directions

St Ola Lake is actually an extension of the larger Limerick Lake to the north. The lakes are found near Highway 62 north of Madoc. Continue on Highway 62 north past the settlement of Gilmour to St. Ola Road. St. Ola Road traverses east from Highway 62 all the way to the southern shore of the lake.

Facilities

From the St. Ola Road, you can reach the boat launch area as well as a tent and trailer park. Both of these facilities are accessible via short access roads that branch north off St. Ola Road. For supplies, there is a very small store just off the highway at Gilmour.

Other Options

If you continue east along St Ola Road past St Ola Lake you eventually reach Weslemkoon Lake Road. Take Weslemkoon Lake Road north about 2 km to **Gunter Lake**. Gunter Lake offers fishing for some nice sized largemouth bass.

Fishing

St Ola Lake is a part of a collection of fine bass lakes found in the area. The lake is formed by the damming of the Mephisto Creek and is quite shallow, making for prime bass habitat. Along with largemouth bass, smallmouth bass are also found in the lake, although in smaller numbers. There is literally an endless array of weed structure available to fish, making for prime top water situations. Popper flies or top water lures such as the jitterbug can produce some fun action on St Ola Lake. Top water action is mainly found during overcast or dusk periods; therefore, a deeper presentation such as a jig is best when the bass are holding deep. Jig type baits are perfect for this type of lake as they are much harder to snag and can be worked through the thick vegetation where the bigger fish hang out.

Adding to the fishery are yellow perch, rock bass and pumpkinseed sunfish. These panfish are typically easy to catch by using a typical bait and bobber set up.

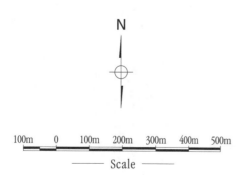

Stoco Lake

Location: Tweed
Maximum Depth: 9.8 m (32 ft)
Mean Depth: 4 m (13 ft)
Way Point: 44° 28' 00" Lat - N, 77° 17' 00" Long - W

Fishing

Being close to a summer tourist town such as Tweed increases the angling pressure on Stoco Lake. Currently, the fishing quality remains fair. Stoco Lake is a shallow lake with an average depth of approximately 3 m (10 ft). Fishing in the lake can be good at times for smallmouth and largemouth bass in the 0.5-1.5 kg (1-3.5 lb) range. Bass are found mainly closer to shore structure in weed beds or off any of the small islands on the lake. Typical bass lures such as jigs and spinner baits can produce decent results.

The three predatory fish found in Stoco Lake also receive the most angling attention. Fishing for walleye and northern pike can be fair, while angling success for muskellunge is hit and miss. No matter which species, there are often some slow periods on this lake. Since walleye are the prime target of anglers, be sure to aid the stocks and practice catch and release, especially if you hook into a spawning sized walleye. If you do plan to fish for muskellunge, ensure you check the regulations as new minimum size limits have been recently introduced.

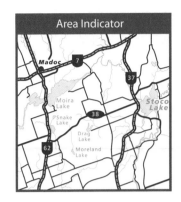

Area Indicator

Directions

This fabulous lake makes up the scenic eastern boundary of the town of Tweed. The lake is easily accessible, as there are several directional signs that can be spotted in town that lead to parts of the lake. Tweed can be reached via Highway 37. Highway 37 can be picked up to the south from Highway 401 near Belleville or from Highway 7 to the north.

Facilities

The lake is a great summer vacation spot with three tent and trailer parks to choose from. A boat launch is also located along the western shore at a small marina found near the inflow of the Moira River. Any needed supplies and roofed accommodation can be found in the town of Tweed.

Other Options

The **Moira River** is an angling alternative that cannot be overlooked. The large river flows into and out of Stoco Lake and both the northern and southern stretches of the river have plenty to offer the angler. The river is easily accessible from numerous areas throughout its entirety. The main sport fish species found in the Moira River are smallmouth bass, largemouth bass, northern pike and the odd muskellunge or walleye.

Species	
Largemouth Bass	Walleye
Muskellunge	Whitefish
Northern Pike	Yellow Perch
Smallmouth Bass	Other

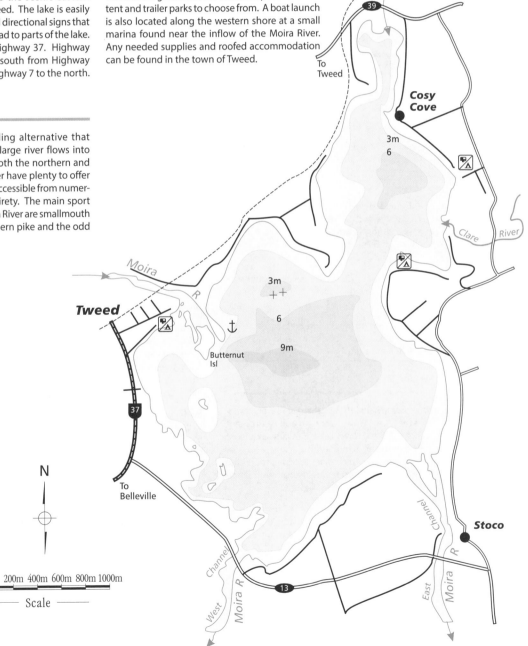

200m 0 200m 400m 600m 800m 1000m

— Scale —

Zone 17

Location: Burleigh Falls
Surface Area: 2,824 ha (6,978 ac)
Maximum Depth: 32 m (105 ft)
Mean Depth: 5.9 m (19.3 ft)
Way Point: 44° 28' 00" N, 78° 43' 00" W

Stoney Lake

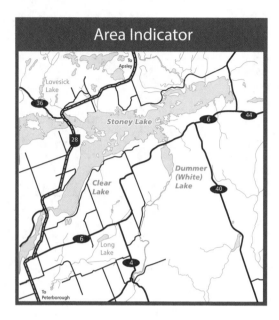

Area Indicator

Species	
Black Crappie	Northern Pike
Brown Trout	Smallmouth Bass
Carp	Walleye
Largemouth Bass	Yellow Perch
Muskellunge	Other

Directions

Stoney Lake is somewhat of a divider between the Great Lake lowlands to the south and the highland areas to the north. The lake or rather lakes are easily reached by following Highway 28 north from Lakefield. The main access area is from the settlement of Burleigh Falls, home to the 28th Trent Severn Waterway lift lock.

To access the southern portion of the lake or Clear Lake, follow Highway 28 north from Lakefield to Young's Point, which is the southernmost limit of Clear Lake. Young's Point is home to lock 27 on the Trent Severn.

County Road 56 to the north and 6 to the south provide alternate access points to the main lake and Upper Stoney Lake. Look for marinas and/or cottage resorts to find launching facilities in these areas.

Facilities

Along with the main boat access area in Burleigh Falls, there are several other boat launch or marinas around the lakes. Crowes Landing and McCrackens Landing are other popular access points to Stoney Lake. Similarly, overnight accommodation is readily found in the area through the many resorts or lodges, private campgrounds and even private cottages for rent around the lake. Inquire locally or search the internet. A good source for local information is www.stoneylake.on.ca.

An interesting attraction found near the northeast shore of Stoney Lake is **Petroglyphs Provincial Park**. The park is a day-use park that helps protect ancient native petroglyphs, carvings in rock bed. There is also a picnic area at the park and a few hiking trails.

Fishing

Also known as Stony Lake, Stoney Lake provides some of the best angling opportunities in the Kawarthas. Stoney Lake actually comprises three interconnected lakes; Upper Stoney Lake to the northeast, Stoney Lake in the centre and Clear Lake to the southwest. This beautiful stretch of water, over 30 kilometres long from Young's Point to the lake's eastern shores, encompasses over 1,000 islands and half a dozen 19th century towns. Stoney Lake is deepest of all the Kawartha Lakes and home to a variety of fish species including walleye, largemouth bass, smallmouth bass, northern pike, muskellunge, yellow perch, brook trout, brown trout, carp and crappie.

The 'Jewel of the Kawarthas' as some call it, was part of the logging highway that moved logs south to Peterborough and area. Steel pins with hooks that were used to tie up the log booms can still be seen anchored in the rock of some of the islands on Stoney. Between 1883 and 1887 the first locks were built at Burleigh Falls.

There are literally hundreds of small islands around the lake, creating navigational headaches for some boaters and fishing hot spots for others. Both smallmouth and largemouth are plentiful in Stoney Lake. Smallmouth bass are renowned for their acrobatic jumps and fighting prowess when hooked. Try surface lures or jigs for added fun. Largemouth bass are brawling fish, aggressive strikers and are mostly found in the warm, weedy, still waters of the big lake. They can be tempted with carefully presented spinnerbaits, plastic worms, or weedless jigs. Live bait such as frogs, minnows or crayfish can tempt any bass. Near the divide between the two lakes, Davis Island is known to produce some nice sized bass.

The most popular sportfish in the area is walleye. They can be found in and around the shoals of Stoney Lake in the summer and in the shallows during the spring and fall. Although they only average 1.5 kg (3 lbs), the odd pickerel tops the scales at 3 kg (10 lbs) on Stoney. Some of the most effective methods include slowly jigging a minnow or worm along a deep water weed line or slowly trolling a Rapala type lure. Near Burleigh Falls and the shoal just south of Big Island are notable holding areas. Walleye are schooling fish so if you catch one stay in that area.

Muskellunge are the dominant predator in Stoney Lake. Growing to over 9 kg (30 lbs), but averaging closer to 3 kg (10 lbs), they can certainly put a challenge when caught. Large lures and spinnerbaits are effective when casting along weed lines with deeper water nearby. Trolling lures such as the Swim Whiz or Believers are the best when worked quickly a good distance from the back of the boat. Try fishing at the end of September and early October to find muskie.

Northern pike can also be found in shallow water along the shores and marshes of Stoney Lake. Pike are suckers for a well trolled lure. Other lures that work include a natural colour Rapala Husky Jerk, soft jerkbaits worked slowly over fallen trees, spinnerbaits or natural baits like minnows and worms. Although their average weight is much smaller, pike over 7.5 kg (25 lbs) are reported in Stoney.

Panfish, such as perch, rock bass and sunfish are perhaps the easiest of all fish to find in Stoney Lake. These fish are excellent for introducing the youngsters to the joys of fishing since they take readily to a worm and hook and can be caught from a dock or shore. Work shallow water with weeds and rocks. Perch like to travel in schools so if you catch one then you are sure to catch another.

A seldom talked about, but common fish species in the Kawarthas, is carp. These big fish can put up quite a fight as the odd one reaches 15 kg (50 lbs) in size. They can be caught using dough balls, corn, worms and various other concoctions. Heavy gear is recommended.

Other Options

For a little change, you can access several fishing lakes north of Stoney Lake via Highway 28. There are quality lakes, such as **Julian Lake,** that can be accessed not far from the highway. Alternatively, if you do not mind a little work, there are literally hundreds of backcountry lakes found to the north that can be reached by 4wd vehicle, canoe or on foot.

Stoney Lake

Location: Burleigh Falls
Surface Area: 2,824 ha (6,978 ac)
Maximum Depth: 32 m (105 ft)
Mean Depth: 5.9 m (19,3 ft)
Way Point: 44° 28'00" N, 78° 43'00" W

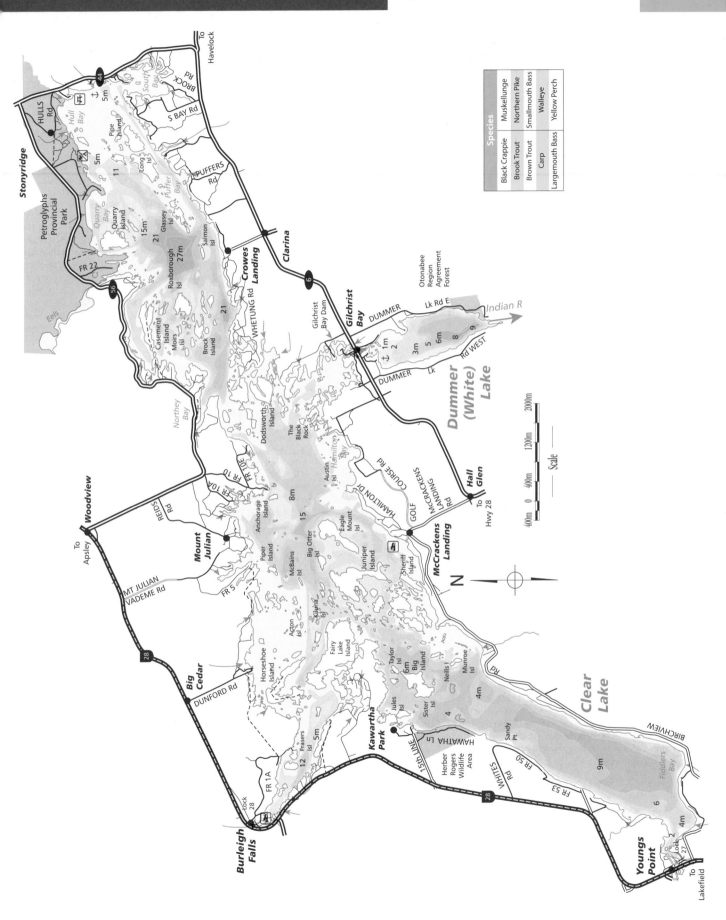

Species	
Black Crappie	Muskellunge
Brook Trout	Northern Pike
Brown Trout	Smallmouth Bass
Carp	Walleye
Largemouth Bass	Yellow Perch

© Backroad Mapbooks

Location: Bobcaygeon
Maximum Depth: 10.6 m (35 ft)
Mean Depth: 4.7 m (15.5 ft)
Way Point: 44° 28′ 00″N, 78° 43′ 00″W

Sturgeon Lake

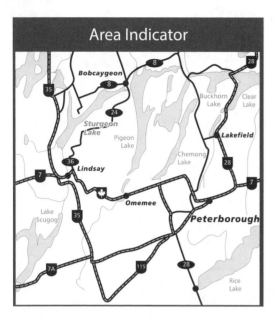

Area Indicator

Directions

Sturgeon Lake is part of the Trent Severn Waterway. Many anglers cruise from lake to lake enjoying the many facilities and good fishing along the waterway. Due to the waterway and easy access, Sturgeon Lake can be busy with boating traffic, especially in the summer.

The main access area to the eastern stretch of Sturgeon Lake is via the town of Bobcaygeon. One of the most direct routes to Bobcaygeon is by taking County Road 17 from the town of Lindsay. County Road 17 travels east and eventually veers north to Bobcaygeon. In the town, there is a boat launch and a marina providing access to the lake. To reach Lindsay, take Highway 35 north from Highway 401 east of the town of Bowmanville.

To reach the west end of Sturgeon Lake, there are two main options. One option is to continue north along Highway 35 from the town of Lindsay. The highway actually passes within a few kilometres of the western shore of Sturgeon Lake providing access to the many side roads to the lake. The other option is to follow County Road 36 from Lindsay. County Road 36 travels north towards the eastern shoreline of Sturgeon Lake. Numerous side roads branch off the county road and provide access to the lake.

Facilities

Boat access areas are readily available along the west end of Sturgeon Lake. There are several marinas available along the eastern and western shorelines of this stretch of the lake. Those looking to overnight in the area will find a couple resorts and private campsites at Snug Harbour and south of the Ken Reid Conservation Area along the Sturgeon River. The **Ken Reid Conservation Area** is accessible off Highway 35 north of Lindsay and offers picnic areas, a beach and washrooms for day-trippers. Organized groups can arrange to camp at the conservation area by calling (705) 328-2271.

There are also a number of boat launch facilities that can be found along the eastern portion of Sturgeon Lake. The main launch area is located in the town of Bobcaygeon. Other launch areas are available at Ancona Point and Verulam Park further to the south. For added boating services, there are a few marinas available along this side of the lake. Overnight accommodation can also be found near Bobcaygeon. Inquire locally or search the internet for Sturgeon Lake accommodations.

Fishing

Sturgeon Lake is another of the popular series of Kawartha Lakes and the Trent Severn Waterway. The Y shaped lake is surrounded by the communities of Fenelon Falls, Lindsay, Sturgeon Point and Bobcaygeon and stretches approximately 25 kilometres (16 miles) from the southern to the northeastern extremes. Similar to most Kawartha Lakes, anglers can find good fishing for smallmouth and largemouth bass, muskellunge and walleye. There are also a good variety of panfish to look for.

The Scugog River flows into the lake at the southern apex, Fenelon River links Cameron Lake to the northwestern end, while Emily Creek empties into the lake at the middle south. The lake outflow is through the Big Bob and Little Bob channels of the Bobcaygeon River at the northeast of the lake.

Walleye are the most sought after sport fish in Sturgeon Lake and fishing for the species is good at times. Walleye are most readily found along shoal areas with some weed growth. Look for weed lines and troll a Rapala or worm harness along these areas to find cruising walleye. Walleye are usually found about a 0.5 metre (1.5 feet) off the bottom, so anything you can do to keep your lure in that range will help. Snap jigging a 3/8 ounce pink jig with pumpkin or chartreuse tail or trolling a floating Rapala with a bottom bounce sinker can produce well too. Walleye can be very suspicious, so use a light line and small hook for better success. The best time to fish is as it is getting dark, as the walleye rise to feed. Productive areas in the east end of Sturgeon Lake are the shoals around Muskrat Island and Hawkers Bay. In the west end, a renowned walleye hot spot is the region south of Fenelon Falls, including Eldery Bay.

Smallmouth and largemouth bass can be found throughout Sturgeon Lake and are predominantly located along shore structure and near weed beds. In particular, Goose Bay is a prime holding area for bass, especially largemouth bass, due to the heavy weed growth in the bay. In heavier weed cover, try working a jig through the weeds in an up and down jigging motion. Even lethargic bass often suck in the passing jig.

Topwater action for largemouth is usually best on calm overcast days or in the evening period. Often the calm before a storm can create a frenzy of action. When topwater action is slow for largemouth bass try jigs, spinnerbaits and crankbaits amid shoreline structure or weed growth.

The other main sportfish found in Sturgeon Lake is muskellunge. Fishing for muskellunge is usually fair for nice sized muskie, especially later in fall. Muskellunge can also be found along weed lines in search of baitfish, especially during the evenings. Larger presentations are needed to lure that big musky. On the flip side, larger lures will limit your incidental catches of other sportfish. A good option for the smaller fish and muskellunge is a Mepps Black Fury.

Another alternative is to try working a jointed Rapala in a Fire Tiger pattern, or an X-Rap Jointed Shad in Gold. Muskie are very sensitive to sound, and scatter when they hear a boat approaching. They will return to where they were once the boat has past, but it is good to have your lure at least 70 metres (200 feet) behind the boat. The jointed lures have a very pronounced swimming motion which can draw strikes from these big predators.

Other Options

Some nearby fishing options include **Pigeon Lake** to the east and **Cameron Lake** to the west. Both lakes are part of the Trent Severn Waterway and are accessible by boat from Sturgeon Lake. Since all the lakes are somewhat interconnected, fishing is comparable to Sturgeon Lake. Populations of smallmouth bass, largemouth bass, walleye and muskellunge inhabit the lakes.

Sturgeon Lake

Location: Bobcaygeon
Maximum Depth: 10.6 m (35 ft)
Mean Depth: 4.7 m (15.5 ft)
Way Point: 44° 28'00"N, 78° 43'00"W

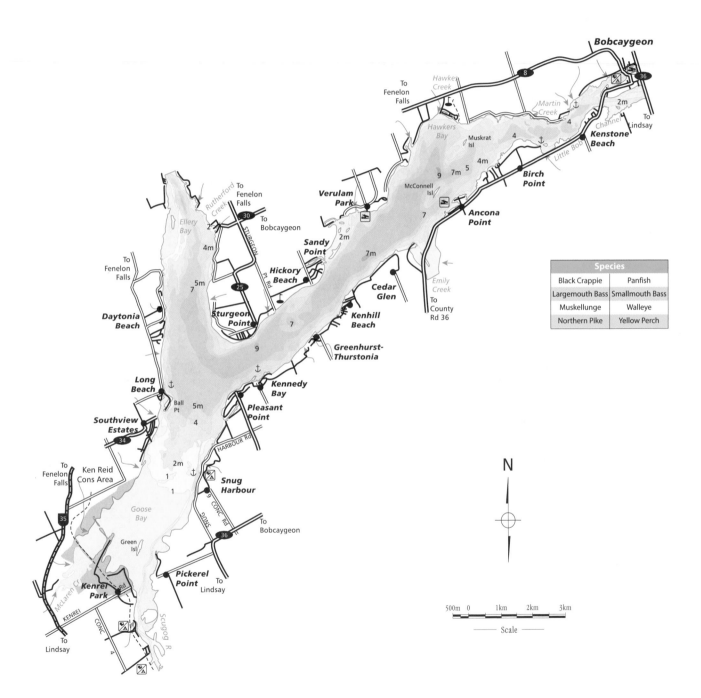

Bobcaygeon

To Fenelon Falls

Hawkes Creek

Martin Creek

2m

To Lindsay

Hawkers Bay

Muskrat Isl

Little Bob Channel

Kenstone Beach

4

Birch Point

9 7m 5

4m

McConnell Isl

Verulam Park

9

7

Ancona Point

Rutherford Creek

To Fenelon Falls

30

To Bobcaygeon

STURGEON

Ellery Bay

4m

2m

Sandy Point

Emily Creek

To County Rd 36

To Fenelon Falls

5m 7

25

Pt Rd

Hickory Beach

Cedar Glen

7m

Species	
Black Crappie	Panfish
Largemouth Bass	Smallmouth Bass
Muskellunge	Walleye
Northern Pike	Yellow Perch

Daytonia Beach

Sturgeon Point

7

Kenhill Beach

9

Greenhurst-Thurstonia

Long Beach

Ball Pt

5m

4

Kennedy Bay

Pleasant Point

Southview Estates

34

HARBOUR Rd

To Fenelon Falls

Ken Reid Cons Area

2m

1

Snug Harbour

CONC Rd 6

SNUG

35

Goose Bay

1

To Bobcaygeon

36

Green Isl

McLaren Cr

Kenrel Park

Pickerel Point

To Lindsay

KENREI

CONC

Scugog R.

To Lindsay

4

N

500m 0   1km   2km   3km
Scale

Zone	18

Location: Sydenham
Elevation: 152 m (500 ft)
Surface Area: 451 ha (1,114 ac)
Maximum Depth: 39.5 m (130 ft)
Mean Depth: 6.8 m (22.3 ft)
Geographic: 44° 25′ 00″ N, 76° 33′ 00″ W

Sydenham Lake

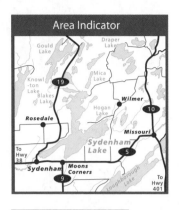

Area Indicator

Species	
Black Crappie	Smallmouth Bass
Largemouth Bass	Yellow Perch
Northern Pike	Other

Facilities

The town of Sydenham has a number of amenities for visitors, including a bank and grocery store. A public boat launching facility is located in town and provides access to the western end of Sydenham Lake.

Visitors wishing to explore the area on foot can enjoy the **Cataraqui Trail** system, which is part of the Trans Canada Trail. This multi-use trail travels right through Sydenham and along the shore of Sydenham Lake. Camping enthusiasts will find the scenic **Frontenac Provincial Park** to the north has many rustic, interior camping areas to enjoy.

Other Options

Hogan Lake is a very small lake that lies just across the Cataraqui Trail near the northeast end of Sydenham Lake. The small lake offers slow to fair fishing for smallmouth and largemouth bass. A small population of northern pike also exists in the lake.

Fishing

Due to its close proximity to Kingston, Sydenham Lake is a popular summer vacationing lake. Fishing pressure in the lake is steady, however, anglers can still have some success throughout the season. Sydenham Lake is a weedy lake providing good cover for all of its resident sportfish. The most active species are smallmouth and largemouth bass, although many a northern pike has shocked bass anglers with big strikes.

Fishing for bass is generally fair for bass that can reach up to 1.5 kg (3.5 lbs). Look for bass to hide in the shallow sections of the lake in any sort of weed cover. The northern and eastern portions of the lake are usually the best holding areas for all three sportfish species.

One method used to catch big northern pike is trolling slowly along weed lines. The best time for pike fishing is during dusk or overcast periods, as the predacious species will cruise into the shallower sections of the lake in search of food. In addition to bass type lures, pike can be enticed to chase after flashy spoons on occasion.

Directions

North of Kingston, Sydenham Lake is the scenic backdrop for the small town of Sydenham. To find the lake, follow Highway 401 to Exit 611 west of Kingston. From the 401, head north along the quieter Highway 38. At the village of Harrowsmith, head east along the Harrowsmith Road (County Road 5). After about 5 km (3 mi) along Harrowsmith Road, you will reach Sydenham and the western shore of Sydenham Lake.

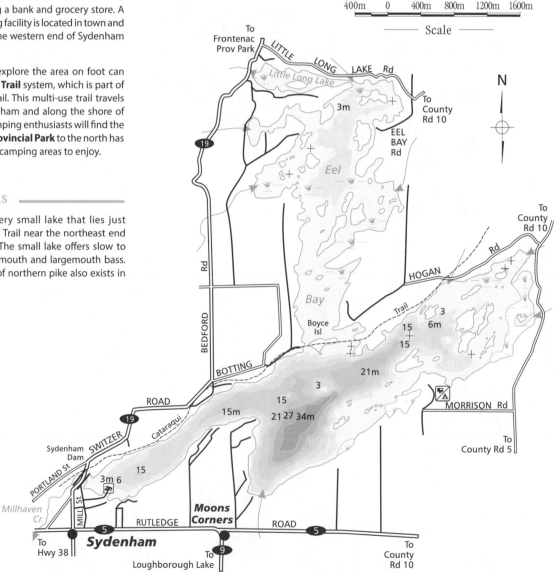

Tallan Lake

Location: 11 km (7 mi) northeast of Apsley
Maximum Depth: 25.6 m (84 ft)
Mean Depth: 12.6 m (41.3 ft)
Way Point: 44° 51' 00" Lat - N, 78° 03' 00" Long - W

Fishing

Some cottages and camps line the shoreline of Tallan Lake, hence fishing pressure is steady throughout the year. The resident smallmouth bass make up the brunt of the angling success. Smallmouth bass average approximately 0.5-1 kg (1-2 lbs) and are found mainly near underwater structure such as rock piles or weed areas. Off the island in the west side of the lake is another productive area.

The other main sport fish species found in Tallan Lake is lake trout. The lake trout are a naturally reproducing strain that is under heavy fishing pressure. Regulations on the lake have been imposed, such as slot sizes and winter sanctuary periods to help the struggling lake trout stocks. If you do intend to fish for lakers, please practice catch-and-release.

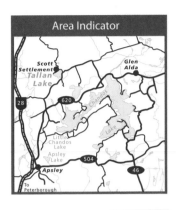

Area Indicator

Directions

North of the town of Apsley, Tallan Lake can be reached by taking County Road 620 east from Highway 28. Look for Clydesdale Road off the north side of County Road 620 and follow Clydesdale Road all the way to Tallan Lake.

Other Options

Clydesdale Lake is accessible via Hobson Road from Clydesdale Road southeast of Tallan Lake. Clydesdale Lake is another cottage destination lake in the area that offers fishing opportunities for smallmouth bass.

Species
Lake Trout
Largemouth Bass
Smallmouth Bass
Yellow Perch
Other

Facilities

A boat launch is available along the northern shore of Tallan Lake via an access road from Clydesdale Road. For overnight camping, **Silent Lake Provincial Park** is located north of Tallan Lake via Highway 28. The park is a full service Provincial Park that offers some scenic lakeside campsites along with services such as flush toilets and showers. The park can be busy during the summer months; therefore, it is recommended to make reservations before arrival. For reservations call (888) ONT-PARK.

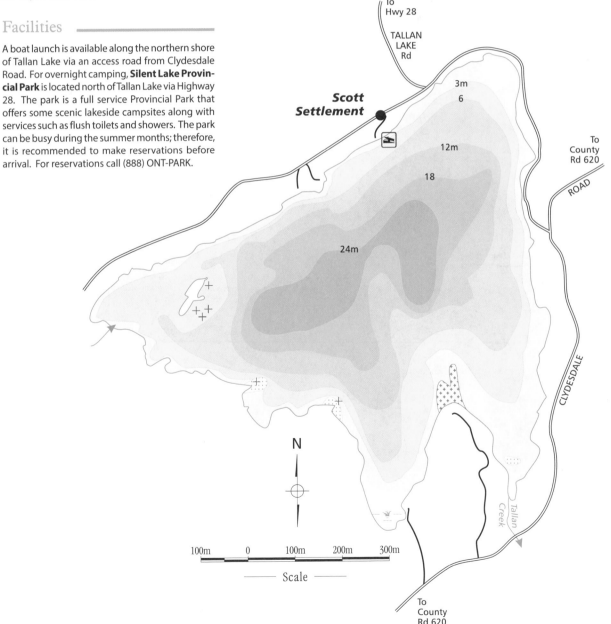

Zone 15

Location: 30 km (18 mi) south of Coe Hill
Maximum Depth: 21m (70 ft)
Mean Depth: 10.7m (35.2 ft)
Way Point: 44° 53′ 00″ Lat -N, 75° 50′ 00″ Long - W

Tangamong & Whetstone Lak

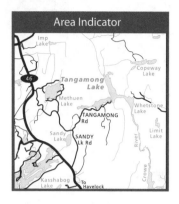

Area Indicator

Species	
Largemouth Bass	Walleye
Muskellunge	Yellow Perch
Smallmouth Bass	Other

Fishing

Both Tangamong Lake and Whetstone Lake are surrounded by private land. The southern shore of Tangamong Lake is highly developed with cottages and camps. Fishing in the lakes is often productive for smallmouth and largemouth bass that can reach over 1.5 kg (3.5 lbs) in size on occasion. Bass can be found throughout the lakes in weedy areas and off the areas with a rocky shoreline. The narrows between Tangamong Lake and Whetstone Lake is a consistent producer of feisty bass.

The other sport fish found in the lakes is walleye and muskellunge. Success for both predators varies but you can usually expect to catch a few walleye during an outing. The 3 m (10 ft) shoal area located in the northern portion of Tangamong Lake is a known holding area for species. The shallow region offers just the right mix of under water structure to attract feeding walleye and musky. The inflow area around the Crowe River is also a good holding area for walleye and muskellunge, especially in spring. In Whetstone Lake, look for walleye along the weed area near the mouth of the Crowe River. Watch for special restrictions on both lakes.

Directions

This collection of lakes is part of the Crowe River system found between Highway 28 and Highway 62. In addition to the public access point on Tangamong Lake, many paddlers reach the lakes by paddling along the Crowe River.

You can reach the access point on the southern shore of Tangamong Lake via Tangamong Road. To find Tangamong Road, first travel north along Highway 28 to Highway 504 near Apsley. Follow Highway 504 east to County Road 46 and head south. About 4 km south along County Road 46 you will meet Sandy Lake Road, which travels south to the junction with Tangamong Road.

Facilities

The access and parking area on Tangamong Lake is found on the southern shore of the lake at **Tangamong Lodge**. There is a small fee for parking and using the canoe/boat launch. Basic supplies and various accommodations are available in and around the town of Apsley. For camping enthusiasts, **Silent Lake Provincial Park** is found to the north of Apsley off Highway 28.

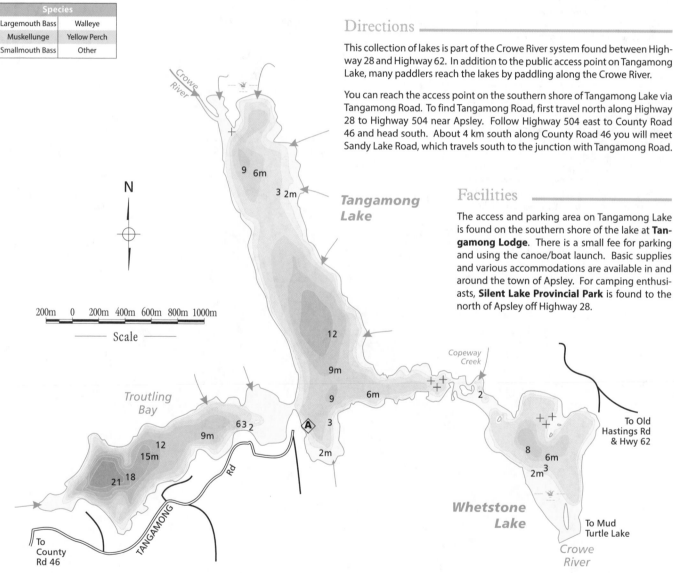

Other Options

At the junction between Sandy Lake Road and Tangamong Road you can easily reach **Sandy Lake**. The small lake is home to a population of smallmouth bass and muskellunge. Alternatively, further south of Sandy Lake, **West Twin Lake** is accessible via County Road 46. West Twin Lake is also inhabited with smallmouth bass and muskellunge as well as largemouth bass.

Thanet Lake

Location: 10 km (6.2 mi) south of Coe Hill
Maximum Depth: 20.4 m (67 ft)
Mean Depth: 8.2 m (27.2 ft)
Way Point: 45° 08′ 00″ Lat - N, 79° 46′ 00″ Lon - W

18 Zone

Fishing

There are a few cottages and camps along the shoreline of Thanet Lake, although the lake remains mainly undeveloped. Fishing in the lake is good at times for smallmouth and largemouth bass in the 1 kg (2 lb) range. Around the island found in the east side of the lake is often a good holding area for both smallmouth and largemouth bass. Try casting a jig or spinner towards the island to find ambush ready bass. Top water action can be experienced in any of the quiet bays. Try top water popping flies and lures during dusk or overcast periods for some exciting bass action.

A natural population of lake trout also exist in Thanet Lake, although the population is quite low similar to most Southern Ontario lake trout lakes. Low populations are the direct result of overharvesting; hence new regulations on ice fishing and catch sizes have been implemented. Please practice catch-and-release.

Directions

Thanet Lake is sandwiched between Highway 28 to the west and Highway 62 to the east. To reach the lake from the west, travel north along Highway 28 to Highway 504 at the town of Apsley. Follow Highway 504 east through the town of Apsley to the junction with County Road 46. Continue east across County Road 46 along Lasswade Road. Just after you pass Henderson Lake off the north side of Lasswade Road, take the first access road off the south side of the road. If you end up at Murphy Corners, you have gone too far.

From the east, follow Highway 62 north past the picnic area on Jordan Lake. The next main road heading west is Steenburg Lake Road North. Follow this road past Murphy Corners and the Dickey Lake turnoff. The next lake to the south is Thanet Lake.

Area Indicator

Species	
Lake Trout	Smallmouth Bass
Largemouth Bass	Yellow Perch

Facilities

There are no developed facilities available at Thanet Lake but rustic Crown Land camping is certainly possible. For supplies, the town of Apsley has plenty to offer, including a grocery and a general store.

Other Options

West Lake can be reached via a short rough portage from the southern end of Thanet Lake. West Lake is surrounded by mainly Crown Land and provides fishing for largemouth bass. Crown Land camping opportunities also exist at the lake.

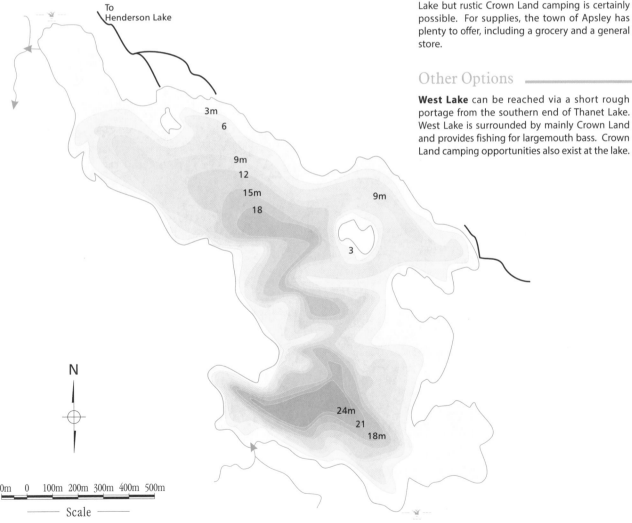

To Henderson Lake

N

100m 0 100m 200m 300m 400m 500m
Scale

Location: 6 km (3.7 mi) east of Godfrey
Elevation: 160 m (525 ft)
Surface Area: 161 ha (398 ac)
Maximum Depth: 32 m (105 ft)
Mean Depth: 11.4 m (37.4 ft)
Way Point: 44° 34′ 00″ N, 76° 36′ 00″

Thirty Island Lake

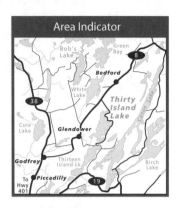

Area Indicator

Species
Largemouth Bass
Northern Pike
Smallmouth Bass
Walleye
Yellow Perch

Fishing

Thirty Island Lake is a picturesque lake that is inhabited by smallmouth bass, largemouth bass, northern pike and walleye. Fishing is fair for bass that can reach 1.5 kg (3.5 lbs) in size. The best way to find smallmouth bass is to cast along rocky shoreline areas and near any of the islands found around the lake. Largemouth bass generally like to stay in shallow bays and frequent weed growth and other shore structure such as fallen trees.

Fishing for northern pike in Thirty Island Lake is regarded as slow to fair for average sized northerns. Pike can be found almost anywhere in the lake, although the best time to fish is during overcast or dusk in the shallow bays. Trolling a flashy spoon can be productive or for aggressive pike try working a top water fly or lure.

Angling success for walleye is generally slow, although there are anglers that claim Thirty Island Lake continues to support a decent population. Look for walleye just off points or along any weed structure. Trolling is the best method to try to find the migratory sportfish.

Directions

Visitors will find Thirty Island Lake northwest of Frontenac Provincial Park. From Kingston or Highway 401, travel north along Highway 38 to the hamlet of Godfrey. At Godfrey, turn east onto Westport Road (County Road 8). After about 5 km (3 mi) along Westport Road, look for one of the many access roads to Thirty Island Lake off to the east. Most roads around the lake are private, so please ensure you request permission before travelling on these roads.

Facilities

Thirty Island Lake is surrounded by private cottages. Please ensure you request permission to access the lake through any private property. For supplies, the villages of Verona and Harrowsmith to the south offer general stores. For outdoor fun, nearby **Frontenac Provincial Park** lies to the southeast of Thirty Island Lake and offers fantastic recreational opportunities. The park has interior camping, paddling, fishing and hiking for visitors to enjoy during the summer months.

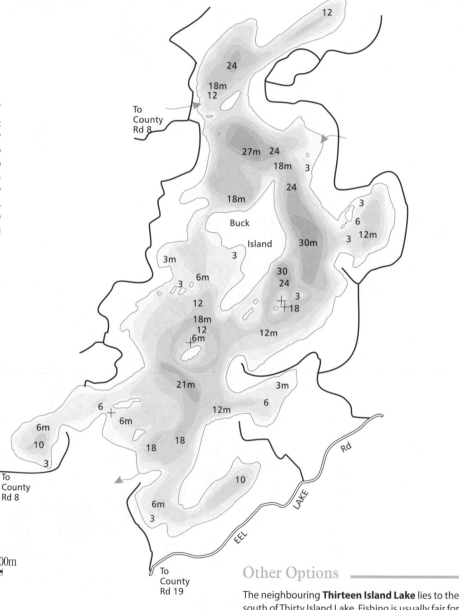

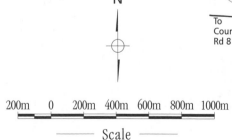

N

200m 0 200m 400m 600m 800m 1000m

Scale

Other Options

The neighbouring **Thirteen Island Lake** lies to the south of Thirty Island Lake. Fishing is usually fair for smallmouth and largemouth bass in the 0.5-1 kg (1-2 lb) range. Northern pike is the other main sportfish found in the lake, while a small population of elusive walleye is rumoured to be out there.

Turtle Lake

Location: 10 km (6.2 mi) north of Burleigh Falls
Maximum Depth: 11.3 m (37 ft)
Mean Depth: 6.5 m (21.3 ft)
Way Point: 44° 39' 00" Lat - N, 78° 15' 00" Lon - W

15 Zone

Fishing

Since Turtle Lake is an interior access lake, the lake receives significantly less angling pressure than other more accessible lakes in the region. Fishing in the lake can be quite good at times for smallmouth bass. There are also a few largemouth bass along with brook trout that were stocked in the past.

Turtle Lake is a deep lake carved out of the surrounding hills. There are a number of rocky shoreline drop-offs that make perfect habitat for smallmouth bass. Another recommended area to sample is near the small rock island found in the middle of the lake. Try working a jig or similar type lure closer to the bottom for the bigger smallmouth. For fly anglers, one fly that is sure to produce results on Turtle Lake is the crayfish imitation. Work the fly off bottom structure in a long quick strip fashion. At times this method can be deadly for smallmouth.

Brook trout were stocked regularly on Turtle Lake to help establish a good spring and fall fishery. Brookies have been known to be quite aggressive at these times of year and can be caught readily from shore with small spinners or even bobber fishing with a hook and worm.

Directions

Turtle Lake is part of a remote access chain of lakes in Kawartha Highlands Provincial Park that can only be found by canoe and portage. The canoe put in is located at the end of Long Lake Road off Highway 28 just south of Apsley. Parking is available for a nominal fee at Long Lake Lodge. To find Turtle Lake, you must paddle west along Long Lake and pass through Loucks Lake then Cox Lake. In total, the trip involves about three portages, with the largest being the 1,503 m (4,931 ft) hike from Cox Lake to Turtle Lake.

Facilities

Part of the **Kawartha Highlands Provincial Park**, this backcountry lake offers a few rustic campsites for canoe trippers and anglers alike. The sites are quite basic, with only a rough fire pit and perhaps a pit toilet. They offer a fantastic way to get away from it all and to enjoy the great outdoors.

Other Options

There are several lakes in and about the area to sample. **Cox Lake** is another interior access lake found to the north. It offers both largemouth and smallmouth bass as well as stocked lake trout. Fishing is reported to be good.

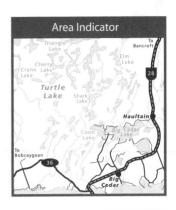

Area Indicator

Species
Brook Trout
Largemouth Bass
Smallmouth Bass

Turtle Lake			
Fish Stocking Data			
Year	Species	Number	Life Stage
2010	Brook Trout	1500	Fry
2009	Brook Trout	500	Fry
2008	Brook Trout	1600	Fry

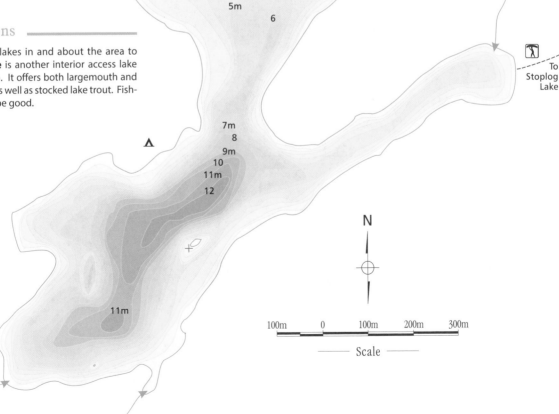

Zone **18**

Location: 14 km (8.6 mi) north of Marmora
Elevation: 198 m (650 ft)
Surface Area: 100 ha (247 ac)
Max Depth: 8.3 m (27.5 ft)
Mean Depth: 7.6 m (25 ft)
Geographic: 44° 52′ 00″ Lat - N, 79° 39′ 00″ Lon - W

Twin Sister Lakes

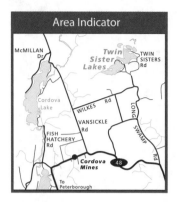

Area Indicator

Species
Largemouth Bass
Muskellunge
Smallmouth Bass
Walleye

Fishing

The Twin Sister Lakes are two side-by-side lakes that are of similar size and fishing quality. There are a few cottages and camps found along the shorelines of both lakes. The main sport fish found are largemouth bass and smallmouth bass. Fishing for both bass species can be good at times for average sized fish. There is plenty of weed structure in the lakes that provide good cover for ambush ready bass. Try flipping a jig through the deeper weed growth, while top water flies and lures can be productive for more aggressive bass. Walleye and muskellunge are also known to exist in the lakes, although fishing for both species is relatively slow.

Facilities

There are no facilities at the Twin Sister Lakes, although any needed supplies can be easily found in the town of Marmora. For overnight accommodation, there are three tent and trailer parks located on the shore of nearby Crowe Lake. For roofed accommodation, there are a few motels that can be found along Highway 7 near the town of Marmora.

Directions

Twin Sister Lakes are part of a series of lakes that help form the Crowe River system. The road leading north to Thompson Lake separates them. You can find the Twin Sister Lakes by following Highway 7 to the town of Mamora. At the town of Marmora, take County Road 33 north from Highway 7. Follow County Road 33 past Crowe Lake to Long Swamp Road. Long Swamp Road is essentially an extension of County Road 33 and traverses north to Twin Sisters Road and Twin Sister Lakes.

Other Options

Just east of Twin Sister Lakes lies **Cordova Lake.** Cordova Lake can be accessed via Vansickle Road from County Road 48. There is a tent and trailer park on the lake and fishing can be decent for both smallmouth bass and walleye. There are rumours of largemouth bass in the lake as well.

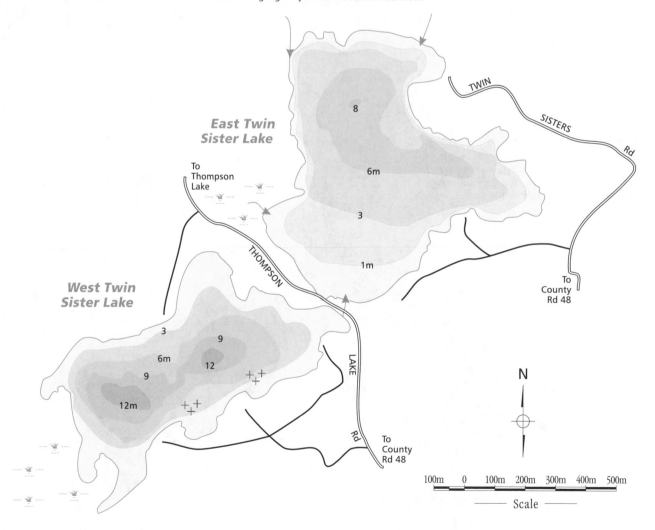

Upper Beverley Lake

Location: 60 km (37.3 mi) northeast of Kingston
Elevation: 94.5 m (310 ft)
Surface Area: 550 ha (1,359 ac)
Maximum Depth: 7 m (23 ft)
Mean Depth: 2.4 m (7.9 ft)
Way Point: 44° 37′ 00″ N, 76° 05′ 00″ W

18 Zone

Fishing

Upper Beverley Lake is a man-made lake created by the damming of the Morton Creek. The lake is quite shallow with an average depth of only 2.5 metres (8 feet). The shallow nature of the lake makes for ideal bass habitat, as there is plenty of weed growth found around the lake. A population of northern pike also exists in Upper Beverley Lake. Regardless of which species you plan to fish for, be prepared to lose some lures or flies, as the weeds love snagging hooks.

Largemouth bass are the main sportfish species found in Upper Beverley Lake, although a small population of smallmouth bass does exist. Fishing is fair for bass that average around 0.5-1 kg (1-2 lbs). The best way to find largemouth is to seek out weed areas and cast along weed lines or right amid the fray. Spinner baits and jigs both work well, although for top water action, try a floating Rapala or popper fly.

Northern Pike fishing is usually slower but these predators can grow to good sizes in Upper Beverley Lake. Similar to largemouth bass, northern pike love shallow, weedy areas and are often found cruising shallow bays with lots of weeds. Spinner baits can work well but pike can be enticed to hit the odd top water presentation, especially at dusk.

Directions

The village of Delta lies between Lower and Upper Beverley Lakes. To reach Delta, travel north from Kingston or south from Smiths Falls along Highway 15. At the hamlet of Crosby, head west along County Road 42. From Highway 15, it is about 15 km to Delta.

Other Options

Eloida Lake or **Lake Eloida** is located to the east of Upper Beverley Lake and can be accessed via the Lake Eloida Road north of Athens. This weedy lake offers anglers the opportunity to fish for northern pike. The pike are not usually very big, although they can be entertaining to catch. There are recent reports that the lake is also inhabited with bass.

Facilities

A public boat launch is found just northeast of the village of Delta along the western shore of Upper Beverley Lake. Look for directional signage for the launch on County Road 42. Those looking to stay in the area will find a country in and a few basic supplies in Delta, or it is possible to stay at nearby Lower Beverley Lake Park on the eastern shore of that lake. The nearby villages of Athens, Portland and Newboro also have plenty to offer visitors.

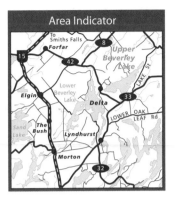

Area Indicator

Species
Black Crappie
Largemouth Bass
Northern Pike
Smallmouth Bass
Yellow Perch

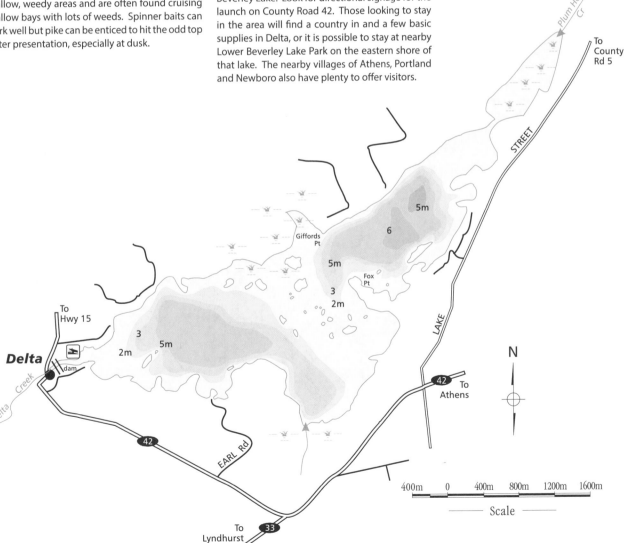

Zone 18
Location: Westport
Elevation: 124 m (408 ft)
Surface Area: 1,363 ha (3,366 ac)
Max Depth: 22 m (72 ft)
Mean Depth: 8 m (26.4 ft)
Way Point: 44° 41' 00" N, 76° 20' 00" W

Upper Rideau Lake

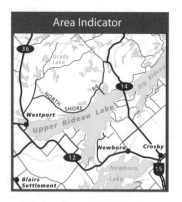

Area Indicator

Upper Rideau Lake		
Fish Stocking Data		
Year	Species	Number
2009	Lake Trout	11,000
2006	Lake Trout	15,000

Fishing

This southern extension of Big Rideau Lake offers fair to good fishing at times for smallmouth bass in the 0.5-1.5 kg (1-3.5 lb) range. Two areas in particular that can be good for bass are Mulvilles Bay near Westport and McNallys Bay along the southern end of the lake. Another hot spot is the 3 m (10 ft) hump found along the southeast end of the lake. The hump is a known attractor for some of the biggest bass in Upper Rideau Lake. Most bass presentations, like spinners, jigs and crayfish imitations, seem to work.

The two other sportfish found in Upper Rideau Lake are northern pike and walleye. Fishing success for both species is slower than for bass. If you are looking for pike, the western end of the lake is the main holding area for these predators. Try along weed lines during dusk, as they will often cruise into the shallows in search of food. Walleye are heavily fished in Upper Rideau Lake and as a result their numbers are quite low. Please practice catch and release in order to help the ailing resident Walleye species.

Directions

Upper Rideau Lake is a popular destination lake that lies to the east of the busy town of Westport. The lake is part of the Rideau Canal Waterway and can be found by following Highway 15 to the hamlet of Crosby. From Crosby, head west along County Road 42. Shortly after passing by the village of Newboro, you will reach the western shore of Upper Rideau Lake at Westport. The eastern end of the lake can be found by taking the Narrows Lock Road (County Road 14) north at Crosby off Highway 15.

By boat, Upper Rideau Lake is connected to Big Rideau Lake to the east and Newboro Lake to the south. Many visitors to the lake come via the Rideau Canal Waterway.

Facilities

Cottages line most of the shoreline of Upper Rideau Lake and the lake is often bustling with boating traffic during the summer months. For boat access on to the lake, a few marinas offer pay per access services. Tent and trailer parks are located near Blairs Point along the southern shore and Carty Point along the northeastern shore of the lake. The nearby villages of Newboro and Westport have plenty to offer visitors, such as accommodations, restaurants, grocery stores and various other retailers.

The **Foley Mountain Conservation Area** can be found on the northwest shore of the lake near Westport. The area is a lovely place to spend a day with picnic sites, a boat launch and several trails, including the famed **Rideau Trail**, to enjoy.

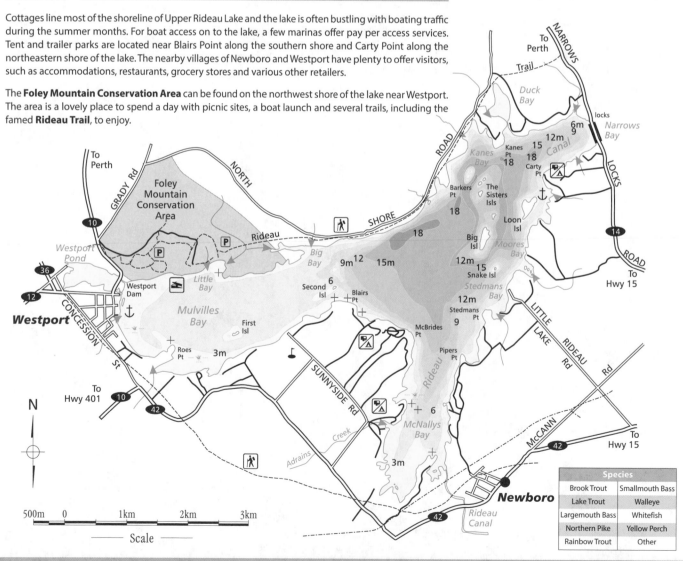

Species	
Brook Trout	Smallmouth Bass
Lake Trout	Walleye
Largemouth Bass	Whitefish
Northern Pike	Yellow Perch
Rainbow Trout	Other

Urbach Lake

Location: 5 km (3 mi) south of Coe Hill
Maximum Depth: 12 m (39.4 ft)
Mean Depth: 6 m (19.6 ft)
Way Point: 44° 50' 00" Lat - N, 77° 49' 00" Lon - W

Fishing

At first glance, Urbach Lake appears to be a very shallow lake that may only support coarse fish species or at best largemouth bass. On the contrary, Urbach Lake is heavily stocked every few years with splake, the lake trout/speckled trout hybrid species. These splake reportedly provide for some good fishing throughout the ice fishing and during spring fishing periods.

The dense population of catchable splake is most active in early spring. Early in the year, try trolling or casting small silver spoons or spinners near the drop off. Later in the year, angling success is usually much slower, although can be productive by trolling through the deep hole in the lake. Morning or evening, seem to be best if trolling for splake during the summer.

Splake are also a good species to target in the winter. At this time, jigging small spoons or jigs tipped with bait can be quite productive.

Facilities

There are no facilities available at Urbach Lake. Overnight camping can be found at the tent and trailer park located north of the lake along the northern shore of Wollaston Lake. Basic supplies can be found in Coe Hill.

Directions

Urbach Lake is a remote lake that lies south of the village of Coe Hill. To find the lake, follow Highway 28 north to Highway 620 at the town of Apsley. Take Highway 620 east past Apsley to the village of Coe Hill. As you travel east past Coe Hill, take The Ridge Road south after the crossing of the Deer River. This road skirts Wollaston Lake, eventually leading to Urbach Lake Lane, which leads to the east side of Urbach Lake. The next road south also leads to the smaller lake, but be careful not to cross private property.

Other Options

If you approach Urbach Lake from County Road 629, you will pass **Wollaston Lake**. Wollaston Lake is a cottage destination lake that is home to a boat launch and tent and trailer park. Largemouth bass, smallmouth bass and lake trout are resident in the lake. Watch for special regulations on lake trout as the population levels are very low.

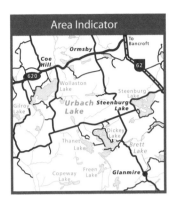

Area Indicator

Species
Largemouth Bass
Splake
Yellow Perch

Urbach Lake		
Fish Stocking Data		
Year	Species	Number
2013	Splake	550
2011	Splake	550
2009	Splake	550

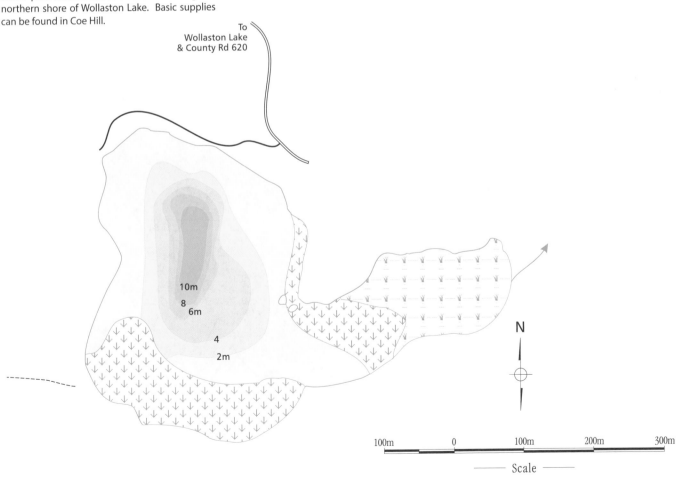

To
Wollaston Lake
& County Rd 620

10m
8
6m
4
2m

N

100m	0	100m	200m	300m

Scale

Location: 35 km (21.7 mi) northwest of Kingston
Surface Area: 599 ha (1,480 ac)
Maximum Depth: 4.3 m (16.5 ft)
Mean Depth: 1.4 m (4.5 ft)
Geographic: 44° 23'00"N, 76° 49'00"W

Varty Lake

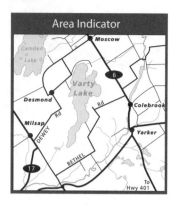

Area Indicator

Species	
Largemouth Bass	Smallmouth Bass
Northern Pike	Other

Fishing

Varty Lake is a good sized lake that lies in the lowland area next to the Frontenac Axis. Since the lake is not far from Kingston or Highway 401, it does receive significant angling pressure throughout the year. Regardless, determined anglers can have a lot of fun on this lake. The lake is inhabited by largemouth bass, smallmouth bass and northern pike. The shallow nature of the lake is ideal for these warm water sportfish, as there is ample weed growth during the summer months.

Fishing success for bass can be good at times for bass up to 1.5 kg (3.5 lbs) in size. Locating weed beds is essential to success. Work jigs or weedless spinner baits through the structure to entice big bass strikes. Northern pike will also be tempted to hit these type of presentations. Normally, the bass will take the slower retrieves, while the pike seem to be angered by a faster more aggressive retrieve.

Directions

Varty Lake is located to the northeast of the town of Newburg not far from Highway 401. Perhaps the easiest way to reach the lake is to follow the 401 to Exit 599 at Odessa. Travel north from the exit along County Road 6 past the village of Yarker. North of Yarker, there are a few access roads off the west side of County Road 6 that lead to the east side of Varty Lake.

Facilities

There are no public access points to Varty Lake, although there are tent and trailer parks that provide boat launching and camping for a fee. Basic supplies can be found in Yarker, while other amenities and retailers can be found in Newburgh to the southwest of Varty Lake.

Other Options

Camden Lake is a similar lake found to the northwest of Varty Lake. Camden is also inhabited with smallmouth bass, largemouth bass and northern pike. Angling success for bass is regarded as fair, while success rates for pike are usually slow. A large portion of the shoreline of Camden Lake is part of the **Camden Lake Provincial Wildlife Management Area.**

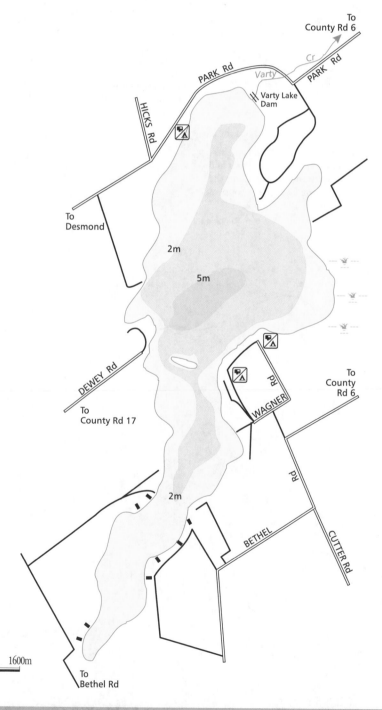

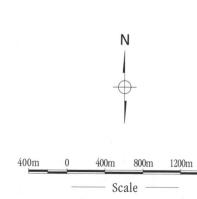

N

400m	0	400m	800m	1200m	1600m

Scale

Victoria & West Victoria Lakes

Location: 30 km (18 mi) southeast of Minden
Maximum Depth: 22.5 m (73.8 ft)
Mean Depth: 9.4 m (31 ft)
Way Point: 44° 51′ 00″ Lat - N, 78° 55′ 00″ Lon - W

Fishing

With the only real access from the Ganaraska Trail, these lakes receive low angling pressure throughout the season. Fishing is known to be productive for both smallmouth and largemouth bass. Look for bass along shore structure, which is abundant around the lakes. Most of the regular bass lures will produce results, including spinner baits, jigs and top water lures. Fly anglers will find these lakes a treat to fish, as the bass are often easy to entice on top water poppers. A good streamer can also work well when the bass are reluctant to come to the top.

In addition to bass, there are yellow perch along with a few rainbow trout in Victoria Lake. West Victoria Lake was stocked in the past with splake, but there have been no recent reports confirming if this species still exists in the lakes.

Directions

Victoria and West Victoria Lakes are hike-in lakes found in the wetlands northwest of Norland. The lakes lie next to the popular, long distance Ganaraska Trail. The eastern trailhead can be found by following Highway 35 north from Lindsay past Norland to Moore Falls. At Moore Falls take County Road 2 (Deep Bay Road) north off Highway 35. Follow Deep Bay Road to a rough access road off the west side of Deep Bay Road, just north of Deep Bay. The access road leads to Lutterworth Lake and a parking area for the trail. Victoria Lake lies approximately 9-10 kilometres from this trailhead, while West Victoria Lake is a short jaunt to the west.

Facilities

Both of these lakes are remote fishing lakes that have no formal facilities available. There are a few rustic Crown Land campsites that have been established over the years. If you do intend to camp at the lakes, be sure to practice low impact camping and please remove any garbage that you bring in or may find.

Other Options

While hiking along the **Ganaraska Trail**, you will pass other remote lakes including **Sheldon Lake**. Sheldon Lake is a Crown Land lake that offers rustic camping and angling opportunities for smallmouth bass and stocked lake trout. The lake is one of the first larger lakes along the trail and is found approximately 3 km west from the parking area at Lutterworth Lake.

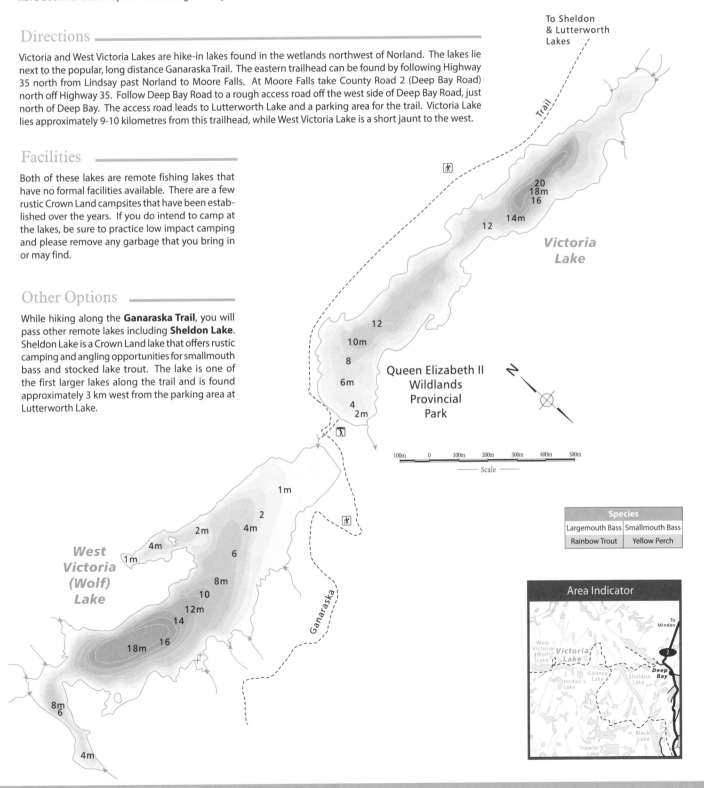

Species	
Largemouth Bass	Smallmouth Bass
Rainbow Trout	Yellow Perch

Location: 16 km (10 mi) south of Trenton
Maximum Depth: 7.3 m (24 ft)
Mean Depth: 4.6 m (15 ft)
Way Point: 44° 01′ 00″ Lat - N, 77° 36′ 00″ Lon - W

Wellers Bay [Lake Ontario]

Area Indicator

Species	
Largemouth Bass	Salmon
Northern Pike	Smallmouth Bass
Panfish	Walleye
Rainbow Trout	Yellow Perch

Fishing

Wellers Bay offers fishing opportunities for mainly bass, walleye and northern pike. Both smallmouth and largemouth bass are found in the bay in fair to good numbers and fishing can be quite productive at times. Bass can reach up to 2 kg (4.5 lbs) and there is definitely a possibility of finding a lunker out there. The many weedy areas around the bay make for prime bass habitat. Look for largemouth bass hunkered in weed beds, while smallmouth tend to frequent underwater structure areas such as shoals, logs or rock piles.

Walleye are the most prized sport fish in the bay and success can be steady at times for some nice sized walleye. Look for walleye along weed lines or along shoal areas. Jigging is a proven, effective method in the region. The key is to find the structure where the walleye are more frequently located near.

Northern pike can be picked up almost anywhere in the bay, although they tend to cruise the shallows at dusk or during overcast periods. Some big pike can be found in Weller's Bay and it is possible to hook into pike in the 5 kg (11 lb) range.

If the fishing is slow for the bigger sport fish, you should be able to find some action in the shallower areas for a variety of pan fish including perch and rock bass. The odd rainbow trout and salmon are also caught periodically in the bay.

Directions

Wellers Bay is part of the renowned Lake Ontario and is a popular wildlife viewing area. To reach Wellers Bay you must first travel to the town of Trenton, which is accessible via Highway 401 west of Belleville. From Trenton, follow County Road 33 south to the town of Consecon and the junction with County Road 39. Take County Road 39 west to the main access area along the south side of the bay.

Facilities

You can find a boat launch just west of Consecon as well as north of Consecon off Smoke Point Road. Along with the boat launch areas, there are a few tent and trailer parks available around the lake. A popular tenting area is the region near Bercovan Beach along the north side of the bay. For supplies and lodging, such as bed and breakfasts, the town of Consecon has plenty to offer visitors.

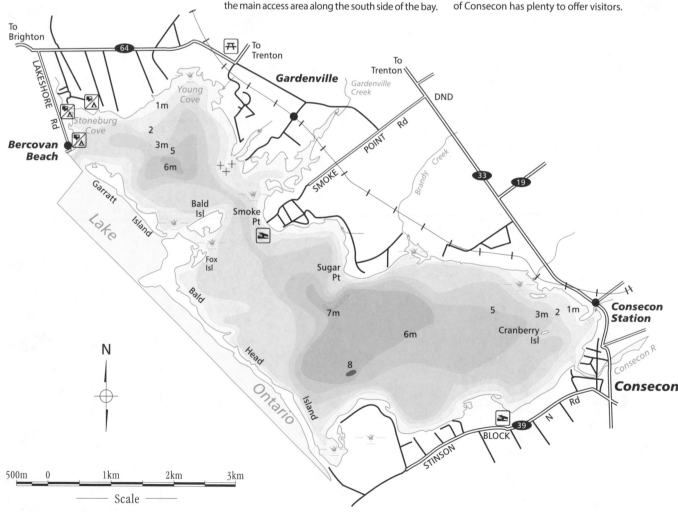

Wensley Lake

Location: 30 km (18 mi) northwest of Ompah
Elevation: 268 m (880 ft)
Surface Area: 571 ha (1,410 ac)
Maximum Depth: 56.3 m (185 ft)
Mean Depth: 22.2 m (72.8 ft)
Way Point: 45° 04' 00" N, 77° 03' 00" W

18 Zone

Fishing

The best opportunity for fishing success on Wensley Lake is for its resident smallmouth bass. Smallmouth bass fishing can be good at times for bass in the 0.5-1 kg (1-2 lb) range. Look for any sort of structure, like fallen logs or weeds, along shoreline areas. Spinners seem to be one of the more effective lures on the clear, spring fed lake as the flashy lure can attract smallmouth from quite a distance. Unfortunately, the clear nature of the water also makes the fish quite fussy during bright summer days.

A natural population of lake trout remains in Wensley Lake, although fishing success for these lakers is generally fair to slow. The best opportunity to catch lake trout is through the ice in winter or in the spring just after ice off. Although you can periodically catch one by casting from shore, trolling small spoons for lake trout is the most effective angling method in the spring.

In order to help lake trout stocks, Wensley (Brule) Lake is regulated with slot size restrictions and special ice fishing regulations. Please check you regulations for details before fishing.

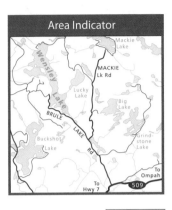
Area Indicator

Species
Lake Trout
Smallmouth Bass

Directions

Wensley Lake is known by many as Brule Lake and is located north of the small village of Plevna. To reach the lake, begin by travelling along Highway 7 to the junction with Highway 509 just north of Sharbot Lake. Travel north along the smaller highway past the village of Danaldson. Shortly after, the highway veers west towards the village of Ompah. Minutes west of Ompah look for Mountain Road off the north side of the highway. Follow Mountain Road north to the Brule Lake Road, which takes you all the way to the southern shore of the lake.

Highway 509 can also be reached from the west via Highways 506 and 41 north of Kaladar and Highway 7. Once on Highway 509, continue north past Plevna to Mountain Road.

Facilities

Just off the Brule Lake Road, you will find a public boat launch and parking area along the southern shore. For a more rustic experience, tour operators have established some cabins and there remains plenty of Crown Land for rustic backcountry camping around the lake. Basic supplies can be found at the local general store in Plevna.

Other Options

Lucky Lake is a much smaller lake that is located just to the east of Wensley Lake. There is a short portage from the eastern shore of Wensley Lake or, if preferred, vehicle access is found off the Mackie Lake Road to the south. Lucky Lake is inhabited with smallmouth bass and a natural population of lake trout. This is one of the few remaining lakes in the area that still supports a natural lake trout fishery, therefore, please practice catch and release and be sure to check for special regulations on this lake.

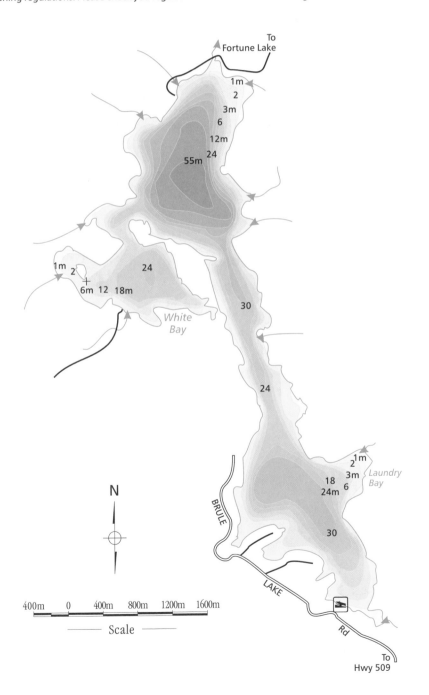

Zone **18**

Location: Weslemkoon
Maximum Depth: 47 m (150 ft)
Mean Depth: 20.3 m (65 ft)
Way Point: 45° 01′00″N, 77° 25′00″W

Weslemkoon Lake

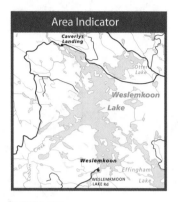

Area Indicator

Species
Lake Trout
Largemouth Bass
Panfish
Smallmouth Bass

Directions

The main access to Weslemkoon Lake is from the small marina located on the southwest shore. To find the marina, follow Highway 62 north from Highway 7 to Weslemkoon Lake Road at the settlement of Gilmour. Follow Weslemkoon Lake Road east all the way to the marina.

Alternatively, there is also a small access point located along the northern shore of the lake near Caverlys Landing. This access point can be accessed from the east of Highway 41 just south of Ferguson Corners.

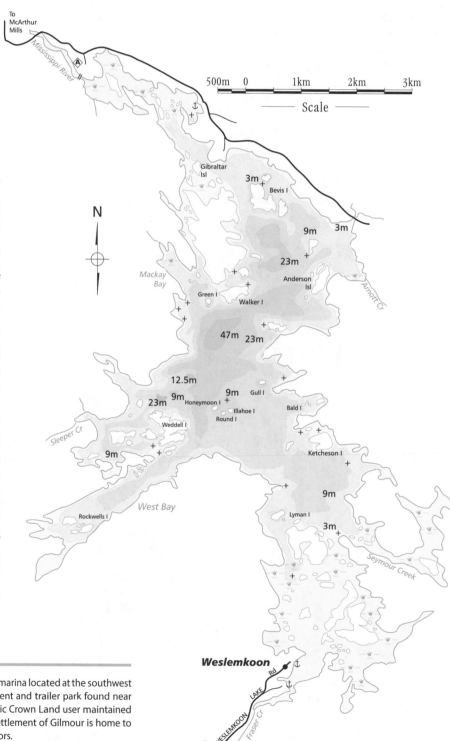

Fishing

As one of the largest water bodies in the area, anglers and cottagers alike frequent Weslemkoon Lake. The lake is riddled with dozens of secluded bays, providing excellent habitat for largemouth and smallmouth bass. Fishing for bass is fair to good at times for bass that can be found to 2 kg (4.5 lb) in size. Smallmouth tend to hold off the islands found around the lake, as the rocky underwater shore structure often associated with the islands is ideal habitat for these fish. Flipping jigs off structure or even crayfish imitation lures and flies can be quite effective in fishing smallmouth. Largemouth bass are also present in the lake is decent numbers and are regularly found in the shallower areas and most notably in the southern shallows.

A natural population of lake trout does exist in Weslemkoon Lake, but fishing is usually quite slow. Trolling along drop-offs next to deeper water (over 20 metres/70 feet) is a proven way to hook up with the odd laker, especially in the warmer months. As with almost every Eastern Ontario lake that is still home to naturally reproducing lake trout, the natural lake trout of Weslemkoon Lake are under siege. Shore development, fluctuating water levels and most importantly, over harvest of the species has brought the lake trout population under severe and continual pressure. Although there are special restrictions on the lake in order to help protect the fragile species, it is highly recommended to practice catch and release whenever possible to help save the species.

Facilities

The main facility found on Weslemkoon Lake is the marina located at the southwest shore. For overnight accommodations, there is a tent and trailer park found near the marina. Alternatively, there are also a few scenic Crown Land user maintained campsites available around the lake. The nearby settlement of Gilmour is home to a small general store and a restaurant for area visitors.

West Lake

Location: 18 km (11mi) west of Picton
Surface Area: 1,534 ha (3,790 ac)
Maximum Depth: 7.6 m (25 ft)
Mean Depth: 2.7 m (9 ft)
Way Point: 43° 55′ 00″ Lat - N, 77° 16′ 00″ Lon - W

20 Zone

Fishing

West Lake is a shallow lake that has plenty of weed growth and other cover throughout the lake. Similar to most Quinte area lakes, West Lake is hit hard for its walleye, although fishing can be fair at times. Look for walleye along weed lines and off the south side of Tubbs Island on occasion. Trolling a worm harness can be effective in a lake like West Lake due to its heavy weed structure. You can literally work the worm harness bait right through weeds. Crankbaits, jigs and other similar baits can also be productive.

Smallmouth and largemouth bass are the two most active sport fish found in West Lake. There is plenty of prime structure to spawn, grow and hide in. Top water action can be exciting at the right times but a tube jig may be the perfect lure to work through the weeds. If your luck is not as productive in the weed beds, try off rock pile structures, such as the rocky shoal found near Tubbs Island.

Adding to the fishery are yellow perch along with some decent sized northern pike and even the odd muskellunge.

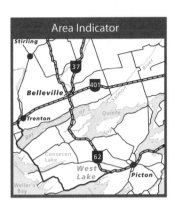
Area Indicator

Facilities

The main attraction to West Lake is **Sandbanks Provincial Park.** The park is one of the most popular provincial parks in the Ontario park system due the massive sand dunes that the park encompasses. The beautiful sandy beaches are a great spot to catch some rays during the heat of summer. For campers, the park offers maintained campsites, flush toilets and showers. The park can be busy; therefore, it is recommended to call (888) ONT-PARK for reservations prior to arrival.

The lake also hosts a boat launch on Tubbs Island as well as a private campground along the eastern shore. Other accommodations and supplies can be found in the village of Wellington.

Directions

The western shore of West Lake is actually part of the popular **Sandbanks Provincial Park**, which separates the water body from Lake Ontario. To find the lake follow Highway 401 to Belleville and head south along Highway 62. The smaller highway eventually intersects County Road 33. The county road leads west along the northern shore of the lake. There is a boat access near Wellington as well as on the southeast shore of the lake on Tubbs Island.

Other Options

The nearby cousin to West Lake is **East Lake,** which can be found to the southeast. East Lake can be reached by following County Road 33 to Picton, then by heading south along County Road 10. East Lake has a boat launch and tent and trailer park for visitors to enjoy while the lake offers fishing opportunities for smallmouth bass, largemouth bass, northern pike and walleye.

Species	
Largemouth Bass	Walleye
Northern Pike	Yellow Perch
Smallmouth Bass	Other

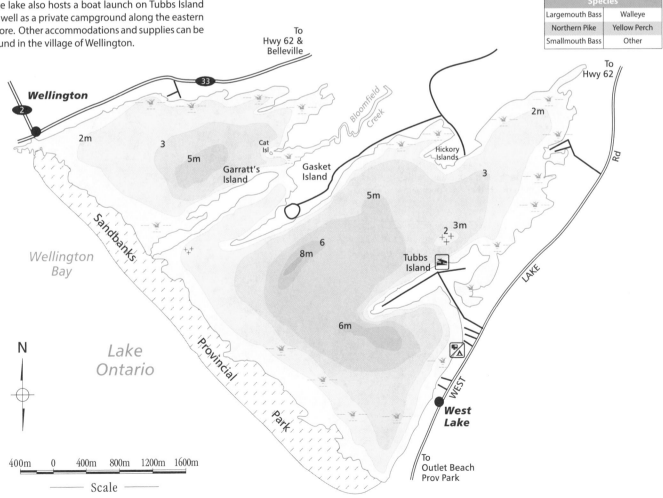

Zone 18

Location: 15 km (9.3 mi) southwest of Arnprior
Surface Area: 2,536 ha (6,266 ac)
Maximum Depth: 9.1 m (30 ft)
Mean Depth: 3.1 m (10.1 ft)
Way Point: 45° 18′ 00″ N, 76° 31′ 00″ W

White Lake- Calabogie

Area Indicator

Directions

White Lake is located near Calabogie Lake, north of the town of Perth. There are a few different access points to White Lake. From the south, the easiest way to find the lake is travel north along Highway 511 from Highway 7 near Perth. Follow Highway 511 to the White Lake Road located south of Calabogie. The White Lake Road travels east to the western shore of White Lake.

From the north, one way to access White Lake is to follow Highway 17 to County Road 2 south of Arnprior. Travel southwest along County Road 2 all the way to the village of White Lake and the northern shore of the lake. Alternatively, County Road 52 leads southeast to the lake from Renfrew.

Facilities

Several cottages, houses, resorts and marinas line the shores of White Lake providing ample places to stay, launch a boat or even rent a boat. Basic supplies, including bait and fuel, are also readily available around this busy cottage country destination. Be sure to surf the internet to find the marina, resort or campground to suit your needs.

Many visitors start their fishing adventure from White Lake Village General Store off County Road 52 at the north end of the lake or White Lake Marina off Bayview Lodge Road. There are also free, but basic public launch sites off White Lake Road along the southwest shore and at Waba Cottage Museum and Gardens Public Boat Launch off Museum Road at the north end of the lake.

Fishing

White Lake is a big, clean lake with many long coves, bays and islands resulting in over 95 km (60 miles) of shoreline to explore. The lake has seen substantial development and is home to many homes, cottages and resorts. Despite the heavy fishing pressure bass, walleye, northern pike and panfish including perch are caught regularly. Anglers looking for a unique fishing opportunity will also be happy to note this White Lake also holds burbot or freshwater ling cod.

Largemouth bass are king in these waters as the shallow nature of White Lake provides plenty of weed growth for largemouth to hide in. Several bass tournaments are held annually and bass up to 2 kg (4.5 lbs) in size are caught regularly. Look for bass along weed lines and even right amid the weeds. Using weedless type lures like a tube jig or weedless spinners can help avoid hook ups. Alternatively, the rocky points near the middle of the lake are a haven for smallmouth bass.

The bays also hide northern pike. A healthy population of 1.5 kg (3-4 lb) pike can be found in these weedy areas waiting for a spinnerbait. Pike are more active at dusk and periodically you can catch a northern off the top with a minnow imitation lure or popper type fly.

Walleye fishing is typically slow on White Lake, but anglers can be surprised occasionally. They are best caught by slow trolling along weed lines near the middle section of the lake early in the season.

Panfish are regularly caught right off the docks by younger anglers. Although smaller in size, they are easier to catch using a bait and bobber or small jig tipped with worms. In addition to perch, there are pumpkinseed sunfish, bluegill and rock bass to catch.

For something different, local anglers often go to their secret hiding places for burbot. These bottom dwelling fish are a popular catch due to their size and great taste. Jigging near creek mouths and other bottom structure is most effective.

Before you head out onto White Lake, be sure to check your regulations. There are specific slot size restrictions in place to aid the walleye population.

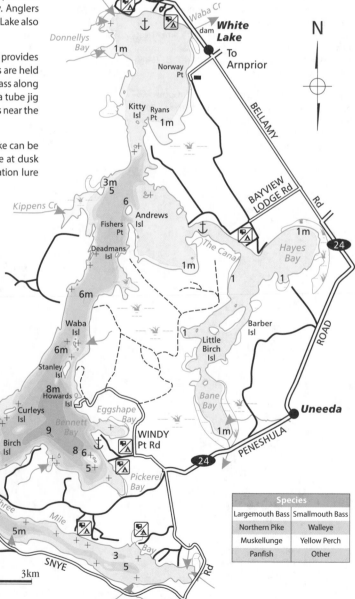

Species	
Largemouth Bass	Smallmouth Bass
Northern Pike	Walleye
Muskellunge	Yellow Perch
Panfish	Other

White Lake- Kinmount

Location: 32 km (19.9 mi) northeast of Norland
Elevation: 305 m (1,002 ft)
Surface Area: 175 ha (432 ac)
Maximum Depth: 10.4 m (34 ft)
Mean Depth: 3.7 m (12.2 ft)
Way Point: 44° 50' 00" Lat - N, 78° 29' 00" Lon - W

15 Zone

Fishing

A few cottages can be found along the shore of White Lake, although the fishing pressure is not overly heavy throughout the year. The most active fishing is for smallmouth and largemouth bass, which can be found to some good sizes on occasion. Largemouth can be found in the long weedy bays hunkered beneath the vegetation ready to ambush top water or subsurface presentations. The southwest bay is also a fine holder of nice size largemouth bass. Smallmouth are often picked up off the two large points that jut out into the lake as well as off the large island.

Adding to the fishery are yellow perch and pumpkinseed sunfish along with the odd muskellunge.

Facilities

There is a boat launch at the dam site found at the north end of the lake. The nearest tent and trailer park is on the shore of Shadow Lake just south of Norland. Supplies and other necessities can also be picked up in Norland.

Directions

White Lake is part of a series of cottage lakes found between Highways 35 and 28, not far from the community of Fortescue. From the west, take Highway 35 north to the town of Norland and turn east onto County Road 45. Follow this country road to the town of Kinmount where the road essentially changes to Highway 503. Continue east along Highway 503 to White Lake Road. Follow White Lake Road east all the way to the rough access near the dam on the north side of the lake. The access is basically suitable for a canoe only. Be sure to watch for private property.

Other Options

Salerno Lake is a popular cottage destination lake that lies due north of White Lake. There are two distinct access roads to Salerno Lake that branch north off White Lake Road. The L shaped lake is inhabited by smallmouth bass, walleye, and muskellunge and to a lesser degree largemouth bass. Fishing is best for smallmouth bass, although die-hard musky anglers can often be found frequenting the lake in search of the big predatory game fish.

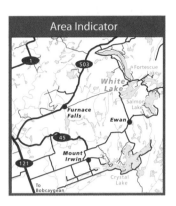

Area Indicator

Species
Largemouth Bass
Muskellunge
Smallmouth Bass
Yellow Perch

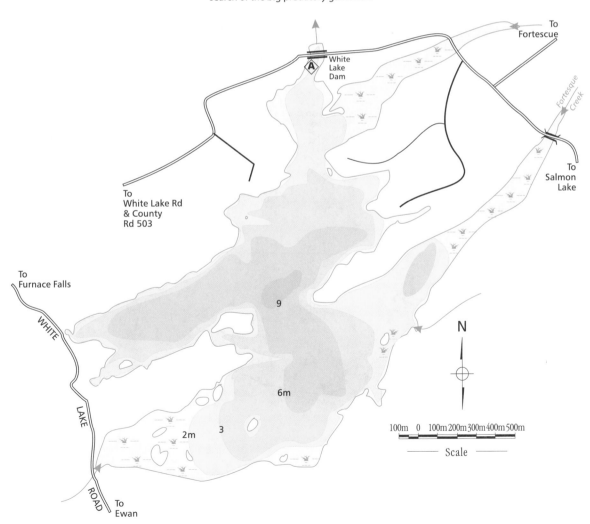

Zone 15

Location: 6 km (3.7 mi) west of Apsley
Maximum Depth: 7.3 m (24 ft)
Mean Depth: 6 m (19.7 ft)
Way Point: 44° 41′00″ Lat - N, 78° 11′00″ Lon - W

Wolf Lake

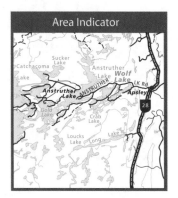

Area Indicator

Species

| Muskellunge |
| Smallmouth Bass |
| Yellow Perch |

Fishing

Found in the Kawartha Highlands Provincial Park, Wolf Lake is a scenic lake with only a few cottages and large stretches of Crown land. The lake is riddled with rocky shoreline and underwater areas providing ideal structure for the resident smallmouth bass. Coupled with the many small islands around the lake, bass have plenty of area to hide in wait for passing bait. Try working jigs off rocky drop offs or off the bottom near rock shoals. You may be surprised by the size of some of these bass.

Muskellunge are also resident in Wolf Lake but fishing success is usually slow for the large predator. They are best caught later in the year using Mepps Black Fury, bucktails or crankbaits. Try working near the bottom over notable shoals or the weedbeds.

Facilities

Home to the **Wolf Lake Canoe Route**, visitors will find a rustic boat launch at the northeast end of the lake. Although there are cottages on the east side of the lake, there are several places to camp including a number of small islands to the west. Roofed accommodations and the odd tent and trailer park can be found on Highway 28 between Lakefield and Apsley. Supplies are readily available in both towns.

Directions

Found in the Kawartha Highlands Provincial Park, Wolf Lake is easily accessed off Anstruther Lake Road. There is a boat launch/access point on the eastern side of the lake, about 5 km from Highway 28. To find Anstruther Lake Road, travel north along Highway 28 from the town of Lakefield or south of Bancroft. Anstruther Lake Road is located off the west side of the highway just south of Apsley.

Other Options

While you are making your way along Anstruther Lake Road to Wolf Lake, you will pass by **Loon Call Lake**. Loon Call Lake is accessible off the south side of road and is another summer cottage lake that can provide decent fishing during the year. The smaller lake is inhabited by largemouth and smallmouth bass, which provide for the bulk of the fishing success. Splake, the hybrid lake trout/brook trout cross, are also stocked in the lake regularly and can be a lot of fun to fish for during the winter months through the ice.

N

200m 0 200m 400m 600m 800m 1000m
— Scale —

To
Hwy 28

LAKE   ROAD

To
Anstruther
Lake   ANSTRUTHER

4

4m

8m

To
Anstruther
Lake

4m

8m

4

To
Crab Lake

Wolfe Lake

Location: 8 km (5 mi) west of Westport
Elevation: 136 m (447 ft)
Surface Area: 943 ha (2,330 ac)
Maximum Depth: 31 m (102 ft)
Mean Depth: 10.4 m (34.3 ft)
Way Point: 44° 41' 00" N, 76° 30' 00" W

Fishing

This popular summer cottage destination was once known for its excellent walleye fishery. However, through the years over fishing has reduced success for walleye to below average levels. Today, the best action comes from the resident bass species. Northern pike and yellow perch round out the warm water sportfish pursued in the lake. There are also brook, lake and rainbow trout, but these species are not really targeted in the lake.

Fishing is fair to good at times for smallmouth and largemouth bass to 1.5 kg (3.5 lbs). Smallmouth are the main bass species found and they like to frequent the numerous rocky underwater structures. There is also ample weed growth to make the ideal setting for some quality bass fishing. Try casting jigs and spinners along underwater rock piles or weed beds for ambush ready bass. A popular set up in this lake is a crayfish imitation fly or lure. Work the crayfish along bottom structure and bass will often suck in your presentation.

Northern pike fishing is generally slow, although a big northern can surprise the odd angler. For pike, try casting spinner baits or jigs along shore structure and near islands. The best time to try for these feisty predators is during the evening when pike cruise into shallows in search of an easy meal.

For the best chance for walleye success, try to locate the shoal areas around the lake. A few of the known hot spots include the 3 m (10 ft) shoal in the southeast corner and the 7 m (20 ft) shoal found in the middle of the lake. These areas tend to attract plenty of baitfish, which in turn attract predators such as walleye. Still jigging off one of these areas can produce good results when the bite is on.

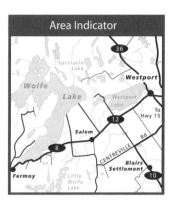

Area Indicator

Species	
Brook Trout	Rainbow Trout
Lake Trout	Smallmouth Bass
Largemouth Bass	Walleye
Northern Pike	Whitefish
Panfish	Yellow Perch

Directions

Visitors can find Wolfe Lake just west of the town of Westport. From the east, begin by following Highway 15 to the junction with County Road 42 at Crosby. Head west along County Road 42 to Westport and look for the Wolfe Lake Road (County Road 8). From Westport, Wolfe Lake is about 8 km (5 mi) west along the Wolfe Lake Road.

To access Wolfe Lake from the west, follow Highway 38 to the village of Godfrey and head east along the Westport Road (County Road 8). The Westport Road eventually changes to the Wolfe Lake Road and passes by the southern end of Wolfe Lake.

Facilities

There is no public boat launch at Wolfe Lake; however, there are a few private resorts and lodges on the lake that offer launching and camping facilities for a small fee. Alternatively, visitors with a small boat or canoe should be able to launch the craft from the side of Wolfe Lake Road along the southern end of the lake. For supplies, accommodations and other facilities, the town of Westport has plenty to offer visitors.

Zone 18

Location: 1 km (0.6 mi) south of Coe Hill
Maximum Depth: 33.5 m (110 ft)
Mean Depth: 13.5 m (44.5 ft)
Way Point: 45° 18′ 00″ Lat - N, 79° 47′ 00″ Lon - W

Wollaston Lake

Area Indicator

Species	
Lake Trout	Northern Pike
Largemouth Bass	Smallmouth Bass

Fishing

Wollaston Lake is an active cottage destination lake with several camps and cottages found along the shoreline. Fishing pressure is consistent throughout the year and angling success remains fairly productive. The main fish species found in the lake are largemouth and smallmouth bass. Fishing for both species is fair for bass that range from 0.5-1.5 kg (1-3.5 lbs). Bass will hold near any sort of underwater or top water cover such as weeds or even boat docks. Another good area to locate bass is off the small island near the middle of the lake.

The two other main sport fish found in Wollaston Lake are lake trout and northern pike. Fishing for both fish is usually slow, although success for pike does pick up on occasion, especially during the spring. Look for pike along weed lines in the evening, especially in the weedier southwest arm of the lake. Trolling spoons, such as a Red Devil, or casting spinner baits can be productive.

There remains a very small natural population of lake trout in Wollaston Lake, although fishing success is limited to mainly the early portion of the season. Due to the fragile nature of the lake trout population; it is recommended to practise catch-and-release whenever possible. Special regulations have been enacted, such as slot sizes and winter fishing restrictions to help aid the trout population.

Directions

You can find Wollaston Lake near the village of Coe Hill east of Apsley. There are two direct routes to the lake. From the west, travel north along Highway 28 from Lakefield to Highway 620 at the town of Apsley. Head east along Highway 620 to Coe Hill. Look for the access road off the south side of Highway 620. If you cross over the Deer River, you have gone too far.

From the east, travel north along Highway 62 past the village of Gilmour to Highway 620. Take Highway 620 west over the Deer River to Coe Hill and to the access road off the south side of the county road. Follow the access road to the boat launch area on the north side of the lake.

Facilities

Along with the boat launch, there is tent and trailer park along the north side of the lake. For supplies, you can find a general store in the village of Coe Hill.

Other Options

If the fishing success is slow on Wollaston Lake, there are a number of nearby lakes in the area. In particular, **Sweets Lake** is found east of Wollaston Lake not far off the south side of County Road 620. The smaller lake offers angling opportunities for largemouth bass.

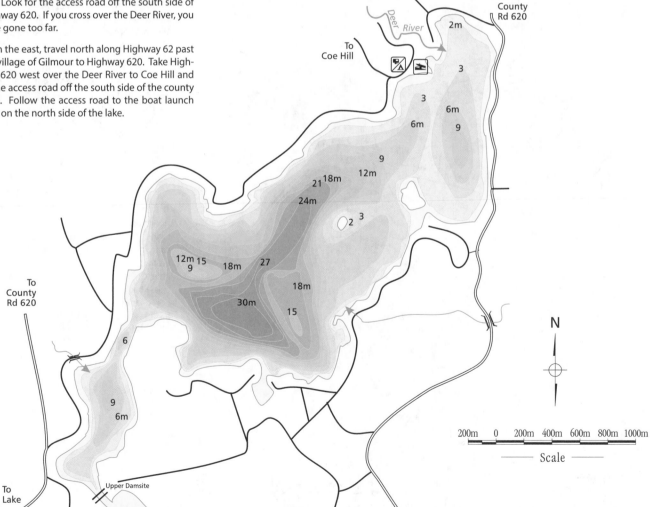

Young Lake

Location: North of Sebright
Elevation: 226 m (741 ft)
Surface Area: 96 ha (236 ac)
Maximum Depth: 10.3 m (34 ft)
Mean Depth: 4.8 m (16 ft)
Way Point: 44° 43' 00" Lat - N, 79° 10' 00" Lon - W

17 Zone

Fishing

Angling success on Young Lake is surprisingly good despite the fact that the lake is easy to access and is fairly small. Fishing is best for largemouth and smallmouth bass, as bass can be found throughout the lake. Weed structure is the best place to look for holding bass; however, it is also possible to find the odd bass holding under shore structure such as cottage docks. You may be surprised when casting a spinner or jig past dock areas.

Walleye, northern pike and muskellunge also inhabit Young Lake. Fishing for walleye and northern pike is generally fair, while musky are usually much harder to find. Walleye average approximately 0.5-1 kg (1-2 lbs) in size, whereas pike and musky can be found in the 3 kg (6.5 lb) range. Some much larger pike and musky are caught and in Young Lake annually. Walleye and northern pike have similar habits throughout the summer months and if you are lucky you can catch a mix of the two. Look for these predators along weed lines; especially at dusk when they move in from the deeper portions of the lake looking for bait fish. There are also a number of significant shoal areas found around Young Lake that should be prime grounds for weed beds and hence bait fish activity. Look for weed growth in the 2-3 m (6.5-10 ft) range of shoals. These areas are usually prime feeding grounds in the evening or during overcast periods.

Other non sportfish species roam the lake such as pumpkinseed sunfish, white sucker and brown bullhead.

Other Options

At the town of Sebright, if you follow Boundary Road (County Road 6) north, you will eventually reach **Riley Lake** and **Kashe Lake.** Both lakes are set amid rockier and rolling terrain than the flatter terrain found near **Young Lake** and **Dalrymple Lake** to the south. The northern lakes offer fishing opportunities for smallmouth and largemouth bass, while a population of walleye and muskellunge also inhabits Kashe Lake.

Directions

This smaller Kawartha Lake is located north of Dalrymple Lake near the village of Sebright. To find the lake from the southwest, first follow Highway 12 to the town of Orillia. In the east end of Orillia, you can find County Road 44 off the north side of Highway 12. Take County Road 44 north approximately 4 km to County Road 45 (Monk Road). Follow County Road 45 east across County Road 169 and past the village of Sebright to the eastern shore of Young Lake. The lake is about 2 km north of Sebright.

Facilities

There is a local community centre along the eastern shore of Young Lake, as well as a boat launch and tent and trailer park. A rough car top canoe access is located along the northern shore via an access road that branches from Boundary Road (County Road 6). Boundary Road can be picked up from County Road 45 in the town of Sebright. Basic supplies are also available in Sebright.

Area Indicator

Species
Largemouth Bass
Muskellunge
Northern Pike
Smallmouth Bass
Walleye
Other

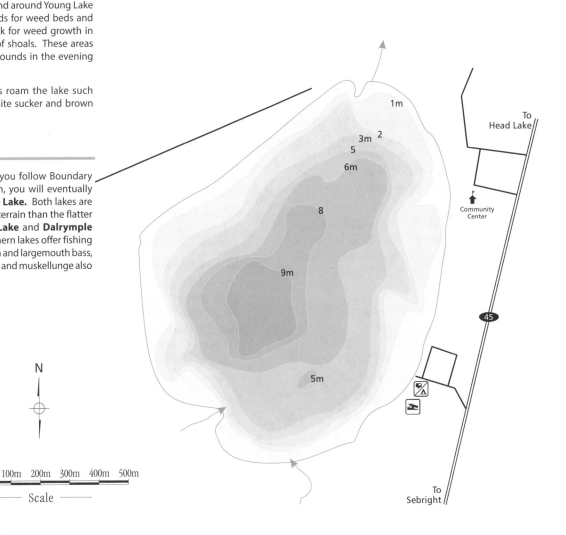

Join
The VOICE of Anglers & Hunters
www.ofah.org

The Ontario Federation of Anglers and Hunters (OFAH) is a powerful advocate for the proud traditions of fishing and hunting, and a world leader in fish and wildlife conservation.

As the VOICE of over 100,000 members, subscribers, supporters and 710 member clubs, the OFAH is the oldest, largest, most influential fishing, hunting and conservation organization in Canada.

The OFAH is a non-profit, non-government, registered Canadian charity. True to its grassroots foundation, OFAH positions are determined democratically by members of all ages, from all walks of life and all parts of Ontario. What brings OFAH members together is their passion for fishing and hunting and a deeply-rooted connection to their outdoors heritage and conservation.

Anglers and hunters belong to the OFAH by choice. For less than the cost of a few cups of coffee a month, their investment in OFAH membership means more time to focus on family, work and hobbies, without the worry of trying to tackle outdoor issues on their own.

OFAH members believe in strength in numbers. They take pride in knowing that their VOICE in the OFAH provides the full-time, professional representation that Ontario's fishing and hunting traditions deserve.

A world leader in Conservation

Since 1928, OFAH members have been the backbone of Ontario's fish and wildlife conservation work. The OFAH has invested millions of dollars to support fish and wildlife conservation projects.

OFAH leadership on projects such as invasive species prevention, habitat restoration, species recovery, fish stocking, and hunter education are admired internationally by our conservation allies. In particular, the OFAH has a worldwide reputation for spearheading three historic conservation achievements – the restoration of wild turkey, elk and Lake Ontario Atlantic Salmon.

You are benefitting from the work of the OFAH when you enjoy Southern Ontario Sunday gun hunting, lakes restored with walleye and salmon, fall turkey hunting, fishing and hunting opportunities on Crown land, additional deer tags, longer archery seasons, and new winter fishing opportunities.

Despite these outdoor victories, years of conservation efforts are threatened by well-funded "anti" groups that are determined to end fishing and hunting. That is why your fellow anglers and hunters need your support.

In the face of ongoing attacks on our fishing and hunting traditions, strength in OFAH membership gives anglers and hunters a VOICE on issues such as access to Crown land, the spring bear hunt, cormorants, invading species, outdoors education, and funding for fish and wildlife conservation programs. How many of these issues are important to you?

Show how much you care about your fishing and hunting future with a membership in the Ontario Federation of Anglers and Hunters.

Join today!

follow us!

If you're not an OFAH member, how is *your VOICE* being heard?

Fishing Tips & Techniques

In addition to the tips under each fish species, we have provided more tips and techniques below. This section is designed to give you a better understanding of the various types of fishing styles as well as a much more elaborate breakdown on fly-fishing. Whether new to the sport of fishing or a Wiley veteran, we recommend reading through this section to pick a few tricks. We also recommend stopping in at the local tackle shop before heading out. They are the ones that know the local tricks and what has been producing well recently.

Bait (Still) Fishing

Probably the simplest way to catch fish and introduce young people or novice anglers to sport fishing is by a technique known as still fishing. When still fishing from the shore or a boat, the angler casts out and waits for a bite. Still fishing can be done with or without the use of a float. Floats (bobbers) can be attached to the line so the baited hook stays suspended in the water. The depth can be adjusted by simply sliding the float up or down the line. The standard red and white ball bobber is effective, although be sure to check out your local tackle store as there are many different types of bobbers now available, including bobbers that will help you cast further from shore.

Casting just beyond the drop-off or around shoreline structure is very effective. In smaller lakes, a one metre (3 to 5 ft) leader with a size 8-12 hook is recommended. Weights should be avoided if possible, as they tend to scare off the fish. If you do need a weight, use 1-3 small split shot weights at least 30 cm (12 in) above the hook. Most fish tend to bite on worms, while other effective baits include leeches or minnows. Other effective baits include maggots and shrimp meat or krill. Alternatively, artificial bait such as powerbait comes in a variety of colours, scents and shapes. The trick is to use the lightest line and smallest hook possible.

Ice Fishing

The ice fishing opportunities in Central Ontario are quite extensive. While some of the more southern lakes have been closed to ice fishing permanently, there remains hundreds of lakes open for ice fishing in the region. Generally speaking, ice fishing is possible from the beginning of January through to early March as long as the ice is safe.

Years ago, ice fishing techniques were quite basic; usually a line on a pole, hook and bait is all you needed. Today, jigging has become one of the most popular fishing methods since live bait is not permitted on many Central Ontario lakes. Jigging is, basically, moving a small spoon or other attractant lure up and down periodically. The idea behind jigging is quite simple; the action of the lure will attract more fish to bite. Jigging may also add light reflection to the lure or even create added sound in the water. These other factors may contribute to the fact that jigging generally produces bigger fish than simply suspending bait.

Other techniques like a tip up contraption and bouncing rod set up have taken the simple rod mount in the ice to new levels. No matter what you choose, it is a good idea to have a smaller rod that is quite sensitive to allow you to see or feel a bite. Some anglers even attach bells or a flag to the rods help alert them of a bite. If practicing catch and release while ice fishing, be sure to be aware of the outside temperature if you are fishing outside of an ice hut. In extreme cold temperatures a fish's eyes will freeze in a matter of seconds basically rendering the fish helpless if released back in the water.

Jigging

Jigging can be an effective method of fishing if you can find where the fish are congregating. Jigging is a popular method of fishing though the ice in winter, although it is also widely used for walleye fishing throughout the open water season as well. Jigging is essentially sitting in a prime location, such as near underwater structure and working a jig head and body up and down to entice strikes. The great thing about jigging is that when the fish are in the area it can work very well, while the downfall obviously is that if the fish are not there, you literally have to wait for them to show up.

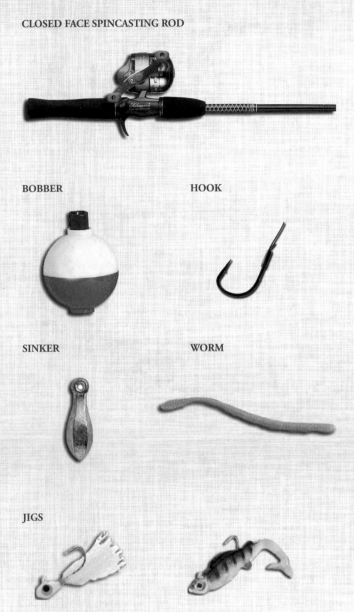

CLOSED FACE SPINCASTING ROD

BOBBER

HOOK

SINKER

WORM

JIGS

In the winter, anglers will jig almost any type of lure through the ice, but outside of the traditional jig head and bait set up, you will also see anglers jigging spoons and other similar type lures. Traditionally, a jig set up consists of a jig head with some sort of bait attached. A jig head is essentially a painted weight with a hook, while the bait can be anything from a minnow or worm to an artificial plastic body in various fashions and colours.

Spincasting

Spincasting is another popular and effective fishing method for all types of water. Essentially, spincasting is the process of casting a line from a rod with a spinning reel. The set up is quite simple making it easy for anyone to learn how to fish and have fun at it.

Most tackle shops offer good reel and rod combinations. It is recommended to go with a lightweight rod and around an 8-pound test line, but this can vary obviously depending on what you are fishing for. The key is to have line light enough to cast effectively

OPEN FACE SPINNING ROD

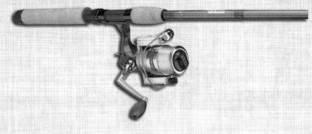

SPOONS

SPINNERS

LAKE TROLL/WORM HARNESS

and tough enough to withstand trolling and landing some fairly large fish. A good idea is to get an open face reel with removable spools. One spool should have light line (6 lb test or lighter) for small lakes and the other heavier line (8 lb or higher) for rivers and trolling.

While open faced reels are still quite popular, closed face reels (bait casters) are definitely the norm out there today and are very effective. Generally, spincasting reels are for lighter fishing duties, while baitcasters can handle the rigors of working bigger fish with bigger line. That is not to say that either one cannot be used in reverse situations, the key is to find which will work best for you. If price is an issue, the cost of a good spinning reel is usually much cheaper than the cost of a same quality bait caster.

Trolling

Trolling is the mainstay of bigger lakes, but also a popular alternative for many smaller lakes. It is a popular fishing method because you are able to cover large areas of water, increasing your chances of success on a lake. Ideally you should use a longer, stiffer rod than traditional spincasting set ups. Eight-pound test is ok for small lakes but you will need heavier line for bigger lakes, especially if using a downrigger.

It is best to troll near structure, along the drop-off or near a mid-lake shallow, such as a sunken island. A depth chart or digital depth finder will help you pinpoint these locations. While it is possible to troll big lakes without down rigging equipment, it can be a challenge, especially as the heat of summer progresses and the fish revert to deep areas of the lake.

If down rigging equipment is not in the budget or not a preferred method, try something like a jet diver or look for specialty trolling weights at your local tackle shop. Alternatively, lead core line and steel line outfits can be quite effective at deep water trolling. These lines are heavy enough to get your presentation down deep and are most effective when used with line counter reels so that you can gauge your depth while trolling. The difference between the two is that lead core line tends to bow while trolling, while steel line does not. Many feel the bowing effect of lead core line can lead to missing strikes, but on the flipside many claim that strikes are much more difficult to detect with steel line. If possible, you should try both systems out to see which one you prefer before buying.

When trolling, simply attaching your spoon or lure to your line may work well, but for lake trout and pike, the addition of a small flasher back from your lure can work wonders. Most notably in the deeper portions of the lake light has a harder time penetrating the water and in turn attracting fish. The addition of a flasher will increase the likelihood of attracting a sportfish to your presentation. For lake trout, silver, copper or gold spoons are the mainstay as they imitate baitfish well. Something like a larger sized Little Cleo, Williams Wabler or similar type spoons can all work well. For northern pike, traditional lake trout spoons can be very productive, however pike also are very attracted to colours like red and yellow. The good old Red Devil and Five of Diamonds spoons are renowned pike favourites.

Fly-fishing

Fly-fishing is not a very popular or at least talked about fishing method in Ontario since many of the fish species in this province are just as easily caught by other fishing methods. Fly-fishing is also the hardest technique to master but once you have caught a fish on fly gear, everything else pails in comparison. Whether it is a small trout or an acrobatic smallmouth bass, the shear excitement of landing a fish with fly-fishing gear is simply exhilarating.

Basically, there are three parts to a fly-fishing outfit: the rod, the reel and the line. Rods come in a variety of lengths and weights, depending on your size and the size of the species you intend to fish. As an example, a 9 ft, 6-weight rod would be an ideal set up for everything from trout to pike up to approximately 5 kg (11 lb) in size. Longer rods are helpful in casting and helping manipulate flies into position, especially on rivers and streams.

When picking up a fly reel, the vast majority of reels (or any that are worth buying) will be weighted similar to the way rods are weighted. The reels are actually made to fit the appropriated rod.

Most fly anglers will have at least a couple fly line alternatives including a floating line and either a medium or fast sinking line. The floating line presents dry flies, as well as subsurface wet flies. A popular option is using sink tip line, which is a combination of sinking and floating line where just the end of the fly line sinks. This type of line allows you to present subsurface flies while retaining the visibility of the fly line on the surface. For surface fishing, some of the best times to fish are during the mayfly and caddis hatches. Trout and whitefish love these insects, but small bass and panfish will take them as well.

Medium sinking lines are ideal for fishing wet flies such as crayfish patterns, nymphs or chironomid pupae near the bottom. The medium sinking line offers the best control when attempting to fish a specific depth, such as along a drop-off or along weed beds for smallmouth bass. Dragonfly, damselfly and even leech patterns can be worked quite effectively this way. Fast sinking lines are ideal for trolling. If you are not familiar with the lake or the fish are few and far between, trolling a fly is a good way to start. Woolly Buggers, streamers and leeches are all good all purpose trolling flies. Work the area just off the drop-off in a figure-eight pattern to vary the direction, depth and speed of the fly.

Regardless of which line you run with, you will also need backing and a leader. The backing is designed to fill up the spool, as well as to act as reserve for when that pike goes for a 100 metre dash. Most people keep 100–150 metres of backing on their reel. The leader is a thinner monofilament line that attaches the thick fly line to the fly. Leaders have a thicker butt that tapers to a thin tippet.

Lures & Flies

At any of your local tackle shops, you will find a seemingly endless array of tackle. From the endless versions of the spinner to the simple jig head and body, it can be a confusing decision. Here is a quick rundown of the lures and flies and what they are mainly used for:

Crankbaits are essentially a piece of painted plastic shaped to wobble when reeled through the water. As with any lure, there are hundreds of different crankbaits on the market. The lure can be productive for a wide variety of sportfish, but most notably for, walleye, pike and bass. The main advantage of any crankbait is its unique movement ability.

Flies are the main component of any trout's diet. Although countless books have been produced on the subject, selecting the right fly is a matter of simply matching the hatch. What you want to do is use a fly that most approximates the insect or baitfish on which the sportfish are feeding. To determine this, spend some time observing the aquatic insects at the lake and try to determine what the fish are rising to and how the insects are moving in the water. If you can not see the adult insect on the water surface then try using a small fine net to scoop up the insects. Once you have discovered what type of insect the fish are feeding on, you should try to determine how the insect moves in the water so you can imitate it. For example, is the adult insect sitting motionless on the water or is it rapidly flapping its wings?

Here is a list of a few recommended flies to include in your fly box. By no means is this exhaustive, but rather a starting base to work from:

Bead Head Nymph is a variation of the halfback or pheasant tail nymph patterns, but is often a little more versatile. The fly is already weighted so it can be fished easily in streams and lakes with either sinking or floating line. The bead head also is an attractant that often glistens in the water attracting attention of predatory fish.

Chironomid (Midge) has quickly become one of the most important flies in the fly box of Western Canadian lake anglers. The fly can also be found in every lake in Ontario and varies in size and colour depending on the lake and time of year. The fly must always be worked very slowly in the part of the water column that depends on what stage of the main hatch is taking place. The big hatches are mainly in the spring, although they are present all year round.

Dragon and Damselfly Nymphs vary in size and colour. Since they are found everywhere, they should certainly be part of every fly box. There are literally dozens of patterns that are used throughout the province and your best bet to know what works is to inquire locally before you head out. These nymphs are often worked deep and even off bottom for cruising trout.

Elk Hair Caddis is a specific caddis imitation fly that revolutionized top water caddis fly fishing in North America. Depending on the time of year your presentations will vary with this type of fly. In the early part of the season, hatching caddis will often flap along the surface attempting to break away. Therefore, your presentation should imitate this. Later in the season when caddis are laying eggs, they will literally smack the water and trout, panfish, whitefish and bass will pounce on them as quickly as possible. The key is to be observant of the hatch and what the flies are doing.

Leeches are a definite must in every fly box since they are found in virtually all lakes in Ontario. Leech patterns are versatile and great for searching lakes. At times, this is all trout are feeding on and even if they are feeding on something else, they will rarely pass up a well-presented leech. This pattern also works very well for bass and walleye at times.

FLY FISHING ROD

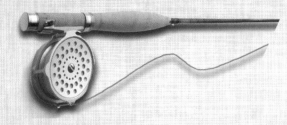

CHIRONOMID

BEAD-HEAD NYMPH

DRAGON NYMPH

ELK HAIR CADDIS

SILI SCUD

WOOLLY BUGGER

Mayfly patterns vary dramatically in size and colour. During a hatch, trout can sometimes be so picky that they will literally pass up your mayfly if it is a size or two too small or a wrong colour. However, the mayfly hatch is a big part of the open water season and a good variety of this fly is needed in your box, especially early in the season.

Muddler Minnow imitates a minnow in distress and is the ideal meal for a wide variety of fish. In general, larger fish seem to like bigger presentations of this fly. The fly is mainly worked below the surface although some anglers have been known to put floatant on them and work them off or just below the top of the water for big aggressive fish.

Streamer is a good versatile pattern for all sportfish species as it imitates baitfish or larger meals that most sportfish thrive on. This fly can be of almost any size and colour, but the key is that it should have a long sleek profile in the water and is used to fish subsurface. While you will see bright coloured streamer patterns out there, typically for Ontario lakes you are looking for a pattern that imitates baitfish.

CRANKBAIT

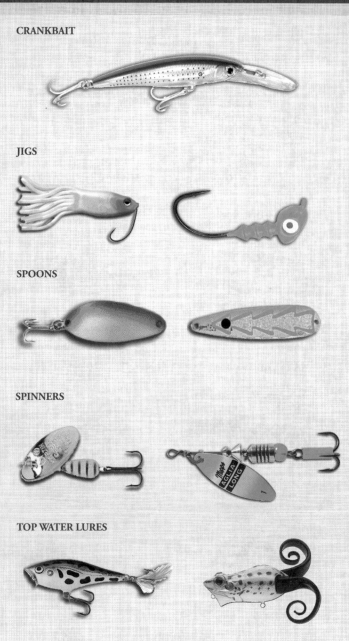

JIGS

SPOONS

SPINNERS

TOP WATER LURES

Woolly Bugger is a good versatile pattern for almost all sportfish in Ontario. This fly imitates larger meals such as a baitfish or leeches and can be effective in both streams and lakes. While the most popular colours are olive and black, other colours and variations, such as a bead head or Egg Sucking Leech, can create a unique fly for that unique situation.

Jigs are made up of a weighted head and plastic body. Both the head and body come in a wide range of colours, shapes and sizes. As with any lure, the key to finding the right shape, size or colour is done mainly through trial and error. Jigs work well for bass and are a favourite lure of walleye anglers. The single hook nature of the jig also works as an effective anti snag type lure. A jig can be worked effectively through weeds, unlike most other lures.

Spinners are one of the most common styles of lures available. A spinner gets its name from one or more metal blades that spin like a propeller when the lure is moving, creating varying degrees of flash and vibration that mimics small fish. The two most popular types of spinnerbaits are the 'in-line spinner' and 'safety pin' spinnerbaits. There are countless variations and brand names such as Mepps and Blue Fox that all produce results. The spinner is a versatile lure proving successful for trout, bass and pike on occasion. The fast action of any spinner is very active and is usually worked quickly within about the 1-3 m (3-10 ft) depth range.

Spoons rank with spinners in terms of sheer numbers of spoons sold. They have been a staple of spincasting since the mid-1800s, and come in a mix of sizes and colours. The basic design of a spoon is simple: an oblong, concave piece of metal with a single or treble hook at the end. Trolling spoons are thinner than traditional casting spoons. There is also a sub-genre of spoons designed to be jigged vertically, rather than trolled or retrieved horizontally. Spoons are more commonly used when fishing for pike and trout; however, they can be productive for other species as well. For pike, the larger presentations with brighter colours, like red or yellow, are the spoons of choice. For trout, smaller silver or gold spoons can be productive with shades of blue, or green. A popular brand name for trout spoons is the Little Cleo, while the Red Devil is a long heralded pike spoon.

Top Water Lures offer some of the most exciting fishing. Top water lures skim the surface of the water to entice fish to grab the lure from the surface of the lake. Top water lures can be quite effective for northern pike, smallmouth bass and largemouth bass. One of the old time favourite brands of top water lures is the Jitterbug.

Releasing Fish- The Gentle Way

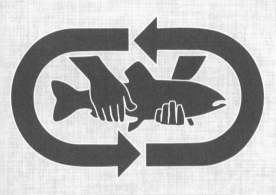

There is a growing trend among anglers to catch and release, unharmed, a part of their allowable catch. As well, more restrictive regulations on specific waters can severly limit the angler's allowable harvest.

A fish that appears unharmed may not survive if carelessly handled, so please abide by the following:

1- Play and release fish as rapidly as possible. A fish played for too long may not recover.

2- **Keep the fish in the water as much as possible.** A fish out of water is suffocating. Internal injuries and scale loss is much more likely to occur when out of water.

3- Rolling fish onto their backs (while still in the water) may reduce the amount they struggle, therefore minimizing stress, etc.

4- Carry needle-nose pliers. Grab the bend or round portion of the hook with your pliers, twist pliers upside down, and the hook will dislodge. Be quick, but gentle. **Single barbless hooks are recommended,** if not already stipulated in the regulations.

5- Any legal fish that is deeply hooked. Hooked around the gills or bleeding should be retained as part of your quota. **If the fish cannot be retained legally, you can improve its chances for survival by cutting the leader and releasing it with the hook left in.**

6- If a net is used for landing your catch, it should have fine mesh and a knotless webbing to protect fish from abrasion and possbile injury.

7- **If you must handle the fish, do so with your bare, wet hands (not with gloves).** Keep your fingers out of the gills, and don't squeeze the fish or cause scales to be lost or damaged. It is best to leave fish in the water for photos. If you must lift a fish then provide support by cradling one hand behind the front fins and your other hand just forward of the tail fin. Minimize the time out of the water, then hold the fish in the water to recover. If fishing in a river, point the fish upstream while reviving it. When the fish begins to struggle and swim normally, let it go.